T0355534

Nine Degrees of Justice

New Perspectives on Violence against
Women in India

Nine Degrees of Justice

New Perspectives on Violence against
Women in India

Edited by
BISHAKHA DATTA

zubaan

Nine Degrees of Justice: New Perspectives on Violence against Women in India
edited by Bishakha Datta

Published (2010) by
ZUBAAN
An imprint of Kali for Women
128 B Shahpur Jat, 1st floor
New Delhi 110049
Email: zubaanwbooks@vsnl.net and zubaan@gmail.com
Website: www.zubaanbooks.com

ISBN 978 81 89884 50 5

Zubaan is an independent feminist publishing house based in New Delhi, India, with a strong academic and general list. It was set up as an imprint of the well-known feminist house Kali for Women and carries forward Kali's tradition of publishing world-quality books to high editiorial and production standards. *Zubaan* means tongue, voice, language, speech in Hindustani. Zubaan is a non-profit publisher, working in the areas of the humanities and social sciences, as well as in fiction, general non-fiction, and books for young adults that celebrate difference, diversity and equality, especially for and about the children of India and South Asia, under its imprint Young Zubaan.

Typeset in Berthold Baskerville 11/13
Jojy Philip, New Delhi 110 015
Printed at Raj Press, R-3 Inderpuri, New Delhi 110 012

Contents

Introduction

If I could rename this book, I would call it *Trespassing in the Nude*; nude because the word instantly evokes images of the body, and much of the violence described in these pages is etched on the body. So much of it is corporeal, or directly related to the body; the physical, material body. And so much of it is related to the body in a larger sense, emanating from society's desire or intention to control women's bodies and sexualities.

In her book *Beyond the Veil* (1987), author and sociologist Fatima Mernissi outlines how traditional Moroccan thinking views the street as male space. A woman who is on the streets is trespassing; she is in male spaces; spaces in which she has no right to be. 'If she enters them, she is upsetting the male's order and peace of mind. She is actually committing an act of aggression against him merely by being present where she should not be.'[1] Women are supposed to be veiled: the Moroccan word for 'unveiled' is *aryana* or nude. Thus an unveiled woman on the street is doubly aggravating the situation: she is nude *and* a trespasser.

The eleven essays and single poem in this selection are also about 'trespassing in the nude', but in a different sense. Every woman in India may not be expected to veil her body, but we are expected to veil our minds, particularly so with respect to our bodies. Yes, we are permitted to make some decisions around bodily functions, such as when we want to go to the toilet. But we are not expected to make any larger decisions about our bodies: from routine everyday ones of how to clothe or feed them to larger ones of how to nourish, cherish, work, entertain, pleasure, sex, protect or control them.

Simply put, we are not supposed to decide how we want to inhabit our own bodies, which at least in a material sense, form the basis of our lives. No, this domain of control, over bodies and lives, is reserved for family, community, society. Any incursion into this territory, any attempt to make our own decisions around our bodies, is viewed as trespass: a 'crime' that must be punished by any means, including violence. In other words, keep her in her 'place'. Any attempt to question this punishment – individually, collectively, through action, resistance or protest – is seen as yet another trespass; a double trespass, almost like trespassing in the nude.

I love books. This book grew out of another book... and another. In the early 1990s, as I began getting involved in the women's movement, I read *The Struggle Against Violence* (1993).[2] Edited by a feminist academic and written by activists, the slim black-and-white volume lovingly explored three campaigns that had taken place in Maharashtra in the 1980s against sex-determination, rape, and the desertion of rural women. What stayed with me long after putting it down was the narrative power of resisting violence, rather than the horror of different forms of violence. Power over horror. The same feeling lingered as I read Ilina Sen's edited volume, *A Space Within The Struggle* (1990),[3] which explored how different social movements looked at the 'women's question'.

Continuing this tradition, *Nine Degrees of Justice* focuses on struggles against violence on women, rather than on violence itself. Violence emerged as a core issue for the fledgling Indian women's movement in the early 1980s with campaigns against custodial rape. Many women who fought for justice then are household names for us now; their struggles an integral part and parcel of feminist lore. Forms of violence that became visible then – rape, dowry deaths, desertion, domestic violence, and sati – still abound.

What may have changed, broadened, or deepened during the last twenty years is our own understanding of violence. We now view patriarchy as cutting across larger forces – poverty, class, caste, religion, conflict, sexuality, ability – and resulting in a range of forms of violence on women. Just think of the past decade: growing economic inequality; drought in Orissa; starvation in Bihar; farmers' suicides in Maharashtra; displacement in West Bengal; communal genocide in Gujarat; conflict in the Northeast and Kashmir; the rise of a state-sponsored militia in Chattisgarh; casteism in Tamil Nadu; fundamentalism in Karnataka; land struggles in Kerala... Women face violence in all of these contexts, so much so that names like Nandigram, Kandhmal, Khairlanji, and Salwa Judum, are now shorthand for particular forms of violence.

If 'violence against women' is now a multi-headed hydra, the acts that underlie this label are systemic and routine, everyday and sporadic. Women experience violence across a wide continuum: in private, public, and virtual domains; from strangers, familiars, and intimates; on streets, in workplaces, homes, war zones, and in the media. Women in India continue to face violence not just because they are 'women', but because they are *Muslim* women, *Dalit* women, women of a particular *tribe* or *ethnicity*, women who are *poor*, or women caught in the crossfire between revolution and the state.

However, as violence has morphed into various forms, so has resistance to it. Struggles against violence now range from the non-violent Gandhian to the digitally networked. Again, let's look at the last decade. In November 2000, Irom Sharmila began her fast-to-death in Manipur demanding the repeal of the Armed Forces (Special Powers) Act. Her hunger strike, which continues, began after the Indian army, with a long history of killings in the Northeast, killed ten young Meitei men in Malom. Groups like the 'mothers' of Manipur, the Meira Paibi, have gone on relay fasts in solidarity and support.

In February 2009, the Pink Chaddi campaign exhorted people to send pink underwear to the head of the Hindu right-wing group, Sri Ram Sene, as a reaction to its members assaulting and molesting two women in a Mangalore pub. During its short-lived six-month lifespan till it was virtually killed by its opponents, it mobilized over 60,000 supporters online, on the Facebook group known as The Consortium of Pubgoing, Loose, and Forward Women. Over 3,000 pink panties were sent to the Ram Sene chief in a shaming action. Reports by women's rights groups showed the growing and systematic communalization of Karnataka, a phenomenon underlying a series of attacks on women.

In between these two landmark struggles, a host of others continue across India. *Nine Degrees of Justice* seeks to explore some of these.

-πε-

Nine Degrees of Justice is not an encyclopedia. It does not aim to be comprehensive. It does not catalogue every form of violence that exists, or every struggle against this. Rather, it explores a selection of struggles against violence on women over the past four decades.

As a second- or third-generation feminist, I see the world both similarly and differently from feminists of earlier (or later) generations. I was born into an analogue world in the early 1960s. The only computers then in use were 'mainframes' that filled entire rooms; they were as large as elephants and only specialists knew how to use them, among them my father. My childhood conversations were on large black instruments that are now called landlines. My penfriends in foreign lands sent me airmail letters with colourful stamps from exotic countries that seemed light years away. My Indian passport said, 'Valid for travel everywhere except South Africa'.

That world no longer exists. The textile mills, which shaped the Mumbai I was born into, are silent behemoths today. The sovereignty of the nation-state is fast slipping away at borderless virtual domains where 'nationality' means nothing. The certainty of the binary – male and female, man and woman – is giving way to the uncertainties of genders: one does not have to be *born* a man or a woman, one can *become* man, woman, trans or something else. If we can move, travel, migrate from one country to another, why can't we move from one gender to another? That too is movement.

Nine Degrees of Justice is set in movements: of women, time, space, points of view, perspectives, certainties. What is movement? That which changes its place or position; that which doesn't remain still or static. Movement does not necessarily mean new replacing old, but new adding to old. Like a rolling stone that gathers new moss without shedding the old; the old more firmly adheres to the stone as new moss gathers on the surface, that's all. Struggles and movements are iterative processes or works in progress. Much like an unfinished building whose foundation, if it is sufficiently strong, does not crumble with each new brick that is placed; shifting instead to accommodate each new brick.

In keeping with this sense of 'movement' then, *Nine Degrees of Justice* explores violences that are 'known' (read: were recognized in the 1980s, e.g. sati), 'accepted' (read: gained recognition in the 1990s, e.g. sexual harassment, armed conflict), 'emergent' (read: may have long existed but are being named and recognized in the 2000s, e.g. right to choice in relationships, lesbian suicides), 'contested' (read: differing perspectives within feminism, e.g. violence against sex workers), and 'new' (read: now emerging with newer technologies or changes, e.g. cyberviolence). Where a known struggle is documented, it is updated, bringing with it newer questions, reflections, thinking, strategies, and insights.

As most of the contributors to *Nine Degrees of Justice* are second- and third-generation feminists, our perspectives also reflect movement dynamics. We ask different questions, think about the same issue a little differently. For instance, one essay looks at legal justice anew, asking if survivor and activist understandings of justice collide or converge. Another essay suggests a re-imagining of feminist conceptions of women in public space by placing 'risk' and 'pleasure' above 'safety' and 'protection'. A third essay repositions women who 'perform sexuality' in the glamour industry not as 'victims', but as working women who strategically navigate the day-to-day violences they face, including the violence of stigma.

Movement is also explored in another way in *Nine Degrees of Justice*: through space. Women who identify as Indian no longer live within the geographical boundaries of the Indian nation-state, but may be part of a rapidly-growing global diaspora of non-resident Indians. South Asian women's groups that exist in several countries today are forging links with women's groups in India, both because we have something in common, and because issues such as the transglobal abandonment of married women demand such connections. In this context, one essay explores the struggle to secure justice for Indian women who face domestic violence in the US, while another explores movement through space by viewing violence in the virtual space of the Internet.

—◊—

If movement is one of the key markers of *Nine Degrees of Justice,* sexuality is the other.

Sexuality and violence have always shared a circular relationship in the lives of women; with sexuality lurking below the surface of issues like the struggles against rape and dowry in the 1980s, sex-selection, child sexual abuse, sexual harassment in the 1990s, and lesbian suicides in the early 2000s. Even so, sexuality has not readily been recognized as the basis of an identity until recently.

We now recognize that women face violence not just because they are *Muslim* women or *Dalit* women, but also because they are *lesbian* women, *transgender* women, women in *sex work,* or *bad* women: women who transgress sexual norms. If caste, class, poverty, religion, and gender are the more familiar axes of marginalization and discrimination, sexuality is clearly another axis along which women are divided – into 'good' and 'bad'. While 'bad' women face violence both as 'sexual subjects' and as 'sexual objects', 'good' women too face violence related to sexuality and reproduction.

On the one hand, women who see themselves as sexual subjects face certain kinds of violence for making their own choices in this area: be it a lesbian woman who chooses her sexual orientation, a straight woman who marries out of her caste, or a transwoman who adopts a child. On the other, women who are seen as sexual objects face other forms of violence, be they sex workers, models, or flight attendants. The dominant moral code classifies both these groups of women as *bad* women: women who are sexually illegitimate, women who have gone beyond the sexual boundaries laid out for them, or trespassed, and must be punished or violated.

At the same time, *good* women continue to face violence, not necessarily for overstepping limits, but because of their gender: because they are women. What is the difference between a housewife who is physically beaten up for producing a daughter and a college student who is emotionally battered for choosing her own lover? None that I can see. Both are being punished for not doing what they are *expected* to do; for not following their socially ascribed roles, for not adhering to their social scripts of gender and sexuality.

But the world is not divided into black and white, and neither are women divided into 'good' or 'bad'. And nor should movements be. Women's movements cannot lay themselves open to the charge that we are a movement of 'good' women, by somehow overlooking or excluding 'bad' women from our struggles. We cannot follow society's moral faultlines or its norms around gender or sexuality in deciding who the movement should represent. In line with this belief, *Nine Degrees of Justice* includes several struggles by women considered 'bad'.

'Words are sacred,' wrote the British playwright Tom Stoppard. 'If you get them in the right order, you can nudge the world a little.' When I think of the essays in this book, six words suggest themselves to me: justice, space, tradition, choice, work, conflict. In my head, the 12 chapters flow in pairs: the first two are about justice, the next two about space, the next pair about tradition, and so on.

Justice, space, tradition, choice, work, conflict are not of course neat, self-contained worlds that maintain their sharp edges, but plasticine shapes that blur, tumble, glide, and

mould themselves into different kaleidoscopic forms. Turn
the lens a touch and you get a different view. Of course, this is
as random as any other ordering. This building of categories
can, like every system of classification, be dug up, redesigned,
and turned into a different edifice. Be that as it may.

Nine Degrees of Justice begins with Farah Naqvi's provocative
essay, 'This Thing Called Justice'. Has using the law led to
justice for women who face violence? she asks. What does
'justice' mean for an individual survivor? What does 'justice'
mean for activists from the women's movement? Do the two
definitions of justice collide or converge? Why, despite the
overwhelming absence of legal victories, do survivors and
activists persist in turning to the law for redress; for that
elusive outcome called 'justice'?

Paired with this is Shamita Das Dasgupta's 'An Intimate
Dilemma', which explores how immigrant Indian women
facing domestic violence in the US often face judicial barriers
in a different legal system. Even when justice is available, it
comes with its own price tag: the stereotyping of culture.
Mainstream Americans have historically viewed immigrants of
colour, especially Asian, as prisoners of their cultures, writes
Das Dasgupta. These cultures are perceived to be surfeit with
vicious patriarchies and provide tacit support to violence against
women. It is not just an immigrant who is tried in a domestic
violence case: his or her culture of origin is also on trial.

Next in sequence are two essays that explore the violences
that women face in two kinds of spaces: the public and the
virtual. In her groundbreaking essay, 'If Women Could Risk
Pleasure', Shilpa Phadke suggests that we need to redefine
our understanding of violence in relation to public space: to
see not rape or sexual assault but the denial of access to public
space as the worst possible outcome for women. Perhaps the
best way for women to enhance claims to public space is not
to seek safety per se, she argues, but to embrace risk and
pleasure while accepting violence as something that must be
navigated in the process of doing so.

So much for the physicality of public space. What does
violence mean in space gone virtual: in the global matrix

created by a billion cables, fibre optic networks, terminals, servers, and other technological artifacts that we experience as cyberspace? Is online violence merely a duplication of offline violence via another platform? asks Sharmila Joshi in 'Untangling the Web'. Or does the nature of cyberspace change the nature and impact of that violence? If so, how? And how can we address such violence without demonizing carrier technologies such as the Internet?

Following these are two essays on tradition: at home and at work. The traditional lineage of male workplaces, which often function like old boys' clubs, subtly condones sexual harassment, says Puja Roy in 'Invisible Yet Entrapping'. Women who complain of sexual harassment are seen as upsetting the gendered status quo. A double trespass: first you're in a male space (or out of place), then you dare complain! How can we confront sexual harassment in workplaces and institutions that remain bastions of male power and privilege? she asks.

Even in these globalized times, the home remains the prime bastion of tradition. Familial restrictions on dress, going out, mobility, work, thought, love, sex, relationships ... all daily curbs that are justified in the name of tradition, as are more extreme forms of violence that occur within the home. In her essay, 'From Roop Kanwar to Ramkunwari', Purnima Manghnani explores four cases of sati that have taken place in India over the past two decades, the challenges they pose, and new strategies to end this practice. In sati cases where the community is clearly complicit, asks she, who should be held accountable: the individual, the family, the community? How can the community see this as a form of violence against women rather than a custom or traditional practice?

From tradition, *Nine Degrees of Justice* veers away towards what families and communities often see as its very antithesis: choice. I refer to individual or personal choice, particularly in matters of love, sex, and relationships. In the last two decades, a number of cases of what are now called 'lesbian suicides' have been reported. These suicides are often the outcome of thwarted choices; thwarted not because of a lack of reciprocity, but because families believe *they* should decide whom their daughters should love. In 'Anatomy of a Suicide', Maya Ganesh delves into the transcripts of one such death in Kerala, powerfully bringing it to life through its detail.

This traditional belief that daughters don't have the right to choose their own lovers is not restricted to lesbian relationships. The past decade has seen a spate of what are mistakenly called 'honour killings', but which are more correctly 'revenge murders'. Many families draw boundary lines that their daughters may not cross. Crossing these lines by asserting one's choice is seen as a direct attack on patriarchal power, parental authority, and community norms. The outcome is often violence, but a violence that communities don't view as violence; a violence that is normalized as reclaiming family honour. In 'Criminalizing Love, Punishing Desire', Rajashri Dasgupta explores this in a heterosexual context.

Where violence against women is concerned, sexuality is almost like the elephant in the room. Everyone sees it, everyone knows it's sitting there behind the violence, everyone ignores it. The next two essays foreground the sexual aspect of women in their professional lives; in their work. In 'Performing Sexuality', Manjima Bhattacharjya looks at the work of young women in the glamour industry in India and some of its violent fallouts on their personal lives and social identities. What does this performance of sexuality entail? What are the cultural tensions surrounding it? What are the coping mechanisms that women in the glamour industry have evolved to manage the social stigma they face as a community and the perceptions of their individual sexuality?

If modelling, or working in the glamour industry, is seen as somewhat illegitimate, sex work is seen as wholly illegitimate. Not as work, not as choice, but as violence. In 'Her Body Your Gaze', Bishakha Datta deconstructs different ways of seeing prostitution as violence: as slavery, as force, as trafficking, and as harm. Reversing the dominant abolitionist gaze that looks in from the outside, she focuses on how violence is viewed from the inside: how sex workers see it; as endemic, but not intrinsic, to prostitution.

The final chapters in *Nine Degrees of Justice* look at conflict.

Political conflict has been an ever-present reality in India since independence. Another elephant silently sitting in the room. Think Kashmir, think the Northeast, think Chhattisgarh. 'It has been an unusually hot summer,' begins Sonia Jabbar's poetic essay, 'River Song', set in Kashmir. 'The sun burns with a fierce, unfamiliar power bleaching the skies white.' Below this burning sun, ordinary women go about their lives, continuing to hunt for the son who 'disappeared', continuing to hold out hope for a return, an answer, some closure. Closure. Solutions. Answers. What happens in their absence? What happens, as the poet Arundhati Subramaniam asks, 'when what is lost is too deep and too irrevocable to be catalogued?' (international.poetryinternationalweb.org. ptw.index.php). Perhaps other ways of writing are needed to sing these voids. In the final selection in *Nine Degrees...* Mona Zote evokes what poetry means to Ernestina, a woman sitting in the hills of Mizoram, 'her head crammed with contrary winds, pistolling the clever stars that seem to say: *Ignoring the problem will not make it go away.*'

—◆—

In June 2009, in an article (in *Tehelka*) on the pending Women's Reservation Bill, development economist Devaki Jain wondered whether the presence of women in politics would automatically mean greater representation of women's issues in the political domain. 'Does the politics of presence get translated into the politics of representation?' she asks.

Underlying the conceptualization of *Nine Degrees of Justice* is a similar question that many women are asking today: Does gender mean representation? Who is a 'woman' where the movement is concerned? Which women does the Indian women's movement represent? This question is often heard by groups of women who see their issues as marginal to the women's movement, among them lesbian women, HIV-positive women, women in sex work, transgender women, and disabled women.

In general, disabled women are simply not regarded as women, an exclusion that is written on their bodies. 'With a "body" that does not "measure up" to society's norms, the situation becomes precariously unbalanced,' writes Anita Ghai in the online newsletter *Infochange* (June 2009 www. infochange.org). She notes that many disabled women feel they face double discrimination, with inadequate representation from both the disability rights movement and the women's movement. The disability movement has consistently ignored reproductive health issues that disabled women face, such as forced hysterectomies in institutions throughout India.

But feminists have also failed to recognize the different experiences of disabled women in a sexist and able society. 'For Indian feminists, disability continues to be synonymous with the identity of being a woman, such that its specific character does not receive its due and is lost in the concern for women's rights in general...' Ghai writes. 'To really hear disabled women's voices, the women's movement has to acknowledge the social, economic, communication, as well as architectural barriers that prevent disabled women from sharing their stories and engaging in a public discourse.'

Nine Degrees of Justice does not adequately represent the violences that disabled women, or many other groups of women face. But it brings many marginal voices, points of view, and perspectives into the fold. I hope these voices will push us to re-examine theories, concepts, and practices that comprise the struggle against violence on women. To expand the frame of what we see, recognize, accept and take on board as violence. To shift our lens so that there are no hierarchies between different forms of violence, with one more important, the other less. No centre, no margins; no good women, no bad. Just a struggle against violence that *all* women face.

NOTES

1. Mernissi, p. 144.
2. Chhaya Datar (ed.) (1993). Calcutta: Stree.
3. Ilina Sen (ed.) (1990): *A Space Within the Struggle*, New Delhi: Kali for Women.

1

This Thing Called Justice

Engaging With Laws on Violence Against Women in India

Farah Naqvi

Question: Bhanwari, your appeal has been pending in the High Court for ten long years. You haven't got anything. Why don't you just let it go?

Bhanwari: I will never leave either them or this case. When I die, if they get off, they get off. But while I am still alive I will never let go of this case. My eyes need to see this thing called justice; only then can I let it go. Otherwise, not. Never.

Bhanwari Devi, Jaipur, 23 March 2007

Much of the early history of what is known as the contemporary women's movement in India has to do with the law. Any discussion on legal engagement with the issue of violence against women brings to mind a host of names: the Mathura case (1974), Rameeza Bi (1978), Maya Tyagi (1980), Bhanwari Devi (1992), Bilkis (2002). The law has been the site of substantive feminist intervention – both in seeking law reform and in litigation.

But has using the law led to justice for women who face violence? What does 'justice' mean for an individual survivor? What does 'justice' mean for activists? Do the two definitions of justice collide or converge? How has feminist-activist engagement with the law changed over the years? Has the nature/site of law changed feminist interventions or have feminist interventions substantively altered the site of the law? And, finally, are there areas of violence against women that we as feminists have neglected?[1]

Feminist-led Law Reform

Women's groups can safely take the credit for an impressive amount of law reform in the area of violence against women. In fact, law reform campaigns in the 1970s mark the emergence of the contemporary Indian women's movement in the public arena. Many of these 'reformed' laws are now taken for granted and one forgets how they came about. But a quick look at some cases is helpful.

In 1972, Mathura, a sixteen-year-old tribal girl from Maharashtra was raped in police custody.[2] In 1974, the Sessions Court let off the accused on the grounds that Mathura was a promiscuous liar and had consented to the 'sex'. The Nagpur bench of the Bombay High Court overturned the acquittal, but in 1979 the Supreme Court reinstated the Sessions Court judgment because Mathura did not raise an alarm and her body did not show enough signs of resistance. At about the same time, the case of Rameeza Bi, who was raped by policemen in Hyderabad in 1978, captured national attention. In 1980, a policeman in Baghpat, Uttar Pradesh tried to molest twenty-five-year-old Maya Tyagi. On being beaten by her husband, he gathered a posse of policemen who shot Maya's husband dead, beat and stripped Maya publicly, and paraded her to the police station where they gang-raped her.

All these cases coalesced into huge protest campaigns by women's groups, with the issue of custodial rape gaining centre-stage. When a rapist has effective 'custody' of the victim, should the norms be the same as in other rape cases? Should the law not acknowledge the excessive power vested in an individual in a position of state authority? Much-awaited reforms in rape laws finally came about in 1983. The Criminal Law Amendment Act introduced four new sub-sections into Section 376 of the Indian Penal Code, including one on custodial rape; this specified that once a crime of rape is established, it is the responsibility of the accused to prove that he is not guilty. It stipulated that the penalty for rape should not be less than seven years, provided for in-camera proceedings, and made disclosure of a victim's identity an offence. Section 114(A) of the Indian Evidence Act was introduced specifically for cases of custodial rape; it stated that if the victim says she did not consent to sexual intercourse, the court would presume she did not consent.[3]

In the early 1980s, women's groups again took to the streets to protest dowry-related cruelty and murders. Kerosene stoves were exploding with alarming regularity in middle-class homes across Delhi and young brides were routinely going up in smoke. The murder of 21-year-old Kanchanbala in 1979, just a year after she was married, provided the trigger. Her angry, heartbroken and determined mother Satya Rani Chaddha became the face of the campaign to introduce reform in dowry laws.

The Criminal Law (Second) Amendment Act 1983 introduced section 498A (cruelty by husband and his family). In defining 'cruelty' it acknowledged both mental cruelty and domestic violence. 498A is the only extant criminal law that covers violence in the home before it actually results in a woman's death. Section 113(A) was also introduced into the Indian Evidence Act – it stated that if a woman committed suicide within seven years of marriage, and there was evidence of cruelty prior to her death, her husband and in-laws would be held responsible for dowry murder unless evidence to the contrary was provided. A 1986 amendment introduced Section 304(B) into the Indian Penal Code, making dowry death a separate and distinct offence.

In 1992 the gang-rape of Bhanwari, a *saathin* (village-level worker) in the government's Women's Development Programme in Rajasthan, led to a national campaign for justice. Bhanwari's job as a *saathin* involved battling tradition in many forms, including the ubiquitous practice of child marriage. When she – a low-caste *kumhar* (potter caste) woman – tried to stop a child marriage in an upper-caste family, tradition hit back. Five upper-caste men from the infant's family gang-raped Bhanwari for daring to challenge their customs.

While the complaint of gang-rape made its way to a criminal court in Rajasthan, women's groups seized the opportunity to raise the issue of sexual harassment at the workplace, since the violence Bhanwari had suffered was a direct consequence of her work. Under the umbrella name of Vishakha, women's groups filed a petition in 1992 in the Supreme Court against sexual harassment that women face in the workplace. The court's historic Vishakha judgment of 1997 issued guidelines to curb such sexual harassment – the first time in India that sexual harassment at the workplace was legally recognized and declared unconstitutional.

The most recent victory for feminist-led law reform has been the Protection of Women from Domestic Violence Act (2005). Initiated and pushed by feminist legal activists, and spearheaded by the Lawyers Collective, the Act provides crucial civil remedies in cases of domestic violence, including protection orders to prevent further violence against the complainant, residence orders entitling a battered woman to stay in the shared household, custody orders giving temporary custody of the children, monetary relief, and compensation orders. (Noteworthy is the fact that the Act expands the notion of a 'shared household' to include unmarried co-habitation, an important dent in the limited notion of marriage as the only valid form of 'family'.) Violation of a protection order is a criminal offence punishable with imprisonment up to two years, or with a fine up to Rs 20,000, or both. Even prior to this Act, feminist lawyers were procuring similar orders (including protection orders and right to live in the matrimonial home) under different provisions of civil law. But the Protection of Women from Domestic Violence Act expands, explicates and places these for women to use as a matter of right under the umbrella of a single law.

Can We Make These Laws Work?
Direct Interventions in Domestic Violence

While feminist-led law reform has covered a broad canvas, the largest arena of direct, on-the-ground feminist action remains marital domestic violence – a response to the simple reality that physical battering and cruelty by husbands and relatives is one of the biggest sources of daily violence in most women's lives.[4] One welcome shift in domestic violence intervention is the move away from the four main metros. Women's groups that intervene in domestic violence are increasingly based in several smaller towns – Jaipur, Chitrakoot, and Kozhikode, among others.

The State has predictably blessed domestic violence intervention 'to keep families and/or married couples together', by setting up counselling centres attached to civil courts. Because 'marriage' is the overarching umbrella within which domestic violence is commonly understood, there is a clear hierarchy – violence by husbands and relatives has become a more recognized social reality; violence within the natal home, including sexual abuse, still remains largely unacknowledged. Both State and society appear reluctant to accept that sexual abuse is 'abuse' and not 'sex' and that it often breaches the boundaries of sexually 'prohibited' relationships namely between brother/sister, father/offspring, uncle/niece/nephew, etc. There are as yet no State 'counselling centres' to deal with this abuse and few women's groups engage with this form of domestic violence in a sustained manner.

The common perception is that women's groups are in the vanguard of vigorous legal prosecution against cruel and violent husbands; that they help survivors in penalizing men through criminal action, by encouraging women to file charges and throw husbands in jail. This is, in fact, far from the truth. Criminal litigation is rarely the first port of call.

Many organizations that intervene in domestic violence first attempt compromise and conciliation, before encouraging women to take recourse to criminal law. Some groups don't 'encourage' criminal action. Others are against criminal action, believing that it actually helps nobody.

Even for organizations who believe that women survivors of domestic violence should take the route of criminal litigation, the structure of the criminal justice system is such that they can do little in terms of the actual legal battle. Since an Indian Penal Code (IPC) crime is a crime against the State, the prosecution is in the hands of State public prosecutors. Women's groups can at best do the dogged follow-up, or help appoint a watching advocate on behalf of the complainant. The progress and outcome of the litigation depends entirely on how sincerely or vigorously the public prosecutor is willing to prosecute; whether or not they have a degree of gender sensitivity; whether or not they are willing to listen to concerns voiced by women's groups or the violence survivor. 'Pursuing' criminal cases is painful work, affording little legal agency, and few feminist lawyers consider it a good use of their energies.

In cases of domestic violence, therefore, feminist organizations enter the courtroom largely for civil relief. Groups like Majlis in Mumbai do this through their own team of in-house lawyers. Anweshi's large team of activists in Kozhikode includes one in-house lawyer who handles all civil work such as divorce, maintenance, custody, etc. Organizations like Vanangana in Uttar Pradesh have developed a regular relationship with independent lawyers through whom they help survivors fight for civil relief.

Majlis in Mumbai specializes in litigation. The Majlis Legal Centre, which started in 1990, now has a team of junior and senior lawyers who directly intervene in cases of domestic violence through trial court litigation in matters of divorce, annulment of marriage, maintenance to wives and children, child custody issues, right of residence in matrimonial home and rights of women in invalid/bigamous marriages. Their annual report states that the 'the aim of the day-to-day litigation is two-fold: (a) To secure the rights of individual women; (b) To create positive precedence and bring in a culture of women's rights within the precincts of courtrooms.' In 2003–04, around

600 women approached Majlis for help in civil matters, and cases were filed on behalf of 175 women. In the Majlis office in Nagpur, there are presently approximately 150 cases pending before the Family Court.

The Anweshi (Women's Counselling Centre) in Kozhikode, one of India's most respected women's groups working specifically on violence since 1993, is firmly opposed to criminal litigation. As its name suggests, counselling and compromise is Anweshi's preferred strategy. Anweshi's annual report for 2005–06 has a category of 'settled' cases but does not have a category of 'convictions'. During this period, 348 new cases came to Anweshi for counselling. A total of 93 cases were 'settled' by Anweshi, while 52 cases, primarily to do with maintenance, custody and divorce, were filed in various [civil] courts. Only 2 cases were filed under section 498A (the criminal offence of cruelty by husbands and relatives). The assumption is that the 498A cases will also be compromised and compounded.

Activists from Anweshi categorically said in a conversation:

We don't want the conviction. No, we don't, we don't. We want to compromise the case before that. So we use 498A as a pressure tactic against the culprit to ask him to come to the negotiating table and [pay] a decent compensation for the peace he has taken away from her. Criminal cases should be the last resort. Why do women come to us?... Because they don't even want to go to a police station, that's why. They are more comfortable with a woman's organization. That's why they come to Anweshi. We don't want a case, they say, so please settle the case for us.

At one level, respecting the agency and choices of individual women means settling a case, if that is what they want. 'Settling' a case on behalf of a violence survivor means bringing the man to the negotiating table and making him agree to certain terms like no physical violence, no negligence, maintenance for the wife and children, and so on. The terms of each 'settlement' are determined according to the specific context of the case. These terms are then written up on a Rs 50 stamp paper, signed by both parties and kept with Anweshi for follow-up in case of any breach.

Anweshi activists explain why their strategy works:

If we give 498A in the petition and the fellow is arrested, then he comes out on bail and for years and years, the case goes on and in the end, the woman… she gives her statement in the court and he gets punished for it. But what does she get? She doesn't get her dowry back; she doesn't get compensation, nothing! Only her vengeance is satisfied by putting him into jail. Her everyday survival problem is not dealt with through this!… So, we feel that this strategy is helping us. By using 498A [as a threat], we are helping the woman to stand on her own, to have her own means for livelihood afterwards.

More than being convicted for the crime of violence, they believe men should be made responsible and pay for their actions in the form of compensation. Anweshi activists take pride in the fact they have not followed a single 498A case all the way to a successful conviction in the group's fifteen-year history:

We will advise women that this is the best way. If you want to go back with the man, 498A case will be a hindrance. If you decide not to go with the man, then we can use 498A to get all your things if he doesn't agree to a marital settlement. So that is our approach.

According to them, only educated, wealthy women who don't have to struggle for material survival would be interested in criminally convicting a man for domestic violence.

If Anweshi responds to women 'who don't want to go to police stations', others work specifically alongside those very police stations. The Mahila Salah Evam Suraksha Kendra (MSESK) is a joint initiative of the Rajasthan police and nine Jaipur-based organizations working on women's rights.[5] Modelled along the lines of the Special Cells for Women and Children in Mumbai, (a joint effort of the Mumbai police and the Tata Institute of Social Sciences, which have been in existence now for over 24 years) the MSESKs are essentially counselling centres inside *mahila thanas* (women's police stations) to help the police in bringing about conciliation between spouses in domestic violence cases.

The non-negotiables include: 'No compromise on the issue of violence against women, principles of self-determination for the client, and no societal pressures of any kind.'[6] The initiative has now spread from Jaipur to ten districts in Rajasthan. MSESK's motive is to help the police approach domestic violence as 'more than just a crime', or as a social situation demanding a multi-pronged intervention. This thinking is very much a contribution of women's rights activists who have worked on the ground with violence survivors – there is a crying need to sensitize the police machinery into offering women in violent situations more than the frightening black-and-white option of 'either you press charges or you go home'. This is a choice few battered women are capable of making at first. They need handholding, emotional and psychological support and assurance of options through counselling. The 2006 figures from the Gandhi Nagar Mahila Thana, where the first MSESK was set up, are revealing. Of 258 women who registered complaints with the MSESK, only 17 went on to file First Information Reports (FIRs) under section 498A. Clearly the MSESK counselling also works largely towards conciliation, rather than in helping women go the legal route.

Activists from Vanangana, a women's group in Chitrakoot district of Uttar Pradesh that has worked with women facing violence for over 15 years, also adopt the 'conciliation between spouses' route in many cases. But Vanangana does not believe in conciliation as a first option. In its experience, much depends on the manner in which options are discussed with a battered woman barely out of a violent situation. Its activists encourage women not to accept compromises with violent, criminally-liable husbands, and the organization's field workers are willing and able to take women through the long difficult legal process.

According to them, many women do seek legal options if that is what is offered to them in the counselling sessions. From 2003 to 2007, 752 of 942 cases registered with Vanangana were domestic violence cases. In 315 cases, after initially approaching Vanangana the survivors and/or their family chose to handle the situation on their own. Of the remaining cases, FIRs under section 498A were lodged in 125 cases, and

non-cognizable reports in 29 cases;[7] seventy-six cases were
solved through mediation, while the counselling process was
still going on in 129 cases. In total, therefore, a little over 10
per cent of Vanangana's cases led to the filing of FIRs; of
these, few reached the trial stage.

The organization cites several reasons for why such few
cases progress beyond the FIR stage: delays in investigation
or shoddy investigation, the filing of final reports by the
police, compromises between parties, survivors losing
interest in following their case because of the huge delays,
and finally a delay in the judicial process itself. In 2006,
Vanangana reviewed the fate of all the FIRs that it had been
instrumental in lodging. A large number were found to be
'under consideration'; in the few that were charge-sheeted,
the trials had not begun. Since all 498A cases are referred
to the family counselling cells attached to the courts in both
Chitrakoot and Banda districts, there is enormous pressure
from the police and the judiciary as well as the community
to compromise – as a result, the phenomenon of witnesses
turning hostile in 498A cases is extremely common.

Exacerbating this is the fact that the Allahabad High Court
appears to have developed a pattern of staying arrests in 498A
cases. Once the accused get a stay, the entire matter goes on
the backburner as far as the police are concerned, and the
accused are basically free to negotiate, pressurize or threaten.[8]
While Vanangana's activists do painstaking, persistent court
follow-up on each case as well as continued counselling, many
women buckle under the dual pressure of an unresponsive
legal system and a hostile social order. Thus the 'success' of
the legal option, even for organizations who believe in this
approach, is clearly dubious.

We have achieved much in terms of law reform. A range
of intervention strategies are clearly on offer: conciliation,
compromise with non-negotiable conditions, the threat
of criminal action, actual filing of criminal cases. Several
organizations work with alternative dispute resolution
mechanisms like Mahila Panchayats and Nari Adalats.[9]
Women's groups today work with survivors, families, the

police and the judiciary. Despite so much work and such a rich history, however, we seem to be no closer to 'legal justice'. Where are the gaps? What are the hard questions we must still ask ourselves?

Between the Pragmatic and the Principled

Today, in effect, many women's organizations do a great deal more counselling and *samjhauta* (brokering compromises) between abusive husbands and battered wives, than prosecuting. This is a direct response to the sad reality that 498A appears to have gradually become a *badnaam* (tainted) law – large sections of the judiciary believe that women either abuse the section or that those bringing 'real' charges against their own husbands must be a bad lot indeed. 'Vindictive little home breakers! What kind of an Indian wife presses criminal charges against her husband for a slap or two!'

This mindset was officially and quite unabashedly, endorsed by a high-level committee set up by the Government of India to recommend 'Reforms of the Criminal Justice System'. Headed by Justice V.S. Malimath, the committee had this to say about section 498A in its influential 2003 report:

This provision is intended to protect the wife from being subjected by the husband or his relatives to cruelty. Cruelty for the purpose of this Section means wilful conduct that is likely to drive the woman to commit suicide or cause grave injury or damage to life, limb or health, mental or physical. It also includes harassment by coercing to meet unlawful demands. This is a very welcome measure. But what has bothered the Committee are the provisions which make this offence non-bailable and non-compoundable.[10]

The woman who lives with the husband and his family after marriage is expected to receive affection and caring and not cruelty and harassment. True to the Indian tradition the woman quietly suffers – without complaining – many inconveniences, hardships and even insults with the sole object of making the marriage a success. She even tolerates a husband with bad habits. But then, when her suffering crosses the limit of tolerance she may even commit suicide. For the Indian woman marriage is a sacred bond and she tries her best not to break it. As this offence is made non-bailable and not compoundable, it makes reconciliation and returning to marital home almost impossible.[11]

Thus, in the long term interests of the 'quietly-suffering' Indian woman, the Malimath committee recommended that 498A be made bailable and compoundable. The Criminal Law (Amendment) Bill 2003 attempted to implement this recommendation but by the time the Bill passed into law in 2005, the provision had been dropped thanks in part to strong opposition by the National Commission for Women in its deposition before the Parliamentary Standing Committee on Home Affairs. So, 498A still remains non-compoundable, on paper but not in practice.[12]

Even if a case is filed, the system itself encourages women to 'compound' the case. Since 498A is technically a non-compoundable offence, i.e., once filed there can be no out-of-court settlement, a battered woman has to file a petition stating that she lied in order to discontinue the case. Women's rights activists have become so acutely aware of this bias that in several cases, they merely ask women to use 498A as a pressure tactic to bring husbands to the negotiating table. The other side of the picture is that women themselves are often loath to press criminal charges, and prefer the softer '*samjhauta*' solution: at least an informal 'settlement' keeps the doors open for a possible reconciliation in the future.

Ultimately it is a chicken and egg story. Did women turn away from 498A, or did the judiciary's tinted view of the section prove too daunting a hurdle? If the law worked for every woman who tried to use it, would it encourage more women to come forward to criminally prosecute for violence within marriage? Is our pragmatic approach actually responding to the needs of all survivors? A women's group working with domestic violence survivors said that when women are told what their 'real' options are, a full one-third of them say:

Is this the only remedy available for me in law? It took me years to decide to go in for legal action, and I thought it will change everything and will give me justice, will punish the people who abused me for years, but it only offers me maintenance![13]

Working the law means walking a fine line between the pragmatic and the principled. In the face of many legal defeats, have activists in the movement gradually downscaled their demands from the high perch of feminist principles far too much? In our search for the 'strategic' solution, are we losing sight of the ideal? Have we abandoned our search for that elusive outcome called 'legal justice'?

The question really is this: Are we as a movement self-editing and turning away from criminalizing a criminal act (wife battery, domestic violence, call it what you will) because we have been unable to make a dent in the essentially intransigent patriarchal biases of the system and judiciary? Instead of hammering away at the patriarchal framework of judges, have we turned away from using 498A to the fullest extent?

Have we ourselves removed this from the menu of options placed before a battered woman – or presented it as less than appetizing? In the present culture of counselling and compromises, we might well negotiate more feminist terms for a violence survivor, but ultimately we are just sending her back home. Surely 'justice' must mean more than this?

Hierarchies of Activism: Decriminalizing Domestic Violence, Criminalizing Rape?

In practice today then, violence within marriage is 'de facto' decriminalized. Marital rape is still not recognized as a crime in India. If you are a woman above sixteen years you can be raped every night by your husband with no recourse to law. While 498A does exist, in practice we are litigating less and less around assault and cruelty. Ergo, the only law we have which criminalizes violence within marriage is gradually becoming redundant. A rape is a rape only outside marriage; an assault on the streets clearly different from an assault at home.

Admittedly, criminal prosecution does not give battered women what they need most and need immediately –

security, a roof over their heads, material support for survival.
Women 'need' basic means to survive. And a large number
of women's groups have based their strategy on this very real
need. It is a valid service delivery, but we cannot believe that
this is 'justice'. Because what women 'need' should not detract
from what they 'want'.

Ironically, groups who routinely broker compromises in
cases of domestic violence are dead against compromising in
cases of rape. Anweshi activists say,

For criminal cases, for rape and all other things we don't use this
strategy (of compromise). Rape is not at all compromisable. But
sometimes, the rapist and the girl's family themselves directly
compromise. They take money and the case is solved. But when
these parties, both of these come to us and say please compromise
for us, we say no. On rape, and especially child rape, we want the
rapist to be punished. That is what we think. Only in 498A, we take
'settlement' as our stand to help the woman.

Since the late 1990s, the organization has been in the
forefront of exposing a sex racket known as the 'Ice Cream
Parlour Case', which had abused young women in Kozhikode.
The case involved influential politicians, officials and sundry
'powerful' people. As a result, the trial was manipulated and
the key players let off. But all the campaigning in the world,
the public exposure and humiliation of the culprits, has not
been satisfying for Anweshi. In this case, they want nothing
less than criminal action and a legal conviction.

Similarly, activists involved in setting up the Mahila Salah
Evam Suraksha Kendras in Rajasthan, many of whom were
critical to Bhanwari's campaign for justice, would never dream
of attempting a *samjhauta* in her case. Vanangana's big legal
battle has been the Ila Pandey child sexual abuse case, which
started in 1999. Nine years later the trial still snakes along in a
Sessions Court. 'Legal justice' does mean something, then.

At one level, everyone believes that a crime must be
punished, and legal conviction has not entirely lost its value.
Legal victory, when it comes, is a powerful high and activists
seek it – despite the long years of slow, tortuous banging of

heads against systemic brick walls. Have we then in our work created a hierarchy of violence? Rape demands criminal conviction; domestic violence less so?

The Paradox of Civil Remedies

Do feminist 'practitioners' of the law (as opposed to theoreticians) then see the law largely as a framework for pragmatic solutions, or a discursive space through which to continue to make 'principles' work? The discussion on civil remedies and the Protection of Women from Domestic Violence Act 2005 is a case in point. The Act, welcomed by scores of activists across the country, meets a deeply felt need for violence survivors: it offers protection orders against violence, and rights to the matrimonial home and custody of children. A Rajasthan-based activist said in a conversation that,

Why did the Domestic Violence Act come? We learnt from 498A that women were unable to take the stress of the police and the court procedure, which can be so endless and in the meanwhile the woman is vulnerable, what does she do with the kids, what does she do with the finance, what does she do for shelter?

But the opening up of a civil option should not mean the closing off of criminal avenues. Bad experience of criminal law cannot be the rationale for civil remedies. According to one activist:

Would you rather focus your energies on finding creative civil remedies that will work for numerous women, or do you want to keep harping on a criminal remedy to batter the institution of marriage just on principle? What do you want? It's a tough one. In winning the battle, are we losing the war? In meeting the 'practical' needs of women, are we losing sight of women's longer-term strategic interests?[14]

Civil remedies like the Domestic Violence Bill must be welcomed on their own terms, as opening up another front in what must be a multi-pronged legal assault on domestic violence; not because they are a substitute for criminal convictions for violence within the matrimonial home. Marriage is, after all, among the institutions most seriously critiqued and questioned by feminist scholarship and activism; the site to be most questioned; the site where patriarchy is reproduced on a daily basis.

'The personal is political' was the war cry of the women's movement; erasing the false public/private divide was what activism was all about. It would be a tragic irony if we now find ourselves strategizing along the same lines of separation when it comes to the law. Even an unspoken acceptance that 'criminal law does not work in the domestic-private space, therefore let's look for civil options' is an admission of defeat; an acceptance that in the domestic-private space women are less than equal, and that a violation of their fundamental right to bodily integrity translates not into punishment for the violator, but only in compensation to her in material terms and perhaps in some assurance of protection from violence in the future.

The fear is, of course, that this tacit acceptance may not be just tacit anymore. Given the culture of informal *samjhautas* that have become the mainstay of domestic violence intervention, having procured civil relief for a woman, how much are we likely to push her towards criminally prosecuting a wife batterer simply because it is 'right','just' and 'feminist' to do so; simply because he is a criminal? Has the movement lost the energy to really make the system work?

Feminist Law Reform: Two Steps Forward, One Step Back?

The purpose of feminist law reforms has presumably been to achieve three things: (a) establish, to the extent possible, feminist principles in the content of the law; (b) create procedures and systems that respond accurately and sensitively to the 'reality' of the average woman who approaches the law; and (c) as a consequence of (a) and (b), achieve greater 'legal' justice, i.e., favourable judgments or convictions, as the case may be.

Yet on the latter ('legal' justice), law reform has yielded little. Legal justice for women remains a mirage. According to the National Crimes Records Bureau (NCRB), the conviction rates for major violent crimes against women – dowry deaths, rape, molestation, and cruelty by husband and relatives – in 2003, 2004 and 2005 were in the range of 18 per cent to 33 per cent (Although it is testimony to the increasingly 'moral' times we live in that for 'immoral' crimes under the Immoral Traffic Prevention Act and the Indecent Representation of Women (Prohibition) Act, the judiciary is substantially more generous, convicting in 82 per cent and 94 per cent cases respectively in 2005).[15]

But NCRB figures, low as they are for so many violent crimes against women, are also somewhat misleading. Legal activists say that conviction rates are impossible to assess accurately since a large number of convictions in such cases are overturned in appeals. It would be a complex statistical formulation to actually follow each case through to its final stage. On rape cases, for example, while NCRB figures claim a 26.1 per cent conviction rate in 2003 and 25.5 per cent in 2005, a more accurate assessment may be closer to a 5 per cent rate of conviction.[16] Clearly then, where rape, dowry murder and domestic violence are concerned, 'justice' is not easily on offer.

Feminist principles in the hands of an unchanged and aggressively anti-feminist system appear to have been counterproductive. To state the obvious: feminist justice needs a large dose of feminist lawyering – not just feminist law reform. But feminist lawyering is among the areas of work most neglected by the women's movement. As a critic said, 'The movement is good at throwing up grand ideas, but stinks at implementation. And legal justice is finally only about making the law work. The focus on law reform is misplaced.'

Despite these patchy results, there is also the predictable view that law reform means more than its quantifiable outcome; campaigns for law reform become an excuse to get a feminist discourse onto a public agenda. Says an activist:

You want changes at the macro level. Now, how do you bring about changes at the macro level? You cannot force them to come with the sheer moral tsunami of a Gandhi. You don't have that sort of moral power... You can't have a Dandi march or salt-making... You'll be yelling at a small little public meeting in Delhi, I'll be yelling over here and hopefully the media might cover us. I think law reform is a very effective tool; that is why without having any glorious and fantastic hope from the law, the women's movement will continue to use it. Besides, law reform may not lead to greater justice, but at least it gives hope of justice.

Apart from the yawning gap between good laws and bad implementation, we need to also critically reflect on the substance of the law reform itself. Perhaps the most serious critique of feminist-led law reform comes from organizations who increasingly work with poor, rural women. They baldly allege, 'Those who spearhead law reform in this country are all urban and middle class and that is the reality they bring to the table.'

Take the Bhanwari gang-rape case, for example. The context was rural, the violence deeply embedded in the village's caste politics. Yet what emerged from the debris of that attack was the Vishakha judgment to deal with sexual harassment in the workplace. While on paper the guidelines refer to both the organized and unorganized sector, the mechanisms proposed (such as complaints committees) make them a virtual non-starter in unorganized sectors like agriculture, where countless rural women routinely face sexual harassment. So far the guidelines have been of some utility in urban, middle-class institutional settings. This is not to detract from the feminist advance made by the Vishakha judgment – merely to point out that although it emerged from a rural context, it has not heralded any significant gain for rural women.

Changes in anti-dowry legislation (the Criminal Law (Second) Amendment Act 1983), a substantial gain for the movement, are also based largely on urban realities. According to the Act, a woman's suicide within seven years of marriage makes a prima facie case for dowry-related murder. The framers of this provision neglected to take into account the fundamental rural reality of child marriage or marriage at a very young age, where the year of the marriage is less important than the year of the *gauna*.[17] For many village women the *gauna* is the effective date from which co-habitation with the husband's family begins. A *gauna* can take place years after the marriage: two years, three years, sometimes even seven years later. As a result the seven-year stipulation of the act can make the law ineffective for them. As feminist activism in rural and *mofussil* India makes its voice heard, substantive and procedural law reform as well as challenges of implementation must take on board a whole new constituency and new concerns.

What does 'Justice' Mean? And for Whom?

Law reform has often been preceded by feminist-led campaigns centred around particular cases. These 'trigger' cases continue to be critical for the women's movement. According to one leading activist,

Whether a campaign actually succeeds or not, the fact that you are bringing a women's issue on to the political agenda, you've already achieved a great deal. You are too small to have a statewide mobilization; you do not affect electoral votes. Campaigns create a public debate, which you as a group are incapable of generating otherwise.

But, does 'success' then mean the same thing for feminist activists and for the survivors on whose behalf or in whose name they act?

It is somewhat startling that the history of feminist-led campaigns, including cases that have entered the annals of feminist folklore, is littered with a series of legal failures. Mathura's case was lost at the very beginning, when in 1978 the highest court in the land acquitted the two policemen who had raped her. Apart from Nagpur-based activists from the Stree Atyachar Virodhi Parishad who last met Mathura in the late 1990s, few women's rights activists today seem to know what happened to her. Rameeza Bi's case also ended in all the policemen being acquitted.[18] Satya Rani Chaddha, an icon of the movement, is today a tired and broken woman, even as we chalk up crucial changes in anti-dowry laws (which emerged out of the campaign surrounding Kanchanbala's

death) in our list of victories. Kanchanbala's husband Subhas
was finally charge-sheeted under Section 306 IPC (abetment
to suicide) in 1991, eleven years after her murder. Convicted
by the Sessions Court, he immediately appealed in the High
Court in 2000. The appeal is still pending, and until it is heard
he remains a free man, out on bail.

Contrary to popular perception, Bhanwari's is also, for
now, a lost case. Her rapists were acquitted on 15 November
1995, and the appeal against their acquittal has been pending
in the Rajasthan High Court for over ten years. Yet she too
is an icon of the movement and it is somehow a common
erroneous perception that we won. A very recent recruit
into the feminist movement said that for her Bhanwari is
a historic figure, much like Mathura remains for an earlier
generation of feminist activists. Did she know that 'legally
speaking', Bhanwari lost? 'What rubbish. She won. I know
she won. We've all always thought we won.' The difference
between 'we won' and 'she won' must be confronted. 'We' (the
women's movement) did make an advance as a consequence
of Bhanwari's case, but 'she' the survivor still waits.

The Ethics of Representation

A feminist legal activist, who has been a part of the movement
for close to half a century, said succinctly, 'We have just done
campaigns, not cases.' Therein lies the gap between the needs
of the movement and the needs of individual survivors –
perhaps one reason that 'legal justice' remains so elusive. While
putting our energies into campaigns purportedly on behalf of a
violence survivor, we seem to have lost sight of the litigation,
of the need for legal victory. A leading feminist academic,
writing about the ways in which (reactionary/patriarchal) legal
discourse can hijack feminist politics, quotes a feminist legal
activist as saying that 'she would rather lose a rape case if in
the process the right kind of debate were made possible.'[19]
But the real question is this: Does the rape survivor care at all
about generating the 'right kind of debate'? When a survivor
starts a legal battle, legal victory is all she wants.

This raises the critical issue of the ethics of representation. In her seminal work, *The History of Doing*, Radha Kumar notes:

While preparations were underway for March 8 demonstrations feminist groups tried to meet Mathura to find out what her own views on the matter were. Two women from Bombay's Forum Against Rape went to meet her and found that though she did not object to the campaign, she was not particularly hopeful either. Though this was a relief, many were shamed by the realization that they had gone so far into the campaign without even wondering what one of its main subjects felt. This had raised the question of representation in a different – and for many, a more painful way: who were we to protest until we had met the woman who was raped and found out whether she wanted a protest or not?[20]

Most women's groups in Delhi or Bombay were unaware of Mathura's existence during the entire time that her case moved from the Sessions Court to the Bombay High Court, and finally to the Supreme Court, It was only when four senior law teachers issued an open letter on 16 September 1979 protesting the Supreme Court's acquittal that women's groups seized upon the issue.[21] According to a Nagpur-based activist who was involved in many phases of the case, Mathura herself had little idea what was going on when the two convicted police constables went in appeal to the Supreme Court:

She was a poor uneducated girl and had no idea what Supreme Court is or High Court is. All she knew was that the policemen were jailed briefly and then let off. She just wanted to leave the bad publicity of being a raped woman behind her and get on with her life.[22]

The same appears to have been true of Rameeza Bi. Vimochana and the Women's Lawyers Association in Bangalore were not involved in helping her fight her case. They emerged only after the acquittal, and filed an appeal against it on their own behalf, although activists in Vimochana say that a group called Stree Shakti Sangathana in Hyderabad was in touch with Rameeza Bi.[23] The tide turned with Bhanwari's case in 1992 where she remained very much at the centre of her campaign. She was informed, aware, and the activists who

spoke on her behalf did so with her consent. They continue to
be in regular contact with her. (In the Supreme Court petition
that led to the Vishakha judgment though, Bhanwari herself
was not a petitioner.) The Bilkis Bano gang-rape and mass
murder case of 2002 (in which the judgment was pronounced
in 2008) has been similarly handled. Bilkis has spoken in her
own voice.

Today the ethics of representation is further complicated
by the demands of twenty four-hour media. Any 'known'
feminist activist is inevitably badgered for a sound byte or
two when a major 'women's case' hits the spotlight. In the
Bilkis case, while the activists who had worked closely with
her for six long years kept a low profile, others who had not
even met her gave sound bytes on the implications of her
legal victory. It is perhaps par for the course. Women's groups
routinely issue public statements of condemnation or support,
often without having met the survivor, or knowing what she
wants – and yes, it is part of their advocacy mandate.

But, who speaks for whom – and when and how – remain
questions in need of urgent debate within the movement. When
does a woman's 'case' become a matter of public concern
and open to public comment? And to what extent does or
should the survivor have control over the public discourse
that she generates? Even if the sound-byte era demands that
any newsworthy story is fair game for public comment, to
what extent should activists be party to these disembodied
constructions of public discourse? Is the survivor no longer
central to the debate? Is the campaign and advocacy more
important than the litigation?

Of course, often times the process of legal engagement
throws up possibilities that were never envisioned at the start
of a campaign, and it would be foolish on our part not to
explore these. A campaign is after all a process, a journey. In
Bhanwari's case, for example, in the very circumstances of her
violation, the movement was presented with an opening at a
crucial political moment. The issue of sexual harassment at
the workplace was gaining rapid momentum in the West and
in international legal circles. In India the phenomenon was

not even legally recognized. The time was right to press for its recognition. During the height of Bhanwari's campaign in 1992, one group of activists (both Delhi- and Rajasthan-based) decided to work closely with Bhanwari in trying to get justice in her criminal case, while another group of Delhi-based legal activists pressed for recognition of sexual harassment at the workplace in the Supreme Court. At the end of the day, we did collectively move the law. But can we be satisfied with a victory that still begs the question: what did and what does Bhanwari want?

Question: Are you happy with the tremendous achievements from your case? And the support and respect you have within large sections of society and the women's movement?

Bhanwari: *'Phark to bahut pada. Mujhe bahut kuch mila. Meri baton ko mana gaya. Lekin duniya ke nyaya se pet nahi bharta. Pet tab bharega jab sarkar nyaya degi'* (It's made a lot of difference. I got a lot. They listened and believed my story. But hunger for justice can never be satisfied with this kind of justice from the world. It will be satiated only when the state gives me justice.)[24]

Locating the Survivor's Voice

Curiously, a series of cases in which the campaign and the survivor spoke in different voices have had to do with Muslim women. The most famous was the Shah Bano case and Shah Bano's infamous reversal of her original stand. In 1985, the Supreme Court granted Shah Bano maintenance under Section 125 of the Criminal Procedure Code. While this was by no means the first judgment of its kind for a Muslim woman, Justice Chandrachud also decided to wax eloquent on the need for a uniform civil code.

In the process, he opened up a hornet's nest. The Muslim right saw it as an attack on their identity. The Hindu right made common cause with 'oppressed Muslim women'. And in 1986, the government played its own cynical politics and brought in a new law: The Muslim Women (Protection of Rights on Divorce) Act that defined the maintenance rights of Muslim women within the limits of Muslim law. Even as feminists of every hue were jumping up and down at the turn of events 'in support of the rights of Muslim women', the Muslim woman at the centre of the storm herself retracted and said she did not want to do anything against her religion.

Shah Bano's is of course a complicated case, which occurred at a complex political moment in our history and is not the subject of the current discussion. More recent history was made by Imrana's case in Muzaffarnagar in June 2005. Raped by her father-in-law, Imrana was reportedly subject to a so-called fatwa stating that she was now *haram* (non-kosher) for her husband but should marry the rapist. The event had women's groups and the All India Muslim Personal Law Board at loggerheads. Meanwhile the pulls of local politics combined with media pressure, forcing Imrana to mutter at various points: 'I shall do whatever the Shariat says...' Perhaps she meant it. Perhaps she did not. Perhaps she was appalled at the suggestion that she live with her rapist but did not want to publicly turn her back on her religious community. Never mind that she had no idea that this was one interpretation of a twisted village-level mullah mind and not a tenet of Shariat law.[25] Who knows what Imrana wanted or under what kinds of social and economic pressures she was surviving? Few bothered to find out.

Women like Shah Bano or Imrana become iconized representations of community in politically-embattled communal situations. They are enmeshed in particular contexts, and in the battle between conservative forces of religion/community and gender rights advocates, they may be unable to articulate their own 'real' desires or understanding. But feminist activists who purportedly lobbied on their behalf have equally accepted them as 'representations of community'. We acknowledge their identity as Muslims but presume their (feminist) acquiescence in trying to re-fashion the salience and/or the meaning of that identity. The question then becomes: Under what conditions of engagement do we as feminist activists earn the right to speak on their behalf?

In other cases, notably that of Mathura in 1974 and Rameeza

Bi in 1978, one is hard placed to locate the survivor's voice at all. The survivor's identity is never fully interrogated, not even by feminist scholars. Mathura was a tribal, Rameeza Bi a Muslim. What role, if any, did these community identities play in these cases that sparked off one of the biggest feminist-led law reform campaigns? Angry protests from her relatives and community followed Mathura's rape; they threatened to burn the Desaiganj police station (then in Chandrapur district, now part of Gadchiroli district in Maharashtra) where the offence took place.[26] That is what led to the filing of first a *panchnama*, later an FIR. As mentioned earlier, women's groups got involved only after the Supreme Court acquittal – almost eight years after the actual incident. But how did this young tribal woman feel about becoming the poster girl for the feminist cause?

A fact often forgotten (or perhaps rarely acknowledged in the first instance) about Rameeza Bi's case is that the same Majlis-e-Ittehadul-Muslimeen (MIM), recently in the news for hurling flowerpots at exiled Bangladeshi writer Taslima Nasreen, was the organization which made Rameeza's case a case at all. The protests following her rape were led not by women's groups but by the MIM. Scores of Muslim protestors led by the MIM carried her husband Ahmad Hussain's dead body, after he had been killed by the police, laid it before the police station, and seized control of the station. Six protestors died when the police opened retaliatory fire. There was mayhem in Hyderabad city. The opposition gheraoed the Chief Minister and a one-man inquiry commission was formed, which finally recommended prosecution of the policemen.[27]

Women's groups enter the picture much later when they file an appeal against the policemen's acquittal, first in the High Court, then in the Supreme Court. They file it on their own behalf – not on behalf of Rameeza. Kannabiran notes that the Rameeza case was an example of a fundamentalist Muslim organization using the violation of a Muslim woman to exert its own (Muslim) muscle in the city of Hyderabad vis-à-vis the State represented then by a Congress government;

that in the battle between MIM and the State, Rameeza was at best a silent pawn.[28]

But even in Kannabiran's own exposition Rameeza's voice is missing. How did this woman herself feel about her dual identity – as a woman who survived violence, or as a Muslim woman who may have been violated because she was both Muslim and woman? If she was a pawn in the hands of fundamentalist Muslims, was she a willing or an unwilling one? And though we must question the very existence of 'free will' and acknowledge women's lack of agency, survivor-centred activism demands that we accept their will at face value. The fact is that both Mathura and Rameeza appear in feminist texts as entirely unmediated, de-contextualized, pure 'woman'; they were violated as 'woman'. They are symbolically appropriated for the feminist cause, without informed consent; their location in a complex socio-political matrix, laden with power and hierarchy, invisibilized.

Justice and the Question of Identity

The invisibilization of identity and power in a crime remains one crucial limitation of the law in general, and of laws to do with violence against women, in particular. We are equal before law, although not equal in society. Law assumes neutrality, and inbuilt into that very neutrality is its failure to provide the elusive outcome called justice – because social arrangements are far from neutral. As young feminists we were taught to believe that when it comes to violence we are ultimately united as women. And a rape is a rape. It is the violation of a woman's bodily integrity. A rape = B rape. But is it all the same? Who rapes, in what situation, what kind of caste, class and religious hierarchies are invoked, what kind of power runs through the rape; how the rape is viewed by courts, by the judges, the lawyers, the policemen, who raped whom and why – surely it does matter?

The Indian Penal Code has no answers to these differentials, which actually determine not only how and why a woman was assaulted, but how her case will be viewed and whether she will get justice. In Indian law The Scheduled Castes and The Scheduled Tribes (Prevention of Atrocities) Act 1989 is perhaps the only piece of legislation that acknowledges the role of identity in a violation. Violations experienced by Dalit women are different from those experienced by non-Dalit women. The Act acknowledges her multiple identities. But this Act is the exception. For the most part, locating rape and domestic violence within the structure of caste and religious community, and bringing identity into the courtroom is a big legal no-no. The women's movement has neither interrogated nor pushed this issue in the realm of the law (apart from the debates surrounding the Uniform Civil Code).

How does one begin to acknowledge many forms of violence faced by women in identity-based terms? Failure to engage adequately with the complex issue of identity in the context of violence against women was hideously highlighted in the Gujarat carnage of 2002. Scores of women were brutally raped and sexually assaulted in myriad ways because they were Muslim, not just because they were women. Even following the anti-Sikh pogrom of 1984, at least five specific affidavits on sexual violence suffered by Sikh women were filed before the Nanavati Commission of Inquiry, when it was finally set up in 2000. But the Indian Penal Code offers no solutions. For one, IPC gives us only Sections 375, 376, 354, and 509.[29] Of these the only serious crime – rape – is spelled out in 375/376 and its definition is limited to acts of penile penetration. The rest (IPC 354 and 509) are mild offences. Much of what was meted out to Muslim women in Gujarat – mutilation of breasts and bodies, insertion of objects into vaginas, stripping and parading – none of it is really a prosecutable crime under Indian law. In recent years women's groups have been debating the need for an expanded definition of sexual crimes. Draft amendments to the laws relating to sexual assault in Section 375, 376, 354 and 509 IPC and the relevant sections of the Code of Criminal Procedure 1973 and the Indian Evidence Act 1872, finalized by the National Commission for Women, are now lying with the government awaiting action. But there is something vital missing in the law – which even the proposed amendments do not take care of – the issue of targeted, identity-based (communal) mass violence; violence against Muslim women because they were Muslim; violence against Sikh women because they were Sikh.

Justice for these survivors is a virtual impossibility. The only survivor of sexual violence in a communal context to have won her case in India is Bilkis Bano, when a Mumbai Sessions court convicted 13 of the 20 accused in 2008. But Bilkis' is a story more about the resilience of one woman and the activists who worked with her, rather than a paean to Indian law. It is a story that takes us from Gujarat all the way to the Supreme Court, to a CBI re-investigation, a transfer of the trial outside Gujarat, and much, much more. Her victory is a symbol only of herself; and also a symbol of the colossal failure of the justice delivery system.

In identity-based crimes against women, the law itself, therefore, limits women's access to 'legal' justice. A corrective to the flawed legal structure was promised by the UPA government when it came to power in 2004, in the form of 'comprehensive' legislation on communal violence. The government's draft, both weak and dangerous and entirely gender-blind, was expectedly roundly criticized by civil society groups. Many separate groups of activists made skeletal alternative drafts, and efforts were made to engage the government in putting together a new draft in partnership with civil society. After close to three years and several activist huddles later, one draft of the Communal Crimes Bill 2008 was handed over to the government in January. At the time of writing, nothing had happened to the Bill.

But the limitation of the law does not quite explain the limited nature of feminist protest. There was little organized protest or anything resembling a feminist-led campaign surrounding the events in Gujarat. Hordes of women's rights activists did not descend upon the streets of Gujarat to scream 'No!' or shout 'Justice!' in the face of one of the worst episodes of communally-motivated sexual brutality against women in modern Indian history. Nothing like this had been seen since the horrors of Partition; yet there was little public display of real feminist anger. Admittedly the crest of the mass-protest era is on a plunge, and the good old street fight has been replaced by The Big Fight,[30] but even behind-the-scenes feminist-led activism and advocacy has been less than robust.

While individual activists who consider themselves a part of the women's movement were both participants and initiators of many of these meetings and discussions around the Communal Violence Bill, women's organizations as a lobby group did not formally respond to the government's Communal Violence Bill, when it was first tabled in Parliament in December 2005. Few kept track of subsequent developments around the Bill. There was no alternative draft bill conceived and 'owned' and pushed by the women's movement. *The Survivors Speak* (Ahmedabad, 2002), the only substantive fact-finding effort to focus exclusively on the impact that the Gujarat carnage had on Muslim women, which had several known feminists on board, was put together at the behest of the Citizen's Initiative, a coalition grouping in Ahmedabad. And apart from the Bilkis Bano case, no other case of sexual violence has been monitored and supported by activists, including legal activists, from the women's movement.[31]

Why is it that a movement for whom rape and sexual violence against women is a core agenda issue, which built its momentum on the issue of sexual violence through dynamic and sustained campaigning, appears to have lost steam when sexual violence unlike any we've known in recent memory exploded on the streets of Gujarat? One can only speculate (a) that feminist activism has not really developed indigenous tools of engagement with community identity-based feminisms; although feminist scholarship in the last decade or so has engaged with the question of identity and identity-based violence, this has not been translated into actual work on the ground; and (b) that feminist-activism has also not developed creative tools of engagement with larger public, political life in which identity-based violence is embedded.

For the most part the entire voluntary sector, including women's groups, has only the most limited engagement with the Muslim community as a whole. There remains a degree of 'othering', and a sense of unease in acknowledging one's own privileged non-minority status. Is there then among feminist activists a nagging sense of discomfort with Bilkis' words:

This judgment is a victory not only for me but for all those innocent Muslims who were massacred and *all those women whose bodies were violated only because, like me, they were Muslim*[32] ...I know that I am not the only one. There are many women out there, whose names and faces I do not know but whose pain I can feel. Through you members of the press, *I want to send a message to all those Muslim women that this is not my struggle alone. It is OUR struggle.* And I know that this important milestone today is the result of all their prayers.[33]

Is her constant proclamation of community identity something only to be tolerated because of the blatant communal circumstances of her violation, but not something to be affirmed? In all private communication with the author, Bilkis has never once articulated her sense of being a 'woman' who suffered a grave injustice. She remains to herself a 'Muslim' first and last. It is that identity which is strongest. Given the movement's troubled relationship with 'the Muslim women's question', can it discursively embrace Bilkis on her own terms? Not appropriate her as a neutral 'woman'- survivor shorn of community identity (like Mathura or Rameeza Bi), but proclaim her as a 'Muslim'-woman survivor who was violated precisely because of an identity she chooses to repeatedly affirm? Survivor-centred activism and identity-based feminism demands just that: creating a discourse of feminism and justice that the survivor is most comfortable with.

The movement's engagement with the larger political domain in which identity-based violence against women is embedded remains very sporadic. The main terrain of intervention on violence against women continues to be almost exclusively the domestic space. One must question whether our emphasis and comfort with 'the personal' space has blunted our desire to engage, even discursively, even just in terms of vigorously foregrounding the gender issue, with the larger, messier, Indian political arena?

It is noteworthy that the 'autonomous' feminist voice has also been muffled on the issue of Nandigram. And the reports of sexual violence in Nandigram have not been amplified, crosschecked, followed up, or turned into feminist-led campaigns to the extent possible. Although an eleven member women's team, including several feminists from Kolkata, undertook a one-day fact-finding journey to Nandigram on 24 November 2007, many months after the violence first erupted, at the time of writing they had only released an interim report. Admittedly the identity-based violence witnessed in Nandigram was different from that of Gujarat, simply because political identities are more mutable than religious-community identity. Even so, it was mass sexual violence that was based on identity. You got raped in Gujarat if you were Muslim. You got violated in Nandigram if you or a member of your family supported the Bhumi Ucched Pratirodh Samiti or the CPM – as the case may be. And yet feminist voices have not merged in national protest. There is still no feminist-led campaign demanding justice and new laws for identity-based mass sexual violence.

This Thing Called Justice

When it comes to violence against women, justice is still just a word. No one appears to be in the justice delivery business anymore – not the State, not women's groups, clearly not even the judges. The justice we speak of is not an alternative form of justice, or validation by a constituency of feminist activists, or the acceptance of one's truth in social forums. One is speaking of 'legal justice' – the kind one gets in a courtroom, the kind survivors wait for with bated breath as the verdict is pronounced. Punishment for the guilty, a vindication of a woman's truth, an acknowledgement of her suffering, an acceptance that a terrible wrong happened, an affirmation by the State and society of a woman's citizenship and equality.

In cases of domestic violence certainly, little of that is on offer. When it comes to domestic violence, the law is used primarily to meet basic survival needs, and justice remains

that remote proverbial cherry that women have perhaps
learnt not even to aspire to. There are many contradictions
to be confronted. On rape, we want criminal convictions; on
domestic violence, well, let's not push it because life must
go on. Even within this problematic hierarchy of violence,
even in cases of rape and sexual assault, convictions, in sheer
hard numbers, do not take place. Activists across the board
agree that women's groups campaign with fervour but fail to
litigate. This is perhaps why the feminist road to legal reforms
is littered with dead cases. We failed to convict before the
reforms, sometimes losing steam on criminal litigation during
campaigns, and we continue to fail in securing legal justice
after getting better laws. On domestic violence we appear to
have taken the 'pragmatic'/civil route; on rape we haven't got
criminal convictions.

The gaps are of course many – the most obvious is that
there are very few feminists present in our courtrooms to
represent women through using the laws we have demanded.
The other yawning gap is the dearth of safe, secure, comforting
shelters for women who escape domestic violence. Where
is the crucial safe space that would enable more women to
pursue criminal prosecution? Government shelters are in a
sorry state, and NGO-run services are few and far between.
And what about life beyond a short-stay home or shelter?
What is the economically sustainable, socially acceptable,
long-term life-choice alternative to the sasural/maika options
for the average Indian woman? The truth is that there is
none. A 'single' woman who has walked out of a violent
marriage, perhaps taking her children with her, is simply
not morally or socially acceptable in India. These are areas
for serious intervention by the women's movement. Clearly,
law reform alone cannot and must not set the agenda.
Because ultimately, who do we represent? When we broker
compromises we say we represent the woman's wishes. And
yet we have historically campaigned around women who
did not know we existed, and more than once forgotten that
victim-survivors want legal vindication more than another
set of shiny new laws.

Admittedly the movement today is more mindful of the ethics of representation. There is greater awareness of the principle of survivor-centred activism. Bhanwari and Bilkis both represent this shift. In both cases, survivor-centred activism has meant a close personal involvement between feminist-activists and the survivor/litigant. Activists have responded not only to legal demands of the case but to a host of personal needs – for emotional and psycho-social support, alternative sources of survival, assistance with food, shelter, health and educational requirements of the survivor's children and family. These forms of support are key ingredients in any extended litigation. Also, crucially, survivor-centred activism entails awareness of the security needs of witnesses – if there is a threat perception, then there has to be an ability to respond either by creating alternative structures of protection or by moving State agencies. In the complete absence of any witness protection system in India, survivor-centred activism means playing that role, and playing it to a logical end.

Survivor-centred legal activism of this kind is of course impossible to sustain for large numbers of violated women. Given the deep and abiding sanction for violence in its many forms in India, any intervention by the women's movement will be but a drop in the ocean. Also, survivor-centred campaigning along with the rise of identity-based activism has had another consequence – the carving out of distinct constituencies of women, with whom 'the women's movement' as a whole engages only peripherally. If working towards legal victories demands intensive engagement at the personal and community levels, then it perforce demands a comfort level with the identity politics within which these lives and communities are embedded. Muslim women, Dalit women, tribal women – each group is evolving their own panel of advocates, located within the larger struggles for tribal rights or minority rights and so on.

So is the women's movement today only a sum of different parts? Issues of representation confound us when we deal with 'identity'. Intersectionality is a trendy concept on paper; we acknowledge that patriarchy rears its head in different ways in different class, caste, and religious contexts, and yet when we campaign, which woman do we have in our minds? Is it Mathura or Bilkis or Maya Tyagi? Or, is it a homogenized, singular, victimized woman, shorn of social-political moorings, inhabiting all possible worlds? The fact is that when it comes to violence against women, nothing is just a 'woman's issue'. The politics of violence is so deeply embedded in the politics of identity (and one does not refer only to communal violence) that 'representing' survivors of violence demands a deeper political engagement.

Activists who knew Mathura over thirty years ago say that the issue at the time was neither tribal rights nor tribal exploitation. It was just plain and simple rape.[34] And yet, given that Gadchiroli is a designated tribal district with a large, and extremely poor, tribal population of 38.3 per cent,[35] one is tempted to speculate how the issue would be articulated if such a case took place today. Would it fall to activists from the 'women's movement' to articulate the issues, or would it be located within movements against tribal exploitation? Would such a case turn out differently if we located our struggle within both: a struggle for the dignified survival of tribal communities as well as the gender-based struggle for justice? It is worth contemplating, on grounds of both effective strategy and feminist survivor-centred principle. We may even come a degree closer to achieving legal justice. And for many survivors, legal justice does still matter. In the words of Bilkis Bano in January 2008, after a Mumbai Sessions Court pronounced a guilty verdict on 13 of the 20 accused, twelve of whom were convicted of gang-rape and murder:

Today I stand before you vindicated. For my truth has been heard. For 20 days I was cross-examined in a courtroom in Mumbai and the courage of my truth saw me through. On Friday 18 January 2008 the Honourable Sessions Judge in Mumbai pronounced a judgment that has finally meant some closure to a long and very painful journey that was forced upon me and my family. Of course, many wounds will never heal but I am stronger today, and for that I am thankful.

Acknowledgements

I would like to thank Huma Khan for her critical intellectual and research inputs into the development of this chapter

Notes

1. This essay draws upon in-depth interviews with activists from several organizations that work on violence against women, including Anweshi in Kozhikode, Majlis in Mumbai, Vanangana in Chitrakoot, and activists from Rajasthan. It also draws upon secondary research as well as structured and unstructured discussions with leading feminists and violence survivors. This essay refers to work being done by what is commonly known as the 'autonomous' women's movement, i.e., organizations and groups that have no formal affiliation with any political party.

2. Literature on the Mathura case variously describes her as being sixteen, seventeen or eighteen years old. In *The History of Doing*, Radha Kumar speaks of Mathura as being a seventeen- or eighteen-year-old. Dr Seema Sakhare from the Stree Atyachar Virodhi Parishad, a women's organization in Nagpur which worked on the case, describes Mathura as being 16 at the time of the incident.

3. Feminists had also demanded that the past sexual history of a victim is irrelevant and should not be allowed into the case proceedings. This provision was finally deleted, but only some twenty years later, in 2003. The issue of rape continues to be central to the feminist agenda. A new sexual assault bill, expanding the definition of rape to include various forms of sexual assault, was recently drafted in consultation with women's groups and the National Commission for Women, and now awaits government assent. Among the important new elements in the draft legislation is the introduction of child sexual abuse (CSA) as a form of violence – an index of increasing awareness and activism on CSA in the last decade.

4. It is estimated that domestic violence affects 40 per cent of women in India (ICRW 1996) and cuts across age, education level, social class and religion (INCLEN 2000).

5. Rajasthan University Women's Association, Women's Research Group, National Muslim Women Welfare Society,

All India Democratic Women's Alliance, All India Progressive Women's Alliance, Mahila Prakosht Samyukta Karamchari Maha Sangh (Rathore), People's Union for Civil Liberties, Vividha: Mahila Alekhan Evam Sandarbh Kendra, National Federation for Indian Women.

6. *See* Mahila Salah Evam Suraksha Kendra, 8.
7. In a non-cognizable report or NCR there is often no arrest before the investigation. In case of an arrest, bail can be procured from the police station.
8. *See* Vanangana 2006, 2007.
9. *See* Duvvury et al, 2002.
10. *See* Malimath Committee Report, para 16.4.1.
11. Ibid., para 16.4.2.
12. Attempts to dilute section 498A continue. In February 2008, the government of Maharashtra mounted an attempt to change the state provision and make 498A compoundable. At the time of writing, the move was being strongly opposed by women's groups in the state. Further, as recently as 12 March 2008 a three-judge bench of the Bombay High Court, while holding that a wife cannot withdraw a 498A charge and that courts cannot allow such a serious offence to be compounded, also held that a high court can exercise its inherent power to quash a 498A complaint in the larger interests of justice, to maintain matrimonial harmony, and to prevent abuse of the legal process (*The Times of India*, New Delhi, 13 March 2008).
13. *See* Vanangana, 2003: 12.
14. In 1985, sociologist Maxine Molyneux distinguished between women's 'practical needs', or what women perceive as immediate necessities such as water, shelter and food, and their 'strategic interests' or fundamental issues related to women's subordination and gender inequities. These are long-term, usually not material, and are often related to structural changes in society regarding women's status and equity. They include legislation for equal rights, reproductive choice, and increased participation in decision-making. While it is possible to change women's 'conditions' by addressing their practical needs, it is difficult to change their 'situations' without addressing women's strategic interests.
15. *See* NCRB, Crimes Against Women, 2003–05.

Nature of Crime	2003		2004		2005	
	Cases Regd.	Conviction Rate	Cases Regd.	Conviction Rate	Cases Regd.	Conviction Rate
Dowry Death	6208	32.4	7026	32.1	6787	33.4
Dowry Prohibition Act	2684	21.2	3592	25.0	3204	25.5
ITPA	5510	86.7	5748	84.8	5908	82.2
Rape	15847	26.1	18233	25.2	18359	25.5
Molestation	32939	30.2	34567	30.9	34175	30.0
Cruelty by husband & relatives	50703	18.1	58121	21.5	58319	19.2
Indecent representation of women	1043	76.7	1378	90.0	2917	94.3

16. *See* Raghuraman, 2005.
17. *Gauna* refers to that point when the bride is formally sent from her natal home to live with her husband's family.
18. In Rameeza Bi's case, the Andhra Pradesh (AP) state government set up a one-man Commission of Enquiry comprised of a former high court judge, who found the policemen guilty of murder and rape and recommended prosecution. The accused moved a plea in the Supreme Court saying that since the inquiry was conducted by a high court judge, the AP judiciary would be biased by his opinion. The Supreme Court transferred the case to the Raichur district court in Karnataka. All the accused were acquitted. The defence lawyers did not deny the rape but brought in Rameeza's past sexual history as its justification. A women's group filed a revision to compel the State to go in appeal. It was dismissed.
19. *See* Menon, 2004, p. 208.
20. *See* Kumar, 1993: 129.
21. The open letter to the Chief Justice of India which triggered off the campaign around Mathura's case was written by Upendra Baxi, Lotika Sarkar, Vasudha Dhagamwar, and Raghunath Kelkar.
22. Author's personal communication with Dr Seema Sakhare, Stree Atyachar Virodhi Parishad, Nagpur. 25 August 2008.
23. Authors' personal communication with Vimochana, February 2008.

24. Interview with Bhanwari Devi, Jaipur, 23 March 2007.
25. *See* Naqvi, 2005.
26. Desaiganj is now part of Gadchiroli district carved out of Chandrapur in 1982.
27. *See* Dutta Madhusree, Flavia Agnes, Neera Adarkar, 1996, pp. 115–18.
28. *See* Kannabiran, 1996, pp. 32–41.
29. 375 IPC – Definition of rape; 376 IPC – Punishment for rape; 354 IPC – Assault or use of criminal force with the intent to outrage women's modesty; 509 IPC – Violating a woman's modesty with word and gesture.
30. The Big Fight is a popular weekly television talk show on the NDTV network in which participants debate current issues. Activists of all hues routinely make an appearance on the show.
31. Of the two substantive efforts spearheaded and 'owned' by the women's movement, one was the International Initiative for Justice (IIJ), which consisted of a panel of feminists from India and abroad to study and place the events in Gujarat in an international perspective. The IIJ study took place a year after the events in Gujarat and the report came out a good eighteen months after the carnage. The second feminist-led effort was the submission to the CEDAW Committee in May 2003. Both efforts have provided crucial international advocacy tools and used international legal instruments to analyse the carnage in Gujarat. Although these initiatives have not had a visible impact on the Indian political space or public discourse, one hopes that the work with CEDAW, in particular, will influence India's legal framework on mass sexual violence in the future.
32. Bilkis Bano's statement to the press in Delhi, January 2008.
33. Bilkis Bano's statement to the press in Ahmedabad, August 2004.
34. Personal communication with Dr Seema Sakhare, Stree Atyachar Virodhi Parishad, Nagpur, 25 August 2008.
35. *See* 2001 Census.

References

Dutta, Madhusree, Flavia Agnes, Neera Adarkar (1996): *The Nation-State and Indian Identity*. Kolkata: Samya.
Duvvury, Nata et al. (2002): *Women-Initiated Community Level Responses to Domestic Violence: Summary Report of Three Studies*. Washington D.C.: International Center for Research on Women.

Kannabiran, Kalpana (1996): 'Rape and Construction of Communal Identity', in K. Jayawardena and Malathi de Alwis (eds.), *Embodied Violence: Communalizing Women's Sexuality in South Asia.* New Delhi: Kali for Women.

Kumar, Radha (1993): *The History of Doing: An Illustrated Account of Movements for Women's Rights and Feminism in India, 1800–1990.* New Delhi: Kali for Women.

Mahila Salah Evam Suraksha Kendra (2002): *Providing Wholistic Redressal to Women Facing Violence.* Jaipur:MSESK.

Malimath Committee (2003): *Report on Reforms of Criminal Justice System.* New Delhi: Government of India, Ministry of Home Affairs.

Menon, Nivedita (2004): *Recovering Subversion: Feminist Politics beyond the Law.* Delhi: Permanent Black.

Naqvi, Farah (2005): 'It's a Woman Thing', *Hindustan Times,* 4 July 2005.

National Crime Records Bureau (2003, 2004, 2005). *Crimes Against Women – 2003, 2004, 2005.* New Delhi: NCRB.

Raghuraman, S. (2005): 'Conspiracy of Silence', *The Times of India,* 8 May 2005.

Vanangana (2003): *Annual Report.* Chitrakoot: Vanangana.

—— (2007): *Annual Report.* Chitrakoot: Vanangana.

—— Vanangana (2006): *Chale To Sahi: Human Rights Work Review 2003–2006.* Chitrakoot: Vanangana.

2

An Intimate Dilemma

Anti-Domestic Violence Activism among Indians in the United States of America

Shamita Das Dasgupta

I write this chapter as an insider of the movement it disusses. In 1985, I was fortunate to participate in the creation of Manavi, the first organization in the United States formed to fight against woman abuse in the South Asian immigrant community. Today, nearly two dozen agencies work across the country offering this community, myriad services, awareness programmes, and a strong agenda for social change.[1] Three culturally-specific shelters for battered women have also been established in recognition of the distinct needs of immigrant women from the South Asian region. In addition, reports in popular media, special issues of academic journals, conference panels, judicial and advocate training, and sessions in professional conventions devoted to domestic violence among South Asian Americans indicate the groundswell of a burgeoning movement.

There is no longer much doubt that efforts to counter South Asian domestic violence represent a force for community accountability and change. My goal here is to briefly describe the nature of household violence within the immigrant Indian community, and the endeavours to eradicate it, against the backdrop of the larger American mainstream anti-domestic violence movement. To better contextualize these endeavours,

I also take a brief look at the history of Indian immigration to the US.

In this chapter, I have used the term 'immigrant' regardless of an individual's formal residency status in the US. An individual is deemed an immigrant in the US not necessarily on the basis of his or her official records, but by visible group (read: ethnic) affiliation. The 'immigrant' category is thus a social construction rather than a legal one. For instance, the people at large may consider a young woman born and brought up in the US, but who traces her cultural roots to India, 'immigrant' because she looks like others in the group who are immigrants. This appears to be the case with second- or third- generation Indians in America. By contrast, even a very recent immigrant from England may not be regarded as an 'immigrant', especially if she is white. Therefore, I have used the term 'immigrant' to denote Indians who may or may not fit the category in terms of legal citizenship.

The Gendered Nature of Indian Immigration

Indian immigration to the US can be traced back to the 1800s when a few citizens from colonized India arrived at its eastern shores.[2] Subsequently, others arrived either directly from India or via the west coast of Canada. Most of these early immigrants were farmers from the Punjab region who found the warm climates of the Pacific coast conducive to their traditional vocation. The virulent racism of the times, which culminated in India being included in the 'Pacific Barred Zone' by the Immigration Act of 1917, and the subsequent repatriation of many Indians, stains the history of immigration to the US from India. This scenario remained more or less unchanged until the easing of immigration rules in the mid-1960s.

The amendments to the Immigration and Nationality Act in 1965 did away with quota requirements and many of the discriminatory regulations of the past, and permitted larger numbers of immigrants from individual countries, especially from those that had hitherto been discriminated against. This set the scene for the arrival of ever larger numbers of people from India.

The influx of Indians to the US began post-1970. The policies of the time clearly privileged highly-educated and technically-trained individuals, thus setting the stage for the conglomeration of a large Indian community of doctors, engineers, and scientists on US soil. Given the gendered nature of education and mobility amongst Indians, the primary immigrants from India were men. Within a very short span of time, these men found occupational and financial success and firmly established themselves in their adopted home by creating a network of linguistically-based community organizations, places of worship, and ways of educating the next generation in their parents' traditions and 'culture'.[3]

Given their rapid and successful adaptation to the new society, mainstream America soon conferred on them the dubious title 'model minority'. The label implied that Indians were a hard-working, family-oriented, problem-free community in need of little help to settle in. The Indian community embraced this descriptor with gusto and in turn endeavoured to live up to it. It became particularly sensitive to the picture it projected of itself to outsiders and attempted to project a pristine and unblemished image.[4] Accordingly, the community became adept at denying all social ills within its ranks, be it disease, crime, divorce, poverty, homelessness, under-employment and unemployment, delinquency, drug addiction, intergenerational conflict, and woman abuse.

While the Indian community in the US was vigilant about concealing all its internal problems from the Western gaze, it was even more watchful about concealing instances of domestic violence, and vociferously denied its existence. The general belief was that away from the structural oppression of extended families, traditional customs, and the patriarchal functioning of Indian society, Indian women were free from gender inequity, repression, and violence. As tyranny within the home was considered a characteristic of the poor and uneducated, the highly successful immigrant community believed affluence and education immunized it against domestic violence.

Consequently, the Indian community became preoccupied with maintaining a distinct collective identity founded on its cultural roots.[5] Individuals who raised concerns that did not fit the 'model minority' image were quickly silenced, marginalized, and dismissed as anomalies. When a young battered mother of two, Amita Vadlamudi, killed her abusive husband in New Jersey in 1981, the community openly mocked her and wrote the incident off as a mishap stemming from the perverse dynamics of that particular family.[6] The first South Asian lesbian and gay organization in New York, SALGA, was repeatedly denied space in the Independence Day parade of the diaspora, the community refusing to acknowledge the very existence of same-sex relationships amongst their members.[7]

The demographics of the Indian community began to change after 1980 when many post-1970 immigrants began to facilitate the passage of their kin to the US.[8] These new immigrants, who migrated with the help of the Family Reunification policy,[9] were frequently less educated than previous immigrants and filled blue-collar occupations such as taxi driving, shopkeeping, and motel management. Many Indian business owners displaced from Africa also began to enter the US around the same time and established their trade here. The infusion of these non-technical workers increased the community's heterogeneity, but class differences based on education, occupation, and economics generated fissures within it.[10]

In the 1990s, the Indian community experienced another wave of new immigration; this time on the part of Information Technology (IT) specialists who were invited in as workers of specialty occupations. This group was issued temporary work visas for a duration of up to six years.[11] The current immigrant Indian community is tri-modally distributed by socio-economic status: the post-1970 technically qualified immigrants constituting the first category; the working class immigrants making up the second; and the temporary specialty work visa holders comprising the third concentration.

Indian women did not reflect the same demographic patterns as their male counterparts. Whereas men entered the country as primary immigrants, most women came to the US as dependents of their male kin; that is, as daughters, wives, or less frequently, fiancées, sisters, and mothers. When single women migrated for education or work, it was to fulfil their families' ambitions rather than to realize their personal goals. Even highly-educated and working women who entered the country to live with their husbands on student (F1) or specialty worker (H1-B) visas, were forced into dependency by the regulations of the US Citizenship and Immigration Services (USCIS).[12] Dependants of such visa-holders are forbidden to work legally regardless of their financial needs.[13] The resultant economic and emotional reliance on men has enormous consequences for women involved in abusive relationships.

The vast majority of Indian women in the US are foreign-born and have entered the country after 1970. They tend to have more in common with later immigrants than the post-1970 financially successful men. According to the 1990 US census, 59 per cent of Indian women over 16 years of age worked outside their families but earned on average the paltry sum of $11,746 per year, a sum below the Federal poverty threshold.[14] The 2000 census reports that 54 per cent of Indian women over 16 years work and have a median annual income of $35,173. By contrast, approximately 79 per cent of men in the community are employed and enjoy a median income of $51,904.[15] This income differential, together with the tradition of surrendering the control of family finances to men, severely limits women's access to necessary resources for independent survival and weakens the abilities of abused women to secure adequate legal representation.

Mapping Domestic Violence among Indians in America

Rekha grew up in a middle-class family in India. When she was 23, she met Sandeep, an immigrant to the US, at a cousin's wedding. He took a liking to her and proposed immediate marriage. Sandeep was seven years older than her but had a good job and promised that he would help her brothers immigrate to the US. He assured Rekha's parents that his elderly parents and siblings lived with him in America and she would not lack company and affection. The wedding took place within seven days of the proposal. Sandeep left for the US 10 days after the wedding with the promise that he would soon sponsor Rekha's immigration. It took nearly a year for Rekha to join her husband there.

The day after she arrived in the US, Sandeep told Rekha that she must immediately find a job and earn her keep. Rekha found a minimum-wage job in a burger joint and worked for 10 hours a day. She had to turn over her paycheck to her husband and received only bus fare to go to work. In addition, she had to cook, clean, shop, and take care of her elderly parents-in-law. Her father-in-law was an invalid suffering from Parkinson's disease and her husband's two younger siblings were in college. Rekha found Sandeep habitually emotionally absent except when his mother complained to him about her. He would then threaten her with deportation and say he would not sponsor her brothers' immigration. He told her that she was fortunate to have been rescued from her life of poverty in India, and should be grateful to him. He also told her that if he threw her out of the house, she would have to live on the streets as a prostitute. Sandeep never actually struck Rekha, but her in-laws would physically abuse her for the slightest mistakes.

Rekha discovered that her husband had been married before and had three children from his previous wife. It was Rekha's responsibility to care for his children over the weekend when they came to visit their father and grandparents. She suspected that Sandeep was still romantically and sexually involved with his first wife and that she herself had only been brought over to the US to serve as an unpaid domestic servant in Sandeep's household.[16]

Although the Indian population vehemently denies the prevalence of domestic abuse among its members, most activists claim it to be the most significant problem facing women in this community. It is only since the mid-1990s and due to the efforts of community-based agencies that researchers and practitioners have begun to focus on the problem of violence within the home among South Asians.[17] The only research to date that provides an inkling of the pervasiveness of woman abuse within the home was conducted among 160 well-educated and middle-class south Asian women in the Boston area.[18] Of these women, 35 per cent claimed that their current male partner had physically abused them at least once during their time together; 32.5 per cent that they had been abused in the course of the past year; 19 per cent claimed that their current male partner had sexually abused them at least once during their time together; and 15 per cent that this abuse had occurred during the past year. A significant majority stated that they were still involved in the abusive relationship.

Accounts of domestic violence-related deaths and near-deaths amongst the Indian community also point to the seriousness of the problem. From 1990 to April 2008, community newspapers reported 81 domestic violence-related murders; 15 murder-suicides; 22 attempted murders; 1 attempted suicide after murder; and 2 perpetrators killed by the police in the act of attacking their partners. In addition, 4 deaths and disappearances of women remain unsolved and suspicious, bringing the total number of fatalities and near fatalities to 125.[19] Notwithstanding such extreme violence, there is little reliable statistical data on the incidence of family abuse amongst the Indian immigrant community. The absence of this itself speaks volumes of the invisibility that shrouds the topic of family violence among Indians in America.

The dynamics of family abuse that South Asian women experience in the US, such as economic control, coercion and threat, intimidation, public derogation, isolation, minimization and denial, and assertion of male privilege, overlap with family abuse in other communities, but their significance varies greatly. For instance, a batterer's threat of blackening his partner's reputation among her relatives might affect an Indian woman differently, as it may entail the possibility of being rejected and even killed by her natal or affinal family. A batterer could also easily intimidate his wife by threatening her with deportation, a threat that is significant at many levels. Deportation might force a woman to return to her country in ignominy as a rejected wife; without her children, financial support, and a viable future; to the wrath or ostracism of her family and community in India. A more abstract threat that has enormous power over Indian women is the accusation of being a traitor to their culture and community. This indictment seems to extract compliance equally from first- and second-generation immigrant women.[20]

The perpetrator of domestic violence in the Indian context is not always the romantic partner. Along with the immediate partner, other members of the affinal family such as parents-in-law, sisters- and brothers-in-law inflict violence on women.[21] As families in the Indian community gradually expand, largely on the basis of the primary immigrants' (read: men's) relatives joining them, women in the US are faced with the proverbial 'mother-in-law' abuse. As families extend in the US, a wife's sources of abuse also widen. Sometimes a husband may only be a passive observer of his wife's battering by his relatives, lending credence to her belief that the removal of other family members from the household would end all violence in her life.[22]

The intersections of violence, gender, culture, immigration, and law lend such complexity to Indian women's lives in the US that only interventions from within the community can hope to succeed. Thus, the successes of Indian community-based organizations, far more restricted in human and financial resources than mainstream American agencies, are due to their ability to deal with these complications with sensitivity. The experience of working against domestic violence in the Indian community in the US throws up three issues: (a) this is a community distinguished by culture and ethnicity with specific agendas that cannot be subsumed under the mainstream ones; (b) woman abuse exists and has its own esoteric nuances in the community; and (c) successful interventions must be infused with culturally, linguistically, and legally-appropriate understanding of the needs of victims, perpetrators, and the community.

Culture as the Guilty Party

In my 22 years of work with Manavi as an advocate, I have found that Indian women in the US have to face both legal and cultural obstacles in their attempt to escape family violence. Although there are over two dozen organizations serving the South Asian community, these are unevenly spread across the country and are principally located on the east and west coasts. Only three culture-specific shelters provide housing to South Asian women and their children who are fleeing abuse or have been displaced by family violence. The numbers of both agencies and shelters are pitifully inadequate to meet the needs of these women.

Many women who have sought the services of local non-South Asian or mainstream agencies end up leaving their shelters hastily, preferring to return to their abusers rather than remaining at these refuges. A number of women have stated that their clothing, speech accents, lack of fluency in English, food and toilet habits and the like have often made them targets of distressing curiosity and denigration by other residents. Some have reported that their arranged marriages are perceived as 'weird' and are assumed to be the cause of their abusers' actions. Many mainstream shelters have limited experiences of dealing with immigration issues and are frequently unable to meet the legal residency needs of South Asian women. They are also at a disadvantage when women require language interpretation and translation. Consequently, even when some South Asian women are ready to leave abusive family situations, they assert that without the support of a culture-specific agency and shelter, they will not leave their homes.

I vividly remember a woman calling from one of the southern states to inquire whether there was space for her and her children in Manavi's shelter in New Jersey as she was considering leaving her violent husband. When we offered to help her find space in a shelter in her own locality, she refused and said that she would leave only if she could enter a South Asian shelter, be it five states away. She firmly declared that she needed a place that understood her 'culture'.

The issue of culture as it plays out in the US courts becomes even more critical for Indian victims of family violence. Immigrants of colour, especially Asians, have historically been viewed by mainstream Americans as prisoners of their cultures.[23] Professor Leti Volpp of American University maintains that violence against women is seen in the US as a marker of Asian cultures. Similarly, South Asian cultures are believed to provide, if not explicit, then tacit support to woman abuse. In contrast, battering among whites is seen as a product of individual acts of bad behaviour or a particular predicament, with culture escaping culpability. Writes professor Uma Narayan:

[C]ulture is invoked in explanations of forms of violence against third world women, while it is not similarly invoked in explanations of forms of violence that affect mainstream Western women ...[W]hen such 'cultural explanations' are given for fatal forms of violence against third world women, the effect is to suggest that third world women suffer 'death by culture'... [F]atal forms of violence against mainstream Western women seem interestingly resistant to such 'cultural explanations'.[24]

The perception that certain cultures are surfeit with vicious patriarchies and consequent brutalities toward women complicates the legal status of both batterers and victims in the US.[25] Depending upon the individual perspectives of law enforcement officers, judges, and attorneys, a battered Indian woman may find her petition falls either on patronizing or disbelieving ears. Judges and attorneys may view Indian batterers as vicious monsters or behaving in a culturally-acceptable way, while the victims may be perceived as scheming harridans or long-suffering broken women in need of rescue. Both extremes attempt to fit the individual into racial/cultural stereotypes and are frequently disproportionate to the actual situation on the ground.

The practice of bringing the entire culture up for scrutiny was adopted by advocates and activists when they needed to support individual battered women's residency petitions under certain immigration laws. In 1997, Manavi initiated its immigration-related programme, Zamin, to channel South Asian battered women's self-petitions for residency in the US. Many abused women had either left or been abandoned by their husbands. However, as dependants of their husbands under certain visa categories, they could not legally stay on in the US unless they could obtain a 'hardship waiver' from the courts. To prove 'extreme hardship' under these laws, a 'cultural expert' had to provide written testimony detailing why deportation would be cruel to the battered petitioner and her children. To be successful, affidavits had to elaborate individual harm in the context of a culture, which could only be accomplished by generally vilifying the culture.

Although quite successful, Zamin has generated significant internal dispute within Manavi. The success of asylum affidavits hinges on explaining the petitioner's victimization and persecution by '...unusually patriarchal and culturally dysfunctional cultures...'[26] Aware that overgeneralizations about cultures bring results, the stipulations of affidavits lay contrary burdens on South Asian activists by compelling them to choose between individual benefit and collective cost, and this issue of benefiting an individual woman at the cost of vilifying an entire culture is a heavy burden for advocates. Although such portrayals may benefit an individual woman by getting her residency application approved, we are aware that in the ultimate analysis they misrepresent and tarnish the entire community and contribute to the intensification of racist and xenophobic biases in the US courts.

Most South Asian advocates, immigration attorneys, and 'cultural experts' recognize that the content requisites of [cultural] affidavits nest at the intersections of race, nation, and ways of life that make a culture the bizarre 'other'.[27] States immigrant rights attorney Anita Sinha:

Asylum applicants who flee from non-Western countries because of gender-related violence find that their cases often turn on whether they can show that the persecution they suffered is attributable to the cultural 'backwardness' of their home countries.[28]

This 'othering' of non-Western cultures is evident in the

value given to types of abuse. Not all forms of violence against women are given equal significance by the immigration services. Violence that seems 'foreign' to US cultures, such as female genital mutilation (FGM), dowry harassment, honour killing, stoning as punishment, and religious persecution hold sway over even the severest form of domestic violence.[29] The minimization of domestic violence, the most common abuse to which women are systematically subjected due to their membership in a group, is a clear indication of the xenophobic and racist slant of the US immigration services. Racism is even more blatant in cases where 'cultural experts' are required to testify in person. Defence attorneys, who often seek 'experts' to explain the cultural background of a battered woman charged with a crime, recognize the race biases in court and tend to reject non-white immigrant witnesses.

Whether in relation to criminal legal issues or asylum, the burden of explaining culture to the courts to support battered women generates profound conflicts for South Asian advocates and cultural specialists. On the one hand, they must accept the responsibility of translating the meaning of battered women's needs to the legal system, and on the other, must guard against universalizing one woman's experiences to characterize and stigmatize an entire culture. As most experts and advocates appreciate, in the vast region of South Asia and its constitutent countries, diversity is the rule rather than the exception. However, asylum adjudicators and defence attorneys hardly seek to draw fine distinctions in the explanation of a culture. Successful petitions carry the implicit message that blanket disparagement of a culture is necessary to win approval.

An Over-Reliance on the Criminal Justice System?

If a victim of domestic violence refuses recourse to the legal system, very few viable options are readily available to ensure her safety. This emphasis on the legal system, to the exclusion of other alternative interventions, places many battered women, particularly in immigrant communities, at a disadvantage. The ability to easily access law enforcement and

to choose legal options to ameliorate a situation of domestic
violence is frequently contingent on an immigrant woman's
experiences with the police in her country of origin, as well
as her community's collective encounters with the police in
America. Non-immigrant women of colour also find the over-
dependence on legal remedies problematic, as many of these
communities have intensely antagonistic relationships with
law enforcement and the legal system.

This emphasis on recourse to the legal or criminal justice
system is a legacy of the mainstream anti-domestic violence
movement in the US which began in the 1970s. In addition to
the creation of a widespread network of safe houses, shelters,
and agencies, this movement concentrated on holding the
state accountable for women's safety.[30] To this end, activists
paid special attention to modifying the criminal justice
system and ensuring that violence perpetrated by intimate
partners was considered a criminal offence.[31] Today, many
advocates and policy-makers consider an order for protection,
mandatory arrest, and subsequent legal penalization in the
courts (e.g., no-drop prosecution policy and evidence-based
prosecution)[32] effective deterrents to battering, as these invoke
the formidable powers of the state.

Although the mainstream movement takes pride in its
success in criminalizing domestic violence, many activists,
particularly activists of colour, believe that the movement has
lost its way by becoming over-reliant on the criminal justice
system.[33] The latter is neither just nor unbiased, and has done
more harm to certain communities than good. Domestic
violence laws and policies differentially affect battered women,
who live at differing crossroads of race, class, sexuality, ability,
and citizenship.[34] Battered immigrant women of colour, caught
at the intersections of these various forces, often fall through
the cracks in the legal and social service systems supposedly
erected to protect all battered women.[35]

Unquestionably, some battered women are alive today
due to the increasing arrests and prosecution of batterers,
as well as criminalization of domestic violence and penalty
enhancements. Nonetheless, these gains have been

accompanied by numerous unintended consequences.[36] Battered women of colour may be paying too high a price for rashly inviting the law-enforcement and legal systems to intervene in their lives.[37] Many activists have therefore been challenging the mainstream anti-domestic violence movement's practice of separating 'domestic abuse' from various other forms of violence perpetrated against women, such as racism, xenophobia, homophobia, imperialism, and police brutality.[38]

'Incite! Women of Color against Violence' (n.d.) has pointed out the absurdity of relying on criminal legal interventions when both the law-enforcement and legal systems perpetrate significant violence against communities of colour.[39] In her report on women's safety in the US, activist–scholar Anannya Bhattacharjee rigorously disputes the wisdom of trusting law enforcement to ensure security within the family.[40] She contends that the state and its law-enforcement and legal systems are responsible for a significant measure of violence in many women's lives, often within the confines of their homes. Bhattacharjee maintains that the boundary between protector and perpetrator is blurred when it comes to the lives of the poor, immigrants, and women of colour.

Indeed, the general increase in arrests of battered women who are charged with domestic violence indicates that the laws that were created to protect women have now been turned against them.[41] Besides, even as the state accepts the responsibility of eliminating battering from women's lives, it creates new categories of abuse that perpetuate the status quo. A case in point is the Immigration Marriage Fraud Amendments of 1986, which ushered in a new type of violence in immigrant women's lives and enabling their abusers to intimidate and control them through threats of deportation.[42]

Immigration, Domestic Abuse, and Interventions

The Immigration Marriage Fraud Amendments (IMFA) of 1986 was passed to reduce immigration through fraudulent marriages to US citizens and legal permanent residents.[43]

IMFA requires a citizen or permanent resident to sponsor his or her foreign-born spouse for legal immigration, but does not issue the 'green card' to the sponsored spouse for two years. Instead, the spouse is issued a conditional permanent residency status. At the end of these two years, the conditions are removed after filing of a joint petition and an interview with immigration officials to establish the marriage as bona fide.

These policies took on frightening aspects for battered immigrant women, who became even more trapped in abusive relationships and were often left to the mercy of their spouses for their permanent residency status in the US. The only relief for battered women in IMFA was the 'hardship waiver', which required them to prove that 'extreme hardship' would result if they were deported. The proof of 'extreme hardship' had to be supported by affidavits from 'experts' who discussed the adverse cultural conditions in a battered woman's native country and the difficulties she and her children might face upon their return.[44]

For women living with abusive spouses who are neither US citizens nor permanent residents, the only option for residency in the US may be petitioning for gender-based (or gender) asylum.[45] Gender asylum is also the only option available to women who are fleeing their native countries to escape domestic battery and persecutory violence. The requirements for gender asylum are extremely prohibitive. Even this tenuous opportunity for women to independently obtain immigrant status noticeably deteriorated after 11 September 2001. A number of changes in the name of 'Homeland Security'[46] cruelly affected Indian women and proved a severe setback in advocacy on behalf of battered women.

Immediately following September '9/11', a new set of obstacles confronted battered Indian women in accessing the legal system, and this particularly disadvantaged Muslim women. The backlash against anyone who looked Arab, which includes Indians, has silenced women by placing on them the responsibility of keeping men safe. This means that if women seek outside help, especially from the law-enforcement agencies, the chances are that they will not only expose their spouses and relatives to prejudicial harassment by the police and other officials, but also open their own lives to harrasment.

As many immigrant men are summarily deported for minor infractions of their visas or other violations of the law (including domestic violence), their wives either have to accompany them back or stay behind as undocumented immigrants without minimal resources or support. By inviting the police, and thereby immigration scrutiny, into the community, these women also run the risk of being ostracized by friends, neighbours, religious and community leaders, and being branded as traitors. Many South Asian anti-domestic violence agencies report that after 9/11 they experienced a significant decrease in the number of women seeking assistance.[47]

In addition to biases in America, discrepancies between the legal systems in the home country and the US often thwart Indian women's bids for safety. Although the legal systems are supposedly reciprocal, local courts in both countries frequently act independently and contrarily to the frustration of abused women. The courts in a petitioner's native country may ignore all legal decisions she struggled to receive in the US and hand her a new set of contradictory judgments related to divorce custody, and property settlement. For example, a batterer, whom a woman has successfully divorced in the US may return to his native country, India, and petition the courts for 'restitution of conjugal rights'.[48] An abusive father may simultaneously lose custody of his children in the US but successfully secure full custody of them in Indian courts. Such disagreements between courts in the countries of origin and residence may occur in the areas of separation, divorce, custody, child support, alimony, and settlement of marital property.

In matters of property settlement, such discrepancies are particularly problematic. As a Manavi advocate, I have noticed that US courts routinely ignore dowry and *mehr* issues that Indian women bring up in their divorce proceedings. As dowry is illegal in India, Indian courts have been considering it as *streedhan* or as a wife's property in divorce disputes and honouring her claim to it, while in the US legal system, there is no such recognition. The US courts have even greater difficulty in understanding the concept of *mehr*, or the sum of money a bridegroom promises to pay the bride either at the time of marriage or later, depending on the contract. Consequently, Muslim women tend to lose this rightful asset in cases of divorce in the US.

To complicate matters, a battered woman's family members and community may ignore all legal rulings and demand her compliance to a very different set of emotional decisions. They may want her to return to her abuser so as not to jeopardize the family's reputation in the community, their own physical and/or economic safety, and/or the possibility of contracting good marital alliances for her siblings. Often, parents and grandparents have pressurized women to reunite with their abusers in order to retain the family's reputation. In the US, religious leaders in a woman's community may pressurize her to maintain her marriage in order that she does not mar the 'model minority' impression. In these situations, a battered woman has few viable choices to establish harmony in her life except through the sacrifice of her own safety.

An Emerging Transnational Issue

Sangeeta quit her prestigious job at an Indian university to join her husband who was leaving for the US. She nurtured hopes of finding employment in the US and, perhaps later, furthering her studies. Once she reached America, she discovered that her visa stipulated that she could neither work nor study and had to be entirely dependent on her husband. Sangeeta was frustrated and Raghuvir, her husband of five years, began to emotionally abuse her. He called her a parasite living on his hard-earned income and demanded that she account for every penny spent on household expenses. Within six months, their conflicts intensified. Raghuvir lost his temper a few times and slapped her. Sangeeta began feeling overwhelmed, helpless, and afflicted by a sense that she had to walk on eggshells around Raghuvir. At this point, he suggested that they return to India for a visit. They both left for Delhi on a three-week vacation.

On reaching Delhi airport, Raghuvir took away Sangeeta's passport along with her visa, return ticket, and all the money she had. He left her stranded and caught the next flight back to the US. Sangeeta reached her parents' home with difficulty where, within a week, she received a divorce notice from Raghuvir's attorney. The notice stipulated that she had to respond to the suit in court within three weeks, otherwise the divorce would be granted ex parté. Sangeeta refused to acquiesce without a fight and wanted a proper financial settlement. However, without a passport and visa she had no way of reaching the US or hiring an attorney to represent her there. She also discovered that she could not get her H4 visa re-issued without Raghuvir's sponsorship. She contacted a women's organization in India, which also was in a quandary about solutions to the situation.

Immigration has given rise to a number of forms of violence against women, such as international kidnapping, trafficking, and abandonment or desertion. Desertion of wives and children has grown significantly in India in the wake of increased global worker mobility. As men living or working in the US are viewed as highly eligible grooms, many Indian parents are eager to arrange their daughters' marriages with them. Men's parents are also eager to have their sons enter such alliances for fear of being presented with non-Indian daughters-in-law. Such marriages are arranged with the understanding that the husband, the primary immigrant, would sponsor his spouse to the US.

The reality is that a large number of Indian women married to non-resident Indians (NRIs) are finding themselves without any resources and justice, discarded by their husbands. In the US such desertions carry little weight as the courts tend to define domestic violence chiefly as physical abuse. As divorce is easily obtainable in the US, American society assumes that a deserted wife should be able to secure a divorce and find work. However, in a country where women's financial and physical well-being is often dependent on their marriages, abandonment could very well constitute violence against women. South Asian community-based agencies have been working to get it recognized as a form of violence against women.

Abandonment has fundamental and far-reaching consequences for married Indian women. It impacts their financial, emotional, physical, and social conditions and makes their lives virtually unlivable. The problem of deserted wives in India has become sufficiently significant to attract the notice of the US State Department, Indian government officials,[49] a number of NGOs, and the international media. Almost every state in India has abandoned wives. For example, the Indian government estimates that over 12,000 women in Gujarat and 15,000 women in Punjab have been abandoned by their NRI husbands.[50] Many of these women have never joined their husbands abroad but have been promised year after year that their immigration will be sponsored. Often, the husbands occasionally visit their wives in India and leave again without ever making an attempt to support or help them emigrate.

Although the plight of the women left back in India by their NRI husbands is most dramatic, there are other scenarios of abandonment that violate women's right to safety and justice. The following are the three most common scenarios: (a) An abusive spouse might abandon his wife without any resources in the host country; (b) a wife may be deceived or coerced to return to the home country and be abandoned there by her husband without any means of re-entry, i.e., without passport, visa, airline ticket, or money; and (c) a husband might leave his wife behind in their home country and visit occasionally with promises of bringing her back (hence the label 'holiday bride').

The transnational issue of abandoned NRI wives and related issues are crises of a globalizing world. It is important for governments to recognize the problems generated by heightened human mobility and to develop policies to deal with these. As the number of abandoned women increases in India, agencies in India and the US are moving towards forging an international collaborative programme. Swayam in Kolkata and Manavi in New Jersey have taken the lead in building an international coalition of organizations that would not only provide immediate services to individual women but also initiate policy changes at governmental levels to protect NRI wives and hold errant husbands accountable. Even though the coalition is at an early stage, its goals promise justice for these women.

Conclusion

Over the past two decades, South Asian organizations have carved out a significant space and brought to the fore women's experiences of family violence. Their work and conversations have forced communities to move out of the somnolence of complacency to critically re-examine traditions and culture as they affect women's lives.

Regrettably, certain pockets of the Indian community seem to have accepted the dominant community's proffered theory connecting domestic violence and cultures. A number of years ago, I attended a political meeting in New York where the chief speaker was the then chief minister of Maharashtra, Sharad Pawar. I asked him about the legal policies on domestic violence he was instituting for the state. The secretary of women and child development responded to the effect that it was taking time to implement its policies because in India, ending domestic violence was a matter of modifying culture whereas in the US it was only a matter of law. Such misperceptions at the highest levels contribute to the muddling of 'government-institutionalized misogyny and religious/cultural practices'.[51]

There are no easy solutions to the myriad problems faced by battered Indian women when they tangle with the US law-enforcement and legal system, yet, these represent the most viable recourse they have in the US for redress. On an individual level, Indian women need to be educated in American legal processes and negotiate the legal system, even though racism, xenophobia, and various other prejudices are an inherent part of this institution. While the mainstream community needs to sharpen its understanding of Indian cultures and socio-political issues, the Indian community must also increase its responsiveness to domestic violence and stand up for the safety of immigrant Indian women.

Notes

1. For a complete list of organizations working on ending violence against South Asian women in the US, see http://www.sawnet. org/orgns/violence.php#National
2. *See* Chandrasekhar, 1982.
3. *See* Agarwal, 1991; Barringer and Kassenbaum, 1989; Helweg and Helweg, 1990; Jensen, 1988.
4. *See* Abraham, 2000; Bhattacharjee, 1992; Dasgupta, 1996, 1998a, 2000a; DasGupta and Dasgupta, 1996.
5. *See* Burek, 1992; Saran and Eames, 1980.
6. *See* Dasgupta, 2000a; 'East Brunswick Woman Arrested for Murder', 1981.
7. *See* Dasgupta, 1998b.
8. 82 per cent of the Indian population in the US has entered after 1980. *See* US Census Bureau, 2004.
9. Reunification of families is a recognized reason for immigration in many countries, including the US. Members of a nuclear family, married partners, unmarried children, and dependent parents of naturalized US citizens become eligible for immigration under this policy. Adult children, as well as married siblings of US citizens, are also admitted under this policy, notwithstanding the horrendous backlog in issuance of visas. The Family Reunification policy is a part of the US Immigration and Nationality Act.
10. *See* Dasgupta, 2000a.
11. This particular visa type, H1-B, is issued to individuals in specialty occupations such as computer technology, health care, and academics. The visa is first issued for a period of three years and is renewable for another three-year period.
12. On 1 March 2003 the Immigration and Naturalization Service (INS) changed its name to United States Citizenship and Immigration Services (USCIS).
13. *See* Shah, 2007; Bhuyan, 2007.
14. In 1990, the US Federal Government delineated that the poverty threshold was $13,359 for a family of four (two adults and two children) and that approximately 14 per cent of the population was under the poverty index. *See* Sawhill, 1993.

15. In 2004, the US Federal Government defined poverty threshold was $19,157 for a family of four (two adults and two children) and 12.7 per cent were below the poverty line. *See* Federal Register, 2006; US Census Bureau, 2007; National Poverty Center, 2006.

16. All names have been changed to protect individual identities. The stories of Rekha and Sangeeta are composites of many cases from Manavi's files.

17. *See* Abraham, 1995, 2000; Dasgupta and Warrier, 1996, 1997; *Journal of Social Distress and the Homeless*, 2000; Krishnan, Baig-Amin, Gilbert, El-Bassel, and Waters, 1998; Raj and Silverman, 2002; *Violence Against Women*, 1999.

18. *See* Raj and Silverman, 2002.

19. *See* Dasgupta, 2000b. The author has collected additional data from published newspaper reports. However, the tally is incomplete and not comprehensive.

20. *See* Dasgupta, 1998b; DasGupta and Dasgupta, 1996.

21. *See* Fernandez, 1997.

22. *See* Raj, Livramento, Santana, Gupta, and Silverman, 2006.

23. *See* Volpp, 2003.

24. *See* Narayan, 1997, pp. 84–85.

25. *See* Chiu, 1994; Dasgupta, 1998a; Maguigan, 1995; Razack, 1998; Sinha, 2001; Visweswaran, 2002; Volpp, 2000.

26. *See* Razack, 1998, p. 20.

27. See Sinha, 2001; Visweswaran, 2002; Volpp, 2000, 2003.

28. *See* Sinha, 2001, p. 1578.

29. *See* Sinha, 2001; Visweswaran, 2002.

30. *See* McMahon and Pence, 2003; Weisberg, 1996.

31. The systematic criminalization of domestic violence cases began in the 1970s, seeking 'to increase the certainty and severity of legal responses, thereby correcting historical, legal, and moral disparities in the legal protections afforded to battered women' (Fagan, 1996, pp. 3–4). To bring about this institutional change, anti-domestic violence activists argued that perpetrators of domestic violence should be apprehended, prosecuted, and punished as sternly as any other violent offender. Criminalization of family assault progressed in three distinct domains: (a) apprehension and criminal punishment of offenders; (b) batterers' re-education or treatment programmes; and (c) availability of legal protection to victims, entitled Order of Protection (OFP) or Restraining Order (RO). By 1980, 47 states had passed laws mandating protection orders for victims and allowing perpetrators to be arrested without

a warrant. The city of Duluth, Minnesota, was the first to institute a mandatory arrest policy in cases involving familial violence. *See* Pence & Shepard, 1999; Pleck, 1989; Zorza, 1992.

32. An Order for Protection (OFP) is a legal directive issued to an abuser to desist from further violent behaviour towards the victim. It may include instructions to stop all communications with the victim as well as maintaining a certain distance from her at all times. Violation of an OFP is considered a crime. Mandatory arrest and no-drop prosecution policies were created to remedy law enforcement's failure to deal firmly with domestic violence and to circumvent victims' non-cooperation with the prosecution of the perpetrators. Mandatory arrest policies deny police officers any discretion and require them to make an arrest in cases where they believe an act of domestic violence has occurred. No-drop prosecution policies require every case of domestic violence to be legally prosecuted regardless of the victim's wishes. Evidence-based prosecution of domestic violence allows a reluctant victim not to be forced to testify against the perpetrator. The prosecution proceeds by relying on objective evidence gathered on the scene of the crime rather than the victim-witness's testimony.

33. *See* Sen, 1999; Eng and Dasgupta, 2003.

34. *See* Coker, 2000, 2001; Dasgupta, 1998a; Mills, 1999; Ruttenberg, 1994; Visweswaran, 2004.

35. Women of dark complexions living in the US coined the term 'women of colour'. The label recognizes race as the principal organizing principle in the US and alludes to the common experiences of darker-skinned women negotiating society in a white-dominated nation.

36. *See* Barak, Flavin, and Leighton, 2001; Bhattacharjee, 2001, 2002; Butterfield, 2002; Eng and Dasgupta, 2003; Ostrowski, 2004; Silliman, 2002.

37. *See* Almjeld, Winter 2003/4; Bhattacharjee, 2001; Incite!, nd; Rodriguez, 2000–1; Sen, 1999; Silliman and Bhattacharjee, 2002.

38. *See* Bhattacharjee, 2001; Dasgupta, 1999; Davis, 1985; Sen, 1999; Smith, 2000–1.

39. *See* Incite!, nd.

40. *See* Bhattacharjee, 2001.

41. *See Violence Against Women,* 2002a, 2002b, 2003.

42. *See* Anderson, 1993; Dasgupta, 1998a; Jones, 1997; Roy, 1995.

43. According to IMFA, if the foreign-born spouse of a US citizen or permanent resident is sponsored for permanent residency and is

married for under two years at the day of his/her entry into the country, s/he will be issued a conditional 'green card'.

44. IMFA was revised by the Immigration Act of 1990 (IMMACT). Under IMMACT, battered women could circumvent their citizen or permanent resident spouses' sponsorships through the 'battered spouse waiver'. To achieve this waiver, battered women had to prove their victimization on the basis of expert evidence of physical abuse or extreme cruelty. The evidentiary requirements for the waiver were complicated and impossible for many immigrant women to satisfy. Notwithstanding the modification to ease immigration issues, IMMACT remained onerous and a bane in battered women's quest for permanent residency. The Violence Against Women Act (VAWA), title IV of The Violent Crime Control and Law Enforcement Act, was passed in 1994 and addressed immigrant battered women's vulnerability to threats of deportation from their abusers. VAWA offered the option of 'self petitioning' to battered women. These 'self petitions' required battered women to substantiate their claims with affidavits of 'extreme hardship' that deportation would result in. Again, cultural experts founded their 'extreme hardship' testimonies on nationwide cultural conditions that would be unfavourable to the well-being of the battered applicant and her children. VAWA II, passed in 2000, has eliminated this 'extreme hardship' affidavit requirement for self-petitioning and added the relief of the U and T visas. Regardless, the responsibility of substantiating abuse for self-petitions and meeting other evidentiary requirements still rests with battered women.

45. *See* United Nations High Commissioner for Refugees' Guidelines On International Protection: Gender-Related Persecution within the context of Article 1A(2) of the 1951 Convention and/or its 1967 Protocol relating to the Status of Refugees. HCR/GIP/02/01, 7 May 2002.

46. 'Homeland Security' refers to a wide governmental effort to protect the US territory from all hazards, internal and external, natural as well as man-made. The goals of Homeland Security are to assess national vulnerabilities, remedy them, and minimize the possibility of damages in case of actual terrorist attacks and other harm. The Department of Homeland Security (DHS) was created in 2002 in the aftermath of 11 September 2001 terrorist attacks.

47. *See* Sthanki, 2007.

48. In India, when one spouse withdraws from the marriage without

'reasonable' excuse, the aggrieved party may go to court and seek restitution of conjugal rights. The expectation is that the couple must give the marriage another try by living together in their marital home. The burden of proof that the withdrawal from marriage was reasonable rests with the party who withdrew from it.

49. The National Commission for Women in India has written a report on problems in NRI marriages, underscoring the issue of deserted wives. In a draft bill submitted to the Ministry of External Affairs and the Ministry of Overseas Indians, the Commission calls for legal understanding between the governments of India and countries where substantial NRI populations reside and suggests some drastic changes to hold abandoning husband accountable. See Khan, 2004.

50. *See Pacific Post,* 2004a, 2004b, 2004c; *NRI Internet,* 2004; Abraham, 2003; *Tribune,* 2004, Khan, 2004.

51. *See* Visweswaran, 2002.

References

Abraham, M. (1995): 'Ethnicity, Gender, and Marital Violence: South Asian Women's Organizations in the United States', *Gender & Society,* 9, 450–568.

Abraham, M. (2000): *Speaking the Unspeakable: Marital Violence among South Asian Immigrants in the United States.* New Brunswick, NJ: Rutgers University Press.

Abraham, V. (2003): 'Married to Despair: Abandoned Wives Lead Hopeless Lives in Kerala Village', *The Week,* 27 July. http://www.the-week.com/23jul27/life11.htm.

Agarwal, P. (1991): *Passage from India: Post-1965: Indian Immigrants and Their Children, Conflicts, Concerns, and Solutions.* Palos Verdes, CA: Yuvati Publications.

Almjeld, K. (2003/4): 'Clear Act Threatens Immigrant Women Victims of Violence', *National NOW Times.* Winter. http:// www.now.org/nnt/winter-2004/clear.html? printable.

Anderson, M.J. (1993): 'A License to Abuse: The Impact of Conditional Status on Female Immigrants', *Yale Law Journal,* 102, 1401–30.

Barak, G., J. Flavin, and P. Leighton (2001): *Class, Race, Gender, and Crime: Social Realities of Justice in America.* Los Angeles: CA: Roxbury Publishing Co.

Barringer, H., and G. Kassenbaum. (1989): 'Indians as a Minority in the United States: The Effect of Education, Occupations and Gender on Income', *Sociological Perspectives*, 32, 501–20.

Bhattacharjee, A. (1992): 'The Habit of Ex-nomination: Nation, Woman, and the Indian Immigrant Bourgeoisie', *Public Culture*, 5, 19–44.

—— (2001): 'Whose Safety? Women of Color and the Violence of Law Enforcement' (A Justice Visions Working Paper). Philadelphia, PA: American Friends Service Committee; Committee on Women, Population, and the Environment.

—— (2002): 'Private Fists and Public Force: Race, Gender, and Surveillance', in J. Silliman and A. Bhattacharjee (eds.), *Policing the National Body: Race, Gender, and Criminalization*. Cambridge, MA: South End Press, pp. 1–54.

Bhuyan, R. (2007): 'Navigating Gender, Immigration, and Domestic Violence', in S. D. Dasgupta (ed.), *Body Evidence: Intimate Violence Against South Asian Women in America*. New Brunswick, NJ: Rutgers University Press, pp. 229–42.

Burek, D.M. (1992): 'National Federation of Indian American Associations', in D. M. Burek (ed.), *Encyclopedia of Associations in the United States*, 26ᵗʰ ed., Part 2, Section 10. Detroit, MI: Gale Research, Inc.

Butterfield, F. (2002): 'Study Finds Big Increase in Black Men as Inmates Since 1980', *New York Times*, 28 August, p. A14.

Chandrasekhar, S. (1982): 'A History of United States Legislation with Respect to Immigration from India', in S. Chandrasekhar (ed.), *From India to America: A Brief History of Immigration; Problems of Discrimination, Admission and Assimilation*. La Jolla, CA: A Population Review Book, pp. 11–28.

Chiu, D.C. (1994): 'The Cultural Defense: Beyond Exclusion, Assimilation, and Guilty Liberalism', *California Law Review*, 82, 1053–125.

Coker, D. (2000): 'Shifting Power for Battered Women: Law, Material Resource, and Poor Women of Color', *U. C. Davis Law Review*, 33, 1009–55.

—— (2001): 'Crime Control and Feminist Law Reform in Domestic Violence Law: A Critical Review', *Buffalo Criminal Law Review*, 4, 801–60.

Dasgupta, S.D. (1998a): 'Women's Realities: Defining Violence Against Women by Immigration, Race, and Class', in R.K.

Bergen (ed.), *Issues in Intimate Violence*. Thousand Oaks, CA: Sage Publications, pp. 209–19.

—— (1998b): 'Gender Roles and Cultural Continuity in the Indian Community in the US', *Sex Roles*, 38, 953–74.

—— (1999): 'Is All Well with Domestic Violence Work in the United States?', *SAMAR*, Spring/Summer, 5–11.

—— (2000a): 'Charting the Course: An Overview of Domestic Violence in the South Asian Community in the United States', *Journal of Social Distress and the Homeless*, 9, 173–85.

—— (2000b): 'Broken promises: Domestic Violence Murders and Attempted Murders in the US and Canadian South Asian Communities', in S. Nankani (ed.), *Breaking the Silence: Domestic Violence in the South Asian-American Community*. Philadephia, Xlibris Corporation: www. Xlibris.com.

DasGupta, S., and S. Dasgupta (1996): 'Women in Exile: Gender Relations in the Indian Community in the US', in S. Maira & R. Srikanth (eds.), *Contours of the Heart: South Asians Map America*. NY: American Writers' Workshop, pp. 381–400.

Dasgupta, S.D., and S. Warrier (1996): 'In the Footsteps of "Arundhat"': Indian Women's Experience of Domestic Violence in the United States', *Violence Against Women*, 2, 238–59.

—— (1997): *In Visible Terms: Domestic Violence in the Indian Context*, 2nd edn. Union, NJ: Manavi, Inc.

Davis, A.Y. (1985): *Violence Against Women and the Ongoing Challenge to Racism*, Freedom Organizing Series # 5. Latham, NY: Kitchen Table.

'East Brunswick Woman Arrested for Murder' (1981): *Star Ledger*, 14 Feb., p. 50.

Eng, P., and S.D. Dasgupta (2003): *Safety and Justice For All: Examining the Relationship between Women's Anti-violence Movement and the Criminal Legal System*. NY: Ms. Foundation.

Fagan, J. (1996): 'The Criminalization of Domestic Violence: Promises and Limits'. Presentation at the 1995 Conference on Criminal Justice Research and Evaluation. Rockville, MD: National Institute of Justice.

Federal Register (2006): 'Current Poverty Rate and Guidelines', 24 January, 71(15), pp. 3848–49.

Fernandez, M. (1997): 'Domestic Violence by Extended Family Members in India', *Journal of Interpersonal Violence*, 12, 433–55.

Helweg, A.W., and Helweg U.M. (1990): *An Immigrant Success Story:*

East Indians in America. Philadelphia: University of Pennsylvania Press.

Incite! Women of Color Against Violence. (nd): Critical resistance– Incite statement: Gender violence and the prison industrial complex. 9 Aug. 2003, http://www.incite-national.org/involve/ statement.html.

Jensen, J.M. (1988): *Passage from India: Indian Immigrants in North America*. New Haven, CT: Yale University Press.

Jones, J.A. (1997): 'The Immigration Marriage Fraud Amendments: Sham Marriages or Sham Legislation?', *Florida State University Law Review*, 24, 679–701.

Journal of Social Distress and the Homeless (2000): Special issue: 'Domestic Violence in the South Asian Immigrant Community', 9(3).

Khan, E. (2004): 'Help Is at Hand for Abandoned NRI Wives', *Ethnic NewsWatch*, xxxv, p. 18.

Krishnan, S. P., M. Baig-Amin, L. Gilbert, N. El-Bassel, and A.Waters (1998): 'Lifting the Veil of Secrecy: Domestic Violence Against South Asian Women in the United States', in S.D. Dasgupta (ed.), *A Patchwork Shawl: Chronicles of South Asian Women in America*. New Brunswick, NJ: Rutgers University Press, 145–59.

Maguigan, H. (1995): 'Cultural Evidence and Male Violence: Are Feminist and Multiculturalist Reformers on a Collision Course in Criminal Courts?', *New York University Law Review*, 70, 36–99.

McMahon, M., and E. Pence (2003): 'Making Social Change: Reflections on Individual and Institutional Advocacy with Women Arrested for Domestic Violence', *Violence Against Women*, 9, 47–74.

Mills, L.G. (1999): 'Killing Her Softly: Intimate Abuse and the Violence of State Intervention', *Harvard Law Review*, 113, 550–613.

Narayan, U. (1997): *Dislocating Cultures: Identities, Traditions, and Third-world Feminism*. NY & London: Routledge.

National Poverty Center (2006): 'Poverty in the United States: Frequently Asked Questions', 18 April 2007. http://www.npc. umich.edu/poverty/#TOP.

NRI Internet (2004): '12,000 cases in Gujarat of women abandoned by their NRI husbands, a figure higher than Punjab', 5 August 2005. http://www.nriinternet.com/Marriages/Desrted_Wife/ 2004/3_Gujrat.htm.

Ostrowski, J. (2004): 'Race Versus Gender in the Courtroom', 5 June 2004. http://www.africana.com/articles/daily/bw 20040504domestic.asp.

Pacific Post (2004a): 'Where Have Our Husbands Gone?', 24 September–5 August 2005. http://www.pacificpost.com/ apnews/news/.

—— (2004b): 'Editorial: Holiday Wives, Abandoned Brides and Runaway Grooms.', 21 October, 5 August 2005. http://www. pacificpost.com/apnews/news/.

—— 'Indian Police Bust Bridegroom Scam', 5 August 2005. http:// www.pacificpost. com/apnews/news/

Pence, E.L. (1999): 'Some Thoughts on Philosophy', in M.F. Shepard and E.L. Pence (eds.), *Coordinating Community Responses to Domestic Violence: Lessons from Duluth and Beyond*. Thousand Oaks, CA: Sage, pp. 25–40.

—— (2001): 'Advocacy on Behalf of Battered Women', in C.M. Renzetti, J.L. Edleson, and R.K. Bergen (eds.), *Sourcebook on Violence Against Women*. Thousand Oaks, CA: Sage, pp. 329–43.

Pence, E.L. and M.F. Shepard (1999): 'An Introduction: Developing a Coordinated Community Response', in M.F. Shepard and E.L. Pence (eds.), *Coordinating Community Responses to Domestic Violence: Lessons from Duluth and Beyond*. Thousand Oaks, CA: Sage, pp. 3–23.

Pleck, E. (1989): 'Criminal Approaches to Family Violence, 1640–1980', in L. Ohlin and M. Tonry (eds.), *Family Violence,* vol. II, 'Crime and Justice: An Annual Review of Research. Chicago, IL: University of Chicago Press, pp. 19–57.

Raj, A., and J. Silverman (2002): 'Intimate Partner Violence Against South Asian Women in Greater Boston.' *JAMWA,* 57, 111–14.

Raj, A., K.N. Livramento, S. Christina, J. Gupta, & J. G. Silverman, (2006): 'Victims of Intimate Partner Violence More Likely to Report Abuse from In-laws', *Violence Against Women,* 12, 936–49.

Razack, S.H. (1998): *Looking White People in the Eye: Gender, Race, and Culture in Courtrooms and Classrooms*. Toronto, Buffalo, and London: University of Toronto Press.

Rodriguez, D. (2000): 'Locked Up, Beat Down', *ColorLines,* 1, 16–17.

Roy, S.G. (1995): 'Restoring Hope or Tolerating Abuse? Responses to Domestic Violence against Immigrant Women', *Georgetown Immigration Law Journal,* 9, 263–90.

Ruttenberg, M.H. (1994): 'A Feminist Critique of Mandatory Arrest: An Analysis of Race and Gender in Domestic Violence Policy', *American University Journal of Gender and the Law*, 2, 171–99.

Saran, P., and E. Eames (eds.) (1980): *The New Ethnics: Indians in the United States*. NY: Praeger.

Sawhill, I.V. (1993): 'Poverty in the United States. The Library of Economics and Liberty: The Concise Encyclopedia of Economics', 18 April 2007. http://www.econlib.org/library/ENC/PovertyintheUnitedStates.html.

Sen, R. (1999): 'Between a Rock and a Hard Place: Domestic Violence in Communities of Color', *ColorLines*, 2, 2 October 2004. http://www.arc.org/C_Lines/CLArchive/story2_1_07.html.

Shah, S. (2007): 'Middle Class, Documented, and Helpless: The H-4 Visa Bind', in S.D. Dasgupta (ed.), *Body Evidence: Intimate Violence Against South Asian Women in America*. New Brunswick, NJ: Rutgers University Press, pp. 195–210.

Silliman, J. (2002): 'Policing the National Body: Sex, Race, and Criminalization', in J. Silliman and A. Bhattacharjee (eds.), *Policing the National Body: Race, Gender, and Criminalization*. Cambridge, MA: South End Press, pp. ix–xxix.

Silliman, J., and A. Bhattacharjee (eds.) (2002): *Policing the National Body: Race, Gender, and Criminalization*. Cambridge, MA: South Asian End Press.

Sinha, A. (2001): 'Domestic Violence and US Asylum Law: Eliminating the "Cultural Hook" for Claims Involving Gender-related Persecution', *New York University Law Review*, 76, 1562–98.

––– (2000): 'The Color of Violence', *ColorLines*, 1, 14–15.

Sthanki, M. (2007): 'The Aftermath of September 11: An Anti-domestic Violence Perspective', in S.D. Dasgupta (ed.), *Body Evidence: Intimate Violence Against South Asian Women in America*. New Brunswick, NJ: Rutgers University Press, pp. 68–78.

Tribune (2004): 'NRI bride mart: Case of runaway grooms', 13 June, 5 August. http://www.tribuneindia.com/2004/20040613/spectrum/main1.htm.

US Census Bureau (2000): *Census 2000*, 2 October 2004, infoplease. com, http://infoplease.com/ipa/A0778584.html.

––– (2004): *'We the People in the United States*. Washington, DC: US Department of Commerce, Economics and Statistics Administration.

––– (2007): *US Population, Census 2000*. Infoplease. 18 April 2007. http://www.infoplease.com/ipa/A0778584.html.

—— (2002a): Special Issue: 'Women's Use of Violence in Intimate Relationships, part 1, 8(11).

Violence Against Women (1999): Special Issue: 'Violence against South Asian Women', part 2, 5(6).

—— (2002b). Special Issue: 'Women's Use of Violence in Intimate Relationships', part 2, 8(12).

— – (2003). Special Issue: 'Women's Use of violence in Intimate Relationships', part 3, 9(1).

Visweswaran, K. (2002): 'Women's Rights as Human Rights: Domestic Violence and the Problem of Culture'. Keynote address, Aarohan: Manavi's First Conference on Domestic Violence in the South Asian Context, New Brunswick, NJ. 13 September.

—— (2004): 'Gendered States: Rethinking Culture as a Site of South Asian Human Rights Work', *Human Rights Quarterly*, 26, 483–511.

Volpp, L. (2000): 'Blaming Culture for Bad Behavior', *Yale Journal of Law and the Humanities,* No. 24, April, 89–116.

—— (2003): 'The Excesses of Culture: On American Citizenship and Identity', Fourth Annual Korematsu Lecture. New York University, NY.

Weisberg, D.K. (1996): 'Introduction' to section 3, 'Battered Women', in D.K. Weisberg (ed.), *Applications of Feminist Legal Theory to Women's Lives: Sex, Violence, Work, and Reproduction.* Philadelphia, PA: Temple University Press, 277–95.

Zorza, J. (1992): 'The Criminal Law of Misdemeanor: Domestic Violence, 1970–1990', *Journal of Criminal Law and Criminology,* 83, 240–79.

3

If Women Could Risk Pleasure

Reinterpreting Violence in Public Space

Shilpa Phadke

It's nigh on impossible to open a newspaper or switch on television news without being assaulted by stories of violence. Violence against women, particularly in public space, captures in droves the breaking news attention of the media. This is of course not intended to suggest that such violence does not take place. Over the past few years, women have been shot at point blank range; thrown off trains, and lost their legs; been sexually assaulted by policemen (a college student, a rag-picker, and a bar dancer separately); and been stalked, raped and killed.[1] These acts of violence are a cause for concern both individually and collectively, and at no point am I minimizing their gravity. At the same time, it is important to position questions of public violence within a larger frame that includes not just public and private violence but also the social, community, family restrictions and self-policing that might not hitherto have been viewed as violence at all.

I have argued elsewhere that questions of violence and safety in public space, especially for women, are inevitably placed in fallacious oppositional binaries: private versus public, safety versus violence, safety versus risk, rational versus risky, where one is cast as the antithesis of the other.[2] I have suggested that for women the private is not necessarily safe, as safety does not include protection from those who are supposed to

protect you, and that anxieties about reputation often lead
women to take risks with physical safety. I have also argued
that it is the insistence on respectability that reinforces these
oppositions in a context where women have little recourse
from private violence, and are themselves often censured for
being unable to prevent public violence.[3]

In this chapter, I re-examine violence, placing it not
in opposition to risk or pleasure but alongside them, to
understand what these terms mean by themselves and
when connected to each other, and their implications for
women's access to public space. My intention is to examine
the publicized version of violence against women and to ask
what other kinds of violence lie in its shadow. The chapter
draws on insights and findings from research conducted by
the Gender & Space Project.[4]

I develop the following arguments: One, that everyday acts
of violence, such as catcalls and comments directed at women
on the streets are linked to more brutal forms of violence such
as rape. Two, that the perception of danger is often sufficient
to prevent women from accessing public space. Three, that
safety and violence are not necessarily opposites, and that
protectionism, particularly one that denies access to the
public, might also be experienced by women as violence.
Four, that risk and violence are not the same and we might do
well to rethink our understanding of these categories. Finally,
in re-imagining risk, violence, and pleasure, I suggest that
for women the best long-term strategy to enhance claims to
public space is to embrace risk and pleasure while accepting
violence as something that must be negotiated in the process
of doing so.

The Violence of Normal Times

...at night, in most large cities, all women are agoraphobic.
                                              Esther da Costa Meyer, 1996

For this section, I borrow the brilliantly evocative title of a
volume edited by feminist legal scholar Kalpana Kannabiran

to draw attention to the fact that the horrifically violent events that have the media in a tizzy are inextricably linked to everyday acts of violence against women: sexual harassment, domestic violence, restrictions on clothing and movement, to name just a few.[5]

How does one understand this notion of 'normal' in relation to gendered violence? Is 'normal' violence the violence that is so ubiquitous that it is no longer worthy of comment? Is it that which is sanctioned by existing power hierarchies and therefore unremarkable? Is it the internalization of these power hierarchies so that certain kinds of violence, exercises of power, appear legitimate?[6] In the context of public space, normalized violence might be seen as the everyday violences that women face when accessing public space. It implies the daily repetitive performance of acts of intrusion and harassment which women are expected to take in their stride. These acts might involve a variety of ideologies, attitudes, and behavioural patterns that underscore the normative idea that women are out of place in public space.

What then is 'normal violence'? Is it the acceptance of the supposed rationality that women are not safe in public space? Is it the restrictions that women place on their own movements? The anxiety that makes women constantly look over their shoulders? A discomfort with darkness (having been told over and over that the night is not safe for women)? The catcalls and comments that women face every day? The conditioning that we should ignore these things and walk on as if nothing happened? Blaming oneself for being harassed: was I wearing the wrong things, looking back in the wrong way, or out in the wrong place? Being unable to access public space without purpose? The denial of open and unquestioned access to public space? In other words, everyday negotiations: how, when, and with whom to commute, when not to be out at all, what to wear, where to walk, how to modify one's gaze, and other strategies that women employ in public space, may all be seen as constituting the realm of normalized violence.

In the larger public discourse, however, violence is only seen to have been committed when women are physically attacked, and to a lesser extent when they are sexually harassed in an explicitly verbal manner. Women however have to deal with the possibility of attack and/or harassment every day, even when it does not happen. This effectively circumscribes their access to public space, yet unless women are actually attacked, no violence is seen to have been committed.

Feminist scholars point out that such normalized violence often leads to situations and states that are then further normalized as female pathologies. Esther da Costa Meyer[7] observes that a social anxiety about the 'place' occupied by women in public 'space' also has an acute impact on women's own anxieties with regard to these public spaces, sometimes to the extent of pathology in the form of agoraphobia, the fear of open spaces. She records that agoraphobia has been interpreted by different authors to suggest fear of the market-place, fear of public squares, dizziness in public squares, and fear of the streets. She argues that agoraphobia often manifests itself in conditions of domesticity – which reinforce women's position within the home and deny them roles in the labour force. This is particularly true of middle-class and affluent women.

Agoraphobia, in this sense, then, can be seen as an allegory for the sexual division of labour and the inscription of sexual difference on to public space.[8] In certain contexts and situations, when the risk of violence against women in public space, real or perceived, is greater, agoraphobia assumes an endemic form. Temporality is also an important factor in determining agoraphobia, as the opening quote of this section by Meyer ominously suggests. In my research in Mumbai, women articulated a heightened anxiety about being in public space at night. This was however, cast as the realistic fear of possible violence and not as pathological, which further demonstrates the erasure of what is seen as 'normal' violence.

The perception of 'normal' violence as unremarkable and something that women simply 'have to deal with' in public is not unconnected to the instances of brutal violence, but has to be seen along a continuum where the existence of 'normal' violence might even condone acts that might be cast as 'abnormal' violence. The day-to-day stares and leers at local railway stations and on trains cannot be seen as separate from assaults on women in the same trains. When I suggest a continuum, I do not mean to imply an easy slide from verbal harassment to rape, or to suggest that they are the same thing. Rather, the prevalence of everyday sexual harassment not only indicates the lack of public space for women but also normalizes violence in public space: she got harassed because she was out of place; she got raped because she was at the wrong place. In both instances, what is really being said is this: she (woman) should not have been in that place. This thinking then allows women to be blamed when they are victims of more brutal attacks. In a similar vein, Kannabiran too has suggested that sudden conflagrations of violence must be understood in the context of this 'ever present violence of normal times'.[9]

Brutally violent crimes against women are part of a range of violent acts against women in public space and stem from women's lack of claim to public space. These acts of violence further contribute to reducing women's access to public space when they are flashed across televisions screens and newspapers, reminding women that they are not safe in the city. The perception of risk is sometimes as significant as the actual existence of risk of violence and media narratives of danger play no small role in circumscribing women's access to public space. In a round-table discussion the Gender & Space Project organized a month after a police constable raped a college girl on Mumbai's Marine Drive, young women said that the wide publicity surrounding the crime would lead to greater policing of their movements and hence decreased mobility in public space. In the violence of normal times, then, for women 'risk' is applicable in its adjectival form, that is, to be at risk, rather than in its verb form, to take risks.

Narrating Danger

Be careful and the world will appear to be good... But in today's superfast world... In the attempt to provide a 'free' atmosphere at home, parents proudly allow girls to wear skimpy clothes and give boys uncontrolled freedom. But there are shards of glass on this modern path... we don't see parents telling their children to tread carefully... There seems to be a competition among young women to show their undergarments in the name of a 'below-waist' fashion... To see girls dangle a cigarette openly is worrisome. If a man is provoked by such clothes, who can one blame?

Saamna (Shiv Sena newspaper), 25 April 2005

This quotation is from an editorial following the Marine Drive rape. It is certainly not representative of the general tone of the media; indeed, it reflects its most conservative and right-wing voice. These conservative voices tend to directly blame women for the violence committed against them. However, the tone of even the most liberal media narratives is one of 'the city under siege' and 'women in danger'. All these narratives of danger contribute towards the evocation of a sense that women are unsafe in the city.

In 'narratives of danger' I include not just the media, which tends to be the most visible, but also state discourses through the police and other functionaries, civil society discourses, and everyday hearsay that circulates through neighbourhood and street conversations. Rosa Ainley points out that perceived threats to safety are different from, although not necessarily less harmful than, 'real threats'. 'Safety' debates, she argues, 'respond to the public's perception of danger, rather than the likelihood of danger itself', making safety inextricably linked to crime prevention.[10] This is often the model used in understanding danger to women: the sense that danger is out there.

The language in which public violence is described exaggerates the level of threat. Take, for example, the headlines from Indian newspapers. 'For women, metro streets are a dark alley,'[11] 'Stalked in sleepless city',[12] 'Fear builds as 10 p.m. nears on the railways',[13] and 'BPO murder: Outsourced fear, women@risk'.[14] Women are inevitably cast in the role of potential victims to be protected. Some recent headlines have been: 'Crime against women',[15] 'Cop molests girl, police beef up security,'[16] 'Home-guard molestation causes safety concerns.'[17]

Even when women conform to the rules demanding purpose and respectability in public space they are still seen to be in danger. In her 1998 study of urban woodlands in Britain, Jacquelin Burgess points out that the media's sensationalization of violent crimes against women and children reinforces the sense of fear and anxiety. One young woman who had been sexually assaulted and then stabbed to death was mentioned in all the focus groups that Burgess conducted. This attack was seen as 'particularly shocking because... [the young woman] was "obeying" all the "rules" – out in the morning with a dog and a young child, and still she was murdered in the most brutal fashion.'[18]

Class affiliations strongly influence the amount of media attention that crimes receive. A police constable's rape of a middle-class college girl in an upper-class area in Mumbai made headlines for several days in April 2005. However, a constable's rape of a teenage rag-picker near Mumbai's international airport only six months later attracted far less media attention.

Perceived respectability and virtue also play a role in how an attack is reported. Innuendoes of 'them having asked for it' surround sexual assaults in public space; these are particularly sharp when the woman is seen as not-respectable. In March 2006, a 52-year-old woman accused Mumbai industrialist Abhishek Kasliwal of raping her in his car during a late-night lift home. A medical examination confirmed both the rape and injuries sustained by the victim. The media avidly covered this case involving an upper-class man until police investigations suggested that the woman was probably a sex worker who was assaulted in the process of selling sex.[19] The reportage then dropped dramatically. Was this because it lost the peg of 'good woman in danger'? Elsewhere, I have argued that sex workers are seen to be taking risks and any negative outcomes are seen as their own fault. Sex workers are seen to be engaging in 'risky' behaviour (risk as verb) and therefore not deserving of protection. In fact, it is society in general and public space in particular that need to be protected from the 'risk' (here noun) of contamination that they represent.[20]

The onus of demonstrating that they 'did not ask for it' continues to rest with women. For instance, an attempt to regulate clothing in colleges was justified in the name of women's safety. One report was headlined, 'Bombay Univ. says mini-skirt ban helps stop rape'.[21] One news report citing the *Saamna* piece quoted at the beginning of this section is entitled 'Women inviting attacks'. Though this piece does not concur with the Shiv Sena view, the headline is misleading and sensational.[22]

Placing this onus on women often prevents women from registering cases against harassment and assault. Two cases, both taking place on New Year's Eve, make this point eloquently. On 31 December 2007, a young woman was molested by a large group of revellers near Mumbai's Gateway of India. On the same day the following year, two women were molested by a crowd of men outside a five-star hotel in Mumbai's Juhu. Press photographers took pictures of both assaults. Both were represented as instances of the growing danger to women in Mumbai. In both cases the women themselves chose not to file cases.[23]

By drawing attention to the ways in which violence against women is sensationalized, I do not intend to suggest that there is no danger at all to women or to deny that the city is becoming a fraught, contested space that is more difficult to negotiate. My intention is to focus on the selective way in which violence against women is highlighted over other kinds of violence, leading to the inevitable conclusion that women might be safer not accessing public space at all.[24] The disproportionate focus on the dangers to women in public space appears to ignore not just the reality that more women face violence in private than in public spaces, but also the reality that more men than women are attacked in public.

Men, however, are rarely represented as being in danger in public space, even when they appear to be specifically targeted. In 2006–07, a homicidal Mumbai serial killer dubbed the Beer Man killed several men; his signature was an empty beer can left next to his victim. However, because men are a taken-for-granted presence in public space, violence against them is generically represented. The focus on sexual safety depicts sexual assault as a special type of crime, and one underlining women's particular vulnerability. The fact that not only women but also men can be raped is something that finds little mention. The Beer Man, for instance, would sodomize his victims before killing them. However, only one newspaper article alluded to men's sexual vulnerability. The others referred to the victims as 'passive homosexuals', without elucidating further. Several men were killed between October 2006 and February 2007 but the case was never cast as one of 'poor men in danger on the streets of Mumbai'.

On the other hand, random instances of violence that might not even be targeted at women particularly often get represented as 'women in danger'. The apparently 'schizophrenic' 'Hammer Man' in Mumbai who attacked women with a hammer and robbed them is a case in point.[25] The coverage of this focused on the safety of women, barely mentioning schizophrenia, mental illness, or the availability of facilities for treatment.

Narratives of danger underscore the point that all women face violence in public space: 'bad' women ask for it, but women who conform are not necessarily safe. These often apocalyptic visions of impending disaster raise the anxiety levels of women on a daily basis, compelling them to strategize about negotiating every square foot of public space they access, constantly looking over their shoulders and stalked by the ghost of crimes past. By reinforcing the notion that women are not safe in public spaces, these narratives of danger both further restrict and normalize women's lack of access to public space. They have the additional effect of sanctioning various kinds of restrictions on women's mobility, by rationalizing them as being for women's own safety. Such protectionism then engenders its own kinds of violence.

The Violence of Protectionism

'Where are the men?' I asked her.

'In their proper places, where they ought to be.'

'Pray let me know what you mean by "their proper places"'.

'O, I see my mistake, you cannot know our customs, as you were never here before. We shut our men indoors.'

'Just as we are kept in the zenana?'

'Exactly so.'

'How funny,' I burst into a laugh. Sister Sara laughed too.

'But dear Sultana, how unfair it is to shut in the harmless women and let loose the men.'

'Why? It is not safe for us to come out of the zenana, as we are naturally weak.'

'Yes, it is not safe so long as there are men about the streets, nor is it so when a wild animal enters a market-place.'

'Of course not.'

'Suppose some lunatics escape from the asylum and begin to do all sorts of mischief to men, horses and other creatures; in that case what will your countrymen do?'

'They will try to capture them and put them back into their asylum.'

'Thank you! And you do not think it wise to keep sane people inside an asylum and let loose the insane?'

'Of course not!' said I laughing lightly.

'As a matter of fact, in your country this very thing is done! Men, who do or at least are capable of doing no end of mischief, are let loose and the innocent women shut up in the zenana! How can you trust those untrained men out of doors?'

Rokeya Sakhawat Hossain, 1905

If the presence of public violence is sensationalized, private violence is often sought to be silenced. Both the visibility of public violence and the erasure of private violence can be seen to have the same goal: that of suggesting that private spaces are the safest spaces for women to be.

Feminist scholars have demonstrated beyond reasonable doubt that women's homes are often spaces of violence and terror for them.[26] Even when women's homes are not overtly or physically violent, safety is inevitably articulated in the language of protectionism, that is, women must be protected from the 'dangerous' outside world. Elsewhere I have argued that such protectionism reflects a concern with women's sexual virtue and sexual safety rather than actual safety. It is rooted in conservative class and community structures, particularly those of sexual endogamy. The fear is as much that women will form consensual relationships with unsuitable men, as it is that women will be attacked against their will.[27] The problem is not necessarily only physical violence or assault, for often women have little protection from those who are supposed to protect them, be it their own families or even the 'desirable' men they marry. In fact, sometimes so peripheral is the question of actual violence to the more pressing issue of avoiding unsuitable alliances and maintaining familial and community 'honour' that families themselves perpetrate violence against those women who transgress these boundaries.[28]

The language of protection and safety hides the real agenda of controlling women's sexuality. As writer Rokeya Sakhawat Hossain suggests in her fictional piece 'Sultana's Dream', rationality is a strange thing. It is possible to present as logical and rational something which is not, by articulating it in a language that makes it appear so: in this instance, as Hossain suggests, the irrationality of locking up potential victims when potential perpetrators freely walk the streets.[29] It would not be rational to suggest that women should not be in the public because they may meet the wrong kind of men, but saying that women are unsafe because of the possibility of violent sexual attack has a kind of altruistic rationality: it is for women's own good. This diktat then covers both possibilities with one stroke: it protects women both from those outside men they do not want to know as well as those they might actually want to know.[30]

Protectionism has yet another problem: it is conditional. Safety becomes a form of exercising control, using the motifs of 'good' versus 'bad' women to determine the right to protection. Articulating safety in the language of morality places all those who do not conform at the risk of violence in public space: sex workers are rendered completely unable to protect themselves by an ideology that defines them as not being worthy of protection. Lesbian women are at risk of censure in sex-segregated spaces if they do not conform to the prescriptions of femininity. Heterosexual women with male partners in public space are vulnerable to assault from the self-appointed guardians of morality. Denying women the right to be in public spaces, to access public services and amenities, to seek pleasure in the simple act of walking their city, I argue, is not just a denial of their citizenship rights, but a form of violence that is especially violent because it is not even recognized as such.

The insistence on respectability, built around concerns of morality creates a situation in which women can be blamed for acts of violence against them. Women can then be seen as being in the 'wrong place', giving the 'wrong signals', wearing the 'wrong clothes', and therefore held responsible for violence committed against them. Even in what appear to be open-and-shut legal cases, accusing voices are raised against women. Thus it was that conservative voices asked why the college girl raped by the constable was in Marine Drive, so far from her home in Ghatkopar.[31]

Similarly, when canoodling couples in Mumbai's public spaces are rounded up and taken to police stations, young women are sought to be shamed by asking whether their parents know what they are up to.[32] As I have suggested elsewhere, for women, the fear of social stigma and the threat to reputation actually enhances the possibility of physical violence by reducing women's capacity to produce safety.[33]

Even when women flout restrictions on clothing, speech, and mobility, similar accusing looks and comments from the family and community stigmatize women's reputations and are a form of psychological violence. In the interests then of both achieving respectability and safety, women often restrict their movements and 'choose' not to venture out on their own. This is a form of self-policing, even imprisonment, that gets defined as a rational choice, not as violence, even though it violates a woman's right and desire to access public space.

There is no objective definition of violence as such. What is defined as violence is highly subjective. Violence that takes place within pre-defined norms and structures of authority – be it the state, community, or family – is normalized as intended to maintain order and therefore not seen as violence at all. Aggression that is sanctioned either by the law or by social norms is seen not as violence but as just retribution. Violence that is officially sanctioned through familial or community authority of whatever kind is then no longer seen as violence. So also the denial of women's access to the public is not about violence but about the rationality of safety, (private safe, public dangerous). If women refuse to accept this rationality of safety then it is presumed that violence is the logical outcome. The fear is not of violence but of uncontrolled violence by unknown persons. This selective labelling of violence, in fact, allows sanctioned familial and community violence to be justified in the name of avoidance of unknown stranger violence. The imposition of safety involves a series of violences which include restrictions in clothing, demeanour, and mobility. These restrictions are justified as being rational and reflect the exercise of a familial and community authority expressed as being in women's best interests. [34]

I would like to argue that acts of extreme coercive violence against women must also be understood in relation to the repressive response that greets women's consensual acts as agents, particularly as sexual agents. Women's actions as sexual agents are often seen as posing a threat to a reified notion of 'Indian culture' and undermining the established order of family, community, and even nation, and these institutions are willing to use violence in order to protect themselves from this threat. The question of violence here then is not about whether it can be prevented, but how it can be managed.

Kathleen B. Jones problematizes our understanding of authority itself. She suggests that an authority based on instrumental rationality, where the mere location of an individual or group in a position of authority entitles them to obedience, is an andro-centric one. She argues that 'the idea of authority as traditional hierarchy makes sense as long as we accept on faith that the need for an ordered efficient, social system takes precedence over any other form of social organization'. This means that established rules and regulations are valued above human relations and, as she puts it, 'the uncertainty of human relationship' is exchanged for 'the certainty of rules'.[35] Quoting Carol Gilligan, Jones suggests that for women the fracture in human connections is what is violent, whereas for men, the connection itself poses a threat. From here Jones argues that 'for men, rule-bound situations, with clear boundaries and limits to aggressiveness are safe: whereas for women, it is precisely this inability to connect, or to affiliate, that represents the dominance of aggression.'[36] While this might appear to be an unnecessarily essentialist view of gender relations and responses, Jones's further observations on how these differing notions of authority are entailed in differing understandings of violence are particularly relevant to my argument.

Though Jones does not directly suggest this, I read her understanding of authority as indicating that were we to open the door to a more subjective, relational, and emotive understanding of authority, we might open the door to more open-ended ways of resolving conflict that might enable us to question established structures of authority. In relation to public space, then, established structures of authority ensure that women are denied access to public space in ways that entail the exercise of sometimes overt, sometimes covert violence. If we acknowledge that even the efforts to prevent public violence entail the use and exercise of violence, we might be able to define the meaning of violence differently. If we are able to see that violence is ever-present, and that only its form differs, then our understanding of risk and violence will dramatically change. This will allow us to recast women's access to public space as an act of negotiation with different kinds of risks, and not as a choice between pure safety and pure danger.

It will then become clear that safety and violence in relation to women's access to public space are not really opposites at all. Because, in the interests of maintaining safety, women might

find themselves subject to all manner of violence. At the same
time, the possibility of engaging public space, of taking on the
unknown, and placing oneself at risk of a violence that may or
may not occur, might in fact offer possibilities for women to
expand their access to public space – and in the process take
a feminist engagement with cities one step forward.

The Feminist Struggle vis-à-vis Violence against Women

Feminists are easily intimidated by the charge that their own pleasure
is selfish, as in political rhetoric which suggests that no woman is
entitled to talk about sexual pleasure while any woman remains in
danger – that is – never.

Carole Vance, 1984

Anthropologist Carole Vance has famously argued that
feminism's success in bringing sexual violence into the public
sphere had also the unintended consequence of suggesting that
women are less sexually safe than ever and that 'discussions
and explorations of pleasure are better deferred to a safer
time'. Vance argues that if as feminists we allow ourselves to
be convinced that our desire for sexual pleasure should be
postponed until all sexual violence is eliminated, we will wait
forever. She suggests that we need to talk of sexual pleasure
even as we battle against sexual violence, and that these two
ends are by no means mutually exclusive. Using this line of
thinking, I argue that we cannot postpone thinking about the
pleasures of courting risk: the pleasures of walking the streets
and viscerally writing the city with our bodies.

When I say pleasure here, I refer to something that
encompasses fun, but is much more than that. Pleasure itself
is highly subjective and is inextricably linked to a range of
choices, including those relating to sexuality, dress, temporality,
matrimony (or not), motherhood (or not), to name some.
Pleasure might be found in solitude as much as in company; it
entails the visceral body as much as the untamed mind; and it
entails activity as much as simply doing nothing.[37]

As Vance suggests, the struggle against violence and the
quest for pleasure cannot be separate things. The quest for

pleasure actually strengthens our struggle against violence, framing it in the language of rights rather than protection.[38] The 'right to pleasure' must always include the 'right to live without violence'. The struggle against violence, as an end in itself, is fundamentally premised on exclusion and can only be maintained through violence, in that, it tends to divide people into 'us' and 'them', and actually sanctions violence against 'them' in order to protect 'us'. The quest for pleasure, on the other hand, when framed in inclusive terms, does not divide people into aggressors and victims and is therefore non-divisive.[39]

However, many feminists fear that if pleasure gets on the agenda, women will lose what we've won with much effort. Feminists have also been wary of being accused of demanding 'things' that are lower down on what Nivedita Menon satirically refers to as the 'hierarchy of oppressions'.[40] A left-of-centre ideology often dominates the women's movement, and the desire for pleasure, especially in a context where people are poor or face violence, is seen as suspect. There is a belief that claiming victim-status allows the movement to win many of the small battles and make gains for women. What is never considered is that this might well mean losing the war. In keeping with this strategy, feminist engagements with city public spaces have, given the instances of violence against women, focused on eliminating the risks of violence as far as possible.

Notwithstanding Reclaim the Night marches, access to pleasure in public space has never really occupied centre stage. There is also a fear that the quest for pleasure, an unknown quantity, might be seen as too threatening to society's ideas of order. It might derail the struggles and undermine the righteous and moral grounds on which the women's movement has fought for women's rights. Therefore, even within the women's movement, women do not place themselves or their desires centre-stage because this would immediately be tagged as selfish, self-serving, and divisive. The quest for the right to enjoyment, fun, or pleasure for its own sake just does not find legitimacy.[41]

In another essay I have drawn on the arguments advanced by Winifred Woodhull and Nivedita Menon.[42] Using a Foucauldian paradigm to understand rape, Woodhull suggests that Foucault spoke in 'favour of desexualizing rape by decriminalizing it, making rape a civil offence akin to any other form of physical attack'. She argues that in Foucault's view this might 'undermine the supposed "prestige" of rape as a grand transgression'. Menon suggests that we need to liberate ourselves from the meaning of rape. She argues that feminist politics must move away from the discourse of 'rape as violation', an understanding that is 'perfectly compatible with patriarchal and sexist notions of women's bodies', to work towards transforming common-sense understandings of rape and sexual violence in general.[43]

Drawing on these positions, I have argued that we need to redefine our understanding of violence in relation to public space: to see not rape or sexual assault but the denial of access to public space as the worst possible outcome for women. Rather than safety, what women would seek instead is the right to take risks, placing their claim in the discourse of rights rather than protectionism. What we might seek then is an 'equality of risk': that is, not that women should never be attacked but that when they are, they should receive a citizen's right to redress, and that their right to be in that space should be unquestioned.[44] Choosing to take risks, even of possible sexual violence in public space, undermines a sexist structure where women's virtue is prized over their desires or agency. Placing the desire for pleasure higher up in the hierarchy of demands than the avoidance of sexual violence challenges the assumptions that women's bodies belong to their families and communities rather than to themselves.

At no point am I ignoring or even minimizing the violence, both sexual and non-sexual, that might potentially occur in the public space, and which has implications for both bodily and psychological trauma. The fear of violence in public space is real. However, we also need to recognize another kind of risk. The risk, should women choose not to access public space more than minimally, of loss of opportunity

to engage city spaces and the loss of the experience of
public spaces. This also includes the risk of accepting the
gendered hierarchies of access to public space and by doing
so reinforcing them. A Bambaiya term that young women in
Mumbai use to describe their friends or peers who are gutsy
is 'daring': *usko bahut* daring *hai* (she has guts). Their tone is
admiring, not derogatory.[45] This suggests that young women
implicitly recognize that there is pleasure to be found in
transgression. What women need then is the right to 'dare';
to take chosen risks in an environment where their 'daring' is
recognized as legitimate.

What would change if women were to demand the right to
public space for no reason at all? What would change if we
chose not to avoid risk but to embrace it as an integral part
of urban living? For this we need to clearly distinguish 'risk'
from 'violence'. Much has been written in women's studies
scholarship on questions of victimhood and agency. Women's
desire to access public space has always been seen in terms of
the potential risk of violence. If we recast risk as agency, as an
act of exercising choices, we place the relationship between
risk and violence in a different context. Not only are risk
and violence not the same thing at all, but being allowed to
take risks will transform our understanding of violence from
something that women must avoid at any cost to something
that women might be willing to risk (verb). Violence might well
be seen not as something to be feared but as something to be
negotiated. We need to revise feminist definitions of violence
to include the denial of pleasure, including that of access to
public space, according it greater priority and legitimacy.[46]

I argue that a citizenship that comes with risk and the
possibility of danger holds the prospect of fuller citizenship for
women rather than a limited and circumscribed one linked to
protectionism and safety. Violence can be contained much more
effectively when risk can be calculated and negotiated rather
than when violence is sought to be dealt with through evasion,
without an understanding of its underlying ideologies.

The problem is not so much that women are at risk (adjective),
but that this risk (noun) is perceived differently, and this has

to do with the different impact that public violence is seen to have on women. If all citizens were equal, then violence and risk would also be equal: that is, the meaning of violence would be universal and risk itself would be democratic, i.e., the same for all. As things stand, everyone is not an equal citizen. If we were to focus our energies on equalizing risk, we might be better served in the quest to expand women's access to public space as citizens.[47]

What would happen if we were to envision city spaces where the predominant discourse is not safety but inclusion? What if we imagined a city where there were no hierarchies of access to public space? Some might see this vision as portending anarchy, but in my perception it holds the prospect of democratizing space and fundamentally questioning the discriminations within class, community, and gender. As feminists, it is time for us to extend ourselves beyond the 'safe' (that is legitimized) spaces of arguments based on eliminating violence and address issues of access and pleasure.

Imagining Another World

The very word 'street' has a rough, dirty magic to it, summoning up the low, the common, the erotic, the dangerous and the revolutionary.

Rebecca Solnit, 2000

In *Street Haunting: A London Adventure*, (1930), novelist Virginia Woolf writes:

No one perhaps has ever felt passionately towards a lead pencil. But there are circumstances in which it can become supremely desirable to possess one: moments when we are set upon having an object, an excuse for walking halfway across London between tea and dinner. … Getting up we say: 'Really I must buy a pencil,' as if under cover of this excuse we could indulge safely in the greatest pleasure of town life in winter – rambling the streets of London.

This is by no means the only instance of a woman seeking pleasure in public space. As far back as ancient Greece, women have sought to find pleasure and even abandon in public spaces. These were often in the guise of ritual festivals, as in Adonia[48] and Maenadism.[49] As Rosa Ainley suggests, 'The city isn't only about danger and fear (woman as perpetual victim), or boredom and limitation (woman as housewife), it is also a site of possibility, pleasure and excitement.'[50] However, because the city is cast as dangerous and because women are not legitimately allowed to be out there for pleasure, even the simple act of walking the streets without purpose is not easily achievable.

The desire to access the city for pleasure is not only a bourgeois inclination, though I acknowledge that it is most immediately meaningful to middle-class women. For lower-class women, it is often private spaces that are at a premium, while upper-class women tend to move from one private space to another, rarely accessing public space at all. The claim to seek pleasure in the city is also a deeply political one that has the potential to seriously undermine the public-private boundaries that continue to circumscribe women's access to and visibility in public space. The claim to pleasure in public space as a right also implicitly means challenging the boundaries between respectable and non-respectable women.

As part of our pedagogic engagement in the Gender & Space Project, we conducted three long courses and several shorter workshops with undergraduate students.[51] In the longer courses, our closing session focused on asking students to imagine their public space utopia. Students were asked to read Rokeya Sakhawat Hossain's 'Sultana's Dream', and then paint for us their own vision of a feminist utopia. Each time we found ourselves facing a completely silent group. They could not imagine another world.

This would alternately bewilder and depress us. Being over a decade older than them, we still had fantasies of a utopic world. In the feedback session, their greatest grouse was that the course had been 'too much feminism'.[52] Among young upper-middle-class women today there is a clear distancing from feminism; some of this linked to the perception of feminism as somehow joyless. The terms our undergraduate participants in workshops used were inevitably negative:

'man-hating', 'anti-beauty', 'anti-family'. As feminists, we know these are simply not true. At the same time, however, it is not untrue that after decades of struggle, while many women can today compete with men in the workspace, when it comes to pleasure, the battle has barely begun.

Since the manufacture of the contraceptive pill there has been a slow and grudging acceptance of women's right to sexual pleasure.[53] The question is whether we can now claim the right to other forms of pleasure. The pleasure of sitting on an unbroken park bench and reading a book or eating a sandwich. The pleasure of walking along the streets at night without constantly looking over one's shoulder. The pleasure of not having to change clothes in a car because your family thinks they are immodest. The pleasure of not having to sneak into your home when you enter the building at 2 a.m. for fear of what the neighbours will say. The pleasure of using a clean well-lit toilet on a public street at 4 a.m. Such forms of pleasure can only come from the right to take risks without the fear of loss of reputation as 'good girls'.

Courting risk, that pleasurable dance of forward and backward, of negotiation and choice, is something to which women have a right. Courting entails active engagement, and implies a reciprocal relationship with the city: of approaching the city with the expectation of enjoyment. This is the right to which we stake a claim as women. As feminists, who have benefitted from the struggles fought by our foremothers, we stake our claim to take the struggle further. It is time to claim not just the right to work but the right to play.

Acknowledgements

This essay draws on the insights and findings of the research towards the PUKAR Gender & Space Project (2003–06) in Mumbai funded by the Indo-Dutch Programme on Alternatives in Development (IDPAD). For more information on the project, please see www. genderandspace.org. Many of the ideas in this essay have been developed in collaboration with my colleagues Sameera Khan and Shilpa Ranade, both of whom have also commented on earlier drafts of this essay. Versions of this essay were presented at workshops

on Gender and Space at JNU, New Delhi in November 2007 and
on Women and the Public Sphere organized by SEPHIS in Baku,
Azerbaijan, June 2008, and I extend gratitude to the participants at
these workshops for their comments.

Notes

1. In October 1998, Jayabala Ashar was thrown out of a running
    train in Mumbai when she refused to part with her purse. Jessica
    Lal was shot dead by Manu Sharma in April 1999 at a Delhi
    restaurant when she refused to serve him liquor because the
    bar had closed. In August 2002, a young mentally-challenged
    girl was raped in a Mumbai local train compartment with four
    men and a woman looking the other way. In April 2005, a
    college student was raped by police constable Sunil More in
    a police cell on Mumbai's Marine Drive. In October 2005,
    in two separate incidents, head constable Chandrakant Pawar
    was accused of raping a 15-year-old rag picker while on duty
    near Mumbai airport; police constable Hameed Nazir Kazi of
    Nerul police station, New Mumbai, was accused of sexually
    abusing a bar dancer. In December 2005, a South African
    model was drugged and taken from the bar of a Mumbai
    hotel by two men, Sunil Multhani and Suresh Krishnani, and
    repeatedly raped.
2. *See* Phadke, 2005.
3. *See* Phadke, 2007.
4. This project explored questions of access to public space for
    women in Mumbai, which is widely recognized as the most
    women-friendly city in the country. The question we began
    with was: If this is indeed the country's safest city, then how
    safe is it and what does it mean for women's access to public
    space? Does access to public space translate into a right to
    public space based on ideas of citizenship?
5. *See* Kannabiran, 2006.
6. This internalization of power hierarchies is often true in
    domestic violence. *See* U. Vindhya, 2006, V. Geetha, 1998,
    Meenakshi Thapan, 1997.
7. *See* Esther de Costa Meyer, 1996.
8. Meyer (1996) suggests that class plays an important role in the
    'geopolitical distribution of agoraphobia over urban space'

(p.148). Susan Bordo (1993) points out that both agoraphobia and anorexia are largely disorders of white middle- and upper-middle class women who have 'the social and material resources to carry the traditional construction of femininity to symbolic excess but who also confront the anxieties of *new possibilities*' (p. 177) (my emphasis). Bordo further argues that agoraphobia presents itself as a parody of twentieth century constructions of femininity which escalated in the 1950s and early 1960s when notions of domesticity and dependency were reasserted as the feminine ideal. She writes: 'The housebound agoraphobic lives this construction of femininity literally. "You want me in this home? You'll have me in this home – with a vengeance!"' (p. 170).

9. *See* Kannabiran, 2006, pp. 2–3. Also, at the University of Montreal in Canada, on 6 December 1989, a gunman entered the engineering building, separated the women and men, declared his hatred of feminists, and proceeded to kill 14 women. Feminists viewed this extraordinarily violent act within the context of other forms of violence against women and connected the crime to the everyday sexism to which women are subjected.

10. *See* Ainley, 1998 p. 94.

11. According to this report, 86 per cent of women in Delhi don't feel safe, and every third woman knows at least one rape/molestation victim, says a recent C-voter survey conducted after the capital witnessed a spate of rape cases in public places. According to Mumbai police records (2001 to July 2002), quoted by the report, the city has seen 306 cases of eve-teasing, 243 cases of molestation, and 229 cases of rape. Chennai had 600 cases of crime against women in the previous year. Delhi recorded the highest number of rape cases among the metros: 447 in 2000, 380 in 2001, and 299 till July 2002, as against Mumbai's 124 in 2000 and 127 in 2001, which ranks second on this list (*Times of India*, 25 August 2002).

12. Amin Patil shot Muhammad Ali Umar Sheikh for allegedly harassing his wife and sister-in-law. The report focused on the increasing incidents of 'eve teasing in the city that never sleeps'. (*Sunday Express*, 28 March 2004).

13. Nisha Shah, a 23-year-old model, wanted to complain to the constable on duty when she tried to alight from a local train at 10 p.m., trapped in a sea of men trying to barge into the ladies

compartment. The constable told her he could not help as he had to sign off duty at 10.30 p.m. (Mumbai Newsline, *Indian Express*, 23 July 2004).

14. A young BPO employee in Bangalore was murdered by the driver of the vehicle (*Times of India*, 17 December 2005).

15. This news report profiles the 'phenomenal rise in crime against women'. According to the National Crime Records Bureau's report, dowry deaths have risen from 5,513 in 1996 to 6,917 in 1998, cases of rape from 14,846 to 15,031, torture from 35,246 to 41,318, molestation from 28,939 to 31046, sexual harassment from 5,671 to 8,123. The National Commission for Women's report says that every 26 minutes a woman is molested, every 54 minutes a rape takes place, every 48 minutes an eve-teasing incident occurs, every 4 minutes a woman is kidnapped, and every 10 minutes another is burnt to death over dowry (*Hindu*, 15 May 2001).

16. The Thane Railway police arrested a constable for allegedly molesting a 20-year-old student in the ladies first class compartment on a Kalyan-bound train in Mumbai (Mumbai Newsline, *Indian Express*, 2 August 2003).

17. This report raised serious concerns about the safety of women home guards who work through the night armed with no more than a lathi. A 19-year-old home guard was on duty at Mumbai's Khar railway station at 8 p.m. when sub-inspector Dilip Bhavar entered the guardroom and allegedly molested her. She later registered a complaint. Bhavar was arrested and let off on bail by a metropolitan court the following day (*Times of India*, 19 August 2004).

18. See Burgess, 1998, pp. 125–26. Burgess uses a British Crime survey to show that the absolute evidence of crime in parks, commons, and open spaces is very low but narratives of any attacks generate anxiety. The 'nature of reports creates the public understanding that strangers have become more dangerous than before, contributing to a general sense that things have got some much worse' (p. 126). This leads to a heightened perception of risk which leads fewer people to use the parks. Fewer people means that those who are there feel more insecure because of the relative isolation.

19. *Indian Express*, Mumbai Newsline, 13 March 2006/14 March 2006; *Times of India*, Mumbai, 14 March 2006.

20. See Phadke, 2005.

21. In the months following the rape of a college girl at Marine Drive in April 2005, this article reported that the ban on mini skirts, tight tops, and shorts will help prevent rape (*Indian Express*, 23 June 2005).

22. *Indian Express*, Express Newsline, 25 April 2005.

23. Women not filing cases may also be linked to the need for privacy, the apathy of the police, or other factors. In the 2008 Juhu molestation case, the then police commissioner, D. N. Jadhav, suggested not only that 'anything could happen anywhere' but also that 'wives' were safe at home (*The Hindustan Times*, 2 January 2008).

24. While women appear frequently as the victims of violence in news reports, they are conspicuously absent in other kinds of reports, socio-political or economic. The 2005 *Global Media Monitoring Project* analysed and compared data from 76 countries covering a total of 12,893 news stories in newspapers, and over television and radio. It concluded that women are dramatically under-represented in the news. 'In stories on politics and government, only 14 per cent of news subjects are women; and in economic and business news only 20 per cent … As victims of war, disaster or crime they outnumber men two to one'. *See* Thornham, 2007, p. 86–7.

25. *The Times of India*, 8 November 2006.

26. *See* Dave, 2006; Karlekar, 1998; U. Vindhya, 1998.

27. *See* Phadke, 2007, where I engage extensively with the gendered and classed discourse of safety and the situation of the 'middle-class, Hindu, upper-caste, heterosexual, married or would-be-married woman' at its centre.

28. *See* Chakravarti, 2006; Chowdhry, 1998.

29. Like Hossain, former Israeli Prime Minister Golda Meir suggested that if women were under threat of attack a curfew should be placed on those causing real danger (men) and not, as her colleagues suggested, on the victims (from *Ms* magazine quoted in Weisman (1994).

30. The articulated fear is of the undesirable heterosexual encounter. Same-sex sexual encounters are not even imagined, as society operates within a hetero-normative world-view.

31. Shiv Sena leader Pramod Navalkar was quoted recalling 'the good old days' when girls from Ghatkopar did not venture out to Marine Drive (*Saamna*, 25 April 2005; *Indian Express*, Mumbai Newsline, 26 April 2005).

32. The Mumbai police have periodically targeted courting couples in the city on ground of obscenity and/or immorality. In November 2004 the police arrested 43 couples on the promenade at Bandra Reclamation for 'indecent behaviour'. In April 2007, the police fined at least 80 persons in a drive against 'indecent behaviour' in the same area.

33. *See* Phadke, 2007.

34. Here I am not suggesting that all families knowingly and wilfully perpetrate violence upon women but rather that most, if not all, families will work within the assumed 'rationality' that the public is unsafe for women, especially young women. While violence is not always intended, this does not preclude women experiencing this curtailment, however benevolently intended, as restrictive, even oppressive.

35. *See* Jones, 1988, p. 123.

36. Ibid., 1988, pp. 125–6.

37. My understanding of pleasure was developed together with Shilpa Ranade and Sameera Khan.

38. I am aware of the limitations of using the discourse of rights in this argument given the feminist critique of rights as being individualistic, reifying liberalism, and often reflecting existing hierarchies of all kinds and thus limiting the terms of the debate. This critique is both valid and very valuable and it is important not to forget it. At the same time, the language of rights is also a powerful tool in promoting greater inclusion and participation in quest of a greater egalitarian citizenship, not least because it has a wide acceptability and for now is perhaps the best way of articulating both the entitlement to be free of violence *and* the claim to pleasure.

39. *See* Phadke, Ranade, and Khan, 2009.

40. *See* Menon, 2005 p. 34.

41. This critique is not however intended to undermine the achievements of the women's movement in India, especially in the struggle against violence. For a detailed discussion on the women's movement's response to violence and the campaign against it, *see* Agnes, 1992; Dave, 2006; Gandhi and Shah, 1992; Kumar, 1993; Phadke, 2003; Sunder Rajan, 2003; Suneetha and Nagraj, 2006. *Also see* Kannabiran and Menon, 2007 for an insightful account that focuses on feminist resistance to violence over the past four decades.

42. *See* Woodhull, 1988; Menon, 2004.

43. *See* Menon, 2004, p. 161.

44. *See* Phadke, 2007.

45. Bambaiya is a unique linguistic blend of Hindi, Marathi, and English widely used in Mumbai with a total disregard for rules of grammar.

46. While very upper-class women have even less access to public space than middle-class women, lower-class women in the Mumbai slums of Dharavi, Behrampada and Bainganwadi have limited access to public space but almost no access to private space, so much so that finding a space even to defecate in privacy is next to impossible. My engagement with staking a claim for public space is made in awareness of the fact that in a context where a large part of their lives are led in the public, for slum women it is private space that is at a premium.

47. My utopian vision of an 'equalized risk' is punctured squarely by Geeta Patel's (2006) work on risk, insurance and sexuality which demonstrates eloquently that in the real world there is little hope of risk ever being equal. She points out that in the number-crunching global economy there are risk-producing persons and there are risk-bearing subjects and that 'risky subjects' and 'communities or pools of people' 'at risk' are produced in particular ways by neo-liberal financial regimes. Patel envisages a response beyond the discourses of risk (p. 54).

48. Richard Sennett (1994) recounts the Adonia festivals in ancient Greece where women mourned the death of a youth well-versed in giving women pleasure. They grew lettuces in little pots on their roofs and allowed them to die, the withered plants mirroring Adonis's death. The ritual mourning however assumed the form of a celebration when women stayed up all night, dancing, drinking, and singing. 'Women wandered from neighbourhood to neighbourhood, heard voices calling them above in the dark, ascended the roofs on ladders to meet strangers... This festival occurred at night in the residential districts with no street lighting... The few candles lit... made it difficult to see others sitting nearby, let alone down the street. It threw a cloak of darkness over transformations wrought on the space of the house. Suffused with laughter in the dark, the roof became an anonymous, friendly territory. It was in this space that women... spoke their desires' (p. 78). The festival briefly allows women to claim the streets and the darkness as their own.

49. In her book *Dancing in the Streets: A History of Collective Joy* (2006), Barbara Ehrenreich explores the link between the Greek god of wine, revelry, and orgies, Dionysus, and women, a link that has the potential to be interpreted through a feminist lens. She writes that Dionysus had a special appeal for women of the Greek city-state, who were 'barred from the pleasures and challenges of public life'. In some accounts of Dionysian worship, the women are called by the god to drop their chores and their children and run into the mountains, and there they engage in a frenzied dance of worship called Maenadism. Dionysus appears to have been worshipped for the joy of the rite itself: for pleasure.

50. *See* Ainley, 1998.

51. All courses and workshops were conducted in Mumbai. Longer courses were conducted at the Department of Sociology, St. Xavier's College (August–September 2004), the fourth-year elective course, Sir J.J. College of Architecture (November 2004–March 2005), and the Department of History, St Xavier's College (March–April 2005). Short workshops were conducted at Sir J.J. College of Architecture (July 2004), Majlis Legal Centre (June 2005), J.J. School of Applied Arts, Mumbai (August 2005), Bachelor of Mass Media, Wilson College (August 2005), Bachelor of Mass Media, SIES College (August 2005), LS Raheja Applied Arts (September 2005), and Russel Square International College (March 2006).

52. Discussing the difficulties of including feminist analysis in social work curricula, Anjali Dave points out that 'since students generally come from middle-class backgrounds and are unmarried, they distance themselves from gender issues' (p.177). Dave's comment regarding the marital status of her students is perhaps contextualized within the framework of her essay which examines domestic violence largely within marital relationships, though this is my conjecture. My own observations both as a lecturer in an undergraduate college and a facilitator of workshops suggest that in a context where heterosexual conjugality is offered as the normative aspirational ideal, many young heterosexual middle-class women certainly wish to be married. Their wariness of feminism and feminists is linked to stereotypes that make them fear becoming like the bra-burning feminists, never to find husbands and therefore forever be excluded from the hetero-normative dream.

53. This is of course offset by voices pointing out that the contraceptive revolution was a male revolution denying women the right to say 'No'. There are however other feminists who point out that one must not discount the gains achieved by the sexual revolution even for women. *See* Ehrenrich et al., 1987.

References

Agnes, Flavia (1992): 'Protecting Women against Violence: Review of a Decade of Legislation, 1980–89', *Economic and Political Weekly,* 25 April, WS19–33.

Ainley, Rosa (1998): 'Watching the dectectors: control and the panopticon', in Rosa Ainley (ed.), *New Frontiers of Space, Bodies and Gender.* London: Routledge, pp. 88–100.

Bordo, Susan (1993): *Unbearable Weight: Feminism, Western Culture and the Body.* Berkley: University of California Press.

Burgess, Jacquelin (1998): 'But is it worth taking the risk? How women negotiate access to urban woodland: a case study', in Rosa Ainley (ed.), *New Frontiers of Space, Bodies and Gender.* London: Routledge, pp. 115–28.

Chakravarti, Uma (2006): 'From Fathers to Husbands: Of Love, Death and Marriage in North India', in Lynn Welchman and Sara Hossain (eds.), *'Honour': Crimes, Paradigms, and Violence Against Women.* New Delhi: Zubaan, pp. 308–31.

Chowdhry, Prem (1998): 'Enforcing Cultural Codes: Gender and Violence in Northern India', in Mary John and Janaki Nair (eds.), *A Question of Silence: The Sexual Economies of Modern India.* New Delhi: Kali for Women, pp. 332–67.

Dave, Anjali (2006): 'Feminist Social Work Intervention: Special Cells for Women and Children', in Kalpana Kannabiran (ed.), *The Violence of Normal Times: Essays on Women's Lived Realities.* New Delhi: Women Unlimited, pp. 172–96.

Ehrenreich, Barbara (2006): *Dancing in the Streets: A History of Collective Joy.* New York: Metropolitan Books.

Ehrenreich, Barbara et al. (1987): *Re-making Love: The Feminization of Sex.* New York: Anchor Press.

Gandhi, N., and N. Shah (1992): *The Issues at Stake: Theory and Practice in the Contemporary Women's Movement.* New Delhi: Kali for Women, p. 57.

Geetha, V. (1998): 'On Bodily Love and Hurt,' in John and Nair

(eds.), *A Question of Silence: The Sexual Economies of Modern India.*
New Delhi: Kali for Women, pp. 304–31.

Jones, Kathleen B. (1988): 'XXXX', in Lee Quinby and Irene
Diamond (eds.), *Feminism and Foucault: Paths of Resistance.*
Northeastern University Press, Boston, p. xxx.

Kannabiran, Kalpana (2006): 'Introduction', in Kalpana Kannabiran
(ed.), *The Violence of Normal Times: Essays on Women's Lived
Realities.* New Delhi: Women Unlimited, pp. 1–45.

Kannabiran, Kalpana and Ritu Menon (2007): *From Mathura to
Manorama: Resisting Violence against Women in India.* New Delhi:
ICES and Women Unlimited.

Karlekar, Malavika (1998): 'Domestic Violence', in *Economic and
Political Weekly,* 33(28): 1741–51.

Khan, Sameera (2007): 'Negotiating the Mohalla: 'Exclusion, Identity
and Muslim Women in Mumbai', *Review of Women's Studies,
Economic and Political Weekly,* 42(17): 1527–33.

Kumar, Radha (1993): *The History of Doing: An Illustrated Account of
Movements for Women's Rights and Feminism in India, 1800–1990.*
New Delhi: Kali for Women.

Menon, Nivedita (2004): *Recovering Subversion: Feminist Politics Beyond
the Law.* New Delhi: Permanent Black.

—— (2005): 'How Natural is Normal? Feminism and Compulsory
Heterosexuality', in *Because I Have a Voice: Queer Politics in India.*
New Delhi: Yoda Press.

Meyer, Esther da Costa (1996): 'La Donna è Mobile: Agoraphobia,
Women and Urban Space', in Diana Agrest et al. (eds.), *The Sex
of Architecture.* New York: Harry N. Abrams, pp. 141–56.

Patel, Geeta (2006): 'Risky Subjects: Insurance, Sexuality and
Capital', *Social Text* 89, no. 4.

Phadke, Shilpa (2003): 'Thirty Years On: Women's Studies Reflects
on the Women's Movement', in *Review of Women's Studies,
Economic and Political Weekly,* 23 October 2003.

—— (2005): 'You Can be Lonely in a Crowd: The Production of
Safety in Mumbai', *Indian Journal of Gender Studies,* 12(1): 41–
62.

—— (2007): 'Dangerous Liaisons: Women and Men: Risk and
Reputation in Mumbai', in *Review of Women's Studies, Economic
and Political Weekly,* 42(17): 1510–18.

Phadke, Shilpa, Sameera Khan, and Shilpa Ranade (2006): Women
in Public: Safety in Mumbai. Unpublished Report submitted to

the Indo–Dutch Programme on Alternatives in Development (IDPAD).

—— (2009): 'Why Loiter? Radical Possibilities for Gendered Dissent', in Melissa Butcher and Selvaraj Velayutham (eds.), *Dissent and Cultural Resistance in Asia's Cities*. London: Routledge.

Sakhawat Hossain, Rokeya (2004; originally published 1905): 'Sultana's Dream', in Maitrayee Chaudhuri (ed.), *Feminism in India*. New Delhi: Women Unlimited, pp. 103–14.

Sennet, Richard (1994): *Flesh and Stone: The Body and the City in Western Civilization*. New York, London: WW Norton & Co.

Solnit, Rebecca (2000): *Wanderlust: A History of Walking*. New York & London: Penguin.

Sunder Rajan, Rajeswari (2003): *The Scandal of the State: Women, Law and Citizenship in Postcolonial India*. New Delhi: Permanent Black.

Suneetha, A., and Vasudha Nagaraj (2006): 'A Difficult Match: Women's Actions and Legal Institutions in the Face of Domestic Violence', *Economic and Political Weekly*, 14 October, 4355–62.

Thapan, Meenakshi (1997): 'Femininity and its Discontents: Woman's Body in Intimate Relationships', in Meenakshi Thapan (ed.), *Embodiment: Essays on Gender and Identity*. New Delhi: Oxford University Press.

Thornham, Sue (2007): *Women, Feminism and Media*. Edinburgh: Edinburgh University Press.

Vance, Carole S. (1984): 'Pleasure and Danger: Towards a Politics of Sexuality', in Carole S. Vance (ed.), *Pleasure and Danger: Exploring Female Sexuality*. Boston: Routledge & Kegan Paul, pp. 1–28.

Vindhya, U. (2006): 'Battered Conjugality: The Psychology of Domestic Violence', in Kalpana Kannabiran (ed.), *The Violence of Normal Times: Essays on Women's Lived Realities*. New Delhi: Women Unlimited, pp. 197–223.

Weisman, Leslie Kanes (1994): *Discrimination by Design: A Feminist Critique of the Man-made Environment*. Chicago and Urbana: University of Illinois Press.

Woodhull, Winifred (1988): 'Sexuality, Power, and the Question of Rape', in Lee Quinby and Irene Diamond (eds.), *Feminism and Foucault: Paths of Resistance*. Boston: Northeastern University Press, pp. 167–76.

Woolf, Virginia (1930): *Street Haunting: A London Adventure*. Harmondsworth: Penguin.

4

Untangling the Web

The Internet and Violence against Women

Sharmila Joshi

The Internet has become a canvas for violence against women. In this global matrix[1] created by a billion cables, fibre optic networks, terminals, servers, and other technological artefacts, women are being stalked, harassed, and threatened.

One of the channels for the violence is email. A woman in Delhi, for example, received anonymous threats over email that the sender would disclose confidential information about her if she did not have sex with him. Graphic emails about real or concocted sexual relationships between women and their colleagues have circulated in offices. Inboxes of women have been flooded with emails from disgruntled men with whom they were in a relationship or from men whose sexual advances they had rejected. One woman in Delhi received emails threatening rape; her daily activities were detailed online together with accounts of exactly how she would be raped.[2]

Impersonation – fraudulently representing someone else – is another mode of online violence, and it has typically followed a pattern in India. Spurned suitors or former boyfriends put up the woman's telephone number, email address, and even photograph and postal address on social networking sites, sometimes making it appear that the woman herself has posted these details. The profile usually says she is available for sex for a fee or free of charge. In May 2006, for example, a man in Mumbai posted photographs of a former

girlfriend on a site for people with common sexual interests.
He wrote that she was available for paid sex. He later told the
police that he did this because she rejected his proposal of
marriage. The woman began receiving persistent calls from
prospective 'customers' who refused to believe her when she
told them that the photograph and message were a mistake.

Such instances of fake profiles are frequently being reported
to the police and in the media. In September 2006, the Thane
police arrested a young man for creating on the Orkut social
networking website a profile of a former classmate.[3] He
uploaded, just for 'mischief', he told the police, the young
woman's photograph, her mobile number, and email address,
and wrote that she was seeking sex. He then sent out emails
to various listservs to publicize the profile. The woman was
inundated with lewd messages and callers demanding sex. In
January 2007, a flight attendant in Delhi discovered an online
profile that called her 'sex-starved' alongside her photograph
in work uniform. This profiler too publicized the profile by
connecting her name on the site to other online communities
and to sites that advertise sex work.

The Internet is also being used in collusion with other
technologies such as MMS, or Multimedia Messaging Service,
and spy cameras; the convergent result of these technologies
then appears on the Internet.[4] Women are being harassed
with photographs or video clips taken without their consent
and posted on the web, or private images recorded with
their consent but put online in the public domain without
their consent. One woman, for example, was threatened
that photographs of her having sex with a boyfriend would
be posted on the Internet, though she had not consented to
the public distribution of the images. In 2005, a video clip of
a woman, ostensibly a Tamil actress, in her bathroom, was
posted on the Internet. A couple in Mysore shot a video of
their sexual encounters, which perhaps a friend got hold of
and forwarded to online message boards.[5] Some cases of
morphing where the face of a woman is morphed on to the
nude or semi-nude body of another woman and then uploaded
(without the consent of either) have also been reported.

According to one newspaper report, video clips or photographs taken with spycams and posted online on subscriber-only sites include images of a girl sitting on the steps outside a cinema hall unaware that her underclothes are showing, a woman bending down to serve guests at a wedding, a girl changing clothes in the trial cubicle of a clothes store, a girl using a public toilet, couples in acts of intimacy in restaurant cubicles, couples on beaches in Goa, couples having sex in hotel rooms. In some of these images, the faces are blurred or deleted. Some of the images are ostensibly of the wives or girlfriends of the male users of these sites. In this online sub-culture of voyeur sites in India, users compete for 'rep (reputation) points' (compliments from other users), a higher number of downloads, and the fame of being prolific. The images on most of these sites are free to download for subscribers, but a few sell the images.[6]

The cyber crime division of the Delhi police receives three or more complaints of such instances every month; a lawyer in Delhi says he receives at least one case of Internet-related sexual harassment, in its diverse forms, every week. In 2006, the cyber crime division of the Mumbai police recorded 16 cases of online threats; 62 cases were registered under defamation (which covers harassment, stalking, and morphing), and there were 21 cases of illegal access and misuse.[7]

As the use of the Internet spreads in India, the number of users reporting such experiences[8] is also growing. Print media reports highlighting such cases and the emergence of cyber crime sections at police stations in several cities perhaps also contribute to the number of cases being reported. At the same time, when only a fraction of the violence and crimes against women that routinely occur in the offline world appears in police records, it would not be inaccurate to surmise that only a fraction of similar Internet-related incidents is actually getting reported.

From the Street to the Screen

Violence against women in India and elsewhere assumes multiple and endemic social forms: physical and emotional, material, and metaphorical. While the Internet may be relatively new, the violence that is now being routed through it is part of a continuum that encapsulates already prevalent elements of the many forms of violence against women.

Several people I spoke to made this observation. 'Nothing that happens on the Net does not also happen elsewhere. What women experience at the workplace or on the street or at home, they also experience on the Net,' says Shuddhabrata Sengupta, a media practitioner and writer at Sarai, a programme of the Centre for the Study of Developing Societies in Delhi. 'The harassment of the streets has come on to the Internet. Every instance of Internet-related violence is also there in our everyday lives,' says Shohini Ghosh, a professor at the AJK Mass Communication Research Centre, Jamia Milia Islamia, Delhi. 'Cyber-stalking is as terrifying as real-life stalking except that the access the Internet provides is different in character. So we will have to evolve new ways of dealing with cyber-stalking because the methods of restraining real-life stalking clearly won't work here.' According to Ashish Saboo, president of the Association of Public ICT Tools Access Providers (which comprises businesses, principally cyber cafes, involved in shared access), 'A girl might find her name and number written on a train or toilet wall; a website is simply a virtual wall; a parallel to the real world.'

The technology, as people dealing with offences committed in the cyber world point out, is only mediating the violence. 'Just as the telephone was and is used for kidnapping threats and demands for ransom, an email may now be sent for the same purpose. Telecommunications is being used to facilitate crime,' says S.D. Mishra, Assistant Commissioner of Police, Delhi, and overseer of its cyber crime division at the end of 2006. According to Sanjay Mohite, Deputy Commissioner of Police investigating cyber crime in Mumbai at the end of 2006, 'The "mindset" of people who commit crimes through the Internet is the same as when they commit other crimes, only the technology has changed.'

However, the harassment that women are encountering through the Internet is also more than just a duplication of what they encounter elsewhere. In the course of its involvement with harassment, the technology is also changing the nature and impact of that violence. The Internet reaches a larger number of people at a greater speed than would, say, a series of letters defaming a woman. A morphed photograph or a counterfeit profile that is online reaches a wider audience more instantly than would a girl's telephone number written by a classmate on a college wall or a morphed photo in a magazine.

Lawyers working on cyber crime to whom I spoke emphasized that this reach of the Internet makes Internet-associated violence against women different from other forms of the same kind of violence. Pavan Duggal, a Supreme Court advocate who specializes in cyber crime, says the reach of material posted online multiplies the magnitude of the potential harm to a woman. In addition, the morphed image or fake profile often remains as an archive in the online public domain. N.S. Nappinai, a Bombay High Court advocate who works on ICT-related issues, also points out that though many of these may be old offences in a new packaging, their reach is wider than similar offences in the offline world, and therefore their effect is greater. She gives the example of the notorious 2004 MMS clip of two Delhi Public School students engaging in oral sex would have in the past perhaps circulated within a small community. With the Internet it reaches a far wider public. When a model's top fell off during a fashion show in 2006, the incident might have soon been forgotten, but video clips shot on mobile phones began to circulate on the Internet. 'This – the wider reach of an occurrence which otherwise would have been localized – makes the impact of such incidents much greater, and that's a major difference,' says Nappinai.

The fallacious assumption that one's activities on the Internet are completely anonymous also encourages users to commit offences. The medium makes criminals of people who might not normally contemplate committing a crime. 'The man may not hold a gun to a cashier's head,' says Nappinai, 'but because he thinks the risk of harassing someone on the Internet is a lot less, he will go ahead and do it.'

Technology, Globalization, Gender

One of the many strands or 'flows' of globalization is the interconnectedness of parts of the global economy that has come about through technological changes; and one of the flanks of liberalization is the opening up of economies to greater private-sector participation. From 1995 to 1998, only the state-owned VSNL (Videsh Sanchar Nigam Limited) provided Internet access in India. After a change in telecommunication policy, private Internet Service Providers (ISPs)[9] entered the market. About 100 out of 350-plus licensed ISPs are now active,[10] although MTNL and BSNL[11] account for 60per cent of subscriber share.

Computations of the number of Internet users in India vary, with debates about how to define a user (daily or weekly? individual or organization?). At the end of June 2006, there were 8.2 million subscribers. The ISP industry calculates that one subscriber translates into 4 to 6 individual users.[12] This works out to (at least) 32 million Internet users in India, if industry estimates are deemed reliable. The highest numbers are in Mumbai and Delhi, and the growth of subscribers has been fastest in smaller cities and towns. The number of Internet users in India was estimated to have crossed 40 million in March 2007.[13]

Although comprehensive demographically-disaggregated data is not available, the majority of users (an estimated 80 per cent) are believed to be men in the 15-35 year age group. Many users access the Internet at their workplace and a few at home, but the common access for individual users – men, and to a much lesser degree women – appears to be cyber cafes. At the end of 2006, there were an estimated 100,000 to 150,000 cyber cafes in India.[14]

The persons that these numbers represent, these producers and consumers of global content, are situated, like everyone else, in a social context that shapes their relationship with the technologies of the Internet. In other words, our relationship with globalization and technology is not separate from our social, economic, and cultural context,[15] which is invariably unequal and discriminatory.

As contributors to science and technology studies have demonstrated, technology is socially constructed and, like other forms of culture, it is in dialogue with social inequalities. That is, technology and gender discrimination are inter-constitutive, each shaping the other. Gender also intersects with other differences, such as class, to modulate the processes of the production and consumption of Internet material.

The dialogic relationship between technology and gender inequalities has been demonstrated in many ways. At the material level of the production of new information and communication technologies (ICTs), women may constitute a significant 21 per cent of the total workforce of 813,000 in India (principally in software and BPO companies),[16] but they are mostly absent from the policy-making and high-end decision-making structures in the information technology (IT) industry.[17] Much of the low-end outsourced and sub-contracted labour of assembling hardware components for the IT industry involves women engaged in piece-rate work. Studies have demonstrated the benefits (greater mobility, an increased household income, and some level of individual economic autonomy) as well as the enduring gender status quo for women (continuing unpaid housework and therefore a greater burden of work, lower salaries than those of men in comparable positions) as producers of information technology.

As users or consumers, the dialogic relationship between technology and gender inequalities is manifest, amongst others, in the fact that an estimated 80 per cent of Internet users in India are male. The violence and harassment of women that is being routed through the Internet is another manifestation of this unequal social equation. Technocratic utopianism, which focuses only on the liberating potential of the Internet, thus obscures the power relations that permeate cyberspace[18] and points to the fallacy of looking upon technology as neutral.

The Spaces of the Internet

If techno-utopia is at one end of the spectrum, its binary is techno-phobia. New media technologies are frequently regarded with suspicion in relation to their destabilizing effect on the social scaffolding. Ghosh describes this as part of a 'cycle of paranoia that has haunted technology down the ages'. Lawyer and media researcher Namita Malhotra points out that cinema was initially regarded as 'evil' and likened to sorcery, and new technologies such as photography were regarded with suspicion. To unilaterally demonize technology in this way obscures its positive potential. Like other technologies, the Internet also encapsulates discriminatory as well as democratizing dimensions for women and for men.

However, women are often regarded only as passive victims of technology, unable to exercise any active control of technologies. This tendency has been extensively criticized. Sociologist Judy Wajcman, who works on technology and social change, writes '[the] emphasis is perhaps too heavily on how technological developments will reproduce gender hierarchies, rather than on the possibility that gender relations may be transformed by new technologies'.[19]

The Internet is used by women – at least 6 million in India[20] – as it is used by other genders, in their intersecting identities and multiple roles: as professionals, as workers, as activists, as social beings, as pleasure-seekers. Women's online activities cover a wide range – networking, forming online communities of solidarity, creating listservs of shared interests, researching and accessing information, online feminist publishing, mobilizing protests and petitions, soliciting business, making online purchases, emailing and communication, meeting new partners, forming relationships, gaming, surfing, blogging, chatting, etc.

Cyberspace is a new social environment that lets women form 'communities of propinquities'[21] without physical proximity; fragmented in physical space, women can come together in cyberspace as groups with shared concerns and interests. In cyberspace women can create separate discursive spaces.[22] Cyberspace allows for electronic forms of resistance by being a space for politically-marginalized groups to publicize causes that are often overlooked by other media, and for 'reduced risk' communication environments, which enable silenced groups to find a voice and use it effectively.[23] While no online activity – especially in a world bifurcated by the digital divide of highly unequal access to such technologies – can by itself bring about social change, such interactions are one, even if an infinitesimal, component in the incremental process of change.

The simulated nature of cyberspace and the relative anonymity it offers also allows women in chatrooms or on shared-interest sites to break with essentialist notions of gender and, if they wish, 'recreate' their gender identity.[24] Some researchers regard this as an important potential of the Internet in subverting gender identities and relations. Cyberspace offers users the choice to select a gender identity irrespective of their material bodies, to 'step outside' constricting gender roles and experiment with new personas, 'to engage in intimacies they may desire but also fear in the "real" world.'[25]

At the same time, the enthusiasm about these possibilities elides existing gender differences and how they contribute to the formation of online identity. Postcolonial theorists have questioned the idea of being able to separate identity from history and bodily experiences.[26] In the online world, as in the real world, issues of personal identity affect how we relate to others, and the same discourses that regulate 'real' bodies in 'real' space continue to circulate in 'virtual' spaces.[27]

Still, because of its peculiar nowhere and everywhere nature, virtual space allows for greater experimentation and communication than many other spaces. Regarding the Internet as only an intimidating, violent space for women could serve to circumscribe cyberspace and its many possibilities for female users. As Mary Flanagan, an artist who works with emerging technology writes, '...the rhetoric surrounding Internet violence is potentially damaging to women's efforts in cyberspace, as the rhetoric itself can act as a tool of terrorization...'[28]

'Images of vulnerable women...,' points out political scientist Jodi Dean, 'have regulatory effects that operate through fear... evocations of the dangers and infections of the Internet may set up barriers to [women's] use and exploration of cyberspace... some discussions of new technologies have less to do with technology than they do with a larger politics of repression and authority that works through the evocation of fear...'[29]

Cyberspace, or e-space, is a discrete mix of public and private spaces. The online world is often accessed in the privacy of the home, or in the relative privacy of an office/cyber café cubicle where the individual user interacts with the computer screen to connect to a public domain. This domain, though not entirely public, has a mix of private 'spaces', such as email communications between two people, and public 'spaces' such as general access websites or social networking sites.

The public/private formulation of social space has long been debated in feminist social sciences. Space has been theorized in various ways: conventionally, the private realm or domestic sphere is construed as women's space; the space of reproduction. The public realm is deemed masculine, the space of production, of citizenship and the state; the location of the public sphere, the realm of visibility and public recognition. This theorization has been substantively questioned. In this 'geography of prescribed and proscribed spaces,' writes social theorist Diana Coole, transgressions of enforced boundaries – which significantly affect women – involve contestations of power, because the 'boundaries are not about geography but about power.'[30]

Space is an important marker of segregation and reinforcement of social power structures, writes sociologist Shilpa Phadke. 'Spaces, both private and public, are hierarchically ordered through various inclusions and exclusions along axes of gender, class, caste, ethnicity, sexuality and disability... Public spaces are seen as spaces of potential sexual danger for women while the private spaces of the home are presented as havens of safety.'[31]

Women's physical independence and mobility is therefore often accompanied by accusations of sexual promiscuity and warnings about the dangers of violence. As Dean suggests, 'The pervasive attention to Net dangers and hostilities may well be a kind of backlash against the successful use of computer-mediated communication by those previously unable to connect with one another.'[32]

The unique mix of spaces created by the online world may require greater study and theorizing, but if women are perceived to be venturing too deeply into the 'public' realm of the Internet, and then indulging in 'inappropriate' behaviours in cyber spaces, the alarm may well serve to regulate their online movements, to prevent their presence and further 'incursion' into a global, public, masculinist cyberspace.

Investigating Cyber Crime

At the same time, the evolving forms of cyber-mediated violence are all too real. Women are having to deal with threatening mails, fake profiles, morphed images, and other forms of harassment. How, then, is this violence that is being routed through the Internet, being addressed?

Women in India with such experiences of violence and harassment have sometimes approached lawyers. Compromises (as a result of reprimands, threats of legal action, undertakings, monetary compensation) have been reached between the woman and the offender. If she approaches the police, it may take the police a few days to work out which section of which law covers the offence, or whether or not a crime has been committed at all. The complaint may then be registered or sometimes during the interim it is withdrawn or 'settled'.

Investigations thereafter typically involve locating the suspect's Internet service provider (ISP) and Internet protocol (IP) address. If the suspect is using a static/fixed IP address,[33] the service provider can point to the user's location. If it is a dynamic/variable address, the ISP provides details of which subscriber was using it at that particular time. The ease and speed of tracing the person varies. If he is hopping from one cyber café to another, he may be more difficult to trace. If different ISPs are involved at the same time in providing access (at different nodes in an online chain), tracing the subscriber may be cumbersome. If the ISP is not based in India, issues of jurisdiction and extradition can make it exceedingly difficult to trace the suspect and the case is sometimes closed.

Locating the ISP and tracing the IP address is one of the first steps in investigating e-crimes. This was done, for example, when in July 2006 a an email was sent to the office of the President of India, threatening to murder him. Also during that very month a young man in Bhopal was arrested after a mail to a Hindi newspaper was traced to him. He claimed responsibility, as part of an organization, for the train blasts in Mumbai. (He reportedly did this just to 'create a sensation'.)

Sometimes, according to ACP Mishra of the Delhi police, cyber crime cops hack into the email account of the suspect (this is called 'ethical hacking' in law enforcement parlance) or they may place the suspect's email id 'under observation'. In a few instances the Delhi and Mumbai police have simply not been able to trace the offender,[34] but in most cases if the person is in India, he or she is eventually traced. According to DCP Mohite of the Mumbai police, in cases of Internet-related sexual harassment, the woman almost invariably knows or has known the offender, which makes it easier to trace him.

'Such crimes are usually the work of someone known to you and involve a backlash of some kind,' says Ashish Saboo. 'Unless it is a public figure, almost all such cases that I have observed did not involve an anonymous person or secret "admirer". It may take time to trace the person, but it is not impossible. In fact, I would say that using the Internet for such offences leaves a greater trail than other methods.'

Many of these offences, N.K. Nappinai points out, are committed from cyber cafés. While it is difficult for cyber café owners to regulate users, she says, 'If the trail stops, the case does not come to a standstill. The police can learn from the complainant who is likely to harass her, and watch the areas he frequents. Cyber criminals presume they are invisible, especially if they go to a café. But if we know who to look for, we can catch them.'

Prosecution and conviction are however quite another matter. Even if the suspect is traced, the case (when it does reach the courts) may be difficult to prove. Defence lawyers could argue about minute differences in time to claim that the subscriber was not actually using the IP address at that time. 'It is difficult to prove the case beyond reasonable doubt because it may be difficult to link the person to the activity or prove the authenticity of the electronic record,' says Duggal. 'In the virtual world, it is easier to create a defence,' says Nappinai, 'The benefit of doubt can be invoked by saying the email was not from me, because there are sites from which you can hack into people's email ids. The 'I didn't do it' defence is potent in cyber crimes.'

In addition, the efforts of the police and the government are focused on offences of e-commerce, and a relatively less robust effort is invested in cases of Internet-related sexual harassment and gender violence.[35] The prevalence of gender bias and the lack of gender sensitivity and awareness during police investigations of cases of offline violence against women are also likely to prevail and shape the investigation of cases of cyber crimes.

In 2004 the Department of Information and Technology of the government of India created CERT (Computer Emergency Response Team, India), primarily to respond to virus attacks and online security breaches. Cyber crime 'labs' in Mumbai and other cities such as Pune and Bangalore focus on problems relating to data theft and cyber forensics. The laboratories train the police to investigate different types of cyber crimes. DCP Mohite however says, 'We don't have enough computer experts in the police force. So our first task is computer literacy. The pace at which technology changes and the pace at which we in the police can move will never match, so we will succeed in stopping cyber crime only to the extent of our knowledge.'

The Law and the Internet in India

Internet-related offences in India fall under the purview of the Information Technology (IT) Act, which came into force on 17 October 2000.[36] This legislation is primarily concerned with matters relating to e-commerce, such as digital signatures, digital data, licensing, regulatory authorities, jurisdiction, credit card frauds, and 'phishing'.[37]

Many e-offences under the IT law are read in conjunction with the relevant portions of the Indian Penal Code (IPC) or other laws. For example, a 2003 software piracy case was registered under the Copyright Act of 1957. The first conviction for a cyber crime in 2002 by a metropolitan magistrate in New Delhi in a case of cheating was registered under Section 419 (cheating by impersonation) and Section 420 (cheating and dishonesty relating to property) of the IPC. The case involved the online purchase of a television set and a cordless telephone using someone else's credit card number.

The IT Act does not specifically cover most aspects of violence against women, such as cyber stalking or impersonation. Section 503 of the IPC ('criminal intimidation') is sometimes invoked in cases of threatening messages sent by email.[38] The first case of this kind was recorded by the Delhi police before the IT Act was passed, under Section 509 of the IPC ('word, gesture or act intended to insult the modesty of a woman'), when a disgruntled colleague of a woman's husband began sexual chats over the Internet using the woman's identity, giving her home telephone number to other chatroom participants and inviting them to call her.

The IT law also does not specifically cover cyber harassment. In one of the first registered cases of this kind, a person complained that people harassed him by telephoning him and asking for 'college girls' for the night. The callers had received messages about his 'business' on their cellphones through a fictitious website. The police eventually arrested a neighbour who was sending the messages because of a quarrel over the parking of a vehicle. The case was registered under Section 292 (which deals with the offence of 'obscenity' and the dissemination/transmission of obscene matter), Section 509 and Sections 499-500 (relating to defamation) of the IPC.

Only Section 67 in the IT Act directly relates to crimes that affect women. The section ('publishing of information which is obscene in electronic form') speaks of transmission of 'material which is lascivious or appeals to the prurient interest if its effect is such as to lead to deprave and corrupt persons...' It provides for a maximum of five years imprisonment for a first offence and a fine of Rs 1 lakh, and imprisonment up to ten years and fine of Rs 2 lakh for a subsequent offence.

This section is a virtual replication of Section 292 of the IPC of 1860.[39] Neither the IPC nor the IT Act substantively clarify what is meant by 'prurient' or 'lascivious'.[40] This section of the IPC has been widely debated for its subjectivity in interpreting what is 'obscene' and its tendency towards censorship, and I will return to this shortly.

The only conviction under Section 67 of the IT Act (until March 2007) came at the end of 2005. A metropolitan court convicted a young man for online 'obscenity', for morphing photographs of a former girlfriend; he was sentenced to three years imprisonment and a fine. The case is in appeal. The other cases cited at the beginning of this chapter are either under investigation or pending in lower courts.

Offences that are not specifically covered by the IT Act are currently dealt with under the IPC, but the IPC itself does not cover crimes like stalking (which gets grouped with harassment). Although the IPC does not restrict the medium to which it can be applied (in this case, the Internet), the law needs to keep pace with the specificities of the new technology-mediated sexual harassment and violence. It also needs to address issues of cross-border jurisdiction if the offender is operating from outside India.[41]

In December 2006, the government introduced a bill in the Lok Sabha to amend the IT Act. Many of the amendments relate to issues like digital data and e-commerce, but other amendments are also related to video voyeurism, 'sexually explicit' material, cyber stalking, offensive messages, and identity theft.

For some, the proposed amendments don't contain strong deterrents, and a more stringent law that carries a heavy liability is required to reduce Internet-related crimes against women. Others are of the view that too many stringent laws don't help. Sengupta says:

The IT Act is invasive and censorial. In cases of sexual harassment, there is the potential to abuse women's consensual sexual presence on the web. If, for example, a woman participates in an erotic chatroom encounter, this could become an opportunity for someone to abuse her and harass her. And as a participant in the chat, the woman may not complain because what she was doing is also illegal under the law. Because if a chatroom is construed to be pornographic, you too are legally vulnerable if you are a participant.

The more the censorship, Sengupta adds, the more difficult it becomes for people to protect themselves:

It creates a gamut of behaviour that is rendered shame worthy, such as a rape victim's sexual history. The censorial intent of the law can make it very difficult for a woman to do anything. She may have consented to a sexual encounter but not to it being photographed or may have consented to being photographed but not to it being publicly distributed. However, this dividing line is blurred because of the clear censorial burden of the law.'

Even if the IT law were amended with an ideal mix of deterrence and less censorial strictures, legal measures by themselves will not curb violence against women. As the experience with other laws in India – relating to, for example, rape or domestic violence – has shown, gender-just laws that are synchronized with changing social conditions are certainly required, but they must be actually implemented and seen to be implemented. This is only one requisite element in the complex churning of progressive social change.

Censorship and the Internet

Censorship and enhanced regulation of the Internet, within or without the IT Act, is a contentious issue, which periodically evokes debates about Article 19 and freedom of expression.[42]

The Indian government, lawyer-media researcher Namita Malhotra points out, has on occasion attempted to block or censor websites or content on some sites. In 2003, entire Yahoo groups were reportedly inadvertently blocked for a week when the government blocked one group that discussed insurgency-related issues in the Northeast. In 2004, there was an attempt to block a Hindu right-wing site because it could have hurt or incited 'religious sentiments'. In July 2006, after the train blasts in Mumbai, in an attempt to block some blogs that were 'inflammatory' in the interests of 'national security' the government ended up temporarily blocking other popular sites. In January 2007, the government objected to a video on YouTube featuring an NRI actor dressed up as Mahatma Gandhi in a provocative portrayal. YouTube responded by withdrawing the video from its site.

Many people (except the police) I spoke to opposed censorship or monitoring of the Internet and Internet-related activities. Cyber café owners, for example, are against moves such as stricter rules for registration, fines, and greater proposed surveillance of cyber cafés, which they believe will become a pretext for harassing them. Already, if someone uses a cyber café to send threatening mail, the café may be raided by the police. A move to ask all visitors to cyber cafés for proof of identity has been opposed on the ground that it would turn away customers.[43]

'So what if a culprit used a cyber cafe?' asks Deepak Maheshwari, an IT professional and former secretary of the Internet Service Providers Association of India.

If he sends a letter from a post office, will you monitor those? Or monitor all Public Call Offices (PCO) if he makes a threatening call from a phone booth? Will you compel PCO owners to ask for identity proof from every customer? There is a move towards over-regulation of cyber cafés. This in fact is a deterrent and will create a black market. Besides, if a woman gives her photo id at a café, that itself can be misused by someone.

The government asserts that such regulations are necessary to monitor terrorism-related activities and sedition. This,

Malhotra argues, would be in addition to the state's subtext of regulating social morality, of shielding young persons from romantic or sexual content over the Internet. In a curious mix of the two purposes, the Pune police has said that foreign intelligence agencies could be using social networking sites in India to 'lure young Indians looking for a companion into parting with sensitive information'.[44]

Long-term and wide-ranging censorship or regulation of the internet is in fact difficult, as the experience of state-mandated blocks on content in China has shown. The Internet involves multiple jurisdictions, servers, portals, ISPs, and ever-changing technologies. Computer users and software professionals can usually find a way around filters and blocks. For example, computer-hacking experts or 'hactivists' in Canada have recently created a programme that will allow Internet users to circumvent government censorship of the web.[45] 'Any kind of censorship is so easy to circumvent,' says Saboo. 'We are fooling ourselves if we think greater censorship is the answer to Internet-mediated crimes.'

The wide prevalence of pornography on the Internet makes the issue of censorship or greater regulation of the medium even more contentious. Pornography which features adults[46] is an area of divergence for feminists. The dilemma centres around the establishment of a balance between defence of the freedom of expression as well as the need to have safeguards against the exploitation and violence of the pornography industry. While the first position does not defend sexism or degradation, the second argues that it is inherent in pornography.

According to Brinda Bose, a Delhi University professor who researches gender and culture, pornography must be placed within the context of patriarchal society, which sees it as 'potentially exploitative of women, exposing and using their bodies for the sexual titillation of the public, and therefore to be condemned'. She writes:

However, a woman's right not to be exploited, degraded and demeaned by the sexual use of her body is counteracted by her right to consensually expose her body in whatever way she deems fit...

Feminism, indeed, has been hard put to locate the specific dilemma that pornography represents, and because any intervention for the purpose of protecting the possibly-exploited bodies of women must necessarily contend with the problems of censorship, in that it restricts freedom of speech and expression, invests an inordinate amount of power in the censor (which is often the State with a specific political agenda of its own) and can never come to a true consensus about what is actually obscene since it is such a culturally variable term...[47]

Therefore, on the one hand, a strand of feminism argues that the notion of obscenity, which is subjective and variable, is singularly, randomly and deliberately used by state agencies and zealous representatives of the right wing to control sexuality and expressions of sexuality which they claim corrupt the moral and social fabric. They invariably exercise this control through targeting the female body. Sexual discrimination and sexism occur along a continuum, and obscenity can manifest in many forms, such as depictions in the media of servile women. Therefore, this strand of the feminist argument states, targeting pornography – which may be sexually explicit but not sexist – only serves to control women and their bodies. This argument condemns the violence and sexism that may underline pornography, but asserts that through consensual participation in pornography, some women may be 'reclaiming' their bodies by selectively exposing them, and they cannot only be construed as passive, subordinated victims of pornographers.

On the other hand, feminists have argued that the notion of consent and the focus on censorial control of the women who feature in pornography takes the debate away from the framework within which pornography operates: pornography is primarily a misogynistic product of patriarchy, created to serve the sexual interests principally of male consumers. Much of the pornography that is available (on film, DVD, and over the Internet) is explicitly violent against women. This violence involves real women's bodies performing acts involving cruelty for the sexual gratification of men. This argument also emphasizes that pornography is a multibillion dollar industry,[48] and its expansion and profit depend on making available to men images of women that are increasingly abusive.

The liberal argument that discusses pornography in relation to abstract rights and principles is disconnected from pornography's grim reality in actual communities. Women's bodies are beaten, burnt, and mutilated, and these bodies can hardly be 'reclaimed', the strands of this argument assert, when pornography occurs along the continuum of discrimination and violence. The critical factor of a woman's consent that is invoked in these debates is deeply problematic. 'Consent' may have come about under extreme circumstances or after coercion. In the gigantic global pornography industry,[49] to assume that all women engaging in pornography are consenting adults would amount to ignoring the brutal truths of the lucrative transnational trade.[50] Whatever the debatable exceptions, pornography is a manifestation of women's oppression, and this exploitation has to be rigorously addressed.

The Contentious Domain of Pornography

A study by Gossett and Byrne (2002) focuses on the content of the images of victims and perpetrators in violent pornography. In 1999-2000, the researchers examined 31 free-to-access Internet sites that had a combination of images and text which recreated physical and verbal abuse and rape. They included only sites that had the words 'rape' or 'forced sex' in their title, text, or Internet address (to separate them from images of sadomasochism that may resemble rape).[51] They write that there was no way of determining whether the sites involved actual incidents or staged depictions of rape. Four sites explicitly stated that the images were real (one of them said, 'This is no joke, they actually raped a girl and made this video'); others left it to the viewer to determine.

The interactive sites invited viewers to choose between various violent depictions of rape, take online part in the torture of the women, and use a variety of weapons and ways of inflicting pain. In the study sample, 34 of the 56 clear pictures of victims depicted Asian women, and many used words such as 'Asian', 'Japanese', and 'Chinese' as their site's selling point.[52] The age and innocence of the victim was also a selling point, with 16 sites advertising the women as young, and 14 sites describing them with derogatory, misogynist slurs.[53]

The researchers write:

The idea that pornography is the sexual representation of unequal power relations is well supported by our findings... The new technology of the Internet dramatically increases the accessibility of pornography – particularly of violent images – and thus debates about the regulation and social consequences of pornography must increase as well. In particular, the implications of the global nature of the Internet and its effect on the content of pornography must be further explored.[54]

A comparable study on violent pornography sites in India or depicting Indians is not readily available.

Concerns about pornographic content on the Internet are valid and difficult to dispute, according to feminist activist Jac S.M. Kee, but an unyielding advocacy of censorship in response to pornography could compromise important cyber spaces. Kee writes:

Privacy can be eroded through such regulation, as well as the vital functions played by the Internet as a digital space for civil society movements to discuss, communicate and mobilize for transformative action. States have employed the discourse of pornography and harm towards women... to justify policing and censorship of digital spaces without actually engaging with the issue on a deeper level.[55]

'Any discussion today about pornography without an understanding of the Internet as a unique and expanding medium for dissemination – with its ease of distribution, access, relatively low cost of production of images, and uniquely interactive options – would be incomplete,' states Kee. Regulating adult pornography on the borderless Internet would be a complex (besides being a contentious) task, which would involve multiple jurisdictions and legal regimes around the world.

Much of the debate on pornography thus often turns away from the nature or consequences of pornography itself and returns to the nature of censorship. As Sengupta says: 'There is a lot of stuff out there [such as explicitly violent pornography] that can be called hate speech or incitement to violence. Censorship does not solve the problem; it only accentuates it. This needs to be countered by other means.'

If the Internet were to be more closely regulated, what are the implications of giving the government greater powers to censor this vast and open medium?[56] The Indian government, in its various colours, is often repressive about what it considers to be unacceptable expressions of sexuality. For example, in 2004, the Maharashtra government banned women dancing in bars in Mumbai because of the 'threat' their work posed to public 'morality'. In 2006 the state stalked four men in Lucknow who used the Internet to meet, and arrested them under Section 377 of the IPC (relating to 'unnatural offences', which criminalizes 'intercourse that is against the order of nature'). In 2006, in the presence of the media, the Meerut police physically and verbally abused intimate couples using a public park. Citing examples of this kind, Malhotra writes, 'It is in this frightening and draconian context, where the state has no compunctions about policing sex and sexuality, that our understanding of censorship has to be located...'

In a neo-liberal world order, arguments for a cutback of the state's role are all too numerous. It is important to carefully separate these arguments for a withdrawal of the state in a free-market utopia, from substantive debates about the role of the democratically elected state on issues such as censorship of the media. It is equally important to steer away from any singular approach of censorship and banning, while simultaneously not silencing the debate about pornography. Regardless of 'consent', if a woman is trapped in a vortex of violence and trafficking, what are her legal remedies and safeguards? How is the line to be drawn between the state's role of policing exploitation but not assuming for itself the right to moral policing?

Considering the Legal Contours

Online and other pornography and its attendant disputatious
debates lie in an area different from that of the Internet-
mediated sexual harassment against women, through
morphing, impersonation and threats that were noted at the
beginning of this chapter. While the turbulent issues relating
to pornography may appear to have no ready answers, the
Internet-mediated violence that women are experiencing must
be addressed. For this, legal remedies are one starting point.

Several amendments to the IT Act, including those that
relate to 'sexually explicit' material, cyber stalking, and
offensive messages, have been proposed.[57] What may be
required, however, is not just partial amendments, but
also a comprehensive new law that 'empowers women in
cyberspace', according to Duggal. A law that would protect
the right to privacy is one possible strategy, which states
that absolutely no information (textual, visual, aural) about
a person can be made public without their explicit consent.
Both women and men are vulnerable to privacy intrusions in
cyberspace. Privacy can be characterized as 'inaccessibility to
others', and the appropriation of a person's name, likeness, or
identity can be defined as an invasion of privacy, along with
unauthorized use of images, of them, their voices, and other
forms of personal identity.[58]

Currently, offences in India that relate to privacy are grouped
under defamation and sexual harassment laws. The IT Act
refers to privacy only in Section 72 ('breach of confidentiality
and privacy').[59] The Supreme Court has however upheld the
right to privacy as an integral part of the fundamental right
to life under Article 21 of the Constitution. 'We don't have a
robust enough provision for the right to privacy in our legal
structure,' says Sengupta,

probably because various legislations in India are designed to be
invasive (such as the anti-terrorist laws). The only real legal remedy is
a right to privacy measure, not draconian laws that get read in terms
of insult to a woman's 'dignity'. The degree of consent is important
in such a law. It means we don't assume complete victimization. A

woman may have consented to being photographed but not to its circulation on the net. These distinctions are important and need to be legally enforced.

Even when breaching privacy 'in public interest' – such as during 'sting' operations by the media – the ethics cannot be escaped, says Ghosh even as she warns against 'quick-fix' remedies like censorship:

Even though classic distinctions between public and private need to be reworked, an individual's consent is critical. If we violate an individual's consent, then what are the larger implications of such an act? What kind of precedent can be set? Does this threaten my right to privacy? If my right to privacy is violated, then I should be able to have access to speedy trials and suitable compensations. The right to free speech and the right to privacy are very different issues.

While too little privacy and a disregard for consent are problematic, too much privacy when operating in cyberspace can also be a problem. As Anita Allen, a supporter of greater privacy rights, cautions, cyber-specific privacy (including anonymity, confidentiality, secrecy, and encryption) 'can obscure the sources of... misconduct, criminality, incivility, surveillance and threat...' and makes it difficult to trace persons who use the Internet to commit crimes against women. Besides, Allen argues, 'Women have often had too much of the wrong kinds of privacy in the sense of imposed modesty, chastity and domestic isolation and not enough privacy in the sense of adequate opportunities for individual mode of privacy and private choice.'[60] Any discussion of a legally-enforced right to privacy in India would need to consider all these nuances before it is formalized.[61]

Any potential privacy law would also need to account for the fact that the nature of the Internet itself militates against privacy. In addition, as attempts to censor the Internet in some countries have shown, laws pertaining to new media technologies are likely to be one step behind crimes, especially because it is difficult to predict the ways in which these technologies will move and who will find what ways to use them. Would then a privacy law, or indeed, any law be adequate? Particularly so in a context where law enforcement tends to be cumbersome?

It would be useful to study the laws that other countries have passed to address cyber crimes, and especially to address crimes against women that are mediated through the Internet. How have they approached the dilemma of controlling the Internet without completely censoring it? Are there better, stronger laws that are inclusive and progressive, and not reactionary? Does the problem in India (in dealing with issues such as online pornography) lie primarily with definitions of obscenity, or does it lie in an unwillingness to institute a comprehensive legal and institutional structure of safeguards against exploitation? Should laws relating to cyber crime be transnational rather than nation-specific? These and other questions need to be explored to formulate approaches to and remedies for cyber crime against women.

Negotiating the Tangled Web

For some time now, there has been a debate about whether Internet servers and portals should be held liable for content. For example, in February 2007 Google India, which owns Orkut (where fake profiles of women have been posted), said it had no control over the content of the site. Responding to a petition in the Bombay High Court about anti-India propaganda on Orkut, Google said, '...it [Google] cannot be considered to be even remotely associated or connected with the website and the contents posted on it.'[62] Lawyers such as Nappinai are of the opinion that if anyone hosts a site, they should be responsible for what it carries. She however adds that the portal or provider is not liable if they show that they have exercised 'reasonable' care and caution.

The debate remains unresolved, though some social networking sites and servers are now employing moderators who will screen 'socially and sexually offensive content' and ensure that 'flirting does not end up in abuse'. Orkut has introduced both human and automated systems to detect 'abuse'. This, however, comes with its own set of questions about policing. For example, an older woman who was looking for younger partners (but presumably not minors) for sex was blacklisted by a moderator in Mumbai because the 'medium is meant for healthy interaction'. Orkut has reportedly begun to issue warnings, suspensions, and termination notices to recalcitrant accounts.[63]

Self-regulation is perhaps one of the most effective measures when using the Internet. Women can themselves try to minimize harassment with more judicious travels through cyberspace. 'If you don't want State regulation,' Nappinai says, 'the alternative is self-regulation.' While this may sound like circumscribing women's online movements, as Phadke notes in the context of city spaces, 'Safety for women does not flow directly from institutional or infrastructural factors, but has to be strategically produced.'[64]

Online encounters and relationships can entail intense self-disclosure because of the assumed 'invisibility' of the virtual interaction. Young women especially tend to be casual about disclosing information about themselves in chatrooms, when they should be taking measures to protect their identity. The details may thereafter be used in ways that they cannot control. 'When you do this, you are signing away your privacy,' says Nappinai. 'And it may come back to you as a virtual stalker. It is a question of you deciding where you want to go and how you protect yourself – just as you would make these decisions when going out late at night.' Ghosh also emphasizes that we must realize the potential and limitations of the Internet and employ it intelligently: 'Just I take measures to ensure that my privacy in my home is not encroached upon, we have to evolve desktop remedies for our own privacy. We – of all sexual identities – have to ask, what really protects me?'

In mid-2007, in two separate cases, a young woman and a teenage boy were murdered in Mumbai. Both were (separately) active on social networking sites, and had left numerous 'scraps' online that detailed their lives. Their online activities were in part related to the circumstances leading to their murders, and, in fact, their online trail partly helped the police to trace the offenders. The cases were a grim reminder of the virtue of exercising caution over the Internet, and being circumspect about revealing details about yourself.

If a woman is being harassed on a social networking site or in a chat session, she also has the option to leave the space. 'You can easily spurn advances on these sites; nobody is going to literally jump on you,' says Ashish Saboo:

You can pick and chose who you chat with, and even then you can choose to remain anonymous. How you manage your communication certainly helps. In fact, on the web most young women manage this very well. However, on the web your face and expressions are usually 'disconnected'. So it is very important not to let your emotions sway you into revealing more about yourself than is necessary, in a way that may later harm you.

Several initiatives are underway that explore and promote more judicious use of the Internet. University and school curricula in some countries have introduced courses that focus on Internet-related issues, including violence against women. The cyber crime division of the Mumbai police has plans to work with the state education department to introduce web-safety programmes in schools; this would include sessions during which police officers talk to students about the perils of disclosure.

Many online and offline groups in different countries – though not, so far, specifically based in India – work on issues relating to women, the Internet/ICTs, and violence. Some groups[65] are working on creating greater awareness of Internet use while asserting the right of women to move freely within online spaces without harassment or threats, campaigning to raise awareness about how ICTs are connected to violence against women, providing strategies to minimize such violence, and generating a discussion about these issues.

The nature of the Internet is also being explored in the artistic realm. For example, novels and plays have been written about call centres in India, and a documentary film has explored the different shades of feminism in India through conversations in a chat-room.[66] In other words, some of the issues relating to the cyber world are being dealt with through artistic expression, if not by the law, and it would be useful to understand what these explorations can tell us about the Internet experience.

The kinds of harassment and experiences described at the beginning of this chapter – when, for example, former boyfriends upload fake profiles of women, or spycams record their movements, or they are stalked by threatening emails – cannot however be addressed only with desktop strategies, and also require comprehensive legal safeguards. This is in addition to the continuing process of addressing, with multi-layered approaches, gender discrimination, sexism, violence, and unequal social relations. Together, these may well contribute to a fuller realization of the potential of cyberspace for women.

Notes

1. Matrix is derived from the Latin for 'womb'. William Gibson's early cyberpunk novel *Neuromancer* (1984) describes virtual space as 'the matrix'; an 'uncontainable, feminized digital frontier and global information network'. *See* Flanagan, 2000.
2. All the examples and experiences in this section were cited in personal interviews or have appeared in newspaper reports.
3. Orkut, Myspace, Facebook, and other popular social networking sites are online spaces for seeking and forming relationships – romantic or otherwise – which may or may not continue into the offline lives of the participants. The user base of networking sites from India, such as Sulekha, Fropper and BigAdda, grew 120 per cent in 2006, according to a newspaper report. *See* Venkatesh, Ganesh, 'Indian social networks are spreading fast, virtually', *Hindustan Times*, 27 August 2007.
4. In cases of domestic violence in some countries, people have reportedly used technologies like spyware and global positioning systems to track their partners' movements by tracing their Internet and telephone usage.
5. Versions vary of how this video came online. It got named *Mysore Mallige* (and elsewhere is called *Coorgi Sweety* or *Love in Karnataka*) and is regarded by its online fans in India as a 'classic' in its genre. A 2007 PSBT documentary titled *What Are You Looking At?* uses this video as a starting point to talk to

a few respondents about the contents of the video and about pornography.

6. *See* Yash, Suvarna, 'Ways of the Indian pervert', *Times News Network*, 3 December 2006.

7. These numbers are not disaggregated by sex.

8. The United Nations Declaration on the Elimination of Violence against Women (1993) defines violence against women as 'any act of gender-based violence that results in, or is likely to result in, physical, sexual or psychological harm or suffering to women, including threats of such acts, coercion or arbitrary deprivation of liberty, whether occurring in public or private life'. Supplementing this is a range of international conventions. Working To Halt Online Abuse, an anti online-harassment movement, explains online harassment as: 'The intentional crossing of [a person's] emotional or physical safety boundaries [that] usually involves repeated communications via email or some sort of instant messaging program after the harasser has clearly been told to go away.' *See* Kee.

9. Internet Service Providers are a conduit between the subscriber and the rest of the internet, a physical link that makes a user a part of the worldwide web/internet.

10. UNDP, 2005.

11. Mahanagar Telephone Nigam Limited (MTNL) and Bharat Sanchar Nigam Limited (BSNL) are government-owned Internet service providers.

12. According to figures provided by Deepak Maheshwari, who was with the ISP Sify, and has worked as secretary of the Internet Service Providers Association of India.

13. From the 'Internet in India' study (2006) undertaken by the Internet and Mobile Association of India and IMRB International.

14. According to estimates made by Ashish Saboo, but not based on a survey. The number of cyber cafés is approximate because until December 2006, cyber cafés in India required only a Shops and Establishments licence and did not have to be registered as cyber cafés; this policy has now changed in Maharashtra and a few other states. The policy is a state subject and varies from state to state.

15. *See* Freeman, 2001.

16. Business Process Outsourcing (BPO).

17. *See* Kelkar et al., 2005.

18. *See* Warf and Grimes, 1997.
19. *See* Wajcman, 2000.
20. From ISP industry figures in the previous section.
21. *See* Warf and Grimes, 1997.
22. *See* Nayar, 2004.
23. *See* Rhodes, 2002.
24. In this context, a much-quoted image in Western feminist literature is Donna Haraway's Cyborg: a cybernetic organism, a hybrid of machine and organism; an image that conjures up a world without gender. Also relevant here is Judith Butler's much-quoted theorization of gender as enacted, as multiple and fluid. Butler and others have argued that gender is not fixed in advance of social interaction, but is constructed *in* interaction (Wajcman's paraphrasing, 2000). As such, all gender is performed, but in cyberspace this performance can be especially orchestrated by the user.
25. *See* Turkle, 1995; Wacjman, 2000.
26. *See* Fernandez, 1999.
27. *See* Rosser, 2005; Bury, 1999.
28. *See* Flanagan, 2000.
29. *See* Dean, 1999.
30. *See* Coole, 2000.
31. *See* Phadke, 2006.
32. *See* Dean, 1999.
33. An Internet Protocol address is the specific 'address' on the web at which you are when you are online. Every device connected to the Internet is assigned a unique four-stage number. This IP address can be used to identify some details such as the region from which a computer is connecting to the Internet. If an ISP issues one IP address to each user, it is called a static IP address. With a limited number of IP addresses and with increased use of the Internet, ISPs now issue addresses out of a pool, and these are called dynamic IP addresses.
34. While this occurs in different kinds of cases, it also happened when a Delhi woman said she was being harassed through the Internet by an ex-boyfriend. In reality, the woman had created a false online trail to implicate him because she wanted to settle old scores, so there was no 'offender'. In some cases, the offender is a woman. For example, in July 2006, the Pune police arrested a girl for posting an 'obscene' profile of a friend

on Orkut because she was interested in the latter's boyfriend and wanted to draw him away from her.

35. In a 2005 UNDP survey, respondents from India said cyber crimes [such as online fraud], spam, and virus attacks were the most important internet governance priorities. *See* UNDP, 2005.

36. This law was preceded by the IT Bill, which in turn was based on the 1997 UNCITRAL (United Nations Commission on International Trade Laws on e-commerce).

37. 'Phishing' refers to the attempt to acquire information, such as bank account passwords and credit card details, by masquerading as a trustworthy person or business in an electronic communication.

38. 'Cyberstalking is defined as unwarranted, threatening behavioural patterns or advances directed by one Internet user against another with the purpose of harassing the other by using the medium of the Internet.' *See* Duggal, 2004. The cases cited in this section are mentioned in this book.

39. The severity of the punishment is greater under the IT Act than under the IPC because of the assumption that dissemination (and the potential impact) is wider.

40. The judgment of the Supreme Court in *Ranjit Udeshi v. State of Maharashtra* (1965) has often been cited for interpretations of Section 292 IPC. The judgment quoted dictionary meanings of obscenity as 'lewd, filthy, and repulsive'. It referred to the test stipulated in the *Regina v. Hicklin* case (1868) which emphasized the potential of the material to 'deprave and corrupt'.

41. Various international efforts exist in this context. For example, the G-8 '24/7' initiative shares information about cyber crimes, criminals, tools, and methods, though it's not a binding convention. The Council of Europe's Convention on Cyber Crime (of which Japan, the US and Canada are members) tries to make national cyber crime legislation more comprehensive.

42. Article 19 (1) (a) of the Constitution of India guarantees the right to freedom of speech and expression to all citizens. It is qualified by 19 (2), which permits the imposition of reasonable restrictions by the state in times of martial law and the declaration of an emergency.

43. According to a newspaper report, the police are teaming up with software companies to install 'key-logger' software and

closed circuit cameras in cafés in Mumbai. Once a user logs in, whatever s/he 'types, sees, browses, and sends from that particular computer will be stored in a file which would be sent to the main server to create a database'. *See* V. Narayan and Sharma Somendra, 'The Net tightens in cafes', *DNA*, 7 May 2007.

44. *See* Yogesh Joshi, 'ISI luring Indians with love on the Net, say police', *Hindustan Times*, 11 April 2007. This article reported the arrest of a young man in Pune who regularly chatted with an invisible 'girlfriend' in Pakistan and, the report says, was in the process of collecting, with the purpose of forwarding to this person, information about 'defence establishments and religious places in and around the city'.

45. If a user in a country with little or no Internet censorship downloads this programme called 'Psiphon', that computer can then be an access point. A user in a restricted-access country can log on to that access-point computer through an encrypted, proxy connection that will leave no lasting history of the sites visited, and gain access to censored sites. *See* Christopher, Mason, 'Program offers way past Net censors'. From the *New York Times*, in *Hindustan Times*, 27 November 2006.

46. This discussion is not venturing into the entirely different issues related to pornography that features children.

47. *See* Bose, 2006.

48. *See* Jensen, 2007.

49. Estimates of the amount of Internet content that is pornographic range from 10 to 60 per cent.

50. The Internet is a field not for pornography alone, but also for trafficking and prostitution. It is widely used both by sex workers who are soliciting customers and by persons/ groups trafficking women for prostitution. Prostitution, like pornography, is a contested area in feminist discourse.

51. These included sites entitled *The Rapist Archive, Torture and Rape Diaries, Real Brutal Rape Videos, Asian Schoolgirl Raped and Tortured, Forced Sex, Forced Submission,* and *Women in Pain.*

52. This is linked to Western stereotypes about Asian women and their marketing as 'passive, yet artful and eager to please'. *See* Gossett and Byrne, 2002. On many of the sites, the perpetrator's face was blurred, but race/ethnicity was of paramount importance in constructing the image of the victim on some of the sites.

53. Some of the sites had a jukebox of choices for the viewer to select, consisting of text descriptions of the kinds of scenes available, such as 'Rape a Woman', 'Japanese Rape Gang Bang', and 'Tortured and Raped in a Barn'. Some sites invited the viewer to directly participate in the rape or physical violence; one site invited viewers to download a 'cyberslave' programme in which the viewer could 'torture her and abuse her anyway you wish'. Other sites used text to create an image: for example, one site showed a young naked girl with an expression of pain along with the caption: 'These teenagers' hell is your pleasure. They are stretched, whipped, raped, and beaten... crushed, twisted, pierced, thrashed, and tortured.... torn and ripped... beaten till bloody... stretched, used as target practice... they scream, cry, and plead'. *See* Gossett and Byrne, 2002. Many of the sites showed the use of weapons for causing physical pain and for rape, including the use of ropes, cloth gags, handcuffs, chains, guns, knives, bats, whips, clothespins, and cages. Some described how the victim was drugged before the rape, some conveyed the use of an electric shock, hot wax, and vaginal mutilation.
54. *See* Gossett and Byrne, 2002.
55. *See* Kee.
56. The *Internet* is a haven for paedophiles. Numerous task-forces and committees in a number of countries have attempted to control online child pornography, but the child pornography and child prostitution industries have found ways of circumventing the controls. The IT Act in India is silent on the issue of online child pornography.
57. An amendment to the IPC, which is being introduced as part of the amendments to the IT Act, includes Section 502A on 'circumstances violating privacy'. These are described as circumstances in which a person 'can have a reasonable expectation that she/he can disrobe in privacy without being concerned that an image is being captured for the public, regardless of whether the person is in a public or a private place. The section provides for imprisonment of up to two years for whoever intentionally captures (though 'videotape, photographs, film, or record by any means'), publishes or transmits the image of the 'private areas' of any person 'without his or her consent'. *See* Manoj, Mitta, 'Govt. for jail for breaching privacy', *Times of India*, 3 February 2007.

58. *See* Allen, 2000.

59. Section 72 of the IT Act ('breach of confidentiality and privacy') says, 'any person who, in pursuit of any of the powers conferred under the IT Act, rules or regulations made thereunder, has secured access to any electronic record, book, register, correspondence, information, document or other material without the consent of the person concerned discloses such... material to any other person...'. That is, Section 72 only refers to authorized persons who have been conferred with powers under the IT Act and who then disclose the information they obtain; it does not refer to the violation of an individual's privacy in cyberspace.

60. *See* Allen, 2000.

61. The concept of privacy has been questioned in some sections of feminist social sciences as an untenable and universalizing liberal ideology, which focuses on anomic individuals; it offers legal equality while ignoring social inequalities that make the exercise of such rights extremely uneven; it assumes clear-cut bounds of privacy when in fact privacy is fluid and contextual.

62. *See* K. S. Manojkumar, 'Google denies any link, responsibility for Orkut content', *Hindustan Times,* 13 February 2007.

63. *See* Mitra, Soubhik, 'City youth are Orkut, Fropper cyber policemen', *Hindustan Times,* 20 January 2007.

64. *See* Phadke, 2005.

65. This particular listing of activities refers primarily to the work of the Women's Networking Support Programme. The WNSP, an initiative of the Association for Progressive Communities, is a global network of about 100 women in 35 countries who support women networking for social change and empowerment through the use of ICTs. It promotes gender equality in design, development, implementation, access to, and use of ICTs, and in policies that regulate them. The programme is part of the APC, a network of organizations that works on human rights and other issues through strategic use of ICT, including the Internet.

66. The documentary, made by Paromita Vohra, is titled *Unlimited Girls.*

References

Allen, Anita L. (2000): 'Gender and Privacy in Cyberspace', *Stanford Law Review*, 52(5).

Bose, Brinda (2006): 'Introduction', in *Gender and Censorship*. New Delhi: Women Unlimited.

Bury, Rhiannon (1999): 'X-clusively Female: The Cyberspace of the David Duchovny Estrogen Brigades', *Resources for Feminist Research*, vol. 27, Issue 1/2.

Coole, Diana (2000): 'Cartographic Convulsions: Public and Private Reconsidered', *Political Theory*, 28(3).

Dean, Jodi (1999): 'Virtual Fears', *Journal of Women in Culture and Society,* 24(4).

Duggal, Pavan (2004): *Cyberlaw: The Indian Perspective*. New Delhi: Saakshar Law Publications.

Fernandez, Maria (1999): 'Postcolonial Media Theory', *Art Journal,* 58(3).

Flanagan, Mary (2000): 'Navigating the Narrative in Space: Gender and Spatiality in Virtual Worlds, *Art Journal,* 59(3).

Freeman, Carla (2001): 'Is Local: Global as Feminine: Masculine? Rethinking the Gender of Globalization', *Signs,* 26(4).

Gossett, Jennifer Lynn and Sarah Byrne (2002): 'Click Here: A Content Analysis of Internet Rape Sites', *Gender and Society,* 16(5).

Jensen, Robert (2007): *Getting Off: Pornography and the End of Masculinity*. Cambridge, MA: South End Press.

Kee, Jac S. M.: 'Cultivating Violence Through Technology? Exploring the Connection between Information Communication Technologies and Violence Against Women', www.genderit. org.

Kelkar, Govind, Girija Shrestha, N. Veena (2005): 'Women's Agency and the IT Industry in India', in N.G. Cecilia and Swasti Mitter (eds.), *Gender and the Digital Economy: Perspectives from the Developing World*. New Delhi: Sage Publications.

Malhotra, Namita: 'Search History: Examining Pornography on the Internet', www.genderit.org.

Nayar, Pramod K. (2004): *Virtual Worlds: Culture and Politics in the Age of Cybertechnology*. New Delhi: Sage Publications.

Phadke, Shilpa (2006): in *Plainspeak,* Issue 1.

—— (2005): 'You Can be Lonely in a Crowd', *Indian Journal of Gender Studies,* 12(1).

Rhodes, Jacqueline (2002): 'Substantive and Feminist Girlie Action: Women Online', *College Composition and Communication*, 54(1).

Rosser, Sue (2005): 'Through the Lenses of Feminist Theory: Focus on Women and Information Technology', *Frontiers*, 25(1).

Turkle, Sherry (1995): *Life on the Screen: Identity in the Age of the Internet*. New York: Simon & Schuster.

UNDP Asia-Pacific Development Information Programme (2005): 'Voices from Asia-Pacific: Internet Governance Priorities and Practices: India'.

Wajcman, Judy (2000): 'Reflections on Gender and Technology Studies: In What State is the Art?', *Social Studies of Science*, 30(3).

Warf, Barney and John Grimes (1997): 'Counter-hegemonic Discourses and the Internet', *Geographical Review*, 87(2).

5

Invisible Yet Entrapping
Confronting Sexual Harassment
at the Workplace

Puja Roy

... we sit in meditation learning to disentangle from a web invisible
yet entrapping...

Jasmin Cori, Witness

When Piyali (name changed) began working in 1988 with a
well known information technology (IT) company in Kolkata,
she was optimistic about achieving success. She was young,
qualified, and interested in learning new skills. Her team
leader was a supportive man who encouraged her professional
growth. Everything seemed positive until the chief executive
officer (CEO) began making demands on her: accosting
her, asking her out, insisting that she accompany him into
an empty room after an office party. He would make small
physical gestures that were offensive to her and from which
she pointedly shied away. When she spurned his advances,
she was taken off the project on which she was working and
put on another providing fewer learning opportunities. When
she asked to complete her ongoing project, she was transferred
to another office.

Piyali then fixed an appointment with the group head but
when she walked into his office, the CEO was already there.
It was evident they had been discussing her. She was told

that she was not performing; a transfer was offered. Realizing the futility of the situation, Piyali resigned. She somehow completed her current project and got a good recommendation and performance bonus from her boss, undermining the CEO's charge of non-performance. Piyali left her first job shaken and degraded. She was aware of the CEO's power in the IT world. Women in the office were wary of him and had learnt to 'deal with it' in their own way. She did not want to jeopardize her job prospects and did not officially complain about the sexual harassment. She resigned and moved on.

Over the past two decades, sexual harassment at the workplace has gained prominence and visibility as a form of gender-based violence, both due to the women's movement and individual women who have fought highly publicized cases.[1] International conventions, conferences, and committees clearly identify sexual harassment at the workplace as a form of gender-based violence in need of urgent attention and intervention.[2]

While it is important to view sexual harassment at the workplace as gender-based violence, it is also essential to strategically address it, bearing in mind its unique and distinct characteristics. This form of violence is unique in that it is a systematic, intrusive, and pervasive mode that is often implicit in its manifestations. It takes place within the context of a person's work or working environment, attacks the very core of her individuality, and has a detrimental effect on her, both professionally and personally. Sexual harassment covers a range of unwelcome behaviours; from subtly offensive body language and verbal abuse to blatant physical harassment. Sexual harassment at the workplace seriously impedes a person's professional growth and her ability to make a significant contribution to society, while eroding her self-esteem and self-confidence.

Catherine MacKinnon (1979) describes sexual harassment as 'the unwanted imposition of sexual requirements in the context of a relationship of unequal power.'[3] The issues that comprise the core of sexual harassment are 'power' and 'sexuality'. Patriarchal and masculine values that wield tremendous power within social structures are firmly imbibed by men and women alike, and taken into the workspace. This often determines how women are perceived: as sexual beings first and as professionals second.

The actual extent and prevalence of sexual harassment at the Indian workplace is yet to be determined. Sanhita, an NGO in Kolkata, estimates that 35 per cent of women in the formal sector in Kolkata have faced some form of sexual harassment.[4] It sees this as the tip of the iceberg, and believes sexual harassment is more widespread than reported. Hengasara Hakkina Sangha in Bangalore and Sakshi in Delhi have found that sexual harassment is widely prevalent in these cities (up to 49 per cent) and that the actual numbers are far greater than the surveys indicate. Sanhita also found that certain forms of sexual harassment – the display of sexually explicit graffiti, making sexually coloured jokes or remarks – are not clearly recognized as sexual harassment.

Gender Discrimination at the Workplace

In India, there is tremendous gender disparity in the workforce. According to the 2001 census, there are 127.05 million women in the workforce, as against 275.46 million men. In urban areas, there are 15.59 million working women, as against 72.26 million working men. This disparity increases in corporate houses, where there are only 4 per cent women at senior management levels.[5] A patriarchal social structure prevents women from entering and remaining in the workforce. Organizations reinforce gendered power inequalities at the workplace in allocating roles and positions to men and women, in attitudes around conduct and dress codes, and in policies, including those relating to promotions.

Are certain women more vulnerable or susceptible to sexual harassment than others? Do single, separated, divorced women face greater harassment? Are younger women more vulnerable? Are those who are vocal, articulate, and potential leaders clear targets? No, this is not necessarily the case. Sexual harassment occurs whether or not a woman is perceived as assertive; there are continual undercurrents of power and control in the workplace that subject women to various forms of harassment, regardless of their leadership positions, how articulate they are, or how compliant to the norms of the workplace.[6]

A report by Saheli, an autonomous women's group in Delhi, states that 'women in the labour force are viewed as a threat to the institution of patriarchy. They are seen as "snatching" men's jobs.' The presence of women in the workforce upsets the patriarchal status quo of men as breadwinners and women as homemakers. A woman is expected to return home from work and continue with her domestic tasks whereas a man is expected to contribute only at the workplace. A working woman is expected to 'juggle both work and family'. If she does so effectively, she is admired; if she does not, her status as a working woman is held responsible. The same judgment is not pronounced on working men. It is still assumed that women should stay at home if they have no economic reason to work. Such patriarchal thought creates a perfect backdrop for sexual harassment to take root and thrive.

The Struggle against Sexual Harassment

The movement against sexual harassment in India began in the 1980s. Mumbai's Forum Against Oppression of Women protested the sexual harassment of nurses and female staff in hospitals, airhostesses by colleagues and passengers, and students in educational institutions. In Goa, Bailancho Saad publicly campaigned against the chief minister who had allegedly harassed his secretary. Several individuals fought sexual harassment; the best-known being Rupan Deol Bajaj, an IAS officer in Punjab who was molested by K.P.S. Gill, a senior police officer, at a party in 1988. In 1996, Shehnaz Sahni filed a case of sexual harassment against her station manager in Saudi Arabian Airlines. Both women won their court cases, although the process took years.

In the 1980s and 1990s, women could only file complaints of sexual harassment under Section 354 of the Indian Penal

Code that dealt with criminal assault to 'outrage a woman's modesty' or under section 509 against words, gestures and acts 'intended to insult the modesty of a woman'. The term 'outrage the modesty of a woman' trivializes the gravity of sexual harassment as a crime and is demeaning to a woman who has faced violence, as she is seen as someone who is a puritan with Victorian values.[7] For example, there was a great deal of debate as to whether Rupan Deol Bajaj's 'modesty' was 'outraged', before the courts could come to a decision.

In August 1997, with the formulation of Supreme Court guidelines, sexual harassment was eventually given the recognition it deserves as a criminal offence. Bhanwari Devi's fight for justice was instrumental in giving rise to these guidelines, more commonly known as the Vishakha guidelines.[8] They represent a landmark in the ongoing struggle to make sexual harassment at the workplace visible and prominent, and remain in place until legislation is passed on the issue.[9]

The guidelines accord formal, legal recognition of sexual harassment at the workplace as a violation of human rights and an aspect of gender-based violence, and comprehensively define the range of behaviours that constitute sexual harassment. Broadly-speaking, any 'physical, verbal, or non verbal conduct of sexual nature' that is unwelcome is considered to be sexual harassment.[10] It is not the intent, but the unwelcome nature, that determines whether an action constitutes harassment.

A synopsis of the 1997 Supreme Court Guidelines:

It is the responsibility of the employer or other responsible persons in the workplace to prevent or deter the commission or acts of sexual harassment, and to provide for the resolution, settlement, and prosecution of sexual harassment by taking all steps required.

Definition: Sexual harassment includes such unwelcome sexually-determined behaviour (whether directly or by implication) as, (a) physical contact and advances. (b) a demand or request for sexual favours, (c) sexually coloured remarks, (d) showing pornography, (e) any other unwelcome physical, verbal, or non-verbal conduct of sexual nature.

Preventive steps: All employers or persons in charge of workplaces, whether in the public or private sector, should take appropriate steps to prevent sexual harassment.

Criminal proceedings: Where such conduct amounts to a specific offence under the Indian Penal Code or any other law, the employer shall initiate action by making a complaint with the appropriate authority. In particular, it should ensure that the victims or witnesses are not victimized or discriminated against while dealing with sexual harassment.

Disciplinary action: Where such conduct amounts to misconduct, as defined by the relevant service rules, disciplinary action should be initiated by the employer.

Complaint mechanism: Whether or not such conduct constitutes an offence under law or a breach of the service rules, an appropriate, time-bound complaint mechanism should be created for redressal of complaints.

Complaints committee: The complaints mechanism should provide, where necessary, a complaints committee, a special counsellor or other support service. The complaints committee should be headed by a woman, and not less than half of its members should be women. The committee should involve a third party such as an NGO or other body familiar with the issue. This committee must make an annual report to the concerned government department regarding the complaints received and action taken.

Workers' initiative: Employees should be allowed to raise issues of sexual harassment at workers' meetings and other appropriate forums. It should be affirmatively discussed in employer-employee meetings.

Awareness: Awareness of the rights of female employees in this regard should be created, in particular by prominently notifying guidelines (and legislation when enacted) in a suitable manner.

Third-party harassment: Where sexual harassment occurs as a result of an act by any third party or outsider, the employer and person in charge will take all necessary steps to assist the affected person in terms of support and preventive action.

The central/state governments are requested to consider adopting suitable measures, including legislation, to ensure that the guidelines laid down by the order are also observed by employers in the private sector.

Complaints Committees: Proactive or Reactive?

The Supreme Court guidelines require each organization or workplace to institute a complaints committee to proactively address sexual harassment. Each committee is to be headed by a woman, half its members should be women, and the committee should include someone who is familiar with the issue of sexual harassment. However, the experiences of women's groups reveal that many workplaces are not following the guidelines, with committees hastily formed when there is a case to be dealt with.[11]

In May 2000, Preeti (name changed), a woman lawyer, accused Rajeev Dhavan, director of the Public Interest Legal Support and Research Centre (PILSARC), of sexually harassing her. She said that once she began spurning his advances, he began criticizing and undermining her work in the presence of fellow colleagues. The work environment grew so hostile that Preeti was forced to resign. Saheli and other women's organizations pressurized PILSARC into instituting a complaints committee, but the one-man committee dismissed the charges. Appeals from Saheli and others to the trustees of PILSARC to institute an inquiry in accordance with the guidelines went unheeded.[12]

In February 2005, an Indian Air Force flying officer, Anjali Gupta, filed a complaint of sexual harassment in Bangalore police station against three of her superior officers. The police did not cooperate in filing a First Information Report (FIR) and advised Anjali to resolve the issue internally. It was only when the High Court ordered a probe into the matter that the Air Force set up an all-male committee to investigate the charges. In the meanwhile, the IAF court-martialled Anjali on charges of misconduct, indiscipline, and embezzling a little over Rs 1000. She was held under arrest. When women's rights organizations protested her arrest and the formation of the all-male inquiry team, a second team was instituted. However, the charges were dismissed and Anjali was cashiered from service, which meant that she lost all rank and privileges and post-service benefits, apart from being dismissed.

Both male and female committee members carry inherent gender biases and prejudices that often compromise a complainant's case. Note this statement by Air Marshall B.K. Pandey (retd.) during Anjali Gupta's case:

It is incumbent on the IAF women officers as a responsible group to preserve and reinforce their reputation as being as focused, dedicated, sincere and capable as their male counterparts. They should assiduously guard against the temptation to employ allegations of sexual harassment as an offensive weapon merely to push the organization on to the back foot, lest it progressively erode their credibility and the IAF begin to regard them not as a pillar of strength but as a millstone around their neck.[13]

Women who head these committees are as susceptible to gender biases as their male counterparts. They need not necessarily support other women, and even if they do, are not sufficiently empowered to proactively lead the team in that direction. What is needed are committees that are trained on gender-based violence and can assess, understand, and analyse a situation and its power dynamics meaningfully.

Issues of caste, sexuality, religion, and gender often play out in the complaints committees, further complicating the issue. In a public sector case, a supervisor who sexually harassed his junior got away by insisting that he was being framed as a Dalit by a woman from a higher caste. Seema[14] from Bangalore is a transgender person who found herself harassed in both her workplaces: in an accountant's office and in a private firm. She attributes this to her gender identity; she was perceived as feminine, different, and sexually vulnerable. A woman from a minority religious community working in a Mumbai multinational firm faced sexual taunts about women from her community. Although she was the head of the complaints committee, she found herself unable to complain, because she felt that her status placed her at a distinct disadvantage.

Even when committees rule in favour of complainants, management does not always back this decision. Bhavna was harassed by her immediate superior in a large public sector company in Bangalore. The complaints committee

found him guilty, but the management supported him when
he challenged the committee's finding. He argued that the
committee did not have male members, that there were no
representatives of scheduled tribes and castes, and that some
of the members were biased towards him. He also complained
that the accusations were vague and that there had never been
earlier complaints against him. Similarly, PILSARC's board
of trustees supported Rajeev Dhavan when he was accused of
sexual harassment. In the well known Seagull case in Kolkata,
the complainant Sutapa Roy was seen as dispensable to a
larger agenda of safeguarding the intellectual interests and
reputation of the publishing house.[15]

'It is a shame that laws made to protect women are
misused,' was a sentiment expressed several times by people
on the website discussing Anjali Gupta's case.[16] Both men and
women seem to feel that if there is a mechanism protecting
women, it is bound to be misused by them. Women who
complain against sexual harassment are first regarded with
suspicion and disbelieved, with the pronouncement that
'there is usually more to the case than meets the eye'.

A major hurdle that prevents committees from functioning
smoothly is the attempt to look for clear proof of harassment
which may be very difficult to come by, given the covert
nature of harassment and the lack of witnesses. It is firmly
ingrained in the minds of management and others at the
workplace that unless the complainant can furnish proof, the
charges cannot be taken seriously. These sentiments usually
succeed in keeping the woman silent, or in many cases, making
her withdraw her charges, because she cannot convince the
committee of the seriousness of the harassment.[17]

The Supreme Court guidelines clearly emphasize that
it is the impact of the harassment (unwelcome) and not
the intent behind it that needs to be considered. Thus, the
emphasis should be on how the woman is affected, not on
the perpetrator's claim of intent. Circumstantial evidence is
acceptable and should be considered. When an organization
refuses to investigate charges of sexual harassment or when
a committee fails to protect the rights of a sexually harassed

woman, she often has to seek assistance from other sources. Both Preeti and Sutapa sought assistance from women's organizations in their struggles against PILSARC and Seagull; it was only because of the Kolkata women's rights network Maitree's intervention and systematic campaigning that Sutapa received some semblance of justice.

Women's rights organizations have resorted to campaigns and collective action to protest sexual harassment. This would not, however, have been necessary if complaints committees functioned effectively. A committee can only be effective if all its members recognize sexual harassment as an act of gender-based violence that violates employees' rights.

Blurred Boundaries and 'Grey' Areas

The assertion of masculine power is almost always the core reason for sexual harassment at the workplace. 'The refusal to recognize women's economic independence and empowerment is one of the principal reasons for violence against women,' says Radhika Coomaraswamy, the first United Nations Special Rapporteur on Violence against Women,[18] and this often expresses itself as sexual harassment at the workplace.

Systemic manifestations of power support and collude with a man and trivialize and doubt a woman's experience of harassment. This 'old boys' club' attitude, a chauvinistic and patriarchal expression of collective male power, that unequivocally embraces the male perpetrator's cause, ensures that it is extremely difficult for a woman facing harassment to receive the support and help of others. The hostile work environment facing a woman who has dared complain reflects this inherent culture of 'frowning upon the person who has upset the gendered status quo' and sends a signal to other women. The fear of facing repercussions, losing a job or promotion ensures their silence.

Biased perceptions exist with regard to women's behaviour in the workplace. A human resource manager I interviewed in Mumbai feels there are 'gray' areas in issues of sexual harassment: the intricacies of a man-woman relationship, miscommunication and misunderstanding, misconstruing a situation, crossing indistinct boundaries. An NGO asserts that women do react in confused ways to male advances, and that this can lead to mixed messages and unclear signals:

Women are culturally not encouraged to discuss sexuality, and hence they are uncomfortable with it. Men, on the other hand, do not always know how to flirt in a way that is pleasing or romantic, but in crude ways that offend a woman. Both men's and women's actions can be misconstrued under the circumstances.

While it is true that society and culture condition men and women into specific gendered roles and behaviours (with males being more powerful, controlling, and assertive), the notion that women are not culturally equipped to 'deal' with their sexuality and men are unable to communicate appropriately while flirting is one way in which the 'culture cloak' is used to justify sexual harassment. Sexual harassment is violence and not a result of sexual miscommunication or social inadequacies. In the experience of those harassed, being assertive and clear about shunning sexual advances does not prevent harassment. The person who harasses is intent on exerting power over a woman's sexuality; he is not attempting to flirt in a crude way just because he is unaware of the etiquette! Similarly, a woman who is harassed needs to be respected for her feelings. These feelings are real and should not be perceived as being the result of a cultural upbringing that restricts her sexuality or sexual expression.

The president of an NGO based in Bihar has a long history of sexual harassment. He would ask women employees, who were often residents on the campus, for sexual favours. If they refused, he would arbitrarily terminate their services. One or two women succumbed in order to retain their positions, others left and found work elsewhere. Those who left complained to a donor, which investigated the situation and stopped funding the NGO. Those who had left were scornful of and hostile towards a particular woman, Devika (name changed), who had succumbed to the president's sexual demands.[19]

However, can the relationship between Devika and her boss be termed 'consensual'? This type of relationship is often based on unequal and exploitative power relationships, where the harasser employs the 'quid pro quo' tactic: promising benefits in return for sexual favours. The key elements of quid pro quo sexual harassment are a demand for a sexual favour and the threat of adverse job consequences if the demand is refused.[20]

Occasionally a woman succumbs when she feels she has little choice in the matter or that this is the only way to obtain privileges and promotions. Unfortunately, she is perceived as a woman who uses her sexuality to get ahead with her boss, and is regarded with hostility or shunned by colleagues. The boss however is not shunned for unfairly using his power and position to exploit an employee.

There is a marked difference between this kind of 'consensual' relationship and the kind where two colleagues in the workplace are romantically involved. It is important to understand that the 'quid pro quo' situation is exploitative, unequal, and violent, while the other relationship is one where both enjoy similar power equations. It is essential to acknowledge this distinction and not perceive all consensual office relationships as potential cases of sexual harassment.

In one large international NGO, employees are asked to inform management when a romantic relationship develops between two employees.[21] In the organization's policy against sexual harassment, employees are discouraged from being romantically involved. One has to seriously question the extent to which a person's individual rights are compromised by this diktat. Preventing sexual harassment at the workplace should not infringe upon an individual's freedom and rights. At the same time, it is important to be vigilant and recognize a violent, controlling, and exploitative relationship of sexual harassment, and not dismiss it as 'consensual'. These complex power equations need in-depth and systematic analysis in order to confront sexual harassment at the workplace.

The Unorganized or Informal Sector

Rajamma (name changed), a 16-year-old girl, worked as a domestic servant in an upper-middle-class household in Bangalore. Her employer would physically harass her while she was working; when she complained to his wife, charges of theft were framed against her and she was put in the police lock-up on the basis of an oral complaint. The domestic workers' union took up her case, had her released, and picketed in front of the employers' house strongly protesting the harassment and demanding that no other person should work there.

The majority of working women in India, 78.4 per cent, work in the informal sector, where sexual harassment remains an invisible reality. SEWA (Self Employed Women's Association), in Ahmedabad has organized several thousands of women in the informal sector in their struggle for equal wages, better working conditions, fair access to markets, and health facilities. According to SEWA, women in the informal sector face sexual harassment on a daily basis. For example, contractors in construction work rarely give women daily work without extracting a sexual favour. A woman who refuses is not accepted for work the next day. Women do complain about harassment to SEWA, but contractors typically deny this, instead blaming women of making false accusations.

Women in the informal sector put up with and regularly live with sexual harassment. Their rights are tenuous and fragile; they are in great need of employment and do not complain when harassment takes place. Most are afraid that such complaints or the stigma attached to them might make them unemployable. Many do not want their families to know about harassment for the same reason. Besides, the power of the perpetrator is immensely strong in the informal sector, since the complainant is usually poor, vulnerable, and in desperate need of work.

SEWA believes that the way forward is to make men and women working in the informal sector more aware of sexual harassment and link it to their struggle for rights. While there are similarities in the situations of women facing violence in the formal and informal sectors, the position of a woman in the informal sector is markedly more vulnerable. However, it is necessary to find solutions to the problems that women face in the informal sector and enable them to confront sexual harassment in a manner that takes into account their life situations, existing realities, and vulnerabilities.

The Way Forward

It has been almost ten years since the Vishakha judgment and the landmark Supreme Court guidelines against sexual harassment. Many women have taken it upon themselves to fight for justice under these new guidelines. However, the process of seeking justice can extract a heavy toll on a woman, both personally and professionally. Struggling alone against a biased and judgmental system is an uphill task, notwithstanding the existence of the guidelines. Given that a woman's personal character, reputation, professional expertise, and social background are minutely examined under a public microscope during the investigation, it is no wonder that women give up and move on to other workplaces rather than pursuing justice for themselves.

What is required is an enabling environment that builds a circle of strength and understanding, lends unequivocal support to those facing harassment, and gives teeth to implementation of the guidelines. There are several ways in which an enabling environment can be built. On 8 June 2005, 10 female students of North Eastern Hill University (NEHU) in Shillong complained that Professor Vivek Srivastava had sexually harassed them. The institution investigated these complaints through a complaints committee initiated by the existing women's cell. It objectively reviewed the evidence and studied available cases of sexual harassment for guidance. It concluded that Professor Srivastava was guilty, terminated his employment, and recommended that the female students who came forward should be rewarded for their courage. The university protected the ten girls who had given evidence by not revealing their identities, a single step that enabled the girls to speak out freely without fear of reprisals.

The Gender Sensitization Committee Against Sexual Harassment at Jawarharlal Nehru University and the Women's Development Cell at Gargi College, New Delhi, are other examples of proactive initiatives in creating an enabling environment. They conduct awareness campaigns on gender discrimination, facilitate workshops on gender and address sexual harassment cases, including those involving people of alternate sexualities. Sanhita, Saheli, Sakshi, Swayam, The Lawyer's Collective, Indian Centre for Human Rights and Law, among other organizations, have conducted research, documented cases of sexual harassment, publicized the issue, campaigned against harassment, and conducted training courses at workplaces.

Women will come forward to complain of sexual harassment if there is an atmosphere of solidarity in the workplace. However, garnering support may not be straightforward, especially if there are dynamics of power and prejudice to contend with at the workplace. Discussions on sexual harassment and collectively voicing disapproval against offensive behaviour will eventually realign power from the perpetrator to those who stand in solidarity against harassment.

The deeper question still remains: How do we tackle the roots of sexual harassment? How do we promote gender equity at the workplace? Men and women enter the workplace, bringing with them values which are highly gendered. Conversations on gender equity should ideally begin at home and be promoted across all the stages of a person's life. The workplace is, however, an environment in which individuals can be exposed to new ideas and ways of thinking notwithstanding their previous gender knowledge, biases, and 'baggage'. Organizational development programmes require an inbuilt focus on promoting gender equity and plurality at the workplace. The key is to prevent sexual harassment, not just to confront it once it occurs. It is imperative for men to form a part of the process sensitization and change, for it is the responsibility of both men and women to promote gender equality at the workplace.

Gender and anti-sexual harassment policies usually exist in formal work environments and not in the unorganized or informal sector. There is an essential need to facilitate the formation of support systems for persons within the unorganized sector, both from within the sector and without. Collective strength, knowledge, and understanding have proven to be important elements in successfully addressing human rights violations, and these aspects need particular focus and intensification.

Every individual has the right to work, practise his or her profession, in an environment free of violence and discrimination. There are complex issues involved in understanding and addressing sexual harassment; but the key is in making the issue more visible and public. Measures to counter the existence of sexual harassment need to be proactive, intensive, and sustained. It is the collective and cohesive responsibility of all, not just of women's rights organizations, to intensify measures and efforts in making the workplace safe, secure, gender-equal, and free.

Notes

1. For example, *Rupan Deol Bajaj* vs *K.P.S. Gill,* 1995.
2. The 1993 World Conference of Human Rights, Vienna, stresses that 'gender-based violence and all forms of sexual harassment and exploitation, including those resulting from cultural prejudice... are incompatible with the dignity and worth of the human person, and must be eliminated'. Other International conventions clearly identify sexual harassment as gender-specific violence that 'seriously inhibits women's ability to enjoy rights and freedoms on a basis of equality with men' (Committee on the Elimination of Discrimination Against Women 1992, General Recommendation 19). The Beijing Platform for Action, which was adopted at the 1995 Fourth World Conference for Women, strongly advocates that governments 'enact and enforce laws and develop workplace policies against gender discrimination in the labour market,

especially... regarding discriminatory working conditions and
sexual harassment.'

3. *See* MacKinnon, 1979.

4. *See* Sanhita, 2001.

5. Survey by the Confederation of Indian Industries, quoted in
Economic Times, 15 December 2005.

6. From discussions with NGOs in Bangalore, Delhi, Kolkata.

7. *See* Kapur, 2005.

8. In 1992 Bhanwari Devi, a woman working in a government
welfare programme in Rajasthan, was gang-raped during the
course of her work; a public furore accompanied the acquittal
of her rapists. The 1997 Supreme Court Guidelines Against
Sexual Harassment at the Workplace were the result of a
campaign and petition by women's rights groups to protest the
gang-rape of Bhanwari Devi.

9. The Department of Women and Child Development is
finalizing a draft bill to ensure that sexual harassment at the
workplace is legally addressed. The bill is seen as a logical
progression from the Supreme Court guidelines and is being
drafted in consultation with NGOs and women's rights
organizations. The women's movement recommends that the
following issues be addressed in the draft bill: (a) The inclusion
of third party harassment, and the rights of students (b) a
procedure of conciliation that does not infringe the rights of the
complainant; (c) the deletion of a section on punishment for
false and malicious complaints which paves the way for further
harassment and perpetuates the myth that women make false
complaints; (d) an obligation on the part of the employer to
promote the right to gender equality, provide appropriate
working conditions and facilities for women employees, in
order to obviate a hostile work environment.

10. *See* Lawyers' Collective, 2004.

11. Experiences of Sanhita, Vimochana, Saheli, Lawyers' Collective.

12. Although a public protest against PILSARC's role in
Preeti's resignation did have a small negative impact on the
organization, it was insufficient to initiate action against Dr.
Rajeev Dhavan.

13. *See Deccan Herald,* 1 May 2005.

14. As an adolescent, Seema felt trapped in a man's body and
would dress in feminine attire. She faced taunts and ridicule
in college, principally from men. She claimed to have been

raped there but did not complain as she was aware that her case would not be taken seriously. She was forced to leave both her work situations and became involved in sex work. Later, she was hired by an NGO based in Bangalore that works for people of alternate sexualities.

15. Sutapa Roy was employed by Seagull Bookstores in Kolkata in 1998. Tapan Banerjee, one of the managing directors of Seagull, began to sexually harass her physically and verbally; this continued till 1999. Sutapa made verbal complaints to the management, who asked her to resign. As a reaction to the sexual harassment charges, and as a result of pressure from Maitree, a women's network, a committee was formed to look into the charges but eventually the verdict went against Sutapa. It was only after persistent campaigning by Maitree that Seagull gave a written apology to Sutapa and paid her compensation.

16 See Amardeep Singh's website, *Anjali Gupta* vs *The Indian Air Force.*

17 From interview with Vimochana, Bangalore.

18. *See* Coomaraswamy, 2005.

19. From the experience of a donor agency operating in Bihar, 1994.

20. *See* Lawyer's Collective, 2004.

21. Taken from a policy document of a large NGO.

References

Chacko, Shubha (2001): *'Changing the Stream: Backgrounder on the Women's Movement in India,* Mumbai: Centre for Education and Documentation.

Coomaraswamy, Radhika (2005): 'Human Security and Gender Violence', *Economic and Political Weekly,* 29 October 2005.

Indhu, S. and S.N. Nagamani (2000): Sexual Harassment at the Workplace, Draft Report. Bangalore: Hengasara Hakkina Sangha and New Delhi: Sakshi.

Jaising, Indira (ed.) (2004): *Law Relating To Sexual Harassment at the Workplace.* New Delhi: Universal.

Kapur, Ratna (2005): *Erotic Justice: Law and the New Politics of Postcolonialism.* New Delhi: Permanent Black.

MacKinnon, Catherine (1979): *Sexual Harassment of Working Women: A Case of Sex Discrimination.* New Haven: Yale University Press.

Narula, Priya and Catherine Slugget (2002): *The Campaign against Sexual Harassment at the Workplace: A Training Manual,* Socio-Legal Information Centre.

Poonacha, Veena and Neeta Raymond (2004): Prevention of Sexual Harassment in Workplaces/Educational Institutions: An Action Research Project Conducted in Sir J.J. Hospital and Grant Medical College. Mumbai: Research Centre for Women's Studies, SNDT Women's University and India Centre for Human Rights and Law.

Patel, Vibhuti (2005): 'A Brief History of the Battle against Sexual Harassment at the Workplace', Infochange News and Features, *www.infochangeindia.org* November 2005.

PUCL (2003): *Human Rights Violations against the Transgender Community.* Karnataka: People's Union for Civil Liberties.

Saheli (1998): *Another Occupational Hazard: Sexual Harassment and the Working Woman: A Saheli Report.* New Delhi: Saheli.

—— (2000): *Sexual Harassment of an NGO Employee: A Saheli Account.* New Delhi: Saheli.

Sanhita (2001): *The Politics of Silence: Sexual Harassment at the Workplace.* Kolkata: Sanhita.

West Bengal Commission for Women, Sanhita (2004): *Implementing Vishaka: A Status Report.* Kolkata: West Bengal Commission for Women.

6

From Roop Kanwar to Ramkunwari

The Agitation against Widow Immolation

Purnima Manghnani

On 4 September 1987, in the village of Deorala[1] in Rajasthan's Shekhawati region, an entire community colluded in the murder of a newly-married teenaged girl. Only 18 years old at the time of her death, Roop Kanwar was forced on to the funeral pyre of her dead husband, 24-year-old Maal Singh, through the use of drugs, coercion, physical force, and community pressure.[2] Approximately 4,000 to 5,000 people from Deorala and its surrounding villages witnessed this immolation, although none of the villagers later admitted to being present during this incidence of sati.[3]

Every year, since India's independence, one widow had been immolated in Rajasthan on average, further perpetuating the myth of sati *mata*.[4] In 1980, there was the well-publicized sati murder of Om Kanwar in Jhadli village, Sikar district.[5] It was, however, Roop Kanwar's death that finally galvanized a strong, even unprecedented response from progressive women's groups, leading to the emergence of an agitation against sati.

There are a number of reasons for this. Given Roop Kanwar's background (she was educated until the tenth standard and came from a well-to-do family in Jaipur), this incident did not conform to the stereotypical image of widow immolation. By 1987, there was a strong presence and network of women's organizations in Rajasthan, partly due to the impetus provided by the Women's Development Programme.[6] Many women's groups were led by Rajasthani women, rather than by activists from outside the state. Groups that had been addressing other forms of violence against women already had a framework in which to locate sati. As feminist scholar, writer, and activist Kumkum Sangari states, 'Sometimes, things coming into a simmer come to a boil quickly.'

One of the most important factors, however, was that women's groups in Rajasthan were not divided on the issue; they all saw this teenage girl's death as a clear case of murder, were all convinced that the guilty should be punished, that any attempts to glorify her death should be pre-empted, and that both the central and state governments were duty-bound to publicly condemn this event. As activist Brinda Karat of the CPI(M) notes:

This is not like the case of Shah Bano, when the women's movement's response was fragmented. There were lots of discussions: How to confront it? How to frame it? There were differences, but it was a united front in its response to the culpability of dominant politics at that time.

The newly organized agitation launched a campaign against sati murders through a variety of means: public demonstrations and protest marches, fact-finding missions and investigative reports, analytical articles in scholarly journals, legal reform, research on the prevalence and nature of sati, reports to the press and other women's organizations, submissions of memos to government bodies, pamphlets explicating feminist perspectives on widow immolation, joint action committees, and discussion forums and debates in villages, communities, and educational institutions. A delegation of representatives from women's groups met then chief minister Harideo Joshi with two demands: one, that the guilty be charged with murder (not abetment of suicide); two, that the *chunari mahotsav*[7] be prevented from taking place. He was utterly unresponsive. A High Court writ petition eventually forced the state government to ban this ceremony, while state and central legislation prohibited sati and its glorification.

If Roop Kanwar's murder highlighted the need for legal reform and the ideological dangers of sati glorification, subsequent cases have raised other conceptual and practical issues and dilemmas: community accountability and collective punishment, volition as a construct, fact-finding as a strategy, and the practice of working within community belief systems. This chapter analyses the debates, discussions, and activism following three sati murders: that of Charan Shah in the remote village of Satpura in Uttar Pradesh (UP) in 1999; that of Kuttu Bai in Patna Tamoli village of Madhya Pradesh (MP) in 2002; and, most recently, that of Ramkunwari in Bahundari village of UP in May 2005.[8] All three cases occured in Bundelkhand, the region that has had, after Rajasthan, the highest prevalence of incidents of widow immolation in India.

Roop Kanwar:
The Debate Over Legal Reform and State Intervention

Roop Kanwar's death clearly demonstrated that a separate law was required to deal with widow immolation. The Rajasthan Sati Prevention Ordinance of 1987 punished both the attempts to commit sati and its abetment, through imprisonment and fines.[9] The Commission of Sati Prevention Act, passed by the central government the same year, is very similar to the state ordinance with regard to punishable offences and punishments. It defines sati as the:

burning or burying alive of (i) any widow with the body of her deceased husband or any other relative or any article of the husband, or (ii) any woman along with the body of any relative, irrespective of whether the act is claimed to be the result of some voluntary act on the part of the widow or woman or otherwise.

Abetment includes inducement to the widow or woman to be immolated or buried alive, participation in any procession related to the commission of sati, presence at the place where sati is committed, and any action that obstructs the widow from preventing her death or the police from discharging their duties to prevent the immolation. The burden of proof of innocence is placed upon the accused, who is not presumed innocent until proven guilty. The glorification of sati is also an offence under this Act, punishable with 1–7 years of imprisonment and a fine of Rs 5,000–30,000.[10]

At that time, some activists and groups vehemently opposed new legislation specifically addressing sati, arguing that it is already punishable under Section 302 (murder) and Section 306 (abetment of suicide) of the Indian Penal Code (IPC). They felt that a new law specific to sati was redundant, that it was critical not to distinguish between sati and murder, and that a separate law would somehow legitimize sati as a phenomenon differing from murder and give it 'a measure of respectability'.[11] Others insisted that a separate anti-sati law was necessary, particularly because the existing law did not address the glorification of sati, which was a critical aspect if the practice was to be brought to an end. Kavita Srivastava, general secretary of the People's Union for Civil Liberties (PUCL) in Rajasthan and its secretary at the national level, was active in the agitation following Roop Kanwar's death. Speaking about the Act, she said:

[A separate law] was necessary. The IPC is not sufficient to prosecute the glorification of sati. We needed a more specific law; a mechanism, to bring to centre stage, to clinch all these practices of eulogizing sati. We needed a mechanism that was directly addressing this form of violence against women... we needed an Act at that point.

While the legislation is problematic, particularly in its attempt to criminalize a woman who survives immolation,[12] it has served as a preventive tool in Rajasthan. Since it was passed in 1987, there has not been a single successful case of immolation in the state. No temple has been built in Deorala to date to deify Roop Kanwar. The melas organized at the Rani Sati Mandir in Jhunjhunu have decreased in frequency and are unable to lure as many people as they hitherto did. Srivastava notes that the proportion of people participating in these glorification activities has significantly decreased and that this is, at least in part, due to the Act. She, however, also attributes this to public interest litigation, specifically against the Jhunjhunu temple, and partly to PUCL's strong links with community members who serve as informants about glorification activities. The temple organizers have been warned in no uncertain terms 'that someone is watching them and that they therefore have to be accountable to the law'.

On the other hand, there have been no convictions under the new legislation in relation to Roop Kanwar's immolation. The six individuals accused of being responsible for her death (including her father-in-law), were arrested and charges of murder and abetment of suicide, levied against them under the Indian Penal Code. In total, 35 individuals – including 3 minors whose cases were handled by the juvenile court – were eventually brought to trial in connection with her death.[13] All the accused pleaded not guilty and charges against them were dropped due to 'lack of evidence'. The trial dragged on for over nine years and the judgment, delivered on 11 October 1996, concluded that it had not been proved that Roop Kanwar was 'forced' to burn on the funeral pyre of her husband; there were not enough witnesses to substantiate that it was either murder or abetment to suicide. The appeal against this acquittal in the Rajasthan High Court is currently pending.[14]

Notwithstanding the lacunae in the implementation of the law, it remains critical to have a specific law against sati, if only because law serves as a 'moral reminder' about what is acceptable and not acceptable. Sati was previously seen as a social practice, not as a crime. As Kumkum Sangari asserts:

Law provides a symbolic horizon about what is right and what is wrong. In the abstract, it does provide for something. We know that the law does not get implemented but it is important to have, nonetheless. The symbolic horizon does have a meaning.[15]

Several activists also challenge the logic that because a law is not optimally implemented, lack of a law is better than having a law. Dr Renuka Pamecha is a professor of political science, member of the Rajasthan University Women's Association, and one of the six individuals who filed a public interest writ following Roop Kanwar's death. She says:

The law, plus the movement... these both go simultaneously. They give strength to each other – the law gives the movement strength and the movement gives the law strength... Just because the government machinery is not responding in the proper way, that does not mean that the law is not necessary. Without law, how can we pressurize the government to implement it? Every law – on a particular situation – is necessary to change the specific cultural ethos of each of those practices. You have to analyse these crimes in their particulars... laws can address this. Every ethos demands a separate law and the proper implementation of that law.

Law also provides legitimacy to the police while responding to what communities see as 'traditional, social, religious, or cultural practices'. In some cases of attempted and successful immolations, the police have faced resistance and, in a few instances, physical violence from members of the community and other spectators. The Women and Media Committee, a fact-finding team of the Bombay Union of Journalists found that police officers themselves have trouble conceptualizing sati as a crime, given the overriding ideology and culture of sati in these regions:

While top police officials have almost all been unanimous in declaring that the offenders in the sati incident would be severely dealt with and punished for murder, they all viewed the continuing practice of sati in a different light: Not all of them considered it a crime as such, but rather the result of a distorted, 'conservative' attitude.[16]

The police officers also feel that not having a specific law to prevent sati has hampered them considerably. 'We are the law enforcing agencies but what can we do if there is no law?' they complain.[17]

Says Gurpreet Deo, deputy secretary of the National Commission for Women and IPS:

If it were not for a specific law, sati would be treated, at the police level, as a regular crime. No special status would be given to it... If there is a special Act dealing with sati, there is no doubt or confusion – the officer is morally obligated to enforce the law. The officer is compelled to act when the law is enacted. Otherwise, the police may not see that sati is murder and the case will be registered as a suicide instead. With the Sati Act, then there is no confusion. It is better to have an Act. When you enact it, you recognize that there is a problem, and you define the problem and declare it as a crime. It assumes, then, a different meaning... The Act [legislation] connects the act [of sati] to the crime. There is no room for interpretation.

Glorifying Sati

Compared to other forms of violence against women, the prevalence and incidence of widow immolation are actually quite rare. However, the impact that one incident of sati has on strengthening the underlying ideology is tremendous, given the glorification that follows an actual event of widow immolation. States Sangari:

Widow immolation is one of the few crimes where ideology is more pernicious and widespread than the actual act of violence. Just one case of widow immolation strengthens the ideology a million times over, where one case of domestic violence does not have that impact. Widow immolation is coded as tradition; symbolically, it is a deeply significant event. There is a large overriding ideology into which it can be fitted. Ideological propagation is really what glorification is.[18]

She writes with co-author Sudesh Vaid: 'Not only is it impossible... to separate the concept from the practice by intellectual fiat, it is the practice which gives substance and social legitimacy to the concept.'[19]

The Commission of Sati Prevention Act (Central) defines the glorification of sati as:

the observance of any ceremony or the taking out of a procession in connection with the commission of sati; the supporting, justifying or propagating the practice of sati in any manner; or the arranging of any function to eulogize the person who has committed sati, or the creation of a trust, or the collection of funds, or the construction of temple or other structure, or the carrying on of any form of worship or the performance of any ceremony thereat, with a view to perpetuate the honour of, or to preserve the memory of, a person who has committed sati.[20]

Despite this Act, 11 individuals charged with the glorification of sati following Roop Kanwar's death were acquitted in

January 2004 in the Special Court on Sati Prevention in Jaipur. This judgment came soon after the Bharatiya Janata Party (BJP) came into power in Rajasthan. The acquitted include the current vice-president of the Rajasthan BJP and former president of the Bharatiya Janata Yuva Morcha (the youth wing of the BJP). The Rajasthan government refused to file a High Court appeal against this acquittal. Four PILs have been filed since.

In Rajasthan in 2005 alone (between March and June), there have been four incidents of glorification. One involves the publication of a tourist brochure by the state government, entitled *Rajasthan Ke Lok Devi Devta*, which encourages tourists to visit certain sati temples. Women's groups see this as an act of glorification that violates the anti-sati law. In June 2005, the Rajasthan state PUCL filed a criminal complaint in the sati prevention court after the local police station refused to lodge an FIR against the state government and the brochure's author. The government withdrew the brochure and ordered seizure of all the copies in stock.

While most women's rights groups supported this action, two individuals I spoke to expressed the following sentiments:

Regarding the recent move to ban the government tourism book with reference to sati... can there be any denial that sati has been a part of our history? Yes, there is mention of sati glorification in this book... but if there is already a temple or memorial stones (*chabutaras*)... can you damage them? What we need to do... we need to tell people that they need different ways of solving their problems, different solutions to their problems, other than worship of sati shrines. In the same way that we tell women how to access health centres and how to fight for access to doctors.

Changing or deleting four lines from a book is very simple. But how do you delete this [event and ideology] from people's memories? It has been inculcated into our minds. In fact, when you do that – when you focus on this book – the belief in sati becomes more strong, more vehement. It reignites these feelings in people.

Charan Shah: Fact-finding Missions, the Definition of Sati, and the Concept of Volition

Since the 1980s, fact-finding missions have been a central strategy of women's groups investigating violence against women. Often, the evidence uncovered by these investigations is used to apply pressure on the police and government to further probe and respond to an incident. Such fact-finding missions also indicate to family and community members that these are 'crimes', not 'social practices'. While fact-finding has been considered a viable and consistent strategy, the investigations carried out in response to the 1999 death of Charan Shah gave rise to a number of critical debates and discussions within the women's movement.

On 11 November 1999, in Satpura Village[21] of Mahoba District in Uttar Pradesh, a 55-year-old Dalit woman named Charan Shah was burnt to death on the funeral pyre of her deceased husband, Man Shah, who had suffered from tuberculosis for over 30 years.[22] Various groups travelled to Satpura to investigate this death but returned with conflicting versions of what had transpired. The AIDWA team[23] concluded that none of the family members were involved in encouraging, inciting, or coercing Charan Shah to join her deceased husband on the funeral pyre. Similarly, Madhu Kishwar concluded that Charan Shah voluntarily chose to immolate herself, and criticized those who demanded administrative action against members of her family and community who, according to them, had 'abetted' a 'crime'. The National Commission for Women came to similar conclusions and classified her death as a suicide, rather than as a 'sati'.

All these teams found that there was no prior intent to commit sati, that there was an absence of the rituals typically associated with act, and that Charan Shah was not wearing her bridal finery at the time of the immolation. According to these reports, Man Shah died at 8 a.m. and was cremated one hour later. While the pyre was engulfed by flames, the male members of the family went to bathe at a nearby stream and Charan Shah remained at home in the company of other women mourners. The story goes that she left her house on her own and went to the cremation site. There, she threw herself onto the burning pyre of her deceased husband, but by the time her absence from the house was noticed it was too late to save her from the flames.

A team of investigators from Saheli, Nirantar, Vanangana, and other independent researchers challenged these conclusions, asserting that the 'facts' surrounding her death were not as simple as they seemed. They noted that testimonies from family and community members varied and contradicted one another, that there were differing accounts of the time of Man Shah's death, that there was a lack of any attempt to save Charan Shah from the burning pyre, and a series of glorification activities followed her death. They disagreed with the classification of the death as a suicide just because it was not associated with the rituals normally observed in satis. As Kumkum Sangari and Uma Chakravarti declare, 'variations in the rituals of widow immolation do not make the event a suicide...'[24]

Many activists argued that the mere fact that no one attempted to save her life by pulling her out from the pyre or provided her with medical care constitutes a direct violation of the anti-sati legislation. As Srivastava states in an interview:

Even if it was too late, she could have been declared dead at a hospital. Why did the villagers not do that? The villagers' mindset and the fact that some of them made offerings at the site amount to a violation of the Commission of Sati (Prevention) Act.[25]

Charan Shah's death sparked off intense public discussion in the print and electronic media. One of the biggest issues centred around the definition of sati and women's volition with regard to the act of sati. A small minority of feminists feel it is imperative to discern whether or not there is an explicit element of coercion in any case of widow immolation. These activists distinguish between 'voluntary' sati as a cultural tradition, and 'involuntary' or 'forced' sati as a crime. As Subhashini Ali of AIDWA stated in an interview with the author,

There have been differences of opinion on this issue... it depends on how you define sati. It is not just a suicide post the death of the husband; there has to be an element of coercion... In Charan Shah's case, there was no element of coercion.

These activists do not generally support the separate anti-sati legislation (as it does not differentiate between voluntary and involuntary immolations), nor the prosecution of family, community, and other witnesses if the woman committing sati genuinely chooses to do so on her own. As Madhu Kishwar notes, 'it is absurd to describe a forced immolation as a sati. Such an act of coercion can only be called murder'.[26]

However, most anti-sati activists say that women are not sufficiently empowered to truly commit sati on their own. Says Dipta Bhog of Nirantar in an interview:

Does a woman really have the agency to kill herself? This viewpoint is problematic. If you look at women's position in society, what agency do they really have? The issue is really a matter of life and someone taking that life, rather than someone taking their own life. Because this is a culturally-sanctioned tradition, you cannot look at it in the framework of sacrifice. You must look at the framework of sacrifice and why it is only located within women's experiences. You must look at the larger phenomenon of sati.

Several activists note that the question of whether death by sati is voluntary or not, is both spurious and immaterial. As one group of authors writes:

Even if it is ultimately proved beyond a doubt... that she herself expressed a desire to immolate herself on the funeral pyre of her dead husband and that she went to her death willingly, without the use of force by anyone else, it must be remembered that she was a product of the society in which she grew up and lived... in much of Indian society, the status of women is so low that there is very little question of women exercising their free will in any aspect of their lives.[27]

Force or coercion is often indirect and can take various forms, including being a mere spectator to an event. Sangari and Chakravarti write:

There is no such thing as 'innocent witnessing' of such an event. It is always collusion. Along with the nature of her death, and the subsequent attempts to worship and glorify it, these facts clearly indicate that the incident cannot be relegated to mere 'suicide'. It is our conviction that force is not merely direct physical force, but also collective pressure in other forms.[28]

Also related to this question of volition is the lure and attractiveness for a widow of being deified. While one activist clearly says that sati is a separate issue from that of the status of widows, several individuals draw connections between the two. Mohini Giri, former chairperson of the National Commission for Women and current chairperson of the Guild of Service, said in a conversation that 'Because widowhood is such a miserable life – a living death – sati is an answer.'

Another significant discussion following the death of Charan Shah centred around caste inequality and caste mobility. AIDWA felt that the caste dimension was critical to examining the death, and feminists should be cognizant of the fact that Dalits are treated more brutally by law enforcement. Others felt that even if this immolation did represent an effort by a lower-caste group to enhance their social status through the appropriation of a traditionally upper-caste practice, such an act cannot be condoned. As Bhog says:

Autonomous women's groups felt that even though the police and government do respond more harshly to Dalits, we still have to be firm on this issue. One needs to be sensitive to class issues, but we cannot see this issue only in light of a Dalit issue. It is a women's issue too – you cannot prioritize one [social category] over the other.

In the cases of Kuttu Bai (2002) and Ramkunwari (2005),[29] similar conflicting views on the nature of the event, the classification of the death, and the punitive measures directed against family and community arose. However, one observation that most investigators have noted is the conspiracy of silence surrounding the deaths, certain inconsistencies in the testimony, and the collective reconstruction by the community of the sequence of events leading up to these immolations.

Many of the activists described these as serious challenges to unearthing the 'true facts' and utilizing fact-finding missions as a key strategy. Bhog asserts in an interview that:

What seems to be emerging is a pattern in how the narratives are constructed. When you go on a fact-finding mission, it becomes very difficult to decipher the facts. The story becomes a community narrative... And people start to believe the story also... there are serious limits to how many facts you can unearth in a sati incident. There are two things... first, there is the community construction of the story. Second, there is the overwhelming denial of witnessing the event. There is also the statement that they were unable to help... There is a particular kind of way the community responds to and reports on the event. Nobody was around at the critical moment when they could have saved her...

Community complicity and the reconstruction of a common narrative are, in all probability, rooted in a genuine belief in sati, community pressure and fear of the law. The police did not file a FIR in response to Charan Shah's death, maintaining that there was no evidence that this was a case of sati or abetment to suicide. They concluded that her death was a case of suicide, resulting from the misery she experienced following the death of her husband. In fact, according to some reports, the police have filed a case against the deceased Charan Shah, under Sections 279 and 309 of the IPC, alleging suicide. Reports also indicate that the local administration has made efforts to prevent community members and visitors to the village from glorifying this death as a sati, having imposed Section 144 of the Indian Penal Code and preventing worship at the sati *sthal*.[30]

Kuttu Bai:
The Notion of Collective Community Accountability

On 6 August 2002, a 65-year-old Yadav woman from Patna Tamoli village in MP's Panna district was murdered in the name of sati.[31] Villagers and members of the family claimed she had insisted on immolating herself along with the body of her dead husband; that she had climbed atop the funeral pyre on her own; that no one could have stopped her because she was determined to commit sati; and that the funeral pyre ignited on its own.

A delegation of representatives from Janwadi Mahila Samiti (an AIDWA affiliate), Samta Mahila Samiti, Madhya Pradesh Mahila Manch, and Bharat Gyan Vigyan Samiti concluded that there were definite elements of coercion and provocation in this case. It noted that Kuttu Bai could not have committed sati on her own; that there was a vested interest in land inheritance on the part of her sons; that it was very unlikely that a woman of her age and with her physical constraints could have ascended the funeral pyre on her own; and that no one made any attempt to save her life.[32]

Instead, the community members, who had gathered to actively witness and support the immolation, intentionally obstructed the police. Following news that a sati was about to occur, the local administration dispatched only two police officers to the site. A 1000-strong mob stoned and obstructed the officers from preventing the immolation or saving Kuttu Bai. The National Commission for Women delegation to Patna Tamoli too concluded that it was a case of sati, but that Kuttu Bai had chosen to die in this manner of her own free will. While the NCW delegation classified this death as a 'voluntary' immolation, it maintained that the practice of sati is 'barbaric' and 'despicable'. Notwithstanding this sati's classification as 'voluntary', the NCW blamed the inaction of the district police force, local leaders, and community members for this tragedy.[33]

Following Kuttu Bai's death, 15 people were arrested and a case of murder was registered against her two sons, in spite of the recommendations of several activists that charges should be framed under the anti-sati legislation and special courts be established to try the accused. Although these arrests were made, there have been no convictions to date. Rather, in response to the community's collusion in Kuttu Bai's immolation, the then chief minister Digvijay Singh imposed economic sanctions against the village for two years, stopping financial assistance to the gram panchayat for many schemes.

Pamphlets providing information about the Sati Prevention Act were distributed in the area.

The economic sanctions received widespread support from other local leaders and politicians. Najma Heptullah, then deputy chairperson of the Rajya Sabha, proclaimed that action should be taken against the entire village: its inhabitants had been spectators, who took no action to prevent this woman's death (which they were ethically and morally obligated to do). 'Everyone knows that defenceless women are drugged and made to sit on their husband's funeral pyres,' she says:

No one does it out of free choice. Does anyone ask a man to show his love for his wife by sitting on her funeral pyre? The practice of sati is monstrous. It is a national shame and the government of Madhya Pradesh should take action against the whole village or at least the people who aided and abetted the whole thing.[34]

The withdrawal of development schemes, however, created many problems for the villagers, including a rise in unemployment that forced many to migrate to urban centres for work. Many development projects were suddenly stopped. Activists agreed that the community must acknowledge and be held accountable for its collective responsibility in the death of Kuttu Bai. However, the question was how, if at all, a community should be punished for this. Was it ethical to impose sanctions against an already impoverished and marginalized Dalit community?

According to the newsmagazine Week, the chief minister stated:

Punitive action against the community was necessary to prevent other cases of sati from taking place. He wondered whether the villagers were now sorry for their act. He insisted that his decision did not go against the democratic norms and that he had only tried to make people realize that they had done something ghastly and inhuman.

While many of the activists and scholars interviewed were in support of the economic sanctions levied against Patna Tamoli, others wondered whether such sanctions would have any real impact on the mindset and awareness of its residents.

Given that this death was widely conceptualized as a collective crime, issues relating to the identity of the 'accused' also arose. The interview excerpts reproduced below demonstrate these varying opinions:

I think it [the economic embargo in Patna Tamoli] is a good thing. While we talk about the role of the state, we must also look at the role and responsibility of the community. Communities are responsible for their actions.

Subhashini Ali, AIDWA

We didn't think this was right... but we are also not sure what else could have been done.

Shalini Joshi, Nirantar

I was happy... because I felt that maybe the panchayat representatives would feel a little accountable. In villages, there is a belief that sati is real and maybe this economic measure makes them question the incident and see it as an act of violence against women. How do you put pressure on people who form the governance of a village?... In collective crimes, who do you fix the blame on? Do you blame the spectators? The family? I think that is the challenge, which is something women's groups have really struggled with. Who should the FIR be filed against? That was a big question.

Dipta Bhog, Nirantar

I have always felt that we need laws that deal with collective violence, which is what widow immolation is. It is good to have a sense of accountability, a feeling that you can stop these things from happening... that there should be a way to stop them... yes, there have to be forms of punishment that take collective violence into account.

Kumkum Sangari

Several people note that sanctions against community complicity and collusion is an essential strategy to address this form of violence against women. They stress the importance of working within indigenous/traditional belief systems and facilitating people's understanding of widow immolation as immoral. This understanding serves as a prerequisite to accountability and punishment. As Sangari affirmed in a conversation:

One cannot do that [breakdown community complicity] without a prior belief in the fact that there is something fundamentally wrong in immolating a woman. We have to first ask: How can the community first see this as a form of violence against women? The community must do that first, before having the capacity to take responsibility.

Ramkunwari:
Working To Change Community Belief Systems

When 75-year-old Ramkunwari of Bahundari village[35] in UP's Banda district burnt to death along with her deceased 80-year-old husband on 7 May 2005, members of Vanangana, a women's rights organization in that area, began talking to the community. Based on the information they gathered, Vanangana submitted a memorandum to the police and an FIR was filed in the organization's name. Although the organization's goal was to secure justice, this action resulted in community anger against Vanangana. A chowkidar who had implicated the family in Ramkunwari's immolation while speaking to Vanangana workers changed his statement when speaking to the police. He accused the organization of forcing him to give the statement.

Reflecting on their handling of the situation, Maheshwari and Pushpa, both activists of Vanangana, note that:

As a strategy – going into the village and getting information from the community itself – actually backfired on us. We should not have used the organization's name and put the organization's reputation at risk. Now, when we go back, the community is obviously upset with us. We actually should have pressurized the police to do their own investigation.[36]

However, pressurizing the police is challenging as a strategy for other reasons. Police representatives and the district magistrate labelled Ramkunwari's death a case of suicide. The district magistrate proclaimed that the media was responsible for sensationalizing the event by labelling it as a 'sati', even though two fact-finding missions[37] had uncovered elements of coercion and pressure. At the time of these

fact-finding missions, no record or report of her death even
existed. According to media reports, the police were aware of
the incident but did not report it.[38] Gurpreet Deo, one of the
members of a National Commission for Women investigation
into the incident, affirms:

The police actually had a good case to prosecute the family for the
destruction of evidence in a murder or sati case. In the Banda case,
one got the impression that they knew what was going on... they
[the police] could've easily prevented Ramkunwari's death, but they
don't want any backlash or anger from the community.

As part of its mandate to challenge caste and gender
violence and uphold human rights, Vanangana has
investigated numerous cases of sati, and has recently begun
collecting accounts of immolations in five villages in the
region. The organization recruits staff from the villages in the
Bundelkhand region, rather than employing outside activists
unfamiliar with local customs and cultural norms. While
other groups feel it is necessary to directly challenge belief
systems, Vanangana works along with community belief
systems, focuses on building rapport and relationships, and
endeavours to locate and support voices of resistance from
within the community; its activists believe that they cannot
impose their own agendas or beliefs upon the community,
even if they disagree with them.

As Pushpa from Vanangana explained in a conversation:

On any issue – whether sati or another – what we have to assess, as
an organization, is whether the issue is the organization's issue or is
it something that has community support. We also have to ask, how
much support community people are giving to the organization to
work on this issue with them. If we want to work with the people on
an issue, there has to be agreement between the people's voice and
the organization's perspective, especially if we are to do community-
level work. If there is anything wrong that happens in the village,
the organization can definitely raise the issue and give their opinion,
say that this is wrong – but unless the community also feels the same
way, it is not really possible to work with them. The organization
works for the people, so until the people are with you, our objective
of working for the people does not hold true.

Sharada Jain, an activist, scholar and teacher based in Jaipur, was one of the first feminists to publicly respond to the death of Roop Kanwar. She notes that working within community belief systems is a good strategy to challenge them. She explains that it is possible to challenge people's beliefs in certain events by utilizing their own notions about those events. For example, she lists questions that should be asked of those who believed that Roop Kanwar attained sati,[39] voluntarily chose to perish with her husband, and did not suffer any pain in the process:

If this was a 'genuine sati,' there should have been lotus petals at her feet. Why was she crying? How could anyone hear her screams for help if the drums were beating so loudly? If she could self-start the fire, then why was lighting the fire so difficult? The fire was going out and her brother-in-law had to light it.

Madhu Sethia (formerly of AIDWA) of Canodia College in Jaipur provides a striking example of how the police handled a case of attempted sati. Rather than the police telling the woman and the others who had gathered to watch her burn on the pyre of her dead husband in no uncertain terms that this practice was wrong, illegal, inhumane, and a violation of human rights and the law, the police officer shrewdly allowed her to proceed but forbade anyone to aid in the lighting of the pyre. 'If this is true, then she will ignite on her own,' he told them. The woman's attempt was unsuccessful and her death was prevented without angering or antagonizing the local people. Sometimes, says Sethia, directly attacking practices and belief systems only leads people to defend them more vehemently.

Challenges in Working against Widow Immolation

Many of the women involved in the Roop Kanwar agitation still recall how the pro-sati lobby defamed and smeared women's organizations and individual activists. Once the issue was catapulted into the public sphere, the debate was polarized into one of tradition versus modernity. Feminists were labelled 'city women' with loose morals: women who smoke, drink, frequent clubs, and are sexually promiscuous. They were labelled as women without any religious beliefs and the slogan '*baal kati* (women with short bob hair-cuts), *bazu kati* (women who wear sleeveless garments), *bhauhein kati* (women who shape their eyebrows)' was used repeatedly against them. Some women received death threats, hate mail, and were physically threatened. Laxmi Kumari Chundawat, a writer, former member of the legislative assembly of Rajasthan, and one of the few Rajput women to publicly condemn the immolation of Roop Kanwar, faced a huge backlash from the Rajput community. Her home was broken into, property destroyed, and innumerable verbal abuses were directed against her.

Activists from Nirantar and Vanangana describe community anger against the ban on the sati-glorification activities and the investigation of cases by 'outsiders'. Members of Bahundari village were angered by police patrolling of the half-built *chabutara* and the prohibition of worship at the site. Other identified challenges include the economic and material incentives to keep this practice alive[40] (the immense revenue generated by sati temples, *melas* (fairs), other sati-glorification activities) and the use of 'right to religion' and 'cultural survival' arguments in favour of sati. These arguments were used predominantly in Rajasthan where the issue of sati became entangled with religious fundamentalism, and where women's bodies have always been used as symbols of cultural and communal identities.

Several activists describe this challenge:

There are some who talk about this in terms of cultural norms. And that is very dangerous because we don't want the discussion to take place along those lines. We want crimes against women to be classified and viewed in that way. Crimes against women have always been justified along these lines and there is no end to this way of reducing crime to this level of cultural norms.

Subhashini Ali, AIDWA

The freedom of religion does not give anyone the right to commit other crimes against humanity. Something that is immoral cannot be permitted under the argument of religious rights.

Ajay Jain, Lawyer, PUCL, Rajasthan

I think this culture argument is an extremely selective one. People's right to culture has to be viewed within the constitutional framework... Culturally, women are unequal in all religions. Should we accept that? If so, then we cannot accept Article 14 – the right to equality. The cultural argument has to be within the constitutional framework. Practices that deny the right to life, to existence – like sati – have to be annihilated...

I am not saying that we need to be looking through a modern eye, but since we are living in a modern state, we've got to have certain parameters of justice and equality. And if there are certain cultural practices that come in the way [of maintaining these parameters], then we have to question them. We cannot blindly be pro-society... people do have the right to determine their own existence, but within a framework of natural justice. It's not that when we are challenging one practice or value – such as the submergence of the identity of a woman with her husband – we are not substituting this with another practice that is also violating.

Kavita Srivastava, PUCL, Rajasthan

We attempted to draw the issue away from Rajput identity towards the issue of women's identity, security, and respect. We wanted to treat it as a 'women's issue'. In fact, the slogan developed and used during the anti-sati public demonstrations frames the issue in this manner. The slogan 'Sawaal hai mahila ki pahchan ka' (It is a question of women's identity) and 'Sawaal hai mahila ke samman ka' (It is a question of women's dignity) helped to galvanize the various groups involved in the movement, as it was something with which everyone identified.

Madhu Sethia and Nirja Misra

Other challenges include the use of this practice for caste mobility by lower-caste groups to increase their social status, the question of justice and punishment (who is to be punished in the case of widow immolation, and how?), and the problematic clauses within the 1987 anti-sati legislation. Madhu Sethia describes in detail the challenge of trying to organize and catalyze resistance from among the 'community', ordinary people:

Sati is a very remote problem for these women, in comparison to their immediate concerns. They will organize very quickly about the immediate concerns of their families and communities. They are already at the bottom of the social structure. Why should they protest the burning of one woman in Deorala?

Conclusion

While incidents of widow immolation continue to occur in parts of north India, the glorification of sati is widespread in regions even where incidents have ceased. The prevention of glorification is an area that requires further work, as it is related to ideology and is deeply embedded in belief systems about what constitutes tradition, communal identity, cultural and religious practice. Work in this area is particularly critical, given the difficulties inherent in bringing about actual change in beliefs. Any strategy utilized to eradicate this gruesome form of gender-based violence must also take into account the larger socio-structural factors that not only give rise to, but propagate and sustain, such cruelty.

Several people have advocated a multi-issue political front and declared that in order to eliminate the practice and glorification of sati, other forms of oppression and violence against various categories of people must also be addressed. As Karat affirms,

it would be completely utterly wrong to have a women's movement that limits the issue to women's and men's position in society. In terms of sati, it is a widow's position and a women's issue, but at the same time, it has been used for political mobilization and is part of an ongoing process of obliterating more progressive traditions. Women's status is not just linked to a male-female issue, but to religion to a great extent. There is a wider context in which this issue should be rooted. One-issue movements may be important to focus on sometimes, but you cannot fight sati without fighting caste discrimination or the appropriation of tradition.

Others have suggested the implementation of permanent programmes on gender inequality, violence against women, and the criminalization of sati in educational institutions. There are also those who feel that larger social structural factors – such as education of girls, integrated socialization of girls and boys, economic independence of women, and the status of widows in Indian society – must first be addressed before other interventions can be meaningful or effective. Regardless of the strategy, it is evident that all forms of violence and oppression based on social categories and constructs are inter-related, and that widow immolation cannot be tackled in isolation.

Notes

1. Deorala is an approximately two hour drive north of Jaipur and falls within Sikar district, one of the three districts comprising the Shekhawati region. The majority of widow immolations that have occurred in Rajasthan in post-Independence India have occurred in that region. In the early twentieth century, instances of sati continued to be recorded there while the practice was gradually diminishing elsewhere in Rajasthan, and during the four decades preceding Roop Kanwar's death, Shekhawati demonstrated an alarming increase in the incidence of sati.

2. Several investigative reports and newspaper articles, including 'Trial by Fire' 1987 by the Bombay Union of Journalists, 'The Burning of Roop Kanwar' (1987) by Madhu Kishwar and Ruth Vanita, and the many articles published in the February 1988 issue of *Seminar* magazine, attest to the fact that strong elements of coercion marked this incident, that Roop Kanwar attempted to escape her premature death and was forced against her will onto the funeral pyre of her dead husband, that hundreds of people actively took part in preparing for her death, that none of the witnesses to this event did anything to prevent this death, and that someone other than Roop Kanwar lit the funeral pyre.

3. The term 'sati' refers to the immolation of a widow on the funeral pyre of her deceased husband. This term is commonly used today to describe both the act and the individual woman who commits this act. In the English language, the most widespread definition is sati as an act, while in Hindi (and other Indian languages) the most frequest use of the term is sati as a person (the woman). According to the original Sanskrit root of this term, it refers to a virtuous, loyal and chaste woman: 'any woman who confines to her husband all thoughts about men, save those that relate to her father' (Hawley, 1994). Some

contemporary scholars and authors only used the term 'sati' to describe the *voluntary* self-immolation of a widow. For the purposes of this chapter, 'sati' is used to describe both the rite and the individual woman who is immolated, whether it was a 'voluntary' or an 'involuntary' act.

4. 'Sati *mata*'(sati mother) refers to the goddess a woman becomes when she commits sati, and is deified. This term is used to refer to 'real' or 'genuine' sati, and those who worship them in 'deified' form believe that they had immolated themselves on their husband's funeral pyres in a past historical time (not mythic time). They are considered to be a 'superhuman form of ancestor' with the power to protect later generations (Hawley, 1994).

5. Om Kanwar's death in 1980 was reported on by two researchers, Kumkum Sangari and Sudesh Vaid, in the *Economic and Political Weekly*.

6. The Women's Development Programme (WDP) was largely funded by UNICEF and launched in six districts of Rajasthan in 1984. The aim of the WDP was to improve the status of and empower women (particularly from disenfranchised sections of society) through the facilitation of their leadership and participation in the planning and implementation of strategies to address their social, health, and development needs and concerns.

7. The *chunari mahotsav* ceremony occurs on the thirteenth day following the 'sati', during which a red veil is placed on a trident at the site of the cremation.

8. The Bundelkhand region is situated along the border between the states of UP and MP. A very well-known incident of sati, that of 17-year old Javitri Devi of Jaari village in Banda district 25 years ago, resulted in the construction of a large temple in 1979. This temple, and the tale of sati it commemorates, continues to draw visitors bringing offerings, offering puja, and receiving blessings.

9. Attempts to commit sati are punishable with imprisonment of one to five years; abetment of sati is punishable with death or imprisonment for life. Fines can be levied for both offences. This ordinance also vests in the collector and district magistrate the power and authority to prohibit certain acts deemed to be related to the practice and glorification of sati.

10. One of the most significant features of the central Act is provision for the creation, structure, powers, and functions of Special Courts for the trial of sati-related offences.
11. *See* Kishwar, 1994.
12. Madhu Kishwar and Ashis Nandy have referred to the law as a 'draconian' one, which has resulted in greater problems than benefits (Kishwar, 1995 and 1999; Nandy, 1994).
13. A total of 37 individuals were actually accused in this murder case, but two died during the intervening years before the judgment was passed.
14. *See* Narasimhan, 1998; Srivastava, 2004.
15. *See* Sangari and Vaid, *Economic and Political Weekly*.
16. *See* Bombay Union of Journalists, 1987.
17. Ibid.
18. Sangari and Vaid, op cit.
19. *See The Economic and Political Weekly*, 1991.
20. *See* Venkatesan, 1999; http://wcd.nic.in/commissionofsatipre vention.htm.
21. Satpura can also be spelt 'Satpurva'. It is a small village with a population of not more than 200, comprising largely Dalit families. It is located 180 kilometres from Kanpur.
22. *See* Jaishree
23. Headed by Subhashini Ali.
24. *See* Sangari and Chakravarti, 1999.
25. *See* Venkatesan, 1999.
26. *See* Kishwar, 2000.
27. *See* Bombay Union of Journalists, 1987.
28. *See* Sangari and Chakravarti, 1999.
29. Refer to the following sections for further details of these cases.
30. *See* Damodaran, 1999. 'Sati *sthal*' refers to the site of the immolation, where worship occurs following the incident.
31. *See* CPI-M, 2002.
32. Ibid.
33. *See* National Commission for Women, 2002.
34. *See Times of India* editorial, 7 Aug. 2002.
35. Bahundari village is located 45 km from Banda (city) and has a mixed population of Yadavs, Brahmins, Dalits, and Sahus, comprising 60 families.
36. According to community and family members, Ramkunwari's husband was cremated in the early evening. Following this,

Ramkunwari went to bathe at a village handpump. She informed other female family members that no one should touch her and she was subsequently left alone. A few hours later, her family discovered she was missing, rushed to the funeral pyre, and found that she had immolated herself; thirteen days after this immolation, a newly-raised platform (*chabutara*) had been built and worship was taking place at the site.

37. A National Commission for Women mission and another comprising representatives of Vanangana, Nirantar, and *Khabar Lahariya* (a rural women-run newspaper) came to similar conclusions: there appear to have been elements of coercion and pressure. It is unlikely that Ramkunwari could have immolated herself, given her old age and physical incapacity; it is unlikely that a grieving widow's absence would have gone unnoticed for several hours (as claimed); people in the village denied witnessing the event; and there was collusion on the part of the police as no arrests were made and the incident was not, in fact, reported.

38. A petition by Vanangana, Nirantar, and *Khabar Lahariya* was sent to the district magistrate and the chief minister of UP. It demanded that: there be a formal inquiry and investigation into the death of Ramkunwari; those involved in this death be penalized under the 1987 Act; the half-built *chabutara* erected to deify Ramkunwari be demolished; all sati *melas* in the region be stopped; educational material on the illegality and inhumanness of this practice be incorporated into the school curricula; and efforts be undertaken by the local administration to educate and raise awareness among the general public about the Commission of Sati Prevention Act.

39. '*Sat*' refers to the supernatural power attained by a woman before she commits the act of sati. A woman who has attained *sat* is believed to possess supernatural powers, including the ability to bless spectators or to curse anyone attempting to prevent her from committing sati.

40. While there are no standardized estimates on the amount of revenue generated by one sati temple or *chabutara*, there is no doubt that the practice of sati results in immense material enrichment of the local community. Roop Kanwar's death generated over a crore rupees in donations alone, and a temple was not even built in her commemoration (Natarajan, 1999).

References

Ali, Subhashini (1999): 'Outlawing Inhuman Practices – I', *The Hindu*, 27 December.

—— (1999): 'Outlawing Inhuman Practices – II', *The Hindu*, 28 December.

Communist Party of India (Marxist) (CPI-M) (2002): 'Strangehold of Obscurantism', *People's Democracy*, vol. 26: 37, 22 September 2002. http://pd.cpim. org/2002/sept22/09152002_mp_sati.htm

Damodaran, P. M. (1999): 'Burning Questions', *Deccan Herald*, 21 November, 1. http://www.hsph.harvard.edu/Organizations/healthnet/SAsia/forums/sati/ articles/burning.html

Das, Veena (1988): 'Strange Response', *Illustrated Weekly*, 28 February, 30–32.

Hawley, John Stratton (ed.) (1994): *Sati, the Blessing and the Curse: The Burning of Wives in India*. New York: Oxford University Press.

Jaishree, Vijaya et al. (Saheli), 'Charan Shah's Immolation: Countering Earlier Reports', *Manushi*: 115. http://www.indiatogether.org/manushi/issue115/nirantar.htm

Kishwar, Madhu (1994): 'A Code for Self: Some Thoughts on 'Activism', Manushi, 85: 5–9.

—— (1995): 'Murder versus Sati', *Hindu*, 1 December.

—— (1999): 'Sati Prevention Act is Draconian, Anti-people', *Times of India*, 1 December.

—— (2000): 'To Those on a New Civilizing Mission', *Hindu*, 3 February.

Kumar, Radha (1995): 'From Chipko to Sati: The Contemporary Indian Women's Movement', in Amrita Basu (ed.) *The Challenge of Local Feminisms: Women's Movements in Global Perspective*. Boulder: Westview Press, 58–86.

—— (1993): 'The Agitation Against Sati, 1987–88', in *The History of Doing: An Illustrated Account of Movements for Women's Rights and Feminism in India 1800–1990*, New Delhi: Kali for Women, 172–81.

Mani, Lata (1989): *Contentious Traditions. The Debate on Sati in Colonial India*, in Kumkum Sangari and Sudesh Vaid (eds.), *Recasting Women: Essays in Colonial History*. New Delhi: Kali for Women, 88–126.

Mishra, Subhash (1999): 'Medieval Madness', *India Today*, 29 November, 31–33.

Nandy, Ashis (1994): 'Sati as Profit Versus Sati as Spectacle: The
    Public Debate on Roop Kanwar's Death', in John Stratton
    Hawley (ed.), *Sati, the Blessing and the Curse: The Burning of Wives
    in India*. New York: Oxford University Press, 131–49.
Narasimhan, Sakuntala (1998): *Sati: A Study of Widow Burning in
    India*. New Delhi: Harper Collins Publishers India.
Natarajan, Jayanthi (1999): 'Sati versus Murder', *Hindu*, 3
    December.
——— (2000): 'Any Kind of Legitimacy to Sati is Dangerous', *Hindu*,
    4 February.
Natarajan, Jayanthi and Ruth Vanita (1990): 'The Burning of Roop
    Kanwar', in Veena Poonacha (ed.), *Understanding Violence*.
    Bombay: Research Centre for Women's Studies (RCWS),
    SNDT Juhu, 42–48.
National Commission for Women (2002): *Report of the Inquiry
    Committee on Sati Incident at Patna Tamoli Village of Panna District
    in Madhya Pradesh*. http://ncw.nic.in/satimp4.htm
Oldenburg, Veena Talwar (1994): 'The Roop Kanwar Case: Feminist
    Responses', in John Stratton Hawley (ed.), *Sati, the Blessing
    and the Curse: The Burning of Wives in India*. New York: Oxford
    University Press, 101–30.
Pachauri, Pankaj (1987): 'Landmark Judgement: Anti-sati Law
    Extended to all Temples', *India Today*, 31 December.
Rajasthan Sati (Prevention) Act, 1987 (No. 40 of 1987), 26 November
    1987, *Annu Rev Popul Law*, 14: 477–82.
Sangari, Kumkum (1993): 'Consent, Agency and Rhetorics of
    Incitement', *Economic and Political Weekly*, 28 (8): 867–83.
Sangari, Kumkum and Uma Chakravarti (eds.) (1999): *From Myths to
    Markets: Essays on Gender*. Shimla and New Delhi: Indian Institute
    of Advanced Study and Manohar Publishers, 341–67; 360.
Sangari, Kumkum and Sudesh Vaid (1994): 'Sati in Modern India:
    A Report', in Kumkum Sangari and Sudesh Vaid (ed.), *Women
    and Culture*. Bombay: Research Centre for Women's Studies,
    SNDT Juhu, 165–81.
Sen, Mala (2001): *Death by Fire: Sati, Dowry Death, and Female
    Infanticide in Modern India*. London: Weidenfeld & Nicolson.
Shukla, Rakesh (2004): 'Sati Glorification: Crime, Society and the
    Wheels of Injustice', InfoChange News and Features, March.
Srivastava, Kavita (2004): 'Burning Down the Law', *Hindustan*.
Tewatia, D.S., Syeda Hameed, Vijay Daksh, and A.S. Bhasin
    (1999): 'Press Reports Twisted Facts Distorting Reality: NCW

Inquiry Team on the Incident of "Sati" in U.P.', *Mainstream*, 27 November.

Times of India (2002): 'A Crime Called Sati (editorial)', 7 August.

Upreti, H.C., and Nandini Upreti (1991): *The Myth of Sati*, Mumbai: Himalaya.

Vaid, Sudesh, and Kumkum Sangari (1991): 'Institutions, Beliefs, Ideologies: Widow Immolation in Contemporary Rajasthan', *Economic and Political Weekly*, 27 April: WS2–18.

Venkatesan V. (1999): 'The Law, and the Facts', *Frontline*, 16: 25, 27 November–10 December.

Venkatesan V., and Venkitesh Ramakrishnan (1999): 'An Act of Desperation', *Frontline*, 16: 25, 27 November–10 December.

Women and Media Committee (1987): 'Trial by Fire: A Report on Roop Kanwar's Death'. Bombay: Bombay Union of Journalists.

7

Anatomy of a Suicide[1]

Maya Ganesh

There are ways of talking about how women experience violence, there are ways women talk about the violence they experience. This is an attempt to do a little of both. I began my career in a feminist 'violence intervention centre' in New Delhi where I heard different truths and voices on violence; personal interactions can give you details but case studies and research reports can create unidimensional martyrs. From where had she got the recipe for the meal she cooked that was hurled against the wall? What was she planning for her mother's birthday the night before her parents locked her out of the house? Which conference was she going to when she began receiving pornographic emails from her co-workers? I often think that women are creatures of detail, enjoying and revelling in the back stories, the tangents, outtakes, asides, digressions. This is also what life is about, and how we tell our stories. Details create whole women.

I realized that I had become desensitized to the point of blandness; 'violence against women' had become a litany of who did what to whom, which sections of the Indian Penal Code were relevant, and how we were going to 'move' this person from personal guilt and shame to personal instrumentality. This story is a tribute to detail, to everydayness, to the varied perspectives and contexts in which violence occurs, to the curious, beautiful twists and turns that bring people to fall in love. This is a story of the violence that two young women in Idukki, Kerala experienced; the story of their love. It is about families and community, gender and sex, fear and ignorance, caste and prejudice, honour, shame and control; all common ingredients in innumerable stories of 'love failure' and its aftermath. There are a multitude of subjectivities and voices here, not just of mothers, fathers, friends, relatives, and community, but also those of the interviewers, transcribers, translators, and of this author. The most obvious in their absence are those of the protagonists Sunita and Anu.[2]

I

The newspaper: *Thodupuzha,* 26 August 2001: A girl and a woman who wished to live together poisoned themselves when they found themselves unable to do so. The dead are Anu (15), daughter of Mulluvelil Kovalan, Moolamattom, Thodupuzha, and Sunita (22), daughter of the demised Mulluvelil Kolumpan. Anu was a tenth standard student at Government High School, Moolamattom, and Sunita had studied to the fourth standard. They were relatives and neighbours, and together poisoned themselves around six o'clock on Friday evening on the bank of the river near Sunita's house. Seeing them vomiting, a neighbour informed the families but by that time they had vanished into the bushes. A search revealed them dead embracing each other on the riverbank near the jungle.

It is said that Sunita behaved like a man right from childhood. She favoured male attire and expressions, would wear dhotis, and kept her hair cut short. They had been in love for two years and had requested their parents to allow them to live as man and wife. The families were strongly opposed to this and filed a complaint at the police station to separate them. They were brought to the police station and were advised on this, but finding that this had no impact, it was suggested that the parents seek the help of a psychologist. The parents took them to a hospital where they were made to stay and be counselled for four days. When they returned they did not abandon the idea of living together, but the families wouldn't comply. They therefore decided to commit suicide. Kanjar police have undertaken the necessary proceedings. The dead bodies have been taken to the *taluka* (block-level) hospital, Thodupuzha, for the post-mortem. Police have recovered the bottle of poison.[3]

The policeman: The entire incident is very unnatural. Sunita dressed like a boy which is not usual for a girl. That's why this relationship is unnatural. However, the bond between the two girls was very strong. Both of them emphatically said they did not want to be separated, but their affliction is not curable. For one thing, they are from a tribal community and the parents are fundamentally opposed to girls living together as husband and wife. Even the educated in society won't be able to accept it, then how can they?

Such a thing has never been heard of in the tribal community. It may exist everywhere else in the world but it is not natural. It is like swimming against the tide. If it was a man and a woman it would have been natural because it is essential for the next generation to come into being. This is not natural; one of the girls was like a man in her attire and in her manner. If it was natural why couldn't they live together as women? Even in their posture at death the girl who was behaving like a male was showing her superior mentality. She was lying on top. This is either their sexual need or a strong friendship. It will wane. Only when there are kids will a relationship be bonded together more closely with love.

Meena (the interviewer): I met Dr Baburajan, the doctor on duty in the *taluka* hospital when the bodies came in. He conducted the autopsy. He pointed out to the police's 'funny' language when referring to the same-sex relationship. He mentioned in his report that death was due to the consumption of a handful of Furidan. An equal amount was found in the bodies of the two girls. Everyone, including him, wondered how they had consumed so much with ease as the pesticide has a very pungent taste and smell.

Death comes painlessly. First the vision blurs and then numbness settles over the body, and then you just drift away. He laughed, saying he was aware of this as he had once had the experience of consuming it. There were some abrasions and scratches on their arms, perhaps because they were lying on the ground. There seemed to have been no force applied to any part of the body. He thought it was crazy that the older of the two girls was wearing a shirt and a lungi (cloth wrap). Personally he didn't think their relationship was unnatural but he did add that medical college courses do not teach anything about this.

The woman on the street: People around said that the children should have been beaten to death rather than cajoled. Of course they never said this to Sunita, but this was the talk amongst themselves; they said that the girls should not have been let loose like this, they should have been killed and thrown into the river. Perhaps they felt that women should not have been behaving in this way.

Sunita's sister Pushpa: Once they had matured they would have changed themselves. After all they were girls. People need not have scolded them like that; need not have said anything about their companionship. Now people are angry with Anu's family, saying, 'Because of you both the children have died.' Now my mother is all alone.

Sunita's cousin Bindhu: Among the things they used to do was tape songs. Sunita had a tape-recorder into which both of them would sing to each other and tape their voices. After all this happened, Sunita's mother came and asked me for the cassette so that she could hear Sunita's voice again.

Sunita's mother Kamala: My child was beaten to death by them. That's how I see it. They should not have frightened the kids so much. They threatened to beat Sunita three or four times. Why is it that my Sunita alone was blamed?

My other daughter Pushpa and her family come here to help with the tapioca preservation. Now with Sunita gone there is so much left to do. Only I am suffering. It's difficult, isn't it ? The most difficult thing is not having anyone to speak to. Now that you are here I have the consolation that I can speak to you. The other children are married and have gone away, so they won't be here to help me all the time. Only my Sunita was there to help me. Now only two cats keep me company.

Pushpa [crying]: Our father died when Sunita was five years old, and since then she has been taking care of our mother. There are three sons-in-law but none of them helped our mother.

Bindhu: Sunita and I used to watch movies together. Actually, a group of us used to go watch movies together. Then some of the women in our group got married, so there was no one with whom to go in a group. During the coffee-picking season Sunita would tell me about the things she would save up to buy with the money she had earned.

Sunita was the youngest of the sisters; the pampered one. Her mother always listened to what she had to say. If Sunita told her mother to stand in one place and not move, her mother would do exactly that. She was quite something. She would sell crops from the field and give her sisters money to buy medicines for their children. Now their mother is alone and the sisters are not very well off. When Sunita was there everything was fine in every way.

Kamala: I have four children: four daughters. Three were married and taken by others. And after that, only I and my other kid were left in the house. I have to go to work from eight o'clock in the morning. I have to buy a kilo of rice, don't I? And don't I need to look after my house? My husband died because he was ill. And from then onwards me and my Sunita were living in this house and taking care of ourselves. Since my kid looked after my house, I was able to go for work. Every task in the house she used to do. And then she used to go to the neighbouring houses and help them. She used to help everybody. Now there is plenty of tapioca left for processing; she used to do the work of four people.

Sunita never quarrelled, but if you fought with her, then she'd fight back. If you talked reason with her, she responded in a like manner, but if someone said to her, 'I will give it to you' – even we won't hold back if somebody comes and says, 'I will give it to you,' will we? Without any reason if somebody comes and says that they want to beat us up, will we allow it? Will we allow anybody to come to our house and fight with us? It was so with Sunita. She never went there and fought with them.

Villasini (associated with the community-based organization Stree Vedi): It is said that Sunita used to do some bad things when she was younger; many tribals are like that: poor living standards, always drinking and making a ruckus. But I think Sunita's family is better. There are however some girls here, as young as 14-15 years, who go with these auto-drivers and jeep-drivers; they give money to the girls and they are exploited... sometimes for as little as a bangle, a dress, a chain. When these girls come back from school in the evening these men are waiting, and the girls go with them. In fact there was a girl from Cherady who came here to act in a blue film while she was still in school. But I think she is married off now. And what I heard is that Sunita made friends with some of these girls, Sunita herself has pointed out these girls to me sometimes.

There was one of these girls who used to call Sunita over the phone at our house and talk to her regularly, but then we began to get afraid and didn't want to land in any trouble because of this. So the next time she called we told her that Sunita was not around. Sunita entered into this relationship after being with those girls. Maybe that's how Sunita developed an interest in all these things. I have also heard that she used to drink. Some people said she was a drunkard but Sajini said that she got drunk only once. She vomited as well and we told her not to drink. I don't know if her mother drinks, but her father died of alcoholism. And her father's brother's wife drinks.

Shaji (a local woman, Villasini's friend): I've known Sunita for six years. She used to do some small chores in our house and run errands for us; things a man would do, like chopping wood, cutting grass for the cows. But mostly she used to come here to watch TV. She used to take care of our children when they were younger. She was like a member of our family and would spend the whole day with us. And since our husbands are business people and would be away, she would come and keep us company at night. And if we had to go somewhere she would look after the house for us.

She was a girl in all her dealings, but she was very strong mentally; a powerful kind of person. She cut her hair short, wore men's clothes, would talk loudly, and whistle. She was a girl but others used to mistake her for a man. But since we knew her intimately we didn't have any such delusions. We never had anything to fear if Sunita was in the house. I think that since she was the youngest in a family of girls they brought her up to be a man. She knew that people used to comment about her dressing and behaving like a man but she didn't have any particular worries about that. But she had this tendency to oppose anything you said to her. If you asked her, 'Sunita do you want your food now?' she'd say, 'No, I don't want anything now.'

Dr Sudarshan (the psychiatrist): When you see the girls' behaviour, they behaved and spoke just like a mature couple. The younger girl was 14 years old and behaved like a mature woman in an old orthodox Hindu family. She spoke in a very controlled way, not like any other adolescent. She wore a *melmundu* (shawl) and was fair. She was like the actress in the movie *Pashi*. Do you know Shobha... the one who committed suicide? She looked exactly like her. Not at all like the photographs in the newspaper. Not an erotic beauty; more homely.

Sasi (Villasini's husband): These are basically lower-class people, quite backward. And the girls from those areas are being exploited sexually. All the school-going girls are used by the auto-drivers. When the girls are on their way to school the men follow them and ask them to come away with them, and in return give them what they want.

These girls were actually addicts; they were addicted to alcohol. Sunita was really an addict. She was going with those taxi-drivers. At that time she formed a relationship with Anu and that's how they became inseparable. Everyone knows this; people have seen it. But it is a shameful thing so parents won't talk about it openly. In fact, Sunita is a girl brought up without a father, and the mother was a drunkard. The mother brought up the girl as a boy as she didn't have any sons. This girl was just like a man: she used to climb trees to pick pepper. Doing all these different men's jobs she could get enough money to do the things she liked in these men's company. That is how she started with Anu as well. There was no intention to marry. They were also *ganja* (marijuana) addicts.

II

Dr Sudarshan: Suicide attempt cases come to the government hospital. Homosexuality is one reason for the suicides, but if there are sexual problems I will never write that in the suicide report. And how many go to the private hospitals? For the young girls from well-to-do families naturally the patients are taken to private hospitals so that outside people do not come to know about it. We hide it in our reports. For this reason the reported rate of suicide is not correct.

The locals: The suicide rate is high in all these communities largely due to economic reasons like increasing debts and land being mortgaged. They are not able to cope. There is also a lot of alcoholism. However, nobody wastes time here: everyone is hard-working, even the tribals. The suicide rate amongst the youth is quite high here. There is poverty, living conditions are poor, and it is difficult to balance expectations with the actual situation in the house. It becomes difficult for elders to meet the expectations and needs of the younger generation, so their relationships become strained. Young people then go off in the wrong direction.

It's the women who commit suicide more frequently because they have very few opportunities to live as they expect to. The rate is much lower in men. There are more suicides in the Adivasi community, the Urali community. The girls of the Urali community are more neglected; when the girls of this community reach the eighth or ninth standard they go in the wrong direction searching for better living conditions. Other people exploit this. I know personally of two or three girls like this. They were promised jobs and then cheated and taken away, and when they return, their lives and futures have been spoiled. Recently there has been a lot of consciousness-raising through the *kudumbashree* (forum of local families). It has had some positive effects.

Damodaran: As a member of the *karayogam* (community leaders' forum), I cannot agree that there is an increase in the suicides of the women in this community. In my whole life this is the first such case I have come across.

III

Bindhu: Sunita used to come to my house for a cup of coffee. From Sunita's house Anu's was not visible. But it was to mine – they were neighbours but it was like 'above' and 'below'. Sunita would come and ask me, 'Can you go call Anu for a few minutes?' Then I would take her to task, saying, 'You go and do your business, I don't have time for all this.' I didn't like it, and if anyone asked me about them I would say that I didn't know anything and not to talk to me about them. I knew about it but I didn't tell anyone. I told them, 'You should not behave like this; aren't you women? If you are a man and a woman you can behave like this, but since you are women you cannot do this.' But they never listened to me. Sunita would say, 'Don't talk to me about all this. I know this.' And she would walk away.

One day she brought me some Malayalam magazines such as *Malayala Manorama* and showed me things written about women living together. She said, 'See, these things happen in the world'. She would keep saying that she would work hard and earn and have a house where just both of them could live.

Kamala: Both of them were seen talking and holding hands together. I never took it seriously. Children usually walk like that, and I thought that these kids too were like that. Anu's

parents, Kovalan and Ammini, were very disturbed by it.
They made a great fuss over it. They used to scold her and tell
her to come straight home after school. Seeing this happen
again and again, Ammini filled her husband with all kinds of
lies, and the husband became enraged.

All these kids were good friends and they used to sleep
together at Velliyotte and also at Thanga's place. Nobody
took it seriously... She's alone here, all her elder sisters are
married off. She just goes off to where there is other children's
company. She can't sit here all the time on her own.

Shaji: She told us that her relationship with Anu was that of a
very close friend but others misunderstood this. Others were
sure that the relationship between Sunita and Anu was that
of a boy and a girl. She wanted to see Anu and talk to her
constantly. They used to meet and talk every day. It's also said
that Anu loved Sunita very much.

After people started talking about it, when Sunita came to
my house, I asked her, 'What is this, Sunita? Is it true what
people are saying about you?' Then Sunita replied, 'The
closeness between us is not what other people see or say. But
I always want to see her. I want to live with her.' Once when
Sunita had put henna designs on her hands she made an 'A'. I
saw it when the children went to inspect her designs. I asked
her who this 'A' was, and she told me that A stands for Anu,
the person who people are cooking up stories about. She
didn't say anything further and I didn't ask.

Anu's classmates: Anu said she was in love with Sunita and
would like to live with her. We advised her against all this.
We felt that maybe since Sunita dressed like a man she had
developed these feelings. Anu was so in love that she even cut
her hand with a knife to write Sunita's name in blood. Once
she did it with a compass from her geometry box.

Villasini: People say they wanted to live together like husband
and wife. It's a special kind of love; maybe more like a mental
closeness. However, I haven't thought enough about it. But
if a woman and a woman marry, then they won't be having

any children will they, and yet there will be a desire to have
children. And hence there will be problems. But how can
they live like that in society? Imagine if they live together....
If there is some emergency, would they be able to walk alone
in the night? Can these girls walk like that in society?

IV

Anu's mother: Nobody can accept two girls living together. It
is shameful for the family. If she loved a man there would not
have been any problem. Senior members of our community
will never allow this. And I cannot accept it; the community
cannot accept it. The death of the girls was inevitable in that
situation. We could not find any solution for this problem.

Dr Sudarshan: Homosexuality is commonly seen in
military barracks when there is a more close association.
Circumstances cause this. It becomes a habit. If we can change
the circumstances then we can divert them to heterosexual
relationships. You see, as Indians we have our own culture. But
aversion therapy is no use because it is very time-consuming.
If the person wants to change their orientation they have to
give the time for it. But if someone really wants to do it there
will be no side effects.

There are other types of cases also; I have seen them
before. Even after marriage two women have come to me
with this problem. They are married, their husbands are in
the Gulf, and these women want to be married to each other.
They want to separate from and divorce their husbands. Their
loneliness has created this stigma. I think one of the women
has a relative in Bangalore, a clinical psychologist, and went
to that person first. Then they came to me. But then one of
the women was wavering. She was scared that if her husband
found out, he would harass the other woman and take away
their child. There are some bisexuals who fall into this
sexuality. Male homosexuals come to me with these problems
more frequently; they want to know what to do when they
have to get married. They have many sexual problems.

Sasi: Women loving women... What is there to say about that? I don't know. Women can have a mental relationship... or more than that... they may not be thinking of a life like marriage? But these are not long-lasting, are they? When we say 'married' we mean that it is to have a secure life for two people and to produce the next generation. This 'woman loving' is a mental thing. If two women live together there might be some kind of difficulties from the men outside and around them. You just think that if you are a woman alone in the house and somebody comes from outside what can you do? If there is a man that will be better; at least there will be some resistance. You just think about walking alone and walking with a man. If a woman is walking alone, some other man will tease her. If there is a man with her...

V

Kamala: Anu's father Kovalan is the son of my husband's brother. My dears, he's actually my husband's brother: they have the same blood. They are blood relatives. If their hands are cut, the same blood flows. All the people here are related on my husband's side. After my husband's death, all of them changed; my husband's people are a bit estranged from me. My husband had made a bit of property. And now I am in debt of Rs 9000. God sees all this. About Rs 4000 I have repaid and Rs 5000 is still standing. Sibling has turned enemy. Let it be so. They even tried to drive me away from here.

Raman: Kovalan threatened Sunita. She was always going there and then there was a quarrel, which led to a fight, and then I interfered. See, I am like a younger brother to him and Anu was like my sister and Sunita was my friend. In fact we used to play cards together regularly. So I tried to tell him, 'This is between women and it doesn't matter what is happening; when they pass this age it will also end. Let Anu complete her studies and then we can marry her off to someone somewhere else.' But he did not take heed; he did not understand. He said that he would not allow Anu to live with that person; better she commit suicide.

I told Anu as well, 'Edi, this won't do; you won't be allowed to live with this girl.' And she replied, 'I don't want to live with anyone else but Sunita, I won't leave Sunita ever.' I warned them, but they didn't listen.

Kamala: Sunita had gone for tapioca preservation work, at *theni chettan*'s (elder brother's) house. When she was carrying tapioca by the house of Kovalan, he started swearing at her. What need was there for him to swear at her? If there was something like that, he should have come and told me. Then Sunita told me, 'Kovalan and Ammini had a fight with me during the tapioca harvesting.'

We had harvested tapioca, and started peeling it by 4 o'clock. But by around 10 o'clock I heard the sound of swearing by *theni chettan*'s house. When I went to look, Kovalan and Ammini together were swearing at her, my dears. The words they used are unknown even to God. They were swearing very loudly, '*Edy, edy, edy, matavale* (slut, prostitute, whore)' very loudly. I ran up to see what was happening. When I went there Sunita was looking dejected. There were 3–4 men by the well, and so were Kovalan and Ammini. All of them were standing on one side and Sunita was standing alone.

When I reached, Kovalan was silent and Ammini was swearing. I just can't repeat the words she used. Even she came out of the mother's womb, and so did I. Like that, her child came out of her womb, and my Sunita out of my womb. Is this what women tell their children? The words she used!! I couldn't tolerate it. I swore back, 'Was your daughter taught in front of the school or behind it?' Why shouldn't I say that? If that kid is a girl, then mine is too. If the mother was just, she would have told Sunita not to walk around with her girl any more. Instead of that what she said was, 'I won't let you live. I will teach you a lesson.'

If they were worried, so was I. So I said, 'For the last two or three months you have been harassing my Sunita. Does Sunita have a man's thing hanging between her legs, and did your girl come out seeing it?' And she told me I should have raised my daughter properly. I replied, 'Don't pull any of your tricks on us. You're not enough to teach propriety to me and my Sunita. You look after your children and your husband, I'll look after mine. If you are the *mootharalli* (boss) then I am a labourer. For the last 30 to 35 years, I have been going to work to raise my children and look after my husband. Even for a kilo of rice, I need to work. I am not wealthy like you.'

Why shouldn't I say that? I have a bit of property, but not like them... If my Sunita was here, she could have looked after the house and I could have gone off to work. And I could have given money to her to buy things for herself, and we could have saved the money she earned. Now I don't have even a ten-paise coin in my hand.

After all this fighting and swearing, just to spite them Sunita told Anu, 'You should come and stay in my house for one day.' Sunita did that intentionally; both of them decided this together, since everyone was fighting and quarreling. I told Sunita that this won't do; that she had to let Anu go. Sunita replied, 'You know what Kovalan was doing to me for the last 2–3 days. He quarreled with me, so I brought her here. And she will never leave this house without my consent...'

They searched for Anu all over but couldn't find her. She came away after they had already slept. Both of them must have decided this earlier. Otherwise how could she come at 10:30 in the night? Sunita never told me what was going to happen. After Sunita brought her here, what could I do? My elder daughter Shaila told me, 'Why didn't you give her two beatings and send her packing?' I couldn't do that. When she was born, I was there in the hospital to look after her. Anu's mother never considered that. God will see to it; what is it to me?

Around twelve o'clock, people came searching for her here. They had already come 3–4 times earlier, but Sunita had asked me to say that they were not here. People were coming and going back till early the next morning. And then Sunita asked me to tell them that Anu is here, that she's not dead. It's true that in my anger I had told them that I did not know where she was. They came by twice and I didn't say anything. Then Sunita asked me to tell them that Anu is not dead. And I told them so, that Anu is not dead, that she's still alive, and that she is here.

They went and reported all this to the *karayogam* members. Around 2–2:30 some 50 people reached here. They had searched all over the place, and once people came to know, they reached here to ask Sunita why she did this.

Kovalan: We saw that they were in Sunita's house and Sunita wouldn't let my Anu go. We asked them to come out but they didn't.

Kamala: For every other thing Kovalan used to threaten Sunita that he would kill her. It is for the elders to see that they don't say things that will raise the anger of the youngsters. Is it not so? He did try to beat Sunita; will she allow that? That anger was in her mind. That was why she brought Anu here. I did ask her to take her back.

For Anu to speak a little, you need to prod her tongue with a stick. Sunita was the only one talking. I kept asking Anu to get out of the house. She just kept crying. Sunita was standing with one leg inside and one leg outside to prevent people from entering the house. Anu was holding her around the waist from behind. And I too was standing there, and I told them: 'You can't enter the house. You can ask them whatever is reasonable from outside.'

When they threatened to beat Sunita she asked Anu to ask them, 'Why, why do you want to beat her?' The men asked Sunita to let her go. And Sunita replied, 'I won't. Why did Kovalan threaten to kill me with a knife? Why did he start quarrelling with me? And every time I let it go. And for that single reason I have brought her here. You can ask whatever you want from where you are standing outside.'

Kovalan was never allowed to enter the house; he was made to stand outside. And then Sunita told them that if they wanted to, they could file a case. She said that even to the *karayogam* members. He came screaming and kicked at the support that was put here, pulled out the thatch. And now look at my house. Let him give me the money to repair my house. If it was you, would you have allowed this to happen?

I swore at him. I told him to make a garland out of mine and Sunita's intestines and give it to his wife. It's true; I was not able to stand it. He wanted to pull down this hut, kill Sunita, and kill me. Is that how neighbours behave? He was a man, and all who came along with him were men, and here I was alone with my daughter. Is that how they should have behaved?

After this big fight, all of them caught and restrained Kovalan. Otherwise he wouldn't have stopped. They took him away. She told them that they won't step out of the house until the police come... They must have planned it then. From then onwards it must have been in their minds.

Kovalan: The door remained closed all night. They were lying on a bed. We asked them to come out but they didn't. We stood guard outside the door. We waited till the morning, and then went and called the police.

Rajan (from the *karayogam*): Between two women it is very difficult, no? The doctor said it is some hormone deviation, when a male hormone is more in women they will be attracted to other women. Or there may be something wrong in their minds. One night at around 1 o'clock, 2-3 people came to my house with Kovalan. He said that his child was missing. When they had been to Sunita's house her mother had said that there was no one there and not to enter the house. I also went there as it was safer that I was there.

There were people surrounding the house so as not to allow the girls to leave. We asked her if there was someone with her. She finally accepted it and said that there was. She was rude and said, 'Come and take her if you want to; just try to come and take her.' I told her not to talk like that and that as the *karayogam* secretary I was ordering her to let the girl go. It would be a big problem for us if we entered a house where there was no other man. Then after some time the mother herself tried to get them out. Then Sunita said that if we tried to catch them they would commit suicide; that she even had a knife and Furidan with her. Then we thought it was better to call the police the next day. We gave five women

the responsibility of being around the house and ensuring that
Sunita and Anu didn't leave. They stayed till 11 o'clock the
next morning, and then the police came from Kanjar and
took them away.

VI

Reshma (the interviewer): The police officer did not want
his interview to be recorded. We saw the police report after
the suicide and it had photographs of the girls after their
deaths. He said the complaint came from Anu's parents.
They said they didn't have any control over the girls and
wanted the police to give them advice. The policeman said
that they told the girls not to live together but they started
crying. They didn't file a complaint because they didn't
want to harass the girls. They just counselled them, but to no
avail. Sunita was so upset. She told the police that she had
no life after this; after undergoing the shame of being treated
like a culprit, and if she had to be separated from Anu. The
police therefore suggested that the parents take them to a
psychiatrist because the girls were tense and depressed. And
then on the way to the psychiatrist's office Sunita tried to
jump in front of a bus.

Kamala: By 10 a.m, they had gone to Kanjar and brought
the police. They were brought out by the police and were
standing there holding hands. The police took Anu by one
hand and Sunita by the other. Each one was put in a different
part of the yard and spoken to separately. And I was talking all
the while, I said whatever came to my mouth. I was scolding
Kovalan: 'There was no need to file any case! If people like
you had come and talked reasonably with the children, we
could have separated them! Only people with money will file
cases! I don't have any money!'
  I didn't want to go, but since my child was being taken, I too
went. I told them not to take the child, and the police replied,
'Sister, we can't do anything. When the case is given, we have to
take it.' And I said, 'But sir, we have not done anything wrong,
so why should we come? We haven't murdered anybody. You

ask the one who filed the petition. Let him come and solve all this. Me and my Sunita are not coming.'

Then they said, 'Sister, you come with us, and we will reach a reasonable solution.' I told them we didn't have any money, but they said that we didn't have to worry about fares. They had a jeep and would take us there and bring us back. They [Sunita and Anu] entered the jeep together holding hands, and the whole way from here to Kanjar they sat holding their hands together. And even in the police station, they did not let go of each other's hands.

In the police station, they told us that we will take the girls to the hospital, and they also told us to have tea before we went to the hospital. So we went to have tea. On the way, a bus was coming from the east. We had already crossed the road and Sunita was on the other side. Sunita leapt in front of the bus. But a man who was standing there by the road, he also leapt with her and caught her. And I said, 'My God, what is happening to you my child? You have changed so much.' If he had not caught her, she would have been beneath the bus. We didn't have breakfast or tea; we returned to the police station.

From then onwards I think both Sunita and I didn't want to live. My life went out of me when I saw Sunita try to jump under the bus, and it's still wandering thereabouts. Till now, my soul is wandering there in search of my Sunita's soul. I'm not peaceful in my heart. That's why I'm wandering in my conversation like this.

VII

Pushpa: The circle inspector told the elders to let them be together and not to create trouble over it; that this happens to everybody. Then they were taken to Vilayil and injected with medicines. They were made ill in their heads; almost lost their sense. It was said that they were mentally ill. But they became very weak after being medicated and then were taken to Pala, to Cherupushpam Hospital. They were shown to doctors there over 2–3 days, and then came back normal.

Kovalan: The doctor in Vilayil said to the girls, 'Now you are not mature. When you turn 18 you can decide if you still want to live together.' But I opposed this. I will not agree to this. The doctor asked Sunita if she can work and earn for Anu, and Sunita said she could. But I won't allow it. I cannot allow it because it is two women. And we are related; we are family.

Dr. Sudarshan: The relatives were curious, so I told them to go out and brought one of my female staff into the room. The relatives had some hostility and contempt towards the girls. They thought it was some ill-learned behaviour. They are tribals, you see. They are not educated and they have their own way of life and they cannot accept this. Even we will have trouble accepting it, won't we? Because I am a psychiatrist, a person working in this position, I am able to accept it. But at the same time, if this is told to my old parents at home they will not accept it.

I told them that only time can change this. If somebody falls in love and if you feel they are wrong, what you can do is to separate them for six months. But if their love is intense and strong, and if you continue to try and separate them, then there is not much use. Even if the relationship is not acceptable to us, we'll be forced to accept it. Or if they do something foolish like attempting suicide then that will be more difficult.

At first I didn't probe into the details. In the first interview we cannot probe like that; only after establishing rapport that can be done. They were open with me and were scared to go to a doctor. Then I said, 'Children, there is no reason to feel afraid. Feel at ease… why should you be scared? People can make mistakes and these can be corrected. Nobody will hurt you here. If you are in love with each other, then separate for six months, and if it still continues then it is for you to decide. And meanwhile you can talk to me in between; don't think that my treatment with you is over after just giving medicines. You are feeling a bit disturbed in your mind, that's why I will give you the small tablets to reduce that disturbance.'

So I had given them some anti-anxiety drugs. I gave them Diazepam: we give this for restlessness, and I just gave them two milligram, not even the adult dose. But after some time they discontinued it. On the third day, the girls came back with the same sort of reactions. It was not exactly a reaction, it was a conversion symptom. The anti-anxiety drugs put you at ease, improve your performance, allow you to be more receptive. It does not lead to those symptoms they were having: all that tension in the neck, rolling, eyes, body losing control. It is not because of Diazepam. When they came back I did not re-admit them. I just gave them a placebo, a vitamin tablet, and sent them back. I am one hundred per cent sure that what happened to them was not a drug-induced reaction.

See, the parents are ignorant about these things, so obviously they will say that the girls came back in a drugged state. Now that the children are no more, they want to get the sympathy of the public. They deserved to be consoled, and I told the parents that. People should have helped them in this matter. But you see, this was a peculiar case. I was also worried that they may try to commit suicide at night because of the way they were talking. So that's why I kept them for observation. In the hospital I told the ward sisters also to watch out for their foolish behaviour at night. You have to be doubly conscious.

Kamala: In the hospital, after examining her, they gave her medicine, and they gave her an injection too. They made her out to be sick when she was not. She was given two pills and an injection. And after that she just entered into a stupor. Earlier, like the moment she was going to jump in front of the bus, she was agitated. By giving her injections and pills, they made her mad when she was really not so.

This Sunita, she was just pulling everything down and creating havoc. Anu was lying quietly in a corner. Sunita was doing somersaults in bed, just like a cow in the shed somersaults without eating anything. Three or four nurses and doctors held her down but she would not lie still. And Sunita said to me, 'Why did you bring me here? I didn't have any sickness. What did you do to me? And why am I shut inside this room? Mother, take me back home immediately. Where am I now? Is this my house? Why are people crowding here like this? Mother where have you brought me? What have you done to me? I want to walk freely in my house. I don't want to stay here, I'm not sick.'

I told her, 'My dear, it is nothing. We will go back home.' I was even more out of my senses than Sunita. And Sunita too was more out of her senses than me. How could it not be so? Seeing all this, my heart was sobbing. Her anxiety entered me and my anxiety entered her. What could we have done; it all turned out to be so. One or two people nearby had told me to take the girls to a witch doctor to separate them. But it just stayed in conversation. Everything happened very quickly; the case was given and then all this happened before we could do anything. But I never took all this seriously. I never thought that it will all end like this. If she had taken at least a cup of black coffee while she was there, it wouldn't have been so painful. But she would neither eat nor drink anything. Sunita was more distressed than me, and can I have anything without her first eating something? My hunger went away seeing her soul. Both of us lost our hunger when she jumped in front of the bus.

They gave us 14 pills, 7 red pills and 7 white pills. But after coming back we never gave her those. Sunita said that she won't take them. After coming here, her tongue kept hanging out, and her eyes were rolling from side to side and she wouldn't eat anything. She just had one cup of black tea, and we came back only the next morning. So for one whole day, she was living on the strength of that one cup of tea.

And if you looked at her face, it was clouded, her eyes had gone into the sockets, and she was not taking anything in.

After two days, she was taken to Cherupushpam Hospital in Pala. And these two sets of pills were also taken along. They told her not to take the red pills, and they gave three other pills. So the red pills were left there, but the white pills were taken back; and we were told if there was any difficulty after taking the new pills, only then the white pills from Vilayil (the first hospital) need to be given. For three days these pills were to be taken.

After taking those pills for three days, Sunita became all

right. It was only after she had taken those pills that she started having hunger. And she started eating *kanni* (thin rice gruel). After coming back everything became normal. But it's said that they still continued their relationship. Anu was taken to her mother's house for two whole months, and then the exams started. Sunita was here and Anu there. And everything was normal.

Pushpa: After the case was given, after the hospital episode, I asked Sunita about it. She said, 'We were simply walking around together for fun and even then they made a case against me. I really don't have anyone else. Mother and I have no one else. We are alone here and if they start behaving like this, then how can I live?' And then she started crying.

VIII

Pushpa: It was the last exam, and after Anu finished all her papers she distributed sweets to her friends, saying that they wouldn't be seeing her again. She came back around 2 o' clock and both children came down to our house. It was said that they were lying down together; they ate, and then they went away.

Kamala: My dear, I can't talk about that Friday. Every Friday we used to go for a film; Sunita used to go there [points to across the stream], and I used to go to Jayan *chettan*'s house around 12 o'clock. It was already 11:45 a.m.. Sunita asked me, 'Ammae, aren't you going for the film,' and I replied, 'Yes I am. Aren't you? Let's go together.' Sunita said that she was going to her uncle's house: Kovalan's house. 'You go above, and I will go there.'

By 11.45 we had our *kanni*. Sunita was standing out in the yard. I closed the door and stepped out into the yard. Sunita was standing there, just at the end of the yard, with one foot planted down on the rock, and the other above. I put some tobacco into my mouth, and then she told me: 'I'm leaving; aren't you going? It's already 11:45 and the film will start within another 15 minutes.'

'I will reach there by 12:10, I will go slowly.'

'You usually reach around 12:30 and miss the first part of the film. Today, go early and see it fully; it's a good movie.

Then I ran up. Upon reaching the post, I turned back. Sunita was still standing there, with one leg above and one leg below, and was looking at me, and I felt *chammal* (something inexplicable) and I couldn't move from there. Usually I used to run the whole way up, and Sunita used to cross the stream running. And I used to start out only after Sunita crossed the river... but that day Sunita was still standing there, and even I stopped near the post. Sunita was standing there looking at me like this, and I stood there looking down at her...

'Why aren't you going, Mother?'

'I will leave after some time. It's not time yet.'

'Leave, Mother leave, it's already time. I'm going to leave now.'

But Sunita stood there looking at me, and I stood there looking at Sunita. Both of us stood there looking at each other. And I wondered what was happening. I was feeling very anxious, like something was choking my heart.

'Mother it's already time, you'll have to run.'

'Why are you standing there looking at me like that? And why are you trying to send me off? Usually I go after you. Today what happened?'

'I will go, Mother.'

I reached up to the yard above, but my eyes were still there. I was looking to see if Sunita had gone, but Sunita was still standing there looking at me. It had never happened like this before. I was apprehensive about why Sunita was standing there like that...

It was around 4:45 p.m. when I came back. I knew nothing, and it was Friday. My God, even in my dreams I never thought that this would happen... My heart was in turmoil: what's happening to Sunita; what's happening to her? I went up half-heartedly. Even while watching the film I was wondering why Sunita was behaving like that. This question came out like a sob from my heart. Usually after coming back from the film, I would prepare dinner. Sunita would return while the dinner was on the stove and we would have our baths. The thing is that on that Friday it was different.

I came back running and poured myself some *kanni*. As soon as I came back and opened the door I saw a mat and pillows on the floor. The window was covered by a sheet, and there was a plate three-quarters full of rice and some plantains on the table. Sunita's umbrella stood by the door, dripping water... I wondered why it was like this. She must have come back early and had her dinner.

Why was it I was feeling so worried? Why was it like this? She had never left the food like this before... Both of us used to eat together; usually she ate only when I ate, and I ate only when she ate... I didn't take it seriously. I put on some water to boil and cleaned the rice... And then I had some rice and fish curry. I wanted to have my bath but I was waiting for Sunita to come back. The water was still dripping from her umbrella. She must have kept it there and gone out.

Raman: Even on the night before her death – but I didn't know she was going to do this – we were playing cards at my house. We usually played cards every night, till about 10 or 12 o'clock. We were playing rummy for Re 1, and she lost Rs 15, but I told her I didn't want the money and she should keep it. But she insisted I take it back. She called me 'mama', but everybody calls me Rama, but that night she insisted I keep the money.

She told me she was going to Eerattupetta the next day, to her uncle's house. And then she said that she would return from there as the real Sunita. She said the same thing to some other women in the area who she calls 'aunties'. Then I told those women not to advise her on ways to kill herself. It was the day after this conversation that she killed herself. I was away all of the next day and came home in the evening. The others told me that the girls had been under the banana plantains and had vomited. There was a pungent smell of vomit there; they had taken poison. We found the banana peels afterwards but it was too dark to see where they had gone.

Shaji: She used to come early in the morning to take the cow out. She didn't come that morning or afternoon or evening. In the evening around 5 o'clock Bindhu came and asked if Sunita was here, and didn't say anything else. Around 6:30, I heard a cry, something unusual, someone shouting, 'I'm being killed, I'm being killed!' and 'Mother, my mother!' But we thought it was one of those tribal people making noises after getting drunk. At night we saw lights in Sunita's house but the stream was full so we couldn't cross and go there. But we had our suspicions. So when this person Raman came the next day saying Sunita was missing, we told him about the cries. They went to investigate and found both of them dead.

Kamala: Everyone was there for the film except Anu. After the quarrels I wasn't speaking to Anu or any of them. If we were sitting close, watching TV or something, I would never look at her face, just looked straight at the TV. And then that evening Bindhu came running to me, saying she wanted to know where Sunita was so she could borrow some money from her. She knew, but she didn't tell me. I kept saying 'Bindhu, what is the matter; are you keeping something from me?' She came back later saying, 'Kunjamma, they are searching for Anu, and Shaji said Sunita didn't go there at all today. Today is such a bad day; today is such a bad day.' That was how I came to know. Couldn't she have told me right in the beginning?

People went searching but the stream was so full of water; it was raining heavily. A terrible Friday it was. The wind was blowing; we thought a landslide had started. They tried from 7 o'clock till 12 that night, but had to stop and come back; it was too bad. They started out again at 5 o'clock in the morning and found them, after an hour, leaning against a rock. I went and took my child in my arms, saying, 'Why did you do this to your mother; who is going to look after her now?' I don't know what happened next, I kept fainting; someone brought me back here... every time I saw her I would faint.

After this incident people even came and asked me, 'Why didn't you tell us? You should have told us. We could have separated them when Kovalan was quarrelling with you.' I never suspected it would turn out like this, that Kovalan would keep nagging my child, and that this would happen. They had made healthy kids sick. It is terrible. God will not forgive.

IX

Was suicide the only choice for these women?

Violence against women means rape, sexual harassment, and bride-burning. Violence also happens every time a woman is married against her will. It happens every time a woman feels guilty for wanting to be happy and every time that a woman must die because she is unacceptable to society. Lesbian suicides are a result of society's attempt to restrict women's choices and control their lives. We protest these deaths as violence against all women. [PRISM, 2002.][4]

Kerala reports the highest suicide rate in India: almost three times the national average. Every day 32 people commit suicide in the state, and the reasons for this are well-documented: lack of opportunities, irregular development, alcoholism, a mismatch between qualifications/ambitions and actual opportunities, and 'love failure', to name a few.[5] J. Devika of the Centre for Development Studies in Trivandrum suggests that suicide in Kerala is a response to frustrations of individual desires and needs in a society that is unable to create opportunities for self-expression, fulfilment, and actualization.[6]

In the context of lesbian suicides this logic seems relevant: women feel there is no opportunity to lead a satisfying life and find acceptance in their communities. Alongside this is a strong mental health industry with student, school, and marriage counselling, psychology and psychiatry being widely accepted across the state. However, according to Sahayatrika, a grassroots network of women in Kerala working on sexuality rights, the mental health industry is rarely sensitized to the contexts of women's suicides.

Sahayatrika's fact-finding on cases of lesbian couples' suicides shows that most suicides are attempted by working-class Dalit or Adivasi women like Sunita and Anu, not only sexually marginalized for their gender and sexual preferences but triply marginalized economically, socially, and politically. Adding androgyny or other manifestations of gender non-conformity to the mix only exacerbates the isolation and violence women like Sunita face. Poverty and language barriers prevent some women from ever leaving the state. Only those who are better educated, middle class, English- or Hindi-speaking generally have better opportunities as single women or as couples. The latter are more likely to leave Kerala if they feel harassed, and the former are more likely to see suicide as the only escape.

An entirely different perspective on lesbian suicides comes from author Giti Thadani[7] who discusses cases from 1979 in Kerala and Gujarat. Thadani's analysis contextualizes lesbian suicides within the mystic traditions of lovers uniting forever in death, a familiar motif in legendary love stories such as *Heer-Ranjha*. In a similar vein of cultural analysis, scholar Ruth Vanita sees suicide as 'an act simultaneously intensely private and public. Committed in private, it is nevertheless public because it draws the scrutiny of society and state.'[8] A suicide by a same-sex couple can be seen as a defiant public enactment of a private love.

Even so, the public enactments by Sunita and Anu, and many others like them across India,[9] raise troubling questions. Did it have to come to this? Was there no other alternative? There are some women who have found ways of fighting back, but often at great personal cost. There are gender non-conforming women who use their masculine appearances to hide, to run, to pass as men. Mini became 'Babu', cut her hair short, and wore men's clothes; she and her lover Sisha escaped to Coimbatore and lived as 'man and wife' till a suspicious neighbour contacted acquaintances back in Kerala. The couple eventually had to deal with the worst of Kerala's salacious media interest in lesbians. 'We have nothing to say to press reporters or to the world. We will say what we have to say to each other. Can't you leave us alone?' Mini is quoted as saying.[10] Similarly, after attempting to pass as a heterosexual couple, Shree Nandu and her wife Sheela had a much more public outing. Violent confrontations with their families appeared on the front pages of most newspapers in the state. This couple, however, had the support of a number of women's organizations across the country, and today at least Nandu feels that she has made a critical journey to 'the other side'; to greater self- confidence and self-assurance.[11]

The overwhelming legitimacy given to marriage, hetero-normativity, and morality has always tended to silence sexual diversity. Reconstructing their story, I ask myself what I would have done had I met Sunita and Anu during the their brief and intense relationship. 'You have a choice,' I would have said. 'There is another way to be.' One of the things that stands out from their story is the immense pressure from all: from family, relatives, co-workers, community elders, everyone. On the one hand, there is love, companionship, friendship, stability and security in these relationships. They are not, however, unconditional, and frequently demand compliance and conformity. Choosing the self over the deep-penetrating reach of family, community, and conventional values can be incredibly difficult. Would Sunita have been able to reconstruct an independent life away from her old mother? Would her mother have understood? Would Anu have found the strength to stand up to her parents? I don't know, but they had to have imagined that option. They had to have imagined, before dying, that there was another way to be.

Acknowledgements

I thank those who contributed their time, views, and experiences to the development of this chapter in its earlier form, particularly Reshma Bhardwaj, Deepa Nair, J. Devika and Nandu in Kerala; Jaya Sharma in Delhi; Ponni Arasu, Sumathy, Sunil, and Lesbit in Bangalore; Bishakha Datta and Meenu Pandey in Bombay.

Notes

1.   This reconstruction is based on a currently unpublished interview transcript of a fact-finding mission undertaken by Sahayatrika between 14 February and 4 May 2002. The

interviews were conducted by Deepa V.N., Meena Gopal, Reshma Bhardwaj, Dr. Jayashree, and Subhash, and translated and transcribed by Prema, Arun and Deepa. Many thanks to Sahayatrika for making these transcripts available.

2. Their names have been changed to protect identities.
3. *See Kerala Kaumadhy,* 2001.
4. People for the Rights of Indian Sexual Minorities, a loose coalition now known as Voices Against 377. www.voicesagainst 377.org
5. *See* Iype, 2004; Bose, 2004.
6. Email interview, 2007.
7. *See* Thadani, 1996: 101–04.
8. *See* Vanita, 2005: 126–27.
9. A recent history of the violence faced by lesbian women includes the much-publicized 1988 case of Urmila Srivastava and Leela Namdeo, two constables in the Madhya Pradesh police who got married in a temple before 40 witnesses. They were identified as 'lesbians' in the local press, which led to their dismissal from their jobs. They were eventually forcibly separated. Similar forms of harassment have dogged couples like Manisha and Tarana, both workers in a leather factory whose employer dismissed them suspecting they were in a relationship. Jaya Verma and Tanuja Chouhan got married but a story in the local Mumbai press revealed their identities and whereabouts; their housing society asked them to leave the premises because they felt that an openly lesbian couple was 'bad for the morals of the building' (Khaitan, 2004). In 1995 Madhu and Manisha got married through a symbolic ceremony; Madhu's parents tried to get her married to a man; she and Manisha fled to Delhi and then to Haridwar where they were eventually arrested by the police. 'Madhu is reported to have said that if the world tried to separate them, they would leave the world' (Thadani 1996:110). In 1998, near Cuttack in Orissa, Mamta Mohanty and Monalisa Mohanti signed a Notarial Certificate of a Partnership Deed to live together. Four days later they consumed a poisonous substance together in an attempt to end their lives, preferring death to imminent separation that would have been brought about by the transfer of Monalisa's father. Mamta survived the suicide bid and was charged with Monalisa's murder on a

complaint filed by her family (Khaitan 2004). More recently, in Uttar Pradesh two lesbian couples were singled out and harassed by their families. In 2005, Usha Yadav and Shilpi Gupta tried to elope to Gujarat when Shilpi's marriage was arranged, but their escape to freedom was short-lived. Shilpi's parents filed a case of kidnapping against Usha and a magistrate in Allahabad forced them to return home. (Mukerjee, 2005). In Kanpur, two young lovers attempted to commit suicide, saying they were in despair because their parents were forcing them to marry men.

10. *See* Vanitha, 2000.
11. Personal interview with Nandu, 2006.

References

Adimathra, J. (2002): 'Women Loving Women: Is Homosexual Love between Women Increasing?', trans. Sahayatrika, *Grihalakshmi,* May 2002.

Fire (2001): 'When Sunita, in Menswear, and Anu, in Love, Mated', Queer Love, *Fire,* 10 September 2001.

Iype, G. (2004): 'South India: World's Suicide Capital', Rediff News, http://www.rediff.com/news/2004/apr/15spec.htm, 17 January 2007.

Kerala Kaumadhy (2001): 'Unable to live together: two women commit suicide', 26 September 2001.

Khaitan, T. (2004): 'Violence Against Lesbians in India', http://www.altlawforum.org/Resources/lexlib/document.2004-12-21.9555696555, 27 January 2007.

Mukerjee, S. (2005): 'Social Taboos Pressure Lesbian Love', BBC News South Asia, 6 June 2005. http://news.bbc.co.uk/1/hi/world/south_asia/4566091.stm, 17 January 2007.

Thadani, G. (1996): *Sakhiyani: Lesbian Desire in Ancient and Modern India,* New York: Cassell.

Unknown (2000): 'Living Together is Marriage?' *Vanitha,* 15–31 October 2000.

Vanita, R. (2005): *Love's Rite: Same Sex Marriage in India and the West,* New Delhi: Penguin.

V.N. Deepa (2005): 'Queering Kerala: Reflections on Sahayatrika', in A. Narrain and G. Bhan (eds.), *Because I Have a Voice: Queer Politics in India.* New Delhi: Yoda, 175–96.

Unpublished and Other Data Sources

J. Devika, Email Interview, April 2007.
Shree Nandu, Interview, Trivandrum, September 2006.
Transcripts of Sahayatrika's fact-findings, conducted by Deepa V.N.
  Reshma Bhardwaj, Dr Jayasree, Meena Gopal, and Subhash:
Moolamattom Fact-Finding, Day 1, 14 Febuary 2002.
Moolamattom Fact-Finding Day 2, 15 February 2002.
Moolamattom Fact-Finding, Day 3, 3 May 2002.
Moolamattom Fact-Finding, Day 4, 4 May 2002.

8

Criminalizing Love, Punishing Desire

Rajashri Dasgupta

6 October 2005. In Rohtak, Haryana, 20-year-old Rekha is readying herself for dinner. She is pregnant. At 8 p.m., there is a quiet knock on the door. Five armed men – her father, two brothers, an uncle and her nephew – barge into the house shouting for her husband, Sanju. Sensing trouble, her elder sister-in-law Manju escapes through the terrace to seek help. The men shoot Anju, Rekha´s younger sister-in-law, through her stomach and chest and beat her mother-in-law on the head with an iron rod. In the midst of the pandemonium Rekha can hear Sanju pleading for his life as the men hold his hands and legs and brutally beat him before shooting him dead.

Throughout the mayhem, her father and uncle stand quietly in one corner of the small room calmly directing the men. They repeatedly curse, 'Kill the *chura* (Dalit). *Izzat mitti me mil gayi, chure ka ghar* (Our honour has become mud in the low-caste house).' Seventeen days after the incident, Rekha gives birth to a boy. 'I saved myself and my baby in my womb by bending over, my shawl covering my stomach, and pretending to be dead on the floor beside Anju,' says Rekha with haunted eyes. 'If the men knew I was pregnant, they would have killed me first. They would never have allowed Sanju's baby to be born: a Dalit in the womb of a Brahmin.' She silently shows me the dried-up stab wounds inflicted all over her frail body.[1] I am going to live,' she says, 'and so will my son'.

A violence more shameful than 'honourable'.

Sanju and Rekha's story is the eternal tale of couples in love who are forced apart by society. It is a narrative of young lovers trapped between their desire, rights guaranteed by the law, and their actual socio-cultural realities. It is a tale of how families, communities, and even state agencies treat love as a criminal activity and lovers as criminals. It is about 'heroic' everyday love, the heroism of defying tradition and resisting parental and kinship authority.

In the course of the past few years, there has been growing concern about the violence faced by couples in India who marry or have relationships of their own choice. Women – unmarried, widowed, or married – who choose their own partners are considered 'indecent', 'loose', or morally lax. Their 'love affairs' or 'love marriages' are treated with distrust and ridiculed as sexual liaisons based on lust, devoid of any family and social responsibilities.

What is prohibited, in particular, are inter-class, inter-religious, inter-caste, and within-*gotra* alliances.[2] As marriage is the only socially-sanctioned sexual relationship, the family arranges it by strictly adhering to these rules and norms. It is the institution of marriage that sustains the caste system. The survival, reproduction, and hierarchy of the caste system depends on endogamy, or marriage within specified caste groups. Linkages through marriage provide the caste system greater social, political, and economic recognition and leverage.[3]

'Marriage is a social rather than an individual act,' argues scholar Prem Chowdhry (2007), 'where the individual's needs, desire, and love are separated from the purely social institution of marriage, an alliance between two families involving material transaction.'

For society, then, marriage is more about getting the right in-laws than picking the right partner to love and live with. Consequently, child marriage, early marriage, arranged marriage, and forced marriage[4] are widely practised to maintain the status quo of social power, family hierarchy, dominance and control over women.

In this context, the assertion of choice, though unintended, is inevitably seen as a direct attack on patriarchal power, parental authority, and community norms. Any display of romantic desire and love is considered to bring 'shame' on 'family honour'. Those who 'breach' the socially-regulated mechanisms of marriage face disapproval, stiff resistance, violence, even death, if and when they choose to marry. 'Any breach in marital links upsets the family and caste support structures,' says feminist historian Uma Chakravarti.[5] 'It changes and threatens the status of the family and the entire caste group.'

With the exclusivity of the caste group getting 'fuzzy', it is no coincidence that opposition is most vicious when a woman from a dominant caste group is in love with a lower-caste man.[6] It is the woman's family – a father, brother, or uncle – that lashes out, ruthlessly, treating a wife, daughter, sister, and her lover or husband as criminals and their love as a criminal activity. As there is a tacit social acceptance of domestic violence, this disciplining of the 'errant' woman is naturalized and the violence shrugged off as the family's 'private and internal affair'.

At the far extreme end of the scale of violence, the 'honour' of the family is asserted by killing the woman. Lesser manifestations encompass beating, harassment, forced confinement, and constraints on movements, friendships, and choice of relationship. These 'honour' codes are also imposed on men, especially on Dalit men or men 'lower' in caste status than their wives. Men too are killed (as in the case of Sanju) or falsely charged with abduction and rape. According to Bhavna Kumar, chief counsellor, National Commission for Women, Delhi, almost half the cases of kidnapping/abduction that parents file against men are false; at least 15 per cent of rape/attempt to rape cases are false charges intended to pressurize couples.[7]

Many couples 'disappear' by eloping to escape their parents' wrath. However, many once gutsy and assertive women do succumb to continuing family coercion and mounting pressure, becoming helpless and fearful; some are driven to commit suicide, others abandon their relationship and return, disillusioned, to their family and meekly submit to an 'arranged marriage'.

The pressure on couples continues to take a toll even after marriage. Such couples suffer greater vulnerability than those in arranged marriages if the relationship proves to be dissatisfying or violent. Disowned by parents, women find it difficult to cope without any family support structures if their marriage sours. Meena Das of Nishtha, an NGO in West Bengal, says that women then question the worth of defying family and parental authority. The feeling of shame is so deeply ingrained that they do not even tell their own children that they married of their own volition.

Following their own bitter experiences, some parents who have themselves had 'love marriages' vehemently oppose their daughters choosing their own husbands. 'My parents fear a repeat of the backlash,' says Sharda of Association for Advocacy and Legal Initiatives (AALI), a Lucknow-based legal aid support group. 'They were exiled from the village when they married on their own. They can't bear to see me suffer and face family ridicule and social boycott again.'

Many women who are estranged from their natal families for marrying against their wishes try to appease their in-laws. From giving up their job to dressing in accordance with the wishes of the family, to restricting their mobility outside the home, women go the extra mile to adjust and to be accepted. The disapproval and violence etched into the collective memory of women acts as a rein, a self-regulatory mechanism.

Courting Cruelty across Caste and Class

7 July 2006. The Supreme Court rules that there is no bar on inter-caste marriage under the Hindu Marriage Act or any other law; and that anyone who harasses/ threatens couples in inter-caste or inter-religious marriages will be prosecuted.[8] The Supreme Court delivers this landmark judgment in the case of Lata Singh, legally a major, who had an inter-caste marriage. It notes that the family of Lata Singh had not only tortured her but had also used the administrative machinery to harass the couple. (In a clear case of caste bias and muscle power, the police had arrested Lata's in-laws for supporting

the couple and refused them bail, rather than arresting Lata Singh's brothers for harassing the couple.)

'This is a free and democratic country,' the court ruling observes, 'and once a person becomes a major he or she can marry whomsoever he/she likes.' If the parents do not approve, the most they can do is cut off social relations. 'But they cannot give threats or commit or instigate acts of violence and cannot harass the person who undergoes such inter-caste or inter-religious marriage.' The court also directs the administration and police authorities throughout the country to ensure that there are no threats and acts of violence against couples who have inter-caste and inter-religious marriages.

In her path-breaking book (2007), Prem Chowdhry has discussed how caste and community structures in rural north India have become increasingly dictatorial and ruthless when young couples challenge customary and family norms. Traditional caste panchayats in Haryana are particularly notorious for breaking up solemnized marriages and preventing marriages on the ground that these violate the practice of exogamy, the rule of prohibiting marriage within a specified group. 'The caste panchayat is a significant source of social control,' says Jagmati of All India Democratic Women's Association (AIDWA), Haryana. 'It enjoys wide-ranging dictatorial powers and frequently imposes justice according to its own definition.'[9]

The self-appointed caste panchayat functions like a parallel judiciary which also metes out punishment. In Haryana, these punishments include killing couples, publicly humiliating them by blackening their faces, shaving their heads, or forcing couples to drink, or dip their nose in, urine. One of the commonest punishments forces a woman to tie a *rakhi* (symbol of sisterhood) on her husband's hand. This marks him as her brother and automatically severs any other relationship between them, including marriage.

Caste panchayats do not hesitate to abuse their powers for their own gain. Haryana's Jhaundi village panchayat, for example, opposed the arranged marriage of Ashish and Darshana. When their child was a year old, the caste panchayat ruled that the couple were '*bhaicharas*' or brother and sister according to village exogamy rules. They asked Darshana to tie a *rakhi* on her husband. Darshana flatly refused and the couple was exiled from the village for three years. AIDWA investigations revealed that the case had nothing to do with violating 'culture'. The panchayat members wanted revenge because Ashish's family had not supported the *sarpanch* during the elections.

Another weapon used against rebel lovers is outcasting or social ostracism, an extreme form of group withdrawal. No man will even allow the 'outcaste' to take water from the well or fire from the oven. 'It is literally social death,' says Abdul Hameed Sheikh, the elected *pradhan* (head) of Gauripur village, West Bengal. 'The threat itself creates fear to conform.' In many villages in West Bengal, parents even perform the *shraadh* (after-death) ceremony to express a ritualistic disapproval and cutting-off of ties.

Religious Hatred Targets 'Mixed' Couples

21 September 2007. The dead body of Rizwanur Rehman, a Muslim graphic designer and teacher is found on the train tracks in the heart of Kolkata, a month after he marries his affluent Hindu girlfriend, Priyanka Todi.[10] In late August, when Priyanka tells her father about the marriage, she faces emotional blackmail from her family. The Todis demand that Rizwanur convert to Hinduism; he agrees. The Todis rake up a long-dead love affair to paint Rizwanur as unreliable; Priyanka does not budge from her position.

When family pressure and emotional blackmail fail, the Todis use their social and business networks to hound the couple. The police threaten a witness to their marriage.

Three times, senior police officers summon the couple to police headquarters to 'persuade' Priyanka to return to her family. Each time, they harass and threaten to arrest Rizwanur if she does not return to her parental home. On 8 September, Priyanka 'agrees' to visit her father for seven days. That is the last time the couple see each other.

On 4 January 2008, the Central Bureau of Investigation (CBI) rules that Rizwanur had committed suicide under 'tremendous mental pressure'. The CBI allegedly points to at least 7 people for abetting the suicide: 4 senior police officers; 2 members of the Todi family, and a friend of Rizwanur's family. It is reported that the Todis had offered a 'friend' of Rizwanur's family Rs 11 lakhs to break up the marriage.

Apart from caste and class, one of the biggest taboos is inter-religious relationships, particularly in cases where Hindu women marry Muslim men. Even in West Bengal, where the Left and democratic social movements have brought progressive changes in people's lives and established rights for women, this taboo remains strongly embedded. 'Violence against such couples, both before and after the marriage, is the norm,' says Chakravarti.

In a similar incident, all hell broke loose on 7 April 2007, when Umar, a Muslim boy in Bhopal, married Priyanka Wadhwani, a Sindhi girl. Political and religious organizations joined the fray to retrieve the claimed 'honour' of the community. Members of the Bajrang Dal, Bhagva Brigade, and other Hindu organizations went to the extent of calling a Bhopal *bandh* (shutdown) if Priyanka was not 'returned'. A Hindu Kanya Raksha Samiti (Protect Hindu Women Committee) was set up in order to 'protect' girls; a Sindhi Panchayat diktat forbade Sindhi girls to cover their faces while going out (which girls usually do to protect themselves from the heat) and to keep mobile phones. Not to be outdone, the Majlis-e-Shura passed an ultimatum to the Muslim community to discipline their children and keep them under control.[11]

The aftermath of the Godhra train-burning incident in Gujarat in February 2002 saw some of the worst cases of inter-religious violence in independent India. Muslim men with Hindu wives were singled out for attack. Groups of Hindu fanatics attacked couples, killed, threatened, and burnt down their houses. On 3 April 2002, Muhammed Riyaz, 34, was hacked to death for being married to a Hindu.[12] Geeta, 30, of Ahmedabad, was stripped in public and stabbed to death on the streets as a lesson to women who dared to breach community norms; her Muslim husband was hospitalized with knife wounds. A Hindu woman married to a Christian man was forced to abort her four-month-old pregnancy.[13]

Vishwa Hindu Parishad (VHP) leader and Bajrang Dal activist Babu Bajrangi of Naroda 'rescues' Patel girls by kidnapping those who marry outside the community; 70 per cent are married to Christian and Muslim men. To date he claims to have 'saved' more than 800 girls. Says NGO activist Rafi of Ahmedabad, 'The girls who have managed to escape from Babubhai's clutches have testified how he captured them and beat them up. He forced them to break off their marriages and those who were pregnant were forced to abort.'[14]

'What is a Man's Life without His *Izzat*?'

There is some discomfort in acknowledging and recognizing the existence of crimes relating to choices in marriage and relationships in India. When I began researching this chapter, many friends and colleagues were surprised. The most common responses were of disbelief: 'But couples do not face honour killing in this country! Perhaps in the rural areas in north India... It's different here... It is more about dowry', or 'Will you do your fieldwork in Pakistan?' While dowry-related violence is seen as 'natural' to Indian patriarchy, violence against relationships of choice is commonly seen as restricted to the Muslim world.[15]

It is perhaps the absence of statistical data, together with the invisibility and lack of recognition of this specific type of violence, that makes intervention difficult. However, violence against couples in relationships of choice is not restricted to a particular caste, to north India, or to rural communities. Evidence of cases reveal that parental or community resistance cuts across religious communities, whether Hindu, Muslim, or Sikh, pervades different social strata in society and is spread across different regions in the country. What differs significantly is the degree of resistance, violence, and the criminality with which families view self-determined marriages and relationships.

According to Pratiksha Baxi, Centre for the Study of Law

and Governance, Jawaharlal Nehru University, Delhi, the diaspora of Asian immigrant communities in the West has been instrumental in highlighting the widespread phenomena of forced marriages and murders that came to be known as 'honour killings'. Contrary to popular belief, an exhaustive study demonstrates that this concept of 'honour' is not confined to only Asian and Arab countries but also permeates Australia, UK, USA, and other societies.[16]

Feminists have challenged labelling this form of violence as 'honour crimes'. The term invokes an adherence to a 'code of honour' and appears to endorse the apparent 'motivation' of the crime. In the process, it masks the inhuman violence and brutality inflicted by the perpetrator on the victim. 'The term carries ideological baggage,' argues Chakravarti. 'It is not adequate to place the word honour within quotes. We need to name the violence more specifically and precisely so as to bring out the brutality of the crime inflicted on women by the family.'[17] Says lawyer and human rights activist Sara Hossain from Bangladesh, 'The term "honour killing" is problematic as it takes on the description adopted by the perpetrator and in reproducing the term obscures the real motivation for the crime or attempted crime.'[18]

One of the most cherished ideals that bind most communities together in India is the idea of *izzat:* honour, reputation, prestige. Linked fundamentally to procreation[19] and the control of female sexuality, this notion of honour is intrinsically linked to both sexes in a most complicated manner. In women, 'honour' is said to reside in their bodies as the safety vault of the family and community, as daughters before marriage and mothers after marriage. 'For the men,' says C.S. Bhan, deputy superintendent of police, Rohtak, Haryana, 'honour is *mouche ka sawal, mouchen oonche rakhen, niche na ho jaaye.*' (Honour is a question of the moustache, of holding it up high.) The *mouche* (moustache) is held high in honour so long as the man is the vault-keeper, decision-maker, able to regulate female honour by controlling women's sexual conduct. Even a whisper of actual, suspected or potential loss of 'honour' in women justifies male aggression and violence.

Thus there is no sign of remorse or shame among the male family members of Rekha's family, now in prison for killing Sanju. 'Sanju's murder is seen as retrieving the lost honour of the family,' says Jagmati, who is helping Rekha fight her case. 'The murderers have in fact become heroes and are considered the moral guardians of the community. Their imprisonment is seen as a supreme sacrifice.' The *mouche*, that had drooped when Sanju dared marry Rekha, now has an upward twist. Says Rohtak's assistant sub-inspector Ram Krishen about the role of Rekha's father, 'For peace, man seeks revenge and feels satisfied. What is the life of a man without his *izzat*?'

Women too adhere to the twin notions of *izzat* and *sharam* (shame), the corollary to honour. Women's subordination to caste and gender oppression, says Chakravarti, is maintained through complicity; there are rewards for collusion and threats for dissent.

Even two years after Sanju's death, Rekha's mother stands on the road publicly cursing and threatening to kill Rekha and her baby son. In private, says Jagmati, Rekha's mother breaks down and wishes the couple had run away to save themselves.

'Laugh, But Don't Make a Sound'

'The greatest danger to the ideology of honour comes from women,' says Chowdhry. 'As upholders of honour, male members of the family must take all decisions on their behalf. This is the only way to control them.' In other words, women's rights to control their own lives, liberty, freedom of expression, association, movement, and bodily integrity are ideas that mean very little in actual practice.

This social anxiety leads to the enforcement of prescribed norms that are neither written scriptures nor rules. The family and society directs and regulates a woman's sexual behaviour and restricts any contact with men outside the immediate family. This 'appropriate' behaviour is meant to preserve a girl's virginity for her husband in a heterosexual marriage, so that the identity and lineage of the children are clearly those of their father.[20] To prevent any 'accidents' or 'disasters' (read falling in love/sexual contact) from occurring, girls are held on a tight leash.

This leash on girls begins early. Young members of Jeevika, an NGO in West Bengal, talk about the dos and don'ts that govern their everyday life from childhood. 'Even a five year-old is scolded for bathing without her panty on,' says young Sreelata. 'We are constantly reminded that when we laugh, our teeth should not be exposed, nor should there be a sound.' As physical and emotional expressions in public are frowned upon, a girl is conscious never to raise her hands to wave her friends goodbye, lean on them, or hug them on the streets.

The tight leash is intended to stifle any autonomy in young girls. It is feared that once autonomy, choice, or freedom is conceded and control slackened, it would be difficult to rein girls in. The ultimate sin is girls exerting their choice of sexual partner against parental consent. Given this fear of 'deviant behaviour', the idea of male guardianship of a woman, whether minor or adult, is never renounced.

While the grip never loosens, what changes is the centre of authority, which is passed on to different male members in the family during successive stages of a woman's life. Before marriage, a girl is under the control of her father or brother; for instance, the Hindu marriage ritual of 'gifting the bride' (*kanya daan*) ensures the protection of her husband. This notion is so entrenched that even the courts sometimes view marriage through the lens of guardianship, rather than that of women's legal or human rights.

However, these apparently immutable norms are contested daily; challenged by intrepid young girls and women. In July 2007, defying the diktat of the school authorities, eight teachers of Bakhrat Girls High School on the outskirts of Kolkata, wore the *salwar-kameez* to work instead of the sari, undeterred by heckling and threats of public humiliation.[21] The gesture destroyed the demure image of the sari-clad woman teacher and threatened the established social order. This is especially so in educational institutions, as it is the first public space into which young girls venture.[22]

Marriage and the Market

'First they (Dalits) grabbed the land, then reservation gave them the jobs, and now they demand the girls.' The caustic comment of a plainclothes Jat policeman in Rohtak police station reflects a mode of social panic. Families control women's sexuality not just to maintain the faultlines of caste, class, religion, and other identities but also in order to maintain economic power. This control is grounded in material conditions as patriarchal families strive to obstruct their daughters from having access to resources.[23]

The arranged marriage-led 'mergers' and strategic family alliances that gave a boost to the economic status of a household are now under threat. The 2005 amendments to the Hindu Succession Act, for instance, treat all agricultural land on par with other property and make Hindu women's inheritance rights in land legally equal to that of men, overriding any inconsistent state laws. This can benefit millions of women dependent on agriculture for survival, argues economist Bina Agarwal.[24] The Act now includes all daughters (including married daughters) as coparceners in joint property under Mitakshara law with the same birthright as sons to share and claim partition of the property while also sharing its liabilities. In addition, the Act makes the heirs of predeceased sons and daughters more equal, by including the children of predeceased daughters, as was already the case for sons.[25]

In a son-preference society, the right to own property can enhance women's security. Property ownership also symbolizes that daughters and sons are equal in the natal family and challenges the notion that the daughter belongs only to her husband's family after marriage. This enhances her social worth, argue women activists, and gives her greater bargaining power in both parental and marital families. 'With girls today enjoying legal rights to inheritance and property, and the right to marry who they wish, families and communities feel endangered,' laughs Surya Bhan, formerly of Punjab University.

The opening up of the market, greater economic

opportunities, bank credits and loans make couples less dependent on families for survival.

'With lesser dependence on the family for economic sustenance, there is a breakdown of the joint family. Young couples are unwilling to follow the family diktat and eager to move away,' says Inderjeet, a social activist in Rohtak, Haryana. Moreover, women's increasing access to education has led to greater autonomy and emancipation. AALI has found that many educated girls from lower middle-class homes in UP are challenging arranged marriages.

Notwithstanding the constitutional guarantees of social and political equality, the continued social and political power of the upper over the lower castes is based on material control.[26] Upper-caste families, long accustomed to power and privileges, fear that marriage by choice will affect not only their social but also their economic domination – by passing property and resources to other caste and social groups. It is against this backdrop that 'honour' operates, with the upper castes trying to keep what they think is rightfully theirs.

However, the processes of political democratization are altering power dynamics at family and community levels. With social hegemony challenged, Dalits are finding more educational and employment opportunities, and depending less on upper castes or their traditional occupations. This social mobility generates aspirations in other domains and also results in inter-caste relationships. 'This is *prem bhalo basher yug*, the age of love and desire,' says Shanti Chakravarty, a member of Jeevika, whose Brahmin son eloped with a lower-caste girl. 'It created a furore. But can we stop them? Can you stop the water of the Ganges from flowing?'

The Distorted Mirror of Media

A recent case that received intense media scrutiny and riveted the nation involves the urban, educated élite: a young Delhi business executive, Nitish Katara is murdered on 17 February 2002. His 'crime'? He was in love with Bharati Yadav, the daughter of D.P. Yadav, a controversial UP politician with numerous charges of murder and spurious liquor deals against him. A card written by Bharati to Nitish reads: 'Chimpu, it's easy to love you: you listen to me without judging... you are so easy to talk to, so easy to feel close to, so easy to love... Happy Birthday – Sweetiepie.'

Even so, in her court testimony in 2006, Bharati denies any relationship beyond friendship with Nitish, possibly out of fear of her family. Nitish was allegedly threatened several times and Bharati was tense about how her family might react to the relationship. According to various media reports, there was a clear class difference between the two groups: the Yadavs had acquired wealth but remained 'rough', while the Kataras were 'refined' but middle-class. In his confession to the police, Vikas Yadav, Bharati's brother, is alleged to have told the police that 'the affair was damaging our family's reputation'.

The media does report on inter-caste marriages, especially those where violence is involved. However, says Chowdhry, there is no 'sympathetic understanding of runaway cases in the Hindi media' except for a few sensitive writers.[27] The Bengali press too swallows the police version verbatim; it does not question whether a young man is actually a 'rapist' or 'abductor' or in a consensual relationship. The tone of such reports is generally sensational and gossipy, reporting how a woman was 'trapped' (not willing) in 'lust' (not love) without probing deeper to understand the vicious grip of the family and community in reining desire. That most couples are driven to suicide is written off as 'preme bhiphol' or 'failure in love' for which the two lovers 'chose' (were not forced) death or 'beche nilen mrityu'. The brutality and the anguish that may have driven a couple to commit suicide is sanitized and death by suicide naturalized.

While condemning such violence, the English press tends to position it amidst an 'intolerant, barbaric India' lurking beneath the surface of the 'incredible India that is making waves all over the world'. This approach stereotypes rural communities as irrational, stagnant, archaic, patriarchal, and unwilling to change, this stagnation or unwillingness to change dragging down the development and progress of a 'shining' urban India. The term 'honour killing' is liberally and unquestioningly used for crimes against couples only in rural communities, not when such violence occurs in urban settings. The media never marked the cases of Nitish Katara and Rizwanur as honour killings. It is as if 'honour' killings and violence are restricted and unique only to rural communities, while the urban élite is free of such traditional notions and archaic customs.

'The media tends to portray such violence as typical backwardness of rural regions refusing to modernize,' says Chakravarti. 'There is seldom any informed opinion or analysis of the patriarchal hurdles at every stage and of customs that perpetuate the violence.' Most of the 'love' stories reported are of doom and gloom, signalling a violent backlash to those who dare to defy; seldom is the resistance, heroism of the couples, and their victory against all odds, highlighted.

Contemporary cinema too explores the dilemma of urban romantic love, where individual desire and aspiration come face to face with social and cultural tensions. According to Professor Shohini Ghosh[28] of Jamia Millia Islamia, New Delhi, the pre-nineties films valorized rebel lovers who resisted family opposition in order to either live or die together. In the films of the 1970s (*Kati Patang, Bobby, Ek Duuje Ke Liye, Love Story*), and the superhits of the 1980s (*Qayamat Se Qayamat Tak, Maine Pyaar Kiya*), family pride and honour are defeated at the altar of love. However, the 1990s 'urban romance' films, as Ghosh calls them, break away from this mould, as duty and family honour triumph over love. Even when the lovers are reunited in the end, it is only after the interests of the family have been served.

In *Hum Aapke Hai Kaun (HAHK)*, for instance, Madhuri Dixit, who is in love with Salman Khan, agrees to marry his brother Rajesh after his wife dies during childbirth leaving behind a little baby. The family's needs come before hers. Ghosh argues that *HAHK* was applauded because it offered an ideal family, where family duty is greater than love, and the 'utopic dream of a happy and supportive community' prevails. The rebellious spirit of the pre-nineties lover is also absent in *Dilwale Dulhaniya Le Jaayenge*. Though Shah Rukh Khan and Kajol love each other, he refuses to elope and marry her against the wishes of the family. He says loftily, *'Main usko chinna nahin chahta, paana chaahta hoon…'* (I don't want to snatch her away, I want to attain her.'). Only when Kajol's father finally relents and agrees to the match are the lovers reunited.

Paternal Judiciary, Litigating Marriage

'For inter-caste love affairs to result in marriage and then for the couple to survive, they require the three Ms,' says Samajwadi Party MLA Dinanath Bhaskar.[29] 'Money, muscle power, and manpower.' His comment reflects both the harsh world confronting romantic love and, more significantly, the yawning gap between the written law and the delivery of justice. A paternalistic judiciary often makes runaway marriages look illegal. The judiciary, argues Chowdhry, often stands as an overarching patriarch and acts on behalf of a woman's male guardians while it criminalizes and constructs female sexuality as essentially transgressive.

The activists of AALI encountered this double standard when they dealt with Rita Dixit's case. Rita, a 25-year-old management graduate, had married her childhood friend, Faizal, a Muslim; her family retaliated by filing criminal charges of kidnapping against Faizal and his family. In fear for their lives and disillusioned by the police harassing Faizal's family, the inter-religious couple approached the judiciary (including the Supreme Court) several times. On 29 March 2000, when Rita went to record her statement, the additional chief judicial magistrate, Lucknow, handed her over into the 'custody' of Nari Niketan, a women's shelter (rather than allowing her to go with her husband). Rita insisted that she wanted to be with Faizal. Ignoring her plea, the magistrate argued that as she had been in the custody of her husband (the 'accused'), she was under duress and in no mental condition to record her statement. The ruling completely ignored the fact that Rita was a major who had married of her own volition.

The court drama climaxed with a reluctant Rita literally dragged by four armed policemen and a woman constable into a police jeep. Members of AALI who had accompanied

Rita held on to her with their 'muscle and women power'. Though the police threatened and abused them, the activists were not cowed down; they approached the district judge who passed an interim order stating that Rita, an adult, could leave Nari Niketan and go with whomsoever she wanted.

The Indian Constitution does not explicitly recognize the right to marry, though it does guarantee a legal framework that guarantees the rights to equality (Article 14), freedom from discrimination (Article 15), freedom of movement, right to residence (Article 19), and right to life and liberty (Article 21). Marriage for both men and women is governed by the personal laws of the five principal religious communities – Hindu, Muslim, Christian, Jewish, and Parsi – while couples of mixed faith can also marry under a specific personal law if they convert.

There are loopholes galore in these laws. For instance, child marriage is recognized under some personal laws even though the Child Marriage Restraint Act, 1954, specifies the minimum ages of marriage as 21 for men and 18 for women, and penalizes underage marriage. Also, although the Indian Contract Act, 1872 (Section 14), provides for consent in marriage, a child's consent is immaterial under these personal laws. What counts is the opinion of her guardian, principally her father. Ironically, however, if the 'child' marries someone of her choice against her parents' wishes, as in the case of Sonu (17 years) of Muzaffarnagar, UP, her guardian can claim her as 'underage' and manipulate the law to render the marriage void![30]

A law that claims to facilitate marriage between couples of different religions without conversion is the Special Marriage Act (SMA) 1954.[31] In reality, however, runaway Hindu couples have found the procedure so complicated and long drawn out that they have resorted to marrying in the Arya Samaj way,[32] a form approved by the Supreme Court. Its bare-bone requirements make it ideal for harassed couples: one hour's notice, proof of age, three photographs, and one hour of puja performed in an Arya Samaj temple before the fire.

In contrast, the Special Marriage Act procedure is time-consuming. A couple has to file a court application with their photographs 30 days before marriage; these are displayed and objections invited. This discloses the intent of couples wishing to marry in secret to avoid harassment. This procedure has worked against couples in inter-religious relationships, with fundamentalist vigilante groups in Gujarat and Delhi making court rounds to 'prevent dishonour' to the community through mixed marriages. Also, a provision in which the police visit a couple's home for 'investigation' before the marriage treats marriage as a criminal activity and the couple as criminals.

Another legal measure that parents routinely use to 'recover' their adult runaway daughters is habeas corpus, a law that is widely used for political prisoners and illegal detention by the state.[33] A husband may also use this provision when his wife is being detained by her natal family. However, the use of habeas corpus needs to be questioned, says Pratiksha Baxi, as it allows a natal family custodial power over women in alliance with the law. Moreover, there are contradictions within the Indian judiciary about the right of an adult woman to choose her partner in marriage. On the one hand, points out Baxi, the family and law courts enforce and encourage reconciliation between a battered woman and her abusive husband in a violent marriage. On the other hand, couples in love marriages may be forced to die, suffer, or endure punishment in state-run institutions.[34]

In reality, a range of laws is used to criminalize love. Ironically, criminal laws intended to protect women from forced marriages are used against these couples. In consultation with resourceful lawyers, a natal family deploys the laws of rape, abduction, and kidnapping against a man. What is most critical in this scenario is the woman's role. To quash criminal proceedings against her lover/husband, what is needed is proof of a woman's age and her consent in the relationship; the girl can issue a statement in court, saying she married of her own volition and that she is a major. 'Otherwise, the marriage is doomed and the boy is sunk,' says Manoj Shukla, a lawyer at the Lucknow High Court. In reality, swear activists, the 'custody' of the woman is vital in helping a couple.

Police and Politicians: And They Are All Honourable Men

Never mind the law. In reality, there are no rules in this game, and the 3Ms – money, muscle and manpower – take over. The police often collaborate with families and register false charges against couples to break up marriages, says AALI's Tulika Srivastav. 'The police refused to believe that I had not kidnapped my wife,' says Tony, a Christian man from Lucknow. 'They arrested and threatened me and immediately started to beat me in the police station.' Tony and his Muslim wife were forced to settle in Benaras.[35]

The Kolkata police reflected similar biases during the Rizwanur-Priyanka case. Although the couple had submitted copies of their marriage and birth certificates and sought police protection from Priyanka's father, this was ignored. Instead the police repeatedly harassed Rizwanur in the presence of a member of the Todi family.

The complicity of the police in maintaining 'culture' runs so deep that even senior police officers do not feel they are doing anything wrong. Political parties play a similar role in maintaining the status quo. Javed Khan, an elected pradhan in a West Bengal village says that families often ask political parties to put pressure on couples. 'Leaders assess the situation, eye the potential electoral power of the families concerned, and calculate the political fallouts,' says Khan. 'This way the parties buy allegiance and hand out patronage.' Haryana chief minister Om Prakash Chauthala refused to take action against a caste panchayat ruling that tried to nullify a marriage by choice. Saying that 'social' groups should act, he washed his hands of all responsibility.

Such cues are picked up by the system. Says Assistant Sub-Inspector Kumar from Rohtak, Haryana, 'We are compelled to live in this society. When couples break norms, there is so much social pressure on the family. There is no alternative for the parents but to murder the boy.'

Posing murder as a choiceless alternative legitimizes the crime. The state cannot however remain a passive spectator to violence, nor can it be termed a private matter. Deputy

Superintendent C.S. Bhan of Rohtak justifies state inaction[36] on the ground that caste practices are 'private matters'. Says Bhan, 'The police do not like to interfere with caste panchayats because they are powerful people, and in large numbers would create a law and order problem.' Says MLA Dinanath Bhaskar, 'If it is *lootmaar* and dacoity, the state can do something to prevent such public violence. But in private matters of *pyar aur rishta* (love and relationship), what can the police do to prevent violence?' Ironically, the entire public machinery is pitched against the private matter of a couple wishing to marry out of choice, but that is never viewed as state violence of another kind.

The Women's Movement: Two Steps Forward, One Step Back

Since the 1980s, a few women's organizations have tried to help women assert their choices in marriage and relationships, says Laxmi Murthy of Saheli, Delhi. Saheli and other Delhi groups were perpetually helping runaway lovers get married in the 1980s and early 1990s. Many women's rights activists have themselves faced stiff parental resistance to their relationships and helped runaway couples in their personal capacities.

Notwithstanding this, NGOs working on women's rights, human rights, and caste rights have yet to see the link between the gamut of issues surrounding the right to marriage, relationships, and sexual choice on the one hand, and violence against women on the other. For instance, the National Commission on Women (NCW) and the National Human Rights Commission (NHRC) have been tardy and ineffective in responding to the numerous cases referred to them. Groups that work on caste discrimination have not taken up inter-caste marriages. 'There is a fragmented and limited understanding of the violation,' says Niti Saxena of AALI. 'As a result there is an absence of rigorous activism on this issue.'

In UP, AALI has done pioneering work in highlighting the issue and supporting women who have exercised their right to choose their own partner. Over the past few years, the group has intervened in, investigated, and documented over 20 cases of violence against women in such situations. AALI is part of the Humsafar network of organizations that is working on this issue in various states.

The 'right to choice in relationships' has yet to get on to the agenda of social movements for many reasons. To begin with, the problem is invisible. A West Bengal group working on violence against women had handled only one such case in ten years. When I approached the West Bengal State Women's Commission, I drew a blank due to the 'absence' of such cases. Conceptually, issues like child marriage are seldom viewed as a denial of a girl's right to choose 'when' to marry.[37] Girls or women who are sold into marriage are seen as victims of 'trafficking', but not as individuals whose right to choose their own relationship has been violated.[38]

Many activists are also 'uncomfortable' with women's assertion of desire and initiative, quite 'different' from a battered victim/shattered-woman-with-no-support, whom they are accustomed to dealing with in violent situations. To cap this, sexuality itself is at the bottom of the priority list for the women's movement, and often seen as diversionary, trivial, and élitist. It is considered a luxury to discuss sexuality when burning issues of poverty, unemployment, religious fundamentalism, are tearing communities apart. Even when sexuality is addressed, it is from the viewpoint of violence, not on the basis of a woman's right to her sexuality.

Feminists often find themselves trapped in a difficult position on this issue. On the one hand, they have questioned the oppressive institution of marriage; on the other, they are accused of promoting marriage. 'At one level we are asserting women's (people) right to relate to/marry whomsoever they want, while at the same time challenging the notion that marriage is the only legitimate or acceptable framework to have sex, intimacy, companionship or raise children,' says Murthy.

According to poet and feminist activist Ruth Vanita,[39] some feminist groups have contributed to a very narrow understanding of sexuality, intimacy, and companionship. In trying to remedy the inherent inequalities of 'triple *talaq* or 'irretrievable breakdown of marriage' as a ground for divorce, or assisting women in bigamous marriages, feminists, she argues, have tended to prop up the institution of heterosexual monogamous marriage to the exclusion of all other arrangements. Says Vanita, 'A residual puritanism also induces us to focus more on the inequalities of polygamy or polyandry than on the sharp inequalities often prevailing in heterosexual monogamous marriages.'

Similarly, notwithstanding the overwhelming presence of caste oppression in people's lives, there is an absence of a deeper understanding of patriarchy operating through the caste system. Few understand the connection between marriage and caste, with marriage reproducing and reinforcing the caste system. 'Both caste and patriarchy are two sides of the same coin,' says Dalit and women's rights activist Ruth Manorama. 'Feminists have failed to centralize caste in their lives.' Similarly, caste groups fail to see the gender issue in caste violence and react to these violations primarily as caste discrimination. 'Each issue, whether of gender or caste, has been left to each movement to be dealt with separately.'

Is the 'invisibility' of caste issues in the women's movement related to its composition and its 'high-caste, high-class' leadership? Alternatively, is it partly predicated on the philosophy of 'the personal is political' resulting in a focus on issues deeply felt by women activists themselves? In the early days, says Murthy, there was less 'third personism' or the urge to go out there and 'do-good-for-our-unfortunate-sisters' kind of social worker attitude. 'While this did retain the passion and energy of autonomous women's groups, there was a huge gap in some areas. Class and caste are two such areas.'

Dare to Win: Keeping the Struggle Going

'What is most required in contentious relationships,' says Mamta of the Humsafar network, 'is a fourth M. Mental power of the couple. Stamina.' Humsafar tries to help couples facing this kind of violence through the following strategies:

Counselling: Inform and prepare the woman about difficulties, including high drama in court, threats by parents to harm the man or threats of suicide; train the couple to face hard questions in court so that they do not buckle under pressure.

Custody: Keep the woman in safe custody, preferably with women activists, out of reach of angry parents so that they cannot intimidate her and create emotional pressure and force her to withdraw from the relationship.

Consent: The woman must give consent to the marriage/ relationship; her statement (under 164 CrPC) is important against the FIR filed by her parents against the boy for abduction and rape of their daughter.

Certificates: Birth or school certificates are essential to prove a woman's age. After the couple's marriage, Humsafar social workers usually advise the couple to leave town to take pressure off them and prevent harassment; parents are kept informed through letters and phone calls about their welfare, the police through the activists.

The NGO Nishtha has evolved a strategy based on its work in the villages of south 24 Parganas, West Bengal. They attempt to convince a harassed couple not to commit suicide, a common phenomenon in the area. They however also persuade them not to run away, for family reconciliation then becomes difficult. If a girl is pregnant and very young, the group suggests abortion and postponing marriage till she is older and the boy gets a job. If she is in late pregnancy, field workers try to convince parents to accept the situation; if they fail, they involve the panchayat[40] members in secret to avoid scandal in the village. However, this strategy has failed in many instances when the boy's passion has 'cooled off', or when the girl is forcibly married off.

AIDWA in Haryana has effectively used the media, workshops, and seminars to spread awareness about the issue of choice in marriage. Today, when AIDWA marches on the streets, holds *morchas* and demonstrations, an indifferent administration is forced to sit up. The year 2004 proved to be a turning point in involving the NCW and NHRC, who in turn exert pressure on the local administration to respond.

The show of resistance had an electrifying impact and caste panchayats got the message that they could not mess around with people's lives. What is required, says Jagmati, is a strong alliance of social groups, movements at various levels, and quick response and relief by the NHRC and NCW.

But for a combination of factors, Rizwanur Rehman's death in Kolkata might have been shrugged off as another simple case of suicide. Sujato Bhadra, a human rights activist of the Association of Protection of Democratic Rights (APDR), immediately alerted the media. The fact that Rizwanur had contacted him on his cell 20 minutes before he was found dead aroused Sujato's suspicions. An alert editor of a Bengali 24-hour television news channel realized the implication of the 'extraordinary' death of an ordinary, law-abiding citizen, and ran the news continuously. Other media houses later picked this up.

People all over Kolkata protested Rizwanur's death and condemned police interference in the private life of two adult citizens. People in his neighbourhood blocked roads and set aflame public vehicles. In the next few weeks, his students and colleagues, human rights groups, women's rights activists, the city's intellectual community, and various citizens' groups held demonstrations, marches, and vigils questioning the shameful role of the police in the entire episode. Over 50,000 signatures were collected during a marathon candlelight vigil in front of St Xavier's college where Rizwanur had studied.

Stung by the public outcry, West Bengal chief minister Buddhadeb Bhattacharya admitted to the media, 'The incident has touched people's hearts. I am not defending any [police] officer. You have seen the social impact and there are several dimensions to this case. There is money power and there is also a communal angle. The government will not compromise.'

There is, however, no place for complacency even in such vigorous movements. As the protests grew louder, there were murmurs of skepticism about Priyanka's role in the entire episode. Like moral custodians, people questioned her for not condemning her father in public and for not living with Rizwanur's mother; it was reported that she looked well and composed, implying a young widow should have been significantly distraught.

This kind of questioning only shows how a woman is doubly victimized by public çensure. It demonstrates the failure to understand the grip of guardianship, the deep emotional bonds and economic dependence of a woman on her family. The unspoken wish to view Priyanka as an icon of 'suffering and sacrifice' or 'courage and defiance' reflect the pressures that a woman faces; she is expected to live up to a certain role and image.

For women, this is an everyday struggle to break free from the strangleholds of *izzat*, guardianship, and *sharam*: strangleholds that result in violence when women make their own choices around love, desire, and relationships. What is required to end such violence is, first and foremost, the recognition that this is as much a form of violence against women as any other. What is necessary to end it is a multi-pronged approach that addresses issues such as honour, shame, sexuality, and challenges the way women are conditioned in specific social and cultural contexts.

Acknowledgements

I am extremely grateful to Uma Chakravarti for the patient hours and the passionate attention she devoted to explaining in detail the issues involved. To AALI and Jagmati for providing generous assistance for my fieldwork, their contacts, discussions, and understanding. To Bishakha Datta who gently encouraged me and kept faith that I would deliver. To Basanti Chakravarty for taking interest, as usual, and for her comments.

Notes

1. Despite severe parental opposition, threats of kidnapping and brutal thrashings, Sanju and Rekha ran away and got married on 9 February 2005. I met Rekha in March 2006 with the help of AIDWA, Haryana. AIDWA is helping Rekha fight the legal case against her natal family and is linking Rekha with organizations to provide shelter and employment. Rekha's father and male family members are in prison.

2. *Gotra* means from the same ancestor. Endogamy *enjoins*
    marriage within specified groups; exogamy *prohibits* marriage
    within specified groups. An arranged match is typically sought
    for couples within the same caste, but outside the exogamous
    category of *gotra*.
3. See Chowdhry, 2007.
4. Forced marriage is different from arranged marriage, the latter
    having the consent of the woman.
5. It is inter-caste *marriage*, rather than inter-caste *alliances*, that
    provokes greater disapproval. Upper-caste men have always
    had sexual relationships with lower-caste women, but there the
    question of marriage, children, and inheritance did not arise.
6. *See* PUDR, 2003. The trend was most significant among the
    cases they have investigated and intervened in between 1999
    and 2003.
7. Personal interview, December 2006.
8. Lata Singh *vs* State of UP, 2006 (6) SCALE 583. Her brothers
    beat up her in-laws and locked up one of her husband's
    brothers for four days without food and water. They forcibly
    took over her family property, continued to issue death threats
    against her husband and their child, and lodged a false case of
    kidnapping and illegal confinement against her husband.
9. AIDWA in Haryana has consistently fought and supported
    couples' rights to 'choice in relationship'. They have challenged
    caste panchayat decisions and organized protests in the state.
10. Rizwanur had struggled from the slums of Tiljala to become a
    graphic designer and a teacher. On 18 August 2007, he married
    Priyanka Todi, a 23-year-old Hindu woman belonging to the
    Rs 200-crore-plus Lux hosiery business family. They married
    under the Special Marriage Act, 1954.
11. *See* Women's Rights Resource Centre, Action Aid India,
    Bhopal, April 2007.
12. *See* PUCL, 2002.
13. *See Asian Age,* 7 June 2003.
14. *See Frontline,* 16–29 December 2006.
15. According to S. R. Ahlawat of Maharishi Dayanand University,
    Rohtak, the issue of violence related to choice is a result of
    the talibanization of culture from Afghanistan to Lucknow,
    wherever Muslims dominate. Personal interview, March 2007.
16. Joint study by The International Centre for Legal Protection
    of Human Rights and Centre of Islamic and Middle Eastern

Law, School of Oriental and African Studies, published in 2001. INTERIGHTS: hcp@interights.org
CIMEL: cimeal@soas.ac.uk website: www.soas.ac.uk/honourcrimes

17. At the time of the interviews in December 2006, both Uma Charavarti and Pratiksha Baxi were toying with the term 'custodial violence' to categorize this specific form of violence.

18. Similarly, activists in the 1980s termed 'sati' as 'widow immolation/murder' as the term 'sati' gave it a certain aura of acceptability that dispersed the reality of it being a heinous crime.

19. *See* Dube, 2007.

20. *See* Sen, 2006.

21. *See Telegraph,* 28 July 2007.

22. In a similar vein, Mukti, 22, the first graduate of Seekh village, Panipat, Haryana, was locked up and beaten for days for expressing her desire to marry her batchmate, a Punjabi. Mukti's father, a Jat, told her to do whatever she wanted to do with the man 'outside the home' but not bring the matter within it, implying she could even have sex with, but not dream of marrying, a man outside her caste. When her father fixed a date to forcefully marry her off to a Jat boy, Mukti ran away. Mukti is now so embittered that she refuses to even marry her lover. 'I want to study to be a lawyer. I want to be free of any guardianship, I do not want to marry.'

23. *See* Prem Chowdhry, 2007.

24. *See* Agarwal, *Hindu,* 25 September 2005.

25. Women's groups point out that the Act is still limited.

26. *See* Chakravarti, 2006.

27. *See* Chowdhry, 2007:11.

28. *See* Ghosh, 2003.

29. Bhaskar is also chairperson of the Schedule Caste/Schedule Tribe Commission in UP.

30. India's ambivalent position on marriage-related matters reflects the lack of state protection to couples, and its complicity with the family and community. India is a signatory to several international human rights instruments like the Universal Declaration of Human Rights (UDHR) that give couples the right to marry of their own choice, besides the fundamental human right guaranteed by the Supreme Court of India in numerous cases. However, although India is a signatory to the Convention on Elimination of All Forms of Discrimination (CEDAW), it

has expressed reservations to those sections directly related to marriage, that is, article 5(a) and article 16, preferring a 'policy of non-interference' in the affairs of a community's culture and religious rights. Legal experts like Supreme Court lawyer Indira Jaising question India's 'reservations', arguing that these subvert the very objectives and purpose of CEDAW.

31. Mohammed Akram, chairperson, Minorities Commission, Lucknow, maintains that no inter-religious marriage is possible until conversion to Islam; marriage under SMA is void. Interview, January 2007.

32. An Arya Samaj priest in Aliganj, Lucknow, said of the marriages he has performed that 25 per cent of the marriages are 'love marriages' and 40 per cent are widow remarriage.

33. 'Habeas corpus' literally means produce in court the body or the person detained.

34. *See* Baxi, 2006.

35. A couple supported by AALI. Telephonic interview with Tony and his wife, February 2006.

36. Interview, March 2007.

37. In West Bengal, every second girl (49 per cent) is married off before she reaches 18 years, higher than the national average of 43 per cent.

38. A few years ago in West Bengal when a family sold their 16-year-old daughter, she refused to marry her 40-year-old 'fiancé'. She was locked up and beaten by his family, and only after 4 days of physical and mental abuse was she rescued by the police and local villagers.

39. *See* Vanita, 2005.

40. Panchayats in West Bengal are elected bodies.

References

Agarwal, Bina (2005): 'Landmark Step to Gender Equality', *The Hindu*, 25 September.

Baxi, Pratiksha (2006): 'Habeas Corpus in the Realm of Love: Litigating Marriages of Choice in India', *Australian Feminist Law Journal*, 25: 59–78. Nathan: Queensland.

Bunsha, Dionne (2006): 'A Serial Kiddnapper and His "Mission"', *Frontline*, 16–29 December.

Chakravarti, Uma (2006): *Gendering Caste through a Feminist Lens: Theorising Feminism*, Maithreyi Krishnaraj (series ed.), Kolkata: Stree.

Chowdhry, Prem (ed.) (2007): *Contentious Marriages, Eloping Couples. Gender Caste, and Patriarchy in Northern India*, New Delhi: Oxford University Press.

Dube, Leela (2007): 'Seed and Earth: The Symbolism of Biological and Sexual Relations of Production', in Prem Chowdhry (ed.), *Contentious Marriages, Eloping Couples: Gender Caste, and Patriarchy in Northern India*, New Delhi: Oxford University Press.

Ghosh, Shohini (2008): 'Married to the Family: Cultural Apprehensions in the Narratives of Film and TV'. *Indian Horizons*, Vol. 55, No. 1, January–March, New Delhi: Indian Council for Cultural Relations, 54–62.

People's Union for Civil Liberties & Vadodara Shanti Abhiyan (ed.) (2002): *Violence in Vadodara: A Report.*

PUDR (2003): *Courting Disaster: A Report on Inter-caste Marriages, Society and State.* Delhi: People's Union for Democratic Rights.

Sen, Purna (2006): 'Crimes of Honour , Value and Meaning', in Lynn Welchman and Sara Hossain (ed.), *'Honour' Crimes, Paradigms, and Violence against Women,* New Delhi: Zubaan.

Shukla, Rakesh (2006): 'Love, Inter-caste Marriage and Criminal Law', *InfoChange New & Features,* www.infochangeindia.org. July.

Telegraph (2007): 'Teachers in Salwar Protest', 28 July.

Vanita, Ruth (2005): *Gandhi's Tiger and Sita's Smile: Essays on Gender, Sexuality and Culture,* New Delhi:Yoda Press.

Welchman, Lynn, and Sara Hossain (2006): *'Honour': Crimes, Paradigms and Violence against Women,* New Delhi: Zubaan.

Women's Rights Resource Centre (2007): 'Report: Action Aid India', Bhopal, April. *See* http://www.actionaid.org/micrositeAssets/india/assets/annual%20report2007.pdf.

Joint study by The International Centre for Legal Protection of Human Rights and Centre of Islamic and Middle Eastern Law, School of Oriental and African Studies, published in 2001.

INTERIGHTS: hcp@interights.org and

CIMEL: cimeal@soas.ac.uk website: www.soas.ac.uk/honourcrimes

9

'Performing Sexuality'

Cultural Transgressions and the Violence of Stigma in the Glamour Economy

Manjima Bhattacharjya

This chapter looks at the work of young women in the glamour industry in India,[*] and some of its violent fallouts on their personal lives and social identities. Being a part of the Indian glamour industry (as a fashion model, commercial model, acting in television serials, music videos, and participating in beauty pageants) involves a certain 'performance of sexuality'. 'Performing sexuality' is literally a gendered performance in which the women present themselves as sensual through a language of poses, actions, or expressions as part of their occupation.[1] This has been traditionally interpreted as the 'sexual objectification of women' in feminist academic and activist discourse. I don't enter the debates around sexual objectification here but focus more on the voices and experiences of women undertaking this performance, and the impact of this on their lives.

[*] This chapter is based on ethnographic interviews conducted over three years with 30 women in the industry between the ages of 17 and 40 living in Delhi and Mumbai, who are involved in modelling on the ramp, for print advertisements and television commercials, in music videos, as well as former beauty pageant winners and contestants. It is drawn from the author's doctoral research on the life-worlds of women working in the glamour economy in India. All names have been changed to protect the identities of those interviewed.

In the first section I briefly examine what this performance of sexuality entails and the cultural tensions around it. The second section investigates the impact of this on their lives and identities. The third section looks at the coping mechanisms that the women have evolved to manage the social stigma they face as a community and the perceptions of their individual sexuality. In the final section I raise some critical questions of sexual moralities that feminists must reflect upon in order to move towards new directions in understanding sexuality and violence.

Sexuality at the Workplace

Modelling, making ads, or the movies... the proximity and the kind of work is very... it's intimate work, you know? The workspace is intimate because you are dealing with clothes, you are standing there half-naked while the designer drapes and drapes. There are twenty other people but you are still in a personal space; it's like doing a movie. You do a kissing scene or you do a love-making scene; there are 52 technicians, but you are still in personal spaces. I think that is why these professions have that slightly dubious quality... and they are slightly dubious, because where else in the world do you get 15 men to watch you when you are changing or while you are getting in and out of a tub 100 times trying to do some shampoo ad or while you are sighing and breathing and your arms and legs are being shown till up here because it's a waxing ad or a cream ad. It's a peculiar profession...

Shaheen, a top TV model in the late 1980s, now an entrepreneur

The glamour industry rests on the creation and perpetuation of a certain image of female sexuality and desire. In modelling, on the ramp, or for print and TV commercials, performance in television, films, music videos, and the associated broad entertainment industry, there is a range of ways in which sexuality is employed. Obvious instances include wearing revealing clothes in ramp shows or fashion shoots, 'suggestive poses', swimwear photographs for a model's portfolio or for a beauty contest, photos in daily tabloid newspapers, men's magazines, issues of sports magazines (such as the *Sports Illustrated* swimsuit issue) or ads which commonly use a sexualized style in the depiction of women's bodies, facial expressions, and other signifiers of sexuality and/or submission.

Such strategies are employed off the ramp or the camera too, for example by the automobile industry.[2] Young women are paid an attractive remuneration to attract crowds by standing alongside cars or motorbikes as salesgirls or attendants, at the annual Auto Expo in Delhi. While the larger automobile manufacturers hire upcoming models from modelling agencies to stand at their stalls, local automobile companies hire young college women. The money offered differs according to the client, and sometimes according to the attire the women are willing to wear: each year newspaper reports reveal 'rate cards' showing that the money paid to women who are willing to wear short skirts or tight-fitting clothes is higher.[3] Paradoxically, along with this, there is a heightened presence of security, the police force, and women police officers to round up 'eve-teasers' based on the implicit assumption that such dress codes will provoke sexual harassment.

In print and television ads, the extent of sexuality to be performed is usually determined by the script, as well as the sexual stereotypes associated with well-entrenched gender roles: such as a mother, wife, or vamp. Within fashion shows, various factors contribute to the level of sexuality that is required to be exhibited or curtailed. Where is the fashion show to be held: in a city or town? Is it to be held in a pub, five-star hotel, makeshift tent, or college auditorium? Who is the audience? What kind of clothes are on show: wedding trousseaus, Western casual wear, lingerie, or swimwear?

Thus, a fashion show with a big designer during fashion week in metros like Delhi or Mumbai will be more 'liberal' than a fashion show for the purpose of entertainment in a smaller city like Ludhiana. Amongst cities too, a show in Aizawl will be designed differently from one at Ludhiana. In Ludhiana, restraint will be exercised in the choreography and choice of outfits to minimize any untoward events (partly based on stereotypes of the sexually-aggressive, virile Punjabi male), while the clothes chosen for Aizawl (where young people are more influenced by Western culture) may be less conservative. Choreographers, designers, and sponsors are usually sensitive to the cultural expectations surrounding a fashion show in any area, and operate accordingly. Says Monica, a former Miss India finalist who has been part of a variety of shows for five years:

I have worked... in Chandigarh, Patiala, Ludhiana, Amritsar, everywhere. I can't tell you how many times we go to Chandigarh! The crowd [there] is actually not ready enough to see the kind of shows we do in Delhi... so when we go there, we do simpler shows. Shows which are like, more covered, because the audience there can't take it. You know, they'll make... unnecessarily they'll create noises and they'll shout... do something... so we don't give them any chance. Our choreographers are very intelligent in that!

Some types of work require more of this performance than others, such as the 'item girls' of Bollywood films, Hindi remix music videos, or regional Punjabi music videos. Recently a new genre of work has emerged: of swimsuit calendars, which involve the models being photographed in exotic locations in swimsuits. These calendars are not publicly available and positioned as 'exclusive' for limited circulation amongst a selected clientele.

Everyday Realities

On the whole, 'performing sexuality' is difficult to avoid (largely because of the competitive nature of the industry and the general standards of available work) and hard to resist, if only for the good money that it offers. Says Nancy, a former winner of the Miss North-East title from Manipur:

See, in India there is hardly any show where you have to show too much skin. I have done bikini shoots, but not shows as there are hardly any lingerie or bikini shows happening here. But the client or choreographer has to be clear on this from the time they get the booking from us. Supposing we get the booking well in advance, they have to tell us if it is a bikini show or a show where there is one round of bikinis or one round of lingerie. It has to be clear from the beginning because there is the question of money: when there is a bikini or a lingerie show, the money increases. If it is a full lingerie show, they normally pay double of what you get for a normal show.

Nancy draws a distinction between a show and a shoot: often a show which is in front of a live audience is more 'dangerous' to 'perform sexuality' in because of the potential for unruly behaviour from members of the audience. A shoot, on the other hand, is a controlled situation, in a more personal space where the model feels safer and more in control. Many models, therefore, agree to wear more revealing outfits in shoots, rather than in shows.

The occupation requires models to be communicative about sexuality and open about its nuances and practical details of how to pose or stand to look most 'sexy' or desirable, and/or use make-up to achieve this effect. A lexicon of suggestive poses are commonly used by the women in the industry: standing with the feet open a certain distance, keeping the mouth/lips open a little more than usual, arching the body in a certain way, tilting the face at an angle against certain lights, posing in front of a blower. A comfortable relationship with the photographer is very important for these shoots to work out well. It is critical that the woman overcomes any inhibitions so that she is able to pose with the correct body language and expressions.

Other than the actual clothes, the effects: such as the oft-used blower in fashion shoots, where a simulated gust of wind causes the hair to blow or clothes to billow glamorously and adds fluidity to a shot, or strong lights that can make an opaque garment transparent, can 'sexualize' an apparently innocuous moment. Vinita, a model, recalls one such incident:

It was this show where I was to wear something from a designer: some material like chiffon. I had to wear it and go on to the blower ... I held my bit down [puts her hand in front of her lap to illustrate] but the blower was on; it blew up too much and showed my back. For two days that's all that people were talking about. It bothers you but only for a day. After that, it's over.

Women from conservative backgrounds often find it difficult to get accustomed to this sort of obvious sexuality at the workplace. Says Shaheen:

A lot of girls come from middle-class, morally heavy backgrounds or small towns where the exposure is just simply – not that they are any different from you and me – but just that they have not had that kind of an exposure. They don't know swimming for example; they've never swum. Now, if you come from a small town where it's cold like maybe Shimla or something, you may not ever need to be in a swimsuit your whole life. But suddenly you come to a city and somebody will say that we need you in a swimsuit and you are like 'What!?'... I worked with a lot of girls who had serious trouble. It is not because they don't have beautiful bodies or they are not beautiful or they don't have fabulous skin, it's just that they have come from spaces where they didn't need to. So there is a battle in their heads.

Negotiating the Bikini

Many women have to consciously work at getting over their inhibitions. Nineteen-year-old Mayuri from Assam, for example, has enrolled for swimming classes and South American salsa dance classes because they will enable her to lose her inhibitions, and get more comfortable with her body; the salsa in particular helping her to be more 'sexy'. Pragati, a middle-class girl from east Delhi actively works to change her attitude. She says:

About wearing revealing clothes, well, I am very adaptive. I just changed my attitude. How? It was easy. I just did it. I don't think that by wearing a bikini I am showing my body, or showing my skin. I am just showing the feel of the garment. This is the change in thinking that happened inside me. I stopped seeing it as skin show. Yes of course my parents said, 'Oh this is wrong, you should not be doing it.' But what can we do now: both me and my sister have done it already! Now there is no point saying anything. Yes, I did feel embarrassed the first time, I was very embarrassed, I thought my brother can be picking it up and looking at it... but then I told myself... I am not showing off my body, just the garment.

Beside the odd bikini shot, the women feel there is far less demand for revealing outfits to be worn on the ramp. There is enough negotiating space for models to express their discomfort with wearing any particular outfit. Choreographers and designers are reasonably sensitive to these constraints and feelings, and often accommodate such requests. Those who are willing to wear more daring clothes are at an advantage because they are in a position to charge more. Many models are clear that while they would do bikini shows or lingerie shoots abroad, they would not wear these in India. As affirmed by Vinita:

Wearing sheer clothes and all is alright to a certain extent. Abroad women walk around topless backstage – it's in their culture. Here, no way. See, you can't suddenly do something that's against your culture. You don't want to show... because it's the way people look at you. You know if you go out with things showing on the ramp, photographers will take a picture of you and put it on the front page so that they can sell their newspaper more! We don't want that.

Anurita in fact learnt the hard way the cultural 'meaning' of modelling in a bikini in India. She recalls:

I thought I was being a proper professional model by agreeing to wear whatever I was asked to and shoot, even if it was a bikini... But I learnt that if you do a lingerie shoot in India, people will only call you for those kind of things, which is really sick... Because I am not a lingerie or bikini model or something, I can shoot well in sarees also! But once you do that kind of work, people think you are fit for that kind of work only which is wrong. It is all in the mind. After that they only call me for condom ads: there is nothing bad about condom ads as such, but I am only getting calls for those kinds of assignments!

The bikini is in fact a recurring motif that symbolizes the ultimate moment of cultural conflict. Mayuri talks about how she was misled into posing in a bikini, something she regrets to this day. She says:

I shot in a bikini because the photographer told me I had to. He said, *'Bikini to folio mein hota hi hai!'* (There is always a bikini shot in a model's folio.) Later I felt, and my colleagues also told me, that I should not have done it. It's not so important for Delhi. If I distribute bikini shots to coordinators, then offers for only that kind of work will come to me. Which is what happened. I did not know anything at the time, so I did it... and started getting all rubbish offers. But I didn't distribute those pictures after that. Bikini shots are important for foreign models, but here in India we are conservative so it is not so important for us...

The Paradox of Agency

Women are often defensive about their choice of assignments, indicating that they see this kind of performance as cultural transgression. The usual defences range from their having 'no choice' to having exercised 'free choice' which is the right of every individual. These two extremes reflect the nuances of 'choice' and 'consent' (and indeed the politics of victimhood and volition) and the realities of women's working lives, where many parameters are considered and weighed against larger goals and desires to arrive at complicated 'choices' that are both free and unfree.

For example, the reason for wearing bikinis in a beauty contest (the most visible and criticized aspect of the profession) is often given as the 'lack of free choice'. Says Monica, a former Miss India finalist:

You know there are certain things that I am not comfortable with personally, so I just go ahead and tell [choreographers], I can't wear it, so if you don't mind, give it to someone else. Otherwise people know that I don't do lingerie shows and all. Because I am not comfortable with it.
Interviewer: But in the swimsuit round you had to wear it...?
In Miss India, yes. That time I definitely wore it. No, because everybody was wearing... it was a pageant; a pageant more than anything else! I am not doing it for fun! It's just an exam. No choice. I think I had to. For that I had to... make myself understand that, ok, I am wearing this and going.

While women absolve themselves of the cultural consequences of their actions with this explanation, they are also aware of the tensions surrounding it. In particular, they are aware of the gaze and intent for disrobing. Even though

wearing a swimsuit to submit the body to scrutiny is an almost
statutory requirement in contests, tensions exist most in the
swimsuit round, as the producers of the model-hunt reality
TV show Get Gorgeous were to discover. Says the producer:

We had the most difficult time with the girls in the swimwear round.
Contestants were not informed beforehand about this and it came as
a surprise for them. They went ballistic, and reacted really violently.
They were like: 'What is this, how can you expect us to wear this…?!'
'This is not a sarong, it's like a handkerchief,' or 'I promised my dad
I wouldn't come on TV in a bikini.' Ultimately we had to leave it
to them – but we told them, you'll lose points, it will reflect in your
marking. Still, only two girls came on stage without the sarong we
had provided with the swimwear, others wore a skirt or trousers
under the bikini top. All of them had a problem, but those who had
been modelling for a while got over it sooner.

The tension is related more to the entanglement of the
self with the family, rather than an expression of personal
inhibitions; i.e., what will the parents say? Traditional parent-
child relations come in the way of what the self wants; and this
has then to be rationalized by being portrayed as a choiceless
career act or a sacrifice that had to be made for the greater
goal. Alternatively, in some instances the issue is just ironed
over or brushed under the carpet so as not to disturb the
cultural child-parent status quo. Says Kavya:

First time I wore a bikini with a small sarong for the contest; it was
funny but it was ok. I did not really feel anything, but I remember I
could only think, 'What will my mother and father say?!' I was quite
concerned. But then I told my mother, and I showed her the picture
– it was not looking bad or anything – but she was not so happy…
I told her not to tell my father. I did not show it to him and she did
not tell him either.

The choice is a considered one, weighed against the level
of ambition and other parameters that are valuable to them.
Admitting this agency, or playing it up, is however guarded
against. In this regard, 'free choice' appears to be more a
reference to a context – of a democracy, a free world, a free
market, a natural extension of modern notions of privacy,

individuality and choice and part of the construction of the 'new Indian woman' – rather than a statement taking complete responsibility for a decision. To the contrary, such an uninhibited and voluntary expression of responsibility is underplayed to avoid aspersions being cast on one's 'character' or being accused of violating cultural norms.

Mayuri has an ambiguous tone when referring to the bikini shot. It is clear that she put considerable effort into it, found it to be quite an exciting experience, and was particularly upset because of the tasteless responses to it.

I had brought the bikini with me, when I came from Assam. You know [in] Guwahati, you get goods from abroad. My cousin sister had got some bikinis. And I bought it from her when I came.

I had never worn a bikini before. So I was very nervous, almost crying after that. But I think that picture of mine is very nice, the expression on the face was also very nice. It's sad that it was taken wrongly... I think I got my Thailand assignment because of that.

Although Mayuri knew her foray into modelling would involve her wearing a bikini and went to some trouble to procure one, she still dramatizes the trauma of the moment: it would seem immodest to make her agency in this too apparent and would bring her in conflict with cultural mores.

Ironically, there is sometimes also a reinterpretation of culture to reconcile with this need of the profession. Shivani, who is from a conservative family in Benaras and modelling for the last three years, says:

I am not that career-oriented, only for time-pass I am in this line... I don't wear anything revealing. My bookers never send me for such shoots. They know my restrictions, they know my limitations, they know that Shivani won't do any shoot with bikini, or the cleavage showing or something like that. Because my parents are not like that. I myself don't have a problem wearing... but ya, I like to maintain my own dignity, my family values, because they expect so much... Still, I did one or two shoots where I was forced to wear a bikini blouse, but it came out properly you know, I wore the coat or something over it, so it wasn't like that kind of [obvious] bikini shoot. Within Indian clothes only.

Under the camouflage of 'wearing Indian only', women are able to get away with much vis-à-vis their families.

In this sense and others, the experience of performing sexuality is full of paradoxes. One is the paradox between the socialized self, that of the 'good woman', and the performance, which imitates the 'bad woman'. Gautami, a winner at the Get Gorgeous model hunt, separates the private person off the camera (invariably a 'good' girl) from the professional model who poses (indecently, as a 'bad' girl would) before the camera, thereby demonstrating the tension that exists between the two personas separated by the eye of the camera:

It's not bad to pose in that kind of [way]. But off the camera, and off all this [the media] if you see that girl in a *salwar* suit, you will never say that she is that [sexual] person... It's ok. If the work requires it, it's ok. It's like play-acting.

At the same time the pragmatic approach of the work being 'like play-acting' leads to clarity in the models' minds about the separation of their inner self with the outer image.[4]

Paradoxically, women also feel that expressing their sexuality through this creative outlet lends them greater confidence, and a sense of pride in the pictures that come out in the way they had envisaged. At certain stages in the process, there are rare moments in which the model's own subjectivity and the creative enterprise come together to create a sense of freedom, sensuality, and empowerment. This is a paradox, and best represented by the response of most of the women that yes, they would like to do an 'item number' but in Samaira's words: 'Like Sushmita Sen... not like Negar Khan. I want to be admired and respected, not lusted after.'

This kind of 'item number' is a metaphor for the paradox of 'performing sexuality': the women want to be desired, want to appear 'sexy', express their sexuality, yet within the limits of physical safety and the safety of an aesthetic gaze that will respect them and look beyond their physicality.

Stigma and Sexual Terror: Facing the Impact

Suddenly the model tag comes on you and suddenly, people feel you
are easy, cheap. Some of the men feel it. They can't believe that you
must be having some values and principles after being a model.

Monica

Both the actual and assumed 'performance of sexuality' that is
part of their occupation have a severe impact on the everyday
lives of women in the industry. Shaheen feels this has always
been the case, even in her time. Part of this is related to the
notion that modelling is not real work, only an extension of
the gendered activity of women dressing up, and any money
that comes from this kind of activity is questionable, or seen
as 'easy money'. She says:

There are outsiders who say to me that 'modelling *mein aap kitne paise
banate ho?*' (So, how much exactly do you make in modelling?) You
know they couldn't imagine you could make this kind of amount of
money without sleeping around. In their heads you were sleeping
around...

This tag is only the tip of the iceberg. Shaheen talks about
the more serious impacts of such stereotyping on the emotional
well-being of the women, including loneliness, depression,
and the fear of being deemed unmarriageable:

These professions are vulnerable professions, acting and modelling
... You are exposing a lot more than a regular girl, in terms of your
body or your views. Your skin is more, your sexuality is more
apparent, and as a result, you are partly viewed as an object, I will
not say completely... because you are indeed flaunting face, skin,
hair, whatever it is, your physical attribute. So you are vulnerable
in this space. It is easy to get men to date you; it's far easier to
get out for dinner and lunches, it's easier to sleep around because
we travel so much. So you have to be very careful that you keep
yourself in a good position. After this when the girls want to settle
down, there's nobody to marry! Men don't want to marry them...
they are happy to date them and take them out and look good with
them in their arms – but don't want to get married to them. You
pay a price for it...

This also leads to a complex relationship between the woman and people around her: especially her family, relatives and male partners (boyfriends, husbands, live-in partners), and a strained relationship with the outside world in which she has to engage prejudices and minimize risks to her reputation. Says Harpreet:

Getting married in India when you are a model is a mammoth job. No man wants to get serious with a model; no man wants the relationship to be legitimate. Most models have broken marriages. I have seen it amongst my peers. Nobody is happy. You leave modelling in case someone does marry you because he or the family will not tolerate it. Or they will keep cribbing till you compromise. Or you go to a *phirangi* [foreigner].They understand better; they don't have a problem if you are posing in a bikini. They don't think like that. They don't think you are a flirt because you are modelling. In my case, my boyfriend has given me a commitment after me being a model but he has set some standards for me... I can't shoot in a bikini... (he says); you can't marry me if you shoot in a bikini. Very few men would do that. It is always that you go by their desire. But otherwise he is really understanding. At least he is committed and I like that. And I think that by just not shooting in a bikini if I can balance my career with my love life it is totally worth it.

Vinita, who was once the model for the Kamasutra condoms advertisement, talks about having problems with her boyfriend over doing a particular ad campaign:

I recently did this print ad for Bed [a lounge bar], and the copy for the ad was 'Would you go to Bed with me?' Quite smart. And my own boyfriend [disbelievingly and slightly hurt about it], said 'I don't think it's right for you to do the ad.' I said, 'Why not? You also work in the film industry.' He said, 'I can't see my wife-to-be, my girlfriend, doing that ...' 'But,' I said, 'what is wrong in that? You have known it from the beginning till now? What has changed now? I'm not going to be in bed with everybody just because it's written over there! This is what I do. I am wearing very respectable clothes, I am covered; there is no skin showing anywhere. There is just the line. Indian men want women who are very subtle, *gharelu* [home-loving] and... I am all that! [in exasperation]. But there's a time for it! I'm also [a professional model]... I cannot disrespect my work.'

Sexual Harassment at the Workplace

The everyday impact of being seen as a sex object both in the workplace and in society at large poses a danger to women's physical and mental well-being in the form of sexual harassment. As Robert Goldman states, 'The very real physical terror which may accompany presentation of the self as an object of desire [is] the fear of rape and violence by misogynous males.'[5] I focus now on this aspect of the undercurrents of 'sexual terror' (also a term used by some of the respondents) that become part of their lives.

There was a general wariness about talking about sexual harassment in the glamour industry.[6] Only in a few instances did women give specific instances. Most of them admitted in passing that they had heard of incidents from their friends and colleagues, but it had never happened to them. Roopali suddenly changes her tone and lowers her voice while discussing this issue.

I don't think that there is any, you know, like if you are talking about sexual harassment or the casting couch kind of thing, I mean, yes, it is definitely happening, but I feel that it's up to a person how they handle it. If we are talking about sexual harassment in the modelling industry or wherever, I feel that it is everywhere. Like even when I was in Singapore Airlines I used to hear stories... I was working for Taj before that for a month as a management trainee, and there also... [voice changes to conspiratorial hush, a bit concerned that she has said too much] I shouldn't be naming it; I'm sure you're not going to... It's okay, right? [Yes, I assure her, indicating it is confidential.] Ok then [voice reverts to normal, and she is back in a more formal mode; it is clear that she is not going to say anything more.] So I mean it is everywhere. People do try to take short cuts and that's why it happens.

Most of the women view sexual harassment as an issue confronting all working women, not just women in the glamour industry:

Interviewer: Is the industry safe for young women?
Monica: See... there are too many answers to this question. I feel that... you have to look after yourself. Industry I don't want to

blame. This is not about this fraternity. It's about all working women
in India. Is it safe for them? They should know it. Nobody else.
Interviewer: Do you think models are exploited in any way?
Monica: I think the answer is the same. It's not all about models. It's
about all Indian women... young women.

While the final 'choice' to refuse such an offer is with the
women, the impact is inevitably that she will not get work
from that source any longer, thereby effectively derailing or
hampering any progress in her career. Says Kavya:

Women have the 'eye', and can understand immediately if someone
is looking at them in the wrong way. And then they keep a distance,
because they can understand him, so that no such situation arises. If
they feel he will ask for sex they have to keep distance. I think you
have to be straight with everybody. And keep an attitude that no one
will misbehave with you. Like if someone tells you, 'Oh it's a give-
and-take relationship,' repeatedly in that way, you can say up front
'What do you mean by "give-and-take"? I give you my services to
show your clothes, and take money from you for that work. It is work,
and that is the give-and-take.' To my mind there is nothing else.

Swati, however, discovered that it was not as simple as that.
In the days before her win at the Gladrags competition, Swati
was approached by the proprietor of a prominent fashion
magazine in Delhi to audition for the cover. A meeting was set
up in the lobby of the hotel Le Meridien. When Swati got to
the lobby she was not able to find him and called his mobile.
He said he was at the bar and she should join him there. In
her words:

I was a little puzzled – why is he sitting in the bar when I specified I
would meet him in the lobby? So anyway I went there. He was sitting
with this other chap. So I sat with him, and he saw my pictures. Of
course I had my make-up on and I was looking however models are
supposed to look. We were talking about money: I told him these
are my rates and this is what I would charge. Then he said, 'Now,
what else could you do for me?' Then I got it. I asked him straight,
'Oh, are you talking about sexual favours?' And he said, 'I think
you're smart enough...' [in sleazy tone]. That's it. I just got up, gave
him one tight slap. It was a shock... you called me here for this?
[incredulous tone] I told him, what do you think of me? My relative

is a well known MLA: I'm going to tell her and I'm going to make your life impossible in Delhi. I just left... Of course I didn't tell anyone about it later.

I was very shaken when I left. I couldn't drive. I met with an accident. [Pause] I couldn't believe it... that this could happen to me! Because sometimes you give certain vibes to somebody. There you can get approached by someone. But knowing myself, when I am not giving that vibe, when I don't fall in that category... then how did he dare to even ask me that question?' I thought about going to the press, but decided there's no point. Every time I look at that magazine and see the girl on the cover [laughs] the same thing just comes to my mind.

Swati's experience shattered her own belief that such offers are made only to 'those kinds of women'. In Swati's head there was a separation between her and women who invited trouble; after this incident she realized that there were no such categories, and such offers were part of the praxis of the industry. This internalized image of the 'bad woman' who would do such a thing is partly why sexual harassment in the industry is a taboo topic, and women do not want to share their experiences about it, or be known as one of 'those kinds of women'.

Ruhi has been modelling for six years and feels that she is losing out on work because of her refusal to cooperate with 'conditions'. At the same time, she feels there is little that can be done to stop it. She says,

I feel like killing them when they make these kind of offers. Once there was a shoot, and they offered me Rs 2 lakhs. I was like, Why? I only charge Rs 6,000–7,000 for a shoot. No, they said, you can keep Rs 50,000 for the shoot. And the rest you know, you need to entertain the client. They don't say you have to sleep with him, they say 'entertain the client'. You need to go for a dinner and things like that. These are the terms they use: 'jo friendly ho' [friendly ones], 'jo bahar hamare saath ghoom sake' [those who can go out with us], 'jisko koi problem na ho' [those who don't have problems with this], and things like that.

Like her, most women do not take action or lodge an official complaint for fear of being dismissed, losing their reputation, or facing hostility or social stigma in the workplace.

Public Harassment

Sexual harassment, innuendoes, indecent proposals, are not matters limited to the casting couch. They also spill over into their personal lives and other aspects of their professional lives, from people outside the industry. Swati recounts some of the experiences of this impact during fashion shows in smaller towns in India:

FTV [Fashion TV] definitely harms the image of models, especially in smaller towns in India. When the public sees Indian girls who are models, they think they are the same as those girls on FTV. We face the consequences of these things. Like when we go for shows in small places – Meerut, Kanpur, Lucknow, Jalandhar – these places are quite difficult. All these guys stand outside the venue in big groups, and after the show, sometimes even during the show, shout comments, pass remarks, usually on the body, so we can hear... like 'hi sexy', 'nice legs', 'nice cleavage', or 'sexy cleavage'. Or *badi* hot *lag rahi thi* skirt *main* (you were looking hot in that skirt). Sometimes even terrible ones, *randi*, slut, whore. Everything. Of course the girls discuss it, talk about it backstage. Usually we ignore it; what else can you do? They usually don't do anything beyond the comments. Once though, we had to say something. It was at the Patiala Heritage Festival, on a college campus. A day before the show some boys came in, sat in the first row and started passing comments while we were rehearsing. It got quite bad, so we had to complain and the choreographer and all had to go up to them and ask them to leave. They were only six boys, it was not a big group so it was ok. These things happen quite regularly in shows especially in the small towns.

Even while on stage in big cities, some of the women recount stories of obscenities being silently mouthed to them or whispered from men in the audience (while they are walking down the ramp and catching their eye), and having to maintain their composure and ignore it while the blood rushes to their head and anger wells up within. Withholding information to maximize safety is one of the strategies used by women. Says Harpreet:

When I meet people, I don't introduce myself as a model... I say I am a student or something. Because men really try to pile on once they know… especially on flights and things. Someone sitting next to you, they ask you what you do. If you say you're a model that's it! They try to pile on, thinking [rubbing her hands in lecherous manner], 'Oh, let's try our luck…!'

Many women feel that this is part of the seamless experience of sexual terror that all women undergo even in public places, while admitting that within the profession there is an added vulnerability. There are often allusions made that women who wear revealing clothes, or do not cover themselves or their 'modesty', will invariably be lynched because of the provocation they will cause to men.[7] Women interviewed for this essay are among those who are easily cited as being in the latter category, and therefore more vulnerable to sexual assault.

My research, on the contrary, indicates that women in the industry do not face any greater sexual assault in public places than other women in similar contexts. Whatever they face is largely unconnected, not to their attire, but to the assumptions related to their occupation. There was no evidence to indicate any incident of physical sexual assault, although there were many incidents narrated of verbal abuse, sexually coloured offers and acts of power in the workplace. More than any actual physical assault, it was the threat of violence or the 'sexual terror' they experienced as part of the general experience of being young, single, working women in an unsafe city like Delhi.[8]

Another form of 'violence' which they experienced was through the global space of the Internet. Say Noelle:

There are also other hazards to being a model: 'Like my brother found some pictures of women in bikinis under my name on the Internet! And they are not me!'

Mayuri's photos (again in a bikini) are also on the Internet, without her permission:

But what happened after that was that there are two-three photographers, without asking me they put those pictures on the website. So people see it and [come with offers]… they ask me and the blood just rushes to my head. I told him few days back to just delete those photos, but he has not done it yet.

This form of technology-related terror forms a new kind of violence against women, and is experienced more intimately by women in the glamour industry. The effects of this we do not yet fully understand. It is not as 'real' as sexual assault but nonetheless creates a sense of sexual terror and has a traumatic impact on the women.

Notes on the Management of Discredited Identity

Interviewer: How do people perceive you when you meet them... when you tell them, 'I am a model'.
Shivani: I don't tell [pat comes the reply].
Interviewer: You don't tell them?
Shivani: No [embarrassed laugh].

In his seminal work of 1963, sociologist Erving Goffman describes stigma as 'an attribute that is deeply discrediting within a particular social interaction'. The person with the attribute is 'reduced in our minds from a whole and usual person to a tainted, discounted one'. Goffman identifies three types of stigma: 'abominations of the body' (physical deformities), blemishes of individual character (evidence or record of mental disorders, imprisonment, addiction, homosexuality, prostitution, and the like), and tribal (stigma related to race/nation/religion). When this stigmatizing attribute is visible or immediately evident or well known, the person becomes 'discredited', whereas when the attribute is not immediately known the person is 'discreditable'.

Goffman explores 'mixed contacts' or how an interaction between 'normals' and the stigmatized play out. In these interactions the stigmatized manage 'social information' (information that the individual conveys about himself through bodily expression in the immediate presence of those who receive the expression) in order to manage their stigma. The already 'discredited' focus on managing the tensions that are generated during social contact, while the 'discreditable' manage information about the 'failing', or as Goffman says, 'to display or not to display; to tell or not to tell; to let on or not to let on; to lie or not to lie; and in each case, to whom, how, when and where'. Various strategies are resorted to, such as 'passing' or the management of undisclosed discrediting information about the self, 'covering', or the use of 'prestige symbols' and 'dis-identifiers' (well-known signs to break a stereotype in a positive way), management of personal identity (such as change in name in the case of entertainers; as Goffman says, the 'average chorus girl changes her name as frequently as her coiffure'), identity documents, and the construction of biography.

Techniques of information control also include the concealment of visible signs that have become symbols of stigma, disconnectedness in biography by maintaining physical distance from a scene, threats to transfer the stigma or even voluntary disclosure through a 'disclosure etiquette': purposeful slips, or wearing of stigma symbols. Through these techniques, Goffman says, the stigmatized must 'constantly strive to adjust to their precarious social identities. Their image of themselves must daily confront and be affronted by the image which others reflect back to them.'

Almost all the techniques of information control are used by women in the glamour industry. All the women stated that they did not reveal their profession to strangers or to landlords or people they meet at social functions, and often tried to 'pass' as media, stylists or other such professionals. To overcome the debilitating effects of stigma, they often build a persona that projects other elements of their personality. As Shaheen says:

You are looked at as an object... but to offset this you have to work doubly hard to make sure that you balance it with an apparent personality and an apparent intelligence and apparent education and apparently other things. You have to work hard to get that side of you up as well. And the moment you do that, then you get the best of both worlds.

'Spectacle and Surveillance':
The Everyday Management of Sexuality

A subtle undercurrent of the life-worlds of women in the industry (as well as women generally in the era of globalization) is the everyday management of their perceived sexuality (or hyper-sexuality in the case of women in the industry), and the concomitant management of potential stigma, at the workplace as well as in public spaces, amongst family and relatives, and society at large.

Women in the glamour industry, and indeed young women in urban India, live precariously between spectacle and surveillance.[9] While they are encouraged to present themselves as sexual, active, autonomous objects to be desired as a spectacle of sorts, they are simultaneously watched or placed under surveillance by the traditional custodians to ensure that boundaries are not crossed.

In her work on public spaces, Shilpa Phadke (see chapter 3 in this volume) shows how new public spaces in metropolitan India, such as pubs, malls, coffee shops, night clubs, multiplexes, etc. (she calls them the 'new spaces of consumption and display'), are spaces to be 'seen' where (upper/middle-class and heterosexual) women enjoy a certain freedom and feel sufficiently safe to indulge their desire to be a spectacle by dressing 'sexily' or behaving in a certain uninhibited fashion. According to Phadke:

While on the one hand women are present in the public in their roles as consumers they are also simultaneously the consumed. In their dress, deportment and gestures, women demonstrate an internalized male gaze. By implication women are expected to simultaneously demonstrate their sexual desirability while ensuring their sexual safety.[10]

However, the moment they step outside these symbols of modern urban development on to the roads or public transport, they are greeted by a different reality in which traditional ways of looking are encountered, alongwith a sense of being under surveillance. Some of the women said the clothes they had to wear during an audition could not be worn to travel to the venue of the audition. Therefore they sometimes wore a shirt over the 'costume' or wore subdued make-up en route to the venue. The distinction that women draw in their minds is clear: the client is entitled to see them as a spectacle, but family and relatives are bound to place them under surveillance. Through a cat-and-mouse game, they will work to get the best of both worlds.

For women in the glamour industry, being in the public eye has both a positive and a negative side in the management of their perceived sexuality. The negative aspect is of course the perceived hyper-sexuality and stigma. Even so, there is the positive side of being seen in public spaces, even on Page Three, which eradicates some of the murkiness from the assumptions surrounding their profession. As Monica says:

> Earlier people who were related to me would say, 'Oh, what kind of work is she doing…' But now they know whatever I am doing, because now it's in front of them. It comes in the newspapers, it comes in the news and it's all out there. So they know that whatever I am doing is…good.

Ensuring that such regular 'outings' are visible in the public domain is part of their management of sexuality: it validates the legitimacy of the job; enables people to connect the work they have (visibly) done and the economic benefits they are enjoying. On the other hand, if they are earning money (from modelling) or engaging in conspicuous consumption, and people around them do not see the evidence of this work (in visible spaces like television or the daily newspaper) they begin suspecting the validity of the claim that the women are actually engaged in modelling.

Women have therefore to 'manage' the perception of their sexuality and the potential stigma it may bring. At the same time they must on this basis take responsibility for their personal safety. Whether it involves acquiring respectability through embracing symbols of good womanhood,[11] or selectively using symbols of availability or singlehood,[12] there is a subtle everyday management at play.

The Problem with Sexual Moralities

Today, the divide between the 'good' woman and the 'bad' woman is blurring in some ways. Women across classes occupy public spaces, more confident of their bodies, fearlessly wearing clothes that they wish to wear, and engage in behaviour that the dominant morality would classify as that of a 'bad woman'! New expressions of moral anxieties (like closure of dance bars in Mumbai, the Shiv Sena on a public rampage separating young couples on Valentines' Day, the imposition of dress codes for girls in colleges and universities) are a response to these developments and arise out of a fear that women are getting out of control, and must be contained.

Morality is also linked to certain kinds of labour performed by women. Certain occupations (especially for women in these occupations) particularly those that involve body work and possible elements of sexuality, are stigmatized. For example, nursing, masseurs, the 'secretary', and obvious professions such as sex work, dancing in dance bars, and also being part of the glamour or film industry. The opposite may hold true for occupations seen to be asexual and therefore highly moral, such as nuns, renunciates, priests, pandits.

This stigma is not just confined to these occupations. All women who go out to work have to cope with this. This is particularly so in the case of jobs involving late hours, night shifts, need to travel, need to wear make-up, or dress in a certain way. Just the fact that women are working outside/ away from the home, beyond (family/male) supervision, is sufficient for moral judgments to be passed. For this reason, migrant women are likely to face an additional stigma, regardless of the occupation they are in.

All women, therefore, who work in the public domain can be placed on a continuum of stigma based on the perception of their sexuality. At one end we could perhaps place the nun or the widow (the desexualized woman) and at the other, the most stigmatized, women engaging in commercial sex. Towards the more stigmatized end of the spectrum lies a cluster of occupations which have an imputed value of immorality, ascribed to them because they are related to the more overt expression or exploitation of sexuality.

I would classify women in the glamour industry somewhere within this cluster (even though many women in the profession do go through their careers without ever utilizing their sexuality in order to make professional strides). Elements of their life, such as stigma, the nature of interaction with the family, their assumed 'hyper-sexuality', the social impact of their objectification, are reminiscent of similar tensions in other sexuality-related professions. For example, a biography of Gulab Bai, a prominent *nautanki* (local travelling theatre/ road-show dance form) artiste from Uttar Pradesh, recounts the lives of women *nautanki* dancers as being on a knife-edge between making independent sexual choices and the notion of sexual availability.[13] Says Varsha Kale, representative of the Bar Girls Association:

The bar girls have swollen feet as they stand in supposedly erotic postures and dance throughout the night. They ward off advances from customers and most of them are secretive about their work, even with their families, for fear of censure and rejection. The number of alcohol and drug abusers amongst them is high as they work in liquor and dance bars; and, worst of all, their work is dependent on the vagaries of youth and looks.[14]

Both accounts are remarkably similar to those emanating from the glamour industry.

The myth that women in the glamour industry are sex objects (especially fashion models who wear revealing clothes, and therefore invite unnecessary attention, even sexual violence and harassment) is linked to the continuing association of 'what women wear' with 'who they are' or 'what type of woman they are'. This only strengthens the discourse of morality that threatens women's freedom today. Most importantly, it catapults women in the industry into a 'hypersexual' category, as women who are sexually aggressive, available, and somewhat less than human. The harassment or stigma they face has more to do with the myths and stereotypes surrounding their chosen profession and the ideas of good women and bad women that continue to have currency in society.[15]

The social impact of the apparent objectification of women in the glamour industry – the harassment, problems in personal relationships, the difficulties in getting married, the stigma, or the sexual terror in the workspace or in public life faced by them, and the sexual terror generally experienced in society by all women – have their roots in these active discourses of sexual moralities. The 'morality' that sees women on the streets who wear Western clothes as provoking men to sexual assault, or that which sees the covering up of women in various forms of purdah as vital to their safety is the same as that which sees fashion models as being sexually available or unmarriageable.

'Sexual objectification and commodification of women' has emerged as the dominant discourse of female sexuality created by globalization and the free market. This discourse does not however take sufficiently into account the subjective experiences and agency of women in the industry, nor offers a relevant critique of the underlying sexual moralities, both of which are critical to challenge the fundamental moralistic assumptions that continue to limit women's lives.

Notes

1. This does not usually carry over into their everyday lives, and is different from 'performing gender' (Butler, 1990) which is practised in everyday life (and which women in the industry also undertake) and refers to a habitus.

2. The automobile industry is, in fact, notorious for its use of women's bodies in advertisements, drawing obvious parallels between a car and a woman's body: both projected as objects of a man's desire.

3. In the India International Trade Fair, women attendants were placed in three groups, A, B, and C, according to appearance and their willingness to wear certain types of clothes. Women in grade A commanded higher rates of up to Rs 1000 a day, and wore Western outfits. Those willing to wear short skirts got a higher pay. Women in grade B were paid Rs 600-750; those in grade C, called the 'saree-suit type', received as little as Rs 150 per day (*Hindustan Times*, 23 November 2004).

4. This is akin to the separation of selves in prostitution and other kinds of body work (lap dancing, masseuse, pole-dancing, and the like).

5. *See* Goldman, 1992.

6. At the time I conducted the interviews, the issue of the 'casting couch' phenomenon (when sexual favours are sought/given at the stage of casting for a film, in exchange for a role) was very much in the public eye because of a sting operation conducted by a TV channel on a prominent television and film actor. As a result, it was immediately assumed that I was seeking information on the casting couch, and the responses were defensive and harsh, often signalling closure of any discussion on the topic, and sometimes closure of the interview itself.

7. The women interviewed had themselves internalized these ideas and repeatedly referred to ways of dressing while reflecting on the impact of being a model in their everyday lives.

8. Sangari (2004) notes that the urban terrain is strongly linked in male imagination to the Westernized woman, 'a blind follower of Western fashion which reduces her to little more than a sexualized body to be gazed at and sometimes, even groped.'

9. The term is used by Montgomery (1998) to refer to the situation of upper-class women in New York in the nineteenth century.

10. *See* Phadke, 2005.

11. For example, Hindu symbols of marriage such as *sindoor* and *mangalsutra* are sometimes even used by non-Hindu women or unmarried women to avoid unwanted attention.

12. For instance, some models hide their married status so that they are perceived as more desirable in the industry; outside the industry, in a public place, such as on board an aeroplane or at a party, they may pretend to be married because they feel it will help them maintain boundaries and enhance their safety.

13. *See* Mehrotra, 2006.

14. Geeta Seshu (2004). 'Dignity No Bar', *Hindu*, 17 September 2004.

15. For instance, even if they are 'modestly dressed', they may still encounter harassment because it is known that they are 'models'.

References

Butler, Judith (1990): *Gender Trouble*. New York: Routledge.

Goffman, Erving (1963; reprinted 1986): *Stigma: Notes on the Management of a Spoiled Identity*. New York: Touchstone (Simon and Schuster).

Goldman, Robert (1992): *Reading Ads Socially*. London: Routledge.

Mehrotra, Deepti Priya (2006): *Gulab Bai: The Queen of Nautanki Theatre*. New Delhi: Penguin India.

Montgomery, Maureen E. (1998): 'Displaying Women: Spectacles of Leisure', in Edith Wharton (ed.), *New York*. New York, London: Routledge.

Phadke, Shilpa (2005): '"You can be lonely in a crowd": The Production of Safety in Mumbai', *Indian Journal of Gender Studies*, 12: 1.

Sangari, Kumkum (2004): 'New Patriotisms: The Beauty Queen and the Bomb', in R. Ivekovic and Julie Mostov (eds.), *From Gender to Nation*. New Delhi: Zubaan.

10

Her Body Your Gaze

Prostitution, Violence, and Ways of Seeing

Bishakha Datta

Results 1-10 of about 476,000 for Kathleen Barry, Female Sexual
Slavery, www.google.com.

This was not the first vegetable to be dropped into the pot.
No, this was more like the secret ingredient that adds magic
to the mush: thrown in as the recipe begins taking shape, as
potatoes, tomatoes, garlic, and onions meld with one another,
yielding their hidden promise, gathering enough heat; hissing,
fizzing, spluttering, thickening into a broth, until it all boils
over into a consummate whole. A familiar taste; something
so well accepted that it is almost commonplace; a taste, a
flavour, an idea as natural as that of night following day, earth
revolving around sun.

It has been 30 years since feminist academic Kathleen Barry
first defined prostitution as a form of female sexual slavery in
her celebrated book of the same name. The clocks have turned
and we've entered a new millennium, but that charge has lost
none of its lustre. Or potency. Or sting. It lingers on, almost
like a childhood taste we never forget. Since 1979, when it
was published, *Female Sexual Slavery* has done everything
a book can be expected to do: gone into multiple reprints,
become a must-read, received the kind of media publicity
that feminist texts only dream of, been endorsed by icons like
Gloria Steinem, featured in virtually every women's studies

curriculum, and been cited by the who's who of women's rights. If popularity is an index of publishing royalty, *Female Sexual Slavery* is queen. Honestly, what more can a book achieve?

Prostitution as Slavery

In abolitionist discourses, prostitution is typically constructed as violence against women in one of three ways: as slavery, as force or coercion, or as harm to body and self. Barry defines female sexual slavery as 'present in all situations where women or girls cannot change the immediate conditions of their existence; where regardless of how they got into those conditions they cannot get out; and where they are subject to sexual violence and exploitation'. It can take place in prostitution or marriage, be 'criminal and clandestine' or 'secret and socially tolerated'. A slave can be a 'prostitute, battered wife, incestuously assaulted child, veiled woman, purchased bride' living in 'an Arab harem, a German eros centre, an American pimp pad, or a suburban home. Wherever it is situated, it brings both monetary gain and personal satisfaction to its perpetrators.'[1]

I do not subscribe to Barry's world-view that 'sexual slavery lurks at the corners of every woman's life', although I do agree with her on one count: men assuming that sex is their right, or that they are sexual subjects, and women existing, as objects, to meet their sexual needs. If patriarchy is the social domination of men, male sex right is its sexual variant. While Barry sees this resulting in sexual slavery, I see it triggering off bedroom politics: with men and women continually negotiating sexual power, as they do in other realms. Slavery exists as an exception in my book, not as a rule: at the extreme edge of a power continuum, where all the walls have closed in and there is no room to turn.

Although Barry writes that female sexual slavery can exist outside prostitution, the focus of her gaze is the prostitute: 'a woman... reduced to her sexual utility.'[2, 3] For her, a prostitute is inevitably a trafficked slave: someone who is purchased, kidnapped, procured, or deceived into prostitution, and then seasoned into the new life through beating, rape, and torture.[4] A poor woman is the most 'susceptible to procurers' and to slavery, which remains slavery *even if she consents*.[5]

Implicit in this paradigm is the belief that a woman never comes to prostitution on her own; she has to be 'seasoned' before being thrown into the pot, like a chicken being tenderized. If 'the craft of slave procurers' includes many recipes (love, befriending, seduction, kidnapping, and purchase),[6] so does seasoning (convincing, brainwashing, indoctrination, verbal abuse, and the inevitable triad of beating, rape, and torture). 'Seasoning is intended to break its victim's will, reduce her ego, and separate her from her previous life. All procuring strategies include some form of seasoning.'[7] Women who are cooked into a shapeless mush are never the same again. 'They suffer the same madness that raped women experience when their victimization is denied and equated with sexual intercourse. It is the same madness undergone by battered wives who are told the police don't interfere in marital disputes.'[8]

Abolitionists who see prostitution as violence often liken it either to rape or to domestic violence. For Barry, prostitution is primarily rape.[9] 'Rape is the primordial core of female sexual slavery... As long as a woman or girl is held in sexual slavery, sexual intercourse is by definition, rape. If one is not free to consent or reject, one is forced... The rape paradigm... forms the social and political context in which victims are sexually enslaved.' Elsewhere, she states that 'rape, as a military strategy and as personal outlet, is inseparable from prostitution.'[10]

Rape. Domestic violence. Slavery. In my book these are three different things that don't necessarily walk hand in hand. For abolitionists, however, such distinctions are trivial distractions on the path to defining victimhood. Halfway through *Female Sexual Slavery*, kidnapped American media heiress Patricia Hearst is suddenly introduced as a proxy for 'enslaved' women in prostitution. Held in captivity in 1974, Patricia was bound, blindfolded, and locked into a closet for 57 days; her captors fed her with her blindfold on and bathed her once a week. Days later she emerged as Tania, a member of the Symbionese Liberation Army (SLA) which had kidnapped her and was famously photographed in a bank robbery with other SLA members.

Patricia Hearst's case is an extreme one; it is scarcely something that vast numbers of women experience. But, does lived experience stand for anything in the face of theory? 'Patricia's experience sheds light on the experiences of women forced into prostitution,' writes Barry.[11] 'The victim becomes another person, not only as a way to handle the situation but as a result of her captors' forced redefinition of her identity...[12] Identification with the enemy is the worst form of depersonalization; it is the loss of freedom to be oneself.'[13]

Is Prostitution Slavery?

Slavery is a big word. A full-barrelled charge with all muskets loaded. It instantly evokes images of a bygone era: 'Negroes', cotton and sugar plantations, the American Deep South; a historical association so strong that it is hard to imagine that slavery can exist today. Yes, slavery is a big word. One is considered a slave only when one is forced to work, owned or controlled by an employer, dehumanized or treated as a commodity, and physically constrained.[14] That's what Anti-Slavery International, a London-based group that has fought slavery since 1839, tells us.

In 1991, the Coalition Against Trafficking in Women (CATW), an abolitionist group that Barry founded, took its case of 'prostitution as slavery' to the United Nations. 'To be a prostitute was to be unconditionally sexually available to any male who bought the right to use a woman's body in whatever manner he chose,' CATW told the working group on contemporary forms of slavery. This unconditional availability and the man's right to do whatever he wanted was tantamount to ownership and slavery.

Anti-Slavery International disagreed with this hypothesis. In a 1997 report, it disputed that the prostitute-client relationship is one of 'ownership' or 'enduring power' or 'unconditional availability'; or that the man can use her body in whatever manner he chooses.[15] Instead, it pointed out that consent is continually being negotiated within each transaction between a sex worker and her client.

Yes, the report said, slavery does exist in situations of debt bondage and child prostitution: 'However, the fact that some sex workers are subject to conditions of slavery does not constitute a logical basis for claims that all sex work amounts to slavery...[16] Rather than facing conditions of slavery, most men and women working as prostitutes are subjected to abuses which are similar in nature to those experienced by others working in low status jobs in the informal sector.'[17]

In viewing prostitution as slavery or captivity, abolitionists often view other low status jobs as freedom. In 2003, over half of the women rescued during a brothel raid in Chiang Mai, Thailand escaped from the shelter they were taken to, within a month of being rescued. Several escaped on the very first day. 'What does it mean that so-called sex slaves often thwart rescue attempts?' asks communication and sociology professor Gretchen Soderlund. 'Is it intellectually and ethically responsible to call every instance of a practice "slavery" when many women involved demonstratively reject the process of protection and rehabilitation, and when they escape from supposed rescuers who aim to force them out of a life of prostitution ("captivity") and into a life of factory work or employment in the low-paying service sector ("freedom")?'[18]

Such articulations typically discount the lived experiences of sex workers: 'When sex workers articulate that they do not believe that "exchanging sexual services for money with multiple partners" is in and of itself sexual slavery or sexual violence, I would like to give them the respect of knowing what they are talking about and their lived experience,' says Meena Seshu, general secretary of the group SANGRAM. 'This in no way compromises my analysis of the male role in any sexual encounter. The potential of *any* sexual encounter turning violent in an unequal space is entirely possible within or outside of commercial sex. The effort in such a case is not to stop the sexual encounter itself but to strive for a space that is respectful of women such that they are not subjects of sexual violence.'

Prostitution as Force

In the 1980s, one set of abolitionists told us that prostitution is slavery. In the 1990s, another set of abolitionists insisted that prostitution is 'the choice that is not a choice'. We were told that no woman can ever 'choose' to be in prostitution; not even as one among a limited set of options, and thus is inevitably forced, coerced, or trafficked into it.

'Sex trafficking is nothing more or less than globalized prostitution,' writes Dorchen A. Leidholdt, co-director of CATW, in *Prostitution, Trafficking and Traumatic Stress* (2003). Writes clinical psychologist and researcher Melissa Farley, editor of this volume, 'Despite the illogical attempt by some to distinguish prostitution and trafficking, trafficking[19] is simply the global form of prostitution.' One writer says that only one per cent of women in the sex industry enter of their own volition, a phenomenon she labels 'casual prostitution'.[20] Closer home, Ranjana Kumari, director of the Centre for Social Research, New Delhi, told a reporter in 2008 that 'only two to three per cent of India's prostitutes enter the profession willingly. These are the high-class girls...'

The ideology of prostitution as force, or trafficking, dominates abolitionist thinking and action across the world. In 2007, a coalition of women's groups released a report tracking the Indian government's progress in promoting women's rights.[21] The report offered no evidence that *all* women are trafficked into prostitution. Nonetheless, it blithely conflated the two, suggested how the Indian government could stop trafficking, and pretended that sex work did not exist by ignoring it. In the 231-page report, there is not even a whisper about improving the working conditions of women in prostitution; this group doesn't exist. When ideological assumptions and half-truths are presented as reality, this is a problem. When an official report by the Indian women's movement ignores the realities of 3 million women engaged in prostitution in India, this too is a problem.

Key to the myth that prostitution = trafficking is the parallel belief that no one can be in prostitution by choice. Coercion, of course! Circumstance, maybe. But choice? Every time a woman says she chooses to be in prostitution, that word is microscopically examined in a way that it never is when a woman says she 'chooses' to be in a marriage arranged by her parents, or in a violent relationship, or when a rag-picker says he 'chooses' to pick rags for a living. It is tacitly presumed that choices can exist in every situation, no matter how coercive, but not in prostitution.

When a poor woman ends up in an ill-paying job in the informal sector, such as domestic or construction work, poverty is seen as context, constraint, or circumstance. However, when the same woman enters prostitution, poverty suddenly becomes 'force': poverty 'forced' her into prostitution. This is a linguistic sleight of hand. How can it be that when women of certain castes and classes become rag-pickers, domestic workers, construction workers, and vegetable vendors, this is seen as a 'choice', but when women of similar backgrounds enter prostitution, this is seen as 'force'? Why do we always isolate the 'choices' of those in prostitution from those that other women make? Prostitution may not be a 'free choice', but surely it is as free a choice as any other?[22]

Free choice is, in any event, a myth. Writes noted economist Amartya Sen,

The existence of choice, does not, of course, indicate that there are no constraints restricting choice. Indeed, choices are always made within the limits of what are seen as feasible... This, however, is *not* a remarkable fact. It is just the way every choice in any field is actually faced. Indeed, nothing can be more elementary and universal than the fact that choices of *all* kinds in *every* area are *always* made within particular limits. For example, when we decide what to buy at the market, we can hardly ignore the fact that there are limits on how much we can spend. The 'budget constraint', as economists call it, is omnipresent. The fact that every buyer has to make choices does not indicate that there is no budget constraint, but only that choices have to be made *within* the budget constraint the person faces. What is true in elementary economics is also true in complex political and social decisions.[23]

Beyond the Force/Choice Dichotomy

Like 'slavery', 'choice' and 'force' are big words. Let's leave them aside for a moment. Let's instead focus on a word that we can wrap our hands around: consent. If choice is the intangible abstraction, consent is its concrete, tangible marker. Consent means saying 'Yes'; giving permission. Yesteryear's politics held consent as immaterial in defining trafficking, which could take place *even if the woman consented.*[24] Today, consent is a gold standard, particularly in the world of sexual politics (even though determining consent remains a grey area: 'She said "no"; he heard "yes".') In 2000 Radhika Coomaraswamy, UN Special Rapporteur on Violence Against Women, stated that

it is the non-consensual nature of trafficking that distinguishes it from other forms of migration... At the heart of this distinction is the issue of consent.[25]... Some women become prostitutes through 'rational choice', others become prostitutes as a result of coercion, deception or economic enslavement.[26]

In the lives they lead, sex workers differentiate between force, choice, and consent through their own experiences. Women in the business understand that what differentiates trafficking from prostitution, or a rapist from a client, is consent, with force or coercion being the absence of consent. Sex workers see prostitution and trafficking as linked, but not the same. Similar to a Venn diagram of two circles, with some areas that overlap and large areas that don't.

Last year, as part of my research for a full-length book on sex work, I interviewed Gouri Roy, a Kolkata-based woman who had entered prostitution twice: she was trafficked the first time, but not the second. The eldest of eight sisters, Gouri was married off when she was 11. Her husband did no work. After a decade of working as a domestic in other village homes, bearing two daughters and a son, and enduring repeated bouts of battering, she began looking for work away from home. A friend of her husband sold her into a brothel in faraway Mumbai. Gouri was then 22. A year later she escaped and returned to her husband's home with some savings. He gladly accepted the savings but threw her out along with their three children.

So what happens now? And if we want to build a hierarchy of horrors, what's worse? Being married at 11? Being beaten up for a decade? Supporting your husband by working through your teenage years? Being sold into a brothel? Or being thrown out when you return? After weighing her options – domestic work, a factory job, prostitution – Gouri went with a friend to Sonagachi, the best-known red-light district in Kolkata.

'What a difference there was between Mumbai and Sonagachi,' says the sweet-faced Gouri, who has sold sex for 13 years. Her Mumbai story was the classic saga of trafficking and debt bondage with elements of slavery. She was forced to have sex with men day and night, and to service the brothel-keeper when she was 'free'. The Rs 15,000 for which she was sold was recorded as a loan to her: whatever she earned went towards repaying this 'loan'. All she could keep were stray tips she was able to hide. She had to eat what she was told, wear what she was told, do what she was told. And, she could never go out. 'If I couldn't do what the customer wanted, he would beat me up,' she recalls. 'When I didn't want to drink, they just pressed my cheeks in, opened my mouth, and poured it in. Like medicine.'

In Sonagachi, on the other hand, Roy is a sex worker. She works fixed hours each day or until she has made enough money. She has floating clients and a few regulars, who are her main source of income. (Like all vendors, regardless of what they sell, sex workers hustle for regular clients who will guarantee them a steady income.) She pays her madam a fixed amount per transaction. Calls in sick once in a while. Occasionally turns down a client. 'I am a human being,' says Roy. 'I too have a place in me from where I can say "No". If I want to spend a day in bed, and not work, I won't.' And she has the small freedoms of everyday life that most of us take for granted. The freedom to eat fish rather than chicken. To wear a red sari rather than a blue one. To visit her children. To see a movie with her lover, who works at a multinational bank.

Many women in prostitution in Kolkata's red-light districts have experienced both trafficking and sex work, and see the distinction. 'My body was readied with mustard oil and cream,' remembers Mala Singh, who was tricked into the trade as a teenager. 'I was not given proper food to eat. It was disgusting. I would not call that sex work.' Singh was sent back home after a police raid, but a hostile reception drove her back to the trade. She now works in Kidderpore, a red-light district by the river Ganges. 'Sex work is what I do now, from a place of liking,' she says.

Gouri Das is another woman who has been through both phenomena, with a marriage and son in between. Extreme poverty made her look for work in her teens, but she's not sure whether she was forced, coerced, or deceived – all core elements of trafficking. 'It would be wrong to say that my neighbour pushed me into it,' she says. 'Although she didn't tell me where she was taking me, I kind of knew.'[27]

Others in sex work have never encountered trafficking. Like Roma Debnath, a married woman with three children who rides the train to Kolkata from her village and back at six each morning and evening. She entertains three or four clients from 10 a.m.–6 p.m. Her husband does not work. (In the trade, she is called a 'flying' sex worker who goes home at night, as opposed to a brothel-based sex worker who lives and works in the brothel). She makes Rs 60–110 for a short 15-minute job, pays Rs 10 to hire a room, and keeps the rest. 'I have to manage my children, my work, my husband, my house. All of it,' she says, like any other working woman who does one shift at work, the other at home. Roma can turn away clients, but not her husband. 'It's not possible,' she says. 'If I'm not feeling good some day, I may not take a customer. But even if I don't feel good, I have to sleep with my husband… Whichever way the husband wants it you have to give it to him, otherwise there's trouble. He thinks it's his right.'

Women like Gauri Roy, Gouri Das, and Roma Debnath can scream themselves blue in the face that sex work is not trafficking, but abolitionists still aren't listening. In 1995, sex worker rights activists at the Beijing conference ensured that every single mention of 'prostitution as violence' in the final conference document was preceded by the word 'forced'. 'The best we could was damage limitation,' writes Jo Doezema of the Network of Sex Work Projects. 'Keeping abolitionist language out of the final document.'[28] The result? CATW's executive director Janice Raymond accused sex workers' activists of 'revising the harm done to women in prostitution into a consenting act'.[29]

Ironically, neither abolitionists nor sex worker activists believe that the forced/free dichotomy is of any value, but for different reasons. Meena Seshu of SANGRAM notes that these categories blur in the everyday lives of those in prostitution: 'A woman can 'choose' to enter prostitution and still face coercion from a client. Or a woman can be 'forced' into prostitution and yet assert her agency in refusing a client. 'Choice' and 'force' are not mutually exclusive positions; both are situations that a woman can encounter and has to negotiate – like any other woman.' All that the free/forced dichotomy may have ultimately done is regroup women in prostitution into 'good' women (forced) and 'bad' women (those who chose); both face violence within prostitution. Any guesses whose violations get taken seriously?

Prostitution as Harm

At the heart of the abolitionist gaze lies the unshakeable belief that prostitution causes harm to *all* women: to those who sell sex and those who don't. A parallel belief is that this harm is caused to the *entire beings* of those in prostitution: to body, self, and soul. 'Objectification' and 'dehumanization' are the twin pillars of this belief system, with the 'harms' of prostitution often being likened to those of pornography.[30]

'In much pornography, people, usually women, become *objects* for another,' remarks Allison Alliter, quoted in

Laurie Shrage's 2007 paper, 'Feminist Perspectives on Sex Markets', on which this section is substantially based. 'To treat someone as merely a body for another's use, without recognizing that she too is a subject with desires, is to treat someone as a subhuman creature or object, and therefore violates her dignity as a human being.'[31] For Catherine MacKinnon, pornography involves men treating women as mere *instruments* in order to satisfy their sexual desires. 'Such treatment, at best, fails to recognize women as free and equal persons and, at worst, *dehumanizes* women and encourages their victimization.'[32]

In a similar vein, Carole Pateman argues that people's bodies and sexual capacities are an integral part of their identity as men and women: thus the woman who works as a prostitute sells her womanhood and therefore herself.[33] Elizabeth Anderson believes that 'the commodification of sexual "services" destroys the kind of reciprocity required to realize human sexuality as a shared good, and may corrupt non-market sexual relationships by promoting the valuation of women in terms of their market worth.'[34] Debra Satz similarly argues that 'if prostitution is wrong it is because of its effects on how men perceive women and on how women perceive themselves. In our society, prostitution represents women as the sexual servants of men.'[35] She conjectures that the negative image of women promoted by prostitution 'shapes and influences the way women as a whole are seen'.[36]

Several feminists and sex workers dispute all these claims: one, that sex work necessarily means objectification or dehumanization; two, that the 'male gaze' reduces women to a sexual class because of prostitution; three, that sex work means selling or 'harming' the body, self, or soul. Questioning whether sexual objectification is always morally objectionable or whether it is only so in certain contexts,[37] Martha Nussbaum identifies seven distinct kinds of actions that may or may not be part of objectification in any given instance: instrumentality, denial of autonomy, inertness, fungibility,[38] violability, ownership, and denial of subjectivity.[39] Some of these actions are always morally problematic, but some of them are acceptable when they are part of a larger relationship entailing mutual respect, she says.

Nussbaum argues that some actions in which we use another's body sexually are consistent with recognizing the person so used as an end and do not involve treating her as a mere object:

Denial of autonomy and denial of subjectivity are objectionable if they persist throughout an adult relationship, but as phases in a relationship characterized by mutual regard they can be all right, or even quite wonderful... In a closely related way, it may at times be splendid to treat the other person as passive, or even inert. Emotional penetration of boundaries seems potentially a very valuable part of sexual life, and some forms of physical boundary penetration also, though it is less clear which ones these are. Treating as fungible is suspect when the person so treated is from a group that has frequently been commodified and used as a tool, or a prize; between social equals these problems disappear...[40]

Similarly, Jennifer Saul explores the possible connection and continuum between objectification (treating people as *things*) and personification (treating things as *people*). She questions earlier feminist claims that men's use of pornographic images entails treating pieces of paper like women, and conflating 'women' with 'inanimate objects'.[41] Mariana Valverde demolishes the primacy of the male gaze as the only lens through which sex, sexuality, pornography, and prostitution can be viewed and understood.

It is true that the 'male gaze' constitutes a large part of sexual relations in our society, but to assume that this objectifying gaze is the only possible meaning of the term 'sexuality'... denies women any position, however precarious, from which to reclaim or invent nonpatriarchal sexual desires.[42]

Nussbaum also questions whether the sale of sexual services genuinely damages the persons who provide them or women as a whole. She points out that two centuries ago, the use of one's artistic talents for pay, such as singing or acting, was regarded as a form of prostitution.[43] She questions seven common claims against prostitution: it involves excessive risks; the prostitute has little autonomy; it violates the prostitute's bodily integrity; prostitution has a destructive effect on intimate, non-commercial relationships; it violates a person's inalienable right to her sexuality; contributes to a male-dominated social order; and relies on the economic coercion of workers. She concludes that the problems associated with prostitution exist in many other forms of work and social practices, such as marriage; thus these problems are not inherent to the work but are often a function of the prostitute's working conditions and treatment by others.[44]

Jo Doezema, of the Network of Sex Work Projects, criticizes abolitionists for framing the 'injury' of sex in prostitution in a circular manner. 'Prostitution is considered always injurious because the sex in it is *dehumanizing*. However, the sex takes on this dehumanizing character because it takes place within prostitution,' she points out. 'In this neat, sealed construction, there is no place for the experiences of sex workers who claim their work is not harmful or alienating … the notion of a prostitute who is unharmed by her experience is an ontological impossibility: that which cannot be.'[45]

Ways of Seeing: Body, Sex, Sexuality, and Self

If abolitionists and sex workers understand the paid sexual encounter differently, it is partly because they understand sex, sexuality, and sexual power itself differently. For many abolitionists, legitimate sex is sex as self-expression, sex with emotion, sex with intimacy, but not sex for money, which is seen as illegitimate.

Writes CATW co-director Janice Raymond, 'To understand how violence is intrinsic to prostitution, it is necessary to understand the sex of prostitution. The sexual service provided in prostitution is most often violent, degrading, and abusive sexual acts.'[46] Clinical psychologist Melissa Farley echoes a similar line: 'The harm she experiences in prostitution is made invisible, described not as sexual harassment, not as rape, not as intimate partner violence, but as "sex". She shuts down her feelings to protect her self. She becomes 'something for him to empty himself into, acting as a kind of human toilet.'[47] Seen through this lens, all *paid sex* becomes rape: 'paid rape',[48] 'bought and sold rape', 'gang rape carried out day after day for years'.

Many sex workers and feminists view sex through a different lens in which all *consensual* sex is legitimate: be it for pleasure, for emotional connection, for intimacy, for sex, for money, for whatever. In this understanding, every sexual act does not have to have a deep connection with self-expression or emotion. What is exchanged in a paid encounter is 'sexual services', or one kind of sex; what is exchanged in a non-paid encounter with a lover, *maalak*, or *babu* may be another kind of sex, with or without emotion and intimacy. Or, it may blur over time; how else does one explain how clients become regulars and then go on to become *maalak*s?

Several feminists also understand that exchanging or selling sexual services does not mean selling the body, sexuality, self, soul, or womanhood. Says a report from Jagori, a women's group in India: 'What are prostitutes selling? The first instinct is to say their body. But this is a sensationalist kind of statement – how much truth is there in that? A construction worker uses her hands, but is she selling her hands? Similarly, if a prostitute is using her body or vagina, is she selling her body? Or is she selling labour, is she selling time, services and skills?' The report goes on to say that a 'prostitute woman may be selling sex, but not her sexuality'.

Power is another term that is understood differently. While abolitionists see sex as a one-way power flow – male power over women – sex workers see power as a two-way flow. 'We cannot entirely disregard the fact that for many women, the first time they felt powerful was the first time they turned a trick,' write Priscilla Alexander and Frederique Delacoste in *Sex Work* (1987).[49] 'Prostitution involves an equation of sex with power: for the man/customer, the power consists of his ability to 'buy' access to any number of women; for the woman/prostitute, the power consists of her ability to set the terms of her sexuality, and demand substantial payment for her time and skills.'

While Tomiye Ishida writes that 'the money earned by prostitutes is a source of economic power',[50] Charlotte Davis Kasl, author of *Women, Sex and Addiction* (1989), writes of the sexual power of prostitution:

The addictive part is the ritual of getting dressed, putting on makeup, fantasizing about the hunt, and the moment of capture. To know that you could go out there and they would come running. What power! Men would actually pay for sex... For women in prostitution... that feeling of power, along with the excitement of living on the edge, is one of the hardest things to give up.[51]

The Power of Construction: Deconstructing the Abolitionist Gaze

If there is one power base that abolitionists have yet to vacate, it is the power to construct prostitution as a mythical dystopia. What else can one call an abolitionist edifice based on a consistent dismissal of the voices, lived realities, and experiences of sex workers? I recently read *Prostitution, Trafficking and Traumatic Stress* (2003), a collection of essays edited by Melissa Farley. The descriptions of prostitution didn't square with sex workers' lived experiences, and the charged language, hyperbolic words, emotionally-loaded sentences reminded me of propaganda.

In 1937, with Nazi propaganda at its peak, a number of social scientists, communication researchers, opinion leaders, historians, educationists, and journalists came together to found the Institute for Propaganda Analysis (IPA) in the US. The IPA was created to 'teach people *how* to think rather than *what* to think', and grew out of the general concern that increasing doses of propaganda were decreasing the public's ability to develop their own critical thoughts. In its publication *The Fine Art of Propaganda* (1939), the IPA identified 'seven common propaganda devices' that would enable the general public to identify propagandistic material. These are:

Name-calling, or the use of derogatory language or words that carry a negative connotation when describing an enemy. This attempts to arouse prejudice.

Glittering generalities, or words that have different meanings for individual subjects, but are linked to highly valued concepts. When these words are used, they demand approval without thought, simply because such an important concept is involved.

Transfer, or an attempt to make the subject view a certain item in the same way as they view another item, to link the two in the subject's mind. This technique is often used to transfer negative feelings for one object to another; false analogies are similar to this.

Testimonials: or quotations or endorsements, in or out of context, which attempt to connect a famous or respectable person with a product or item. Testimonials are very closely connected to the transfer technique, in that an attempt is made to connect an agreeable person to another item.

Plain folks, or an attempt to convince the public that a particular view reflects those of the common person and works for the benefit of the common person.

Card stacking, or selective omission, which entails presenting only information that is positive to an idea or proposal and omitting that which is contrary to it.

Bandwagon, or an appeal to the subject to follow the crowd; to join in because others are also doing so. This technique seeks to convince the subject that one side is the winning side, because more people have joined it.

In later years, much after the IPA had closed down in 1942, communication researchers added on four other common propaganda devices:

Assertion, or an enthusiastic or energetic statement presented as a fact, although not necessarily true. This often implies that the statement requires no explanation or back-up, but that it should merely be accepted without question at face value.

Lesser of two evils, a technique that seeks to convince us of an idea or proposal by presenting it as the least offensive option.

Pinpointing the enemy, or an attempt to simplify a complex situation by presenting one specific group or person as the enemy. Although there may be other factors involved, the subject is urged to simply view the situation in terms of clear-cut right and wrong.

Simplification, or reduction of a complex situation to a clear-cut choice involving good and evil, or either/or, or black and white.

Many statements in *Prostitution, Trafficking and Traumatic Stress* employ one or more of the propaganda devices cited above. Name-calling and transfer, for instance: as substantiated in my endnotes, prostitution is called and likened to every possible horror: war,[52] rape in conflict,[53] incest,[54] torture,[55] all in the introduction alone. In other chapters, prostitution is likened to domestic violence,[56] captivity,[57] death,[58] and gang rape.[59] In different breaths, prostitution is also referred to as a 'harmful traditional cultural practice',[60] 'a toxic cultural product',[61] 'colonization of the body',[62] and a 'violation of women's dignity and bodily integrity'.[63]

Testimonials – in the form of prostitute voices – are sometimes used, but only when these echo abolitionist thinking. Says one woman in prostitution: 'He had judged me like he'd judge cattle at a fairground, and that's revolting, it's sickening, it's terrible for the women. You can't imagine it if you've never been through it yourself.'[64] This reminds me of everything from school socials or proms to arranged marriages in India, but that's another story. Says another: 'I'm only the genitals they use. They could just as well have bought themselves one of those blown-up dolls. I'm nothing. I'm just a piece of shit.'[65]

My intent is not to dismiss or diminish these prostitute voices in any way, shape or form: I truly see prostitution not as a Grand Narrative with a single reality, but as a complex institution with multiple realities and competing narratives, each with its own integrity. We know that the lives of women in prostitution are lives like any other, including pain and pleasure, exploitation and empowerment, victimhood and volition, coercion and choice. These lives are not only black (pain, exploitation, victimhood, coercion) or only white (pleasure, empowerment, volition, choice). They are grey. My intent is only to point out the dangers of reducing these greys and pinks and reds and greens into permanent blacks.

Writes sex worker Jo Doezema, 'The testimonies of prostitutes thus assume the status of absolute truth. However, only certain versions of prostitutes' experiences are considered "true"'. Alternatively, as Shannon Bell puts it, 'the prostitute body is fit into a theorized totality of feminist space; there is no space for the prostitute herself as speaking subject, particularly if her speech might contradict the feminist construction of her body.' (I would substitute 'feminist' with 'abolitionist', but the point remains the same.)

'Pinpointing the enemy' is another weapon in the abolitionist arsenal. The enemy is clearly 'men', in the form of pimps and clients. This enemy is pinpointed via a mix of devices: assertions, glittering generalities, name-calling, transfer, and simplification. Just words and sentences. No evidence. No proof. Consider these statements:

The strategies of political torturers: debilitation, dread and dependency, read like a pimp's manual.[66]

The pimp might be among the world's most common instructors in the arts of torture.[67]

Pimps break women down emotionally, psychologically, and physically before they turn women out into prostitution.[68]

Pimps control her sense of self, often to the extent of completely controlling her identity.[69]

In a classic combination of false analogy and transfer, pimps are also compared to batterers, and by extension, prostitution to domestic violence.

Men who batter women in their homes and pimps who batter women in prostitution use torture techniques consistent with those described in an international summary of torture, in which torturers deprive their victims of social support, eliminate stimuli other than those controlled by the captor, and block noncompliant behaviours.[70]

Like battered women, prostituted women seek emergency care for broken bones, burns, fractured skulls and other physical injuries.[71]

Prostituted women have multiple batterers where non-prostituted women have one batterer.[72]

Let's not miss what's going on here. Prostitution is not being analogized to *marriage*, with the claim that domestic violence occurs in both, but to *domestic violence* itself.

Needless to say, in this mythical playing field of prostitution as death, war, and captivity, where batterers, abusers, and torturers run rife, women in prostitution are themselves depicted as 'sexualized puppets'.[73] Never mind the violence of this characterization. Just tie up this box of horrors with a red ribbon of generalized assertions and the package is complete:

Violence is the norm for women in prostitution. Incest, sexual harassment, verbal abuse, stalking, rape, battering and torture – are points on a continuum of violence, all of which occur regularly in prostitution. In fact, prostitution itself is a form of sexual violence that results in economic profit for those who sell women, men and children.[74]

Yes, violence is a part of prostitution; no contest. The incidence of violence within prostitution is disproportionately high; no contest. Farley's own study of 475 prostituted people in five countries found that 71 per cent of women in prostitution were physically assaulted, 63 per cent were raped, and 68 per cent met the criteria for post-traumatic stress disorder.[75] 'But when a former prostitute reports that while working as a prostitute she or he was beaten by a spouse, was addicted to drugs, and was defrauded by employers, she or he is not describing *prostitution*,' writes Jo Weldon, director of the International Sex Workers' Media Watch (SWIMW). 'She or he is describing *domestic violence, drug addiction* and *labour violations*.'[76]

This tendency to confuse 'part', 'norm', and 'whole' is rarely evident when describing phenomena other than prostitution. For instance, it is well known that 40 per cent of married women in India face domestic violence: do we take this to mean that marriage equals violence? We know that heterosexual relationships are the norm throughout the world; does that mean homosexuals don't exist? This may appear to be quibbling over words and numbers, but it's not. If language shapes our ideas, these ideas shape understandings and realities. I may not agree with Janice Raymond on much else, but I do agree with her that 'if reality hangs on the thin thread of language, this debate is no mere semantic quarrel'.[77]

Challenging the Gaze: The Violences of Stigma

Intrinsic: belonging to the essential nature or constitution of a thing
Endemic: prevalent in a particular field, area, or environment[78]
Merriam Webster Online Dictionary

Although violence is viewed as intrinsic to prostitution, I would argue that it needs to be more accurately understood as *endemic* to prostitution. Widespread, not inbuilt. There is a world of difference between the two; malaria may be endemic to parts of India but that doesn't make it intrinsic, inbuilt; something that just is and cannot be changed. The pied hornbill may be endemic to the western Ghats but is still not intrinsic to the Ghats (even though it seems so, having lived there for decades). Rather, it is endemic to the region: characteristic, prevalent, belonging to. It is not built into the fabric of the Ghats; if the habitat changes sufficiently, the pied hornbill can over time become extinct.

Violence is *endemic* to prostitution largely because stigma is also *endemic* to it. If 'the acts perpetrated on women in prostitution... psychologically define her as object, as degraded, as "cunt", as "filthy whore", it is because of the stigma attached to the act.' This stigma is rooted in a series of interlocking gazes: a societal gaze that perceives prostitutes as debauched, deviant, wanton, and weak; a religious gaze that considers prostitution a sin; a legal gaze that sees it as a crime; and an abolitionist gaze that characterizes sex workers as 'throwaway women'. When prostitutes swallow these nuggets and spit them out as self-descriptions, the contempt of the stigmatizer becomes the self-loathing of the stigmatized, inscribed on the body like crucifixion wounds or stigmata. Consider these self-descriptions:

Garbage cans for hordes of anonymous men's ejaculations.

Interchangeable with plastic blow-up sex dolls complete with orifices for penetration and ejaculation.

Empty holes surrounded by flesh, waiting for a man's deposit of sperm.[79]

Miller and Schwartz have identified four rape myths relating to prostitution: that 'sex workers are unrapeable' (meaning if she has consented to multiple partners, she has given up the right to refuse other partners or other acts); that 'no harm is done'; that 'they deserve to be raped'; and that 'all sex workers are the same'.[80] If such social stigma makes it easier to sexually assault prostitutes, judicial stigma means lower rape complaints, and near-zero convictions. Rape convictions for *all* women are anyway abysmally low in India; widely estimated at less than 5 per cent. However, at least other women, not all, but some, can file complaints. At least there is an acknowledgement that these women can be raped. At least these rapes (barring those in marriage) are legally recognized as crimes, even when not redressed.

When social and judicial stigma couple with abolitionist stigma to insist that a specific encounter cannot be rape – that all prostitution is rape – who loses out? Both women in prostitution who are raped and those who are not. By creating a superstructure of 'prostitution as rape', abolitionists do not stop prostitution. Rather, they muddy the waters. They spoil the broth. And they diminish the experience of anyone who has ever been raped within or outside prostitution.

Remember the 52-year-old woman in Mumbai who accused industrialist Abhishek Kasliwal of offering her a late-night ride and then raping her in his car? Public and media sympathy stayed with her until she was outed as a prostitute. Somehow, this reduced the severity of the charge in the minds of lawmakers; she became less of a 'good woman' in the eyes of the law. Besides, as 'good woman' usually equals 'woman', less of a woman, and therefore less deserving of justice. What is the conceptual difference in the logic of abolitionists who talk of 'throwaway women' and that of judges who say that 'a woman who goes out on the street and makes a whore out of herself opens herself up to anybody'? None that I can see.

By not engaging with these question, activists somehow round off this picture. When all of us loudly protest the rape of every woman – *Dalit*, tribal, married, single, straight, lesbian, Muslim, Hindu, old, young – but are silent each time a sex worker is sexually assaulted, our actions speak louder than our words. What we end up saying is this: women in prostitution are not worth representing. In doing so, we play God, dividing women into good and bad, deserving and undeserving, pure and polluted. Wouldn't it be more meaningful, as Nussbaum suggests, if 'we oppose the stigmatization of sex work rather than oppose sex work for its contribution to the stigmatization of women?'

Shifting the Gaze: Violence as Sex Workers See It

In March 2009, Meenakshi Kamble, a woman in prostitution from Sangli, presented her understanding of violence to an international gathering of feminists, human rights advocates, people in sex work, and sex workers' rights activists. Meenakshi is a member of VAMP, a collective of over 5500 rural women, men, and transgenders in prostitution and sex work.

Meenakshi spoke of three categories of violence that VAMP members routinely encounter. She spoke of *state violence*: from the police, municipal officials, the public health system, judges, and lawyers. She spoke of *societal violence*: the abusive language, stigma, and discrimination that she and her children face, violence from thugs, private doctors, market players, and anti-sex work activists and NGOs who forcibly rehabilitate adult women 'rescued' in sex work and prostitution. And she spoke of *violence within prostitution*: abusive clients and those who take too much time to ejaculate, demands for sexual acts that the women may not agree to or be uncomfortable with, coercion and the fear of being raped, and exploitation by brothel owners.

In the past decade, sex workers' rights groups in India have fought back against the violence they have always faced. In 2001, when a policeman in the Karnataka town of Nippani threatened to rape Shabana Kazi and 'tear apart her vagina', there were massive street protests in Sangli. In 2004, sex workers protested the demolition of their homes along with those of other migrants in Baina. In 2005, hundreds of women in prostitution in Sangli marched to the collector's office to protest against Restore International, an international NGO, for harassing and terrorizing them.[81] In 2008, police in Bangalore forced about 100 *hijras* (eunuchs) out of their homes, suggesting a spreading pattern of prejudice-driven violence and abuse in the city. Also in 2008, armed hooligans torched a brothel in Sitamarhi, and 250 sex workers and their families lost their homes.

Nippani, Baina, Sangli, Bangalore, and Sitamarhi are to the sex workers' rights movement what Mathura, Maya Tyagi, Rameeza Bi, Maya Tyagi, Bhanwari, and Bilkis are to the women's rights movement: those rare moments when silent immobility is finally stirred into angry protests, simmering till it boils over into massive mobilizations against injustice.

The pot still continues to simmer on the stove. Potatoes, tomatoes, garlic, and onions continue to meld with one another, yielding their hidden promise, gathering enough heat; hissing, fizzing, spluttering, and thickening into a broth. But there's one difference now: it's thirty years later. That old familiar broth – prostitution as violence – doesn't taste the same. It has lost its flavour. It palls on the tongue. It curdles, like milk gone sour.

It is time for a new recipe.

Notes

1. *See* Barry, 1979: 40–41.
2. Ibid., xii.
3. While the 325-page book does devote a chapter to slavery within some forms of marriage, its focus is prostitution and pornography (which is defined as a form of prostitution, akin to how other abolitionists understand it: as 'prostitution in pictures'.)
4. *See* Barry, 1979: 4–5.
5. Ibid., 61.
6. Ibid., 87.
7. Ibid., 93.
8. Ibid., 118.
9. Rape is the primordial core of female sexual slavery.

10. *See* Barry, 1979: 40–41, 75.
11. Ibid., 148.
12. Ibid., 150.
13. Ibid., 151.
14. http://www.antislavery.org/homepage/antislavery/faq.htm.
15. *See* Bindman, 1997. 'The 'right of ownership' implied by 'unconditionally sexually available' and 'in whatever manner he chose' is not possible in this relationship.
16. Ibid.
17. Ibid.
18. *See* Soderlund, 2005: 66.
19. Although there is no agreement on the definition of trafficking, it is agreed that the basic elements include violence, deception, coercion, deprivations of freedom of movement, abuse of authority, debt bondage, forced labour, and practices akin to slavery, and other forms of exploitation or use of force http://www.savethechildren.net/nepal/key_issues/traffdefinition.html
20. *See* Leidholdt, 177 in Farley, 2003.
21. *Convention on the Elimination of All Forms of Discrimination Against Women.* This report is supposed to act as a check and balance: questioning state inaction and offering recommendations to advance the rights of Indian women. It was presented to the CEDAW Committee on 18 January 2007 in New York.
22. *See* Bell, 1994: 111.
23. *See* Sen, 2006: 14.
24. *See* Doezema, 1998.
25. *See* Coomaraswamy, 2000.
26. Ibid., 41.
27. This is the phenomenon that one writer calls 'soft trafficking': 'In the sex establishments of Mumbai, one comes across enough indications of soft trafficking. Many, perhaps most, of the brothels and beer bars contain girls from the same state, the same region, often the same village. You can find Meghalayan or Tamil beer bars where many of the girls have known each other from childhood. You can find Nepali brothels where all the girls are from the same village in Sindhupalchowk district…
It is known that recruitment of new girls is often done by older prostitutes returning to their home villages. They are not dragging strangers off the streets to Bombay; instead they

are bringing over their own family members or neighbours...
Trafficking with the complicity of the family and the girl's
foreknowledge may also be the result of family indebtedness...
It is also clear that soft trafficking has become a widely accepted
cultural practice and that more and more families knowingly
and willingly send their children to brothels in response to
their own poverty.' John Fredrick, 'Deconstructing Gita', p. 15,
Himal, October 1998.

28. *See* Doezema, 1998: 34.
29. *See* Raymond, 1998.
30. This entire section is substantially based on Laurie Shrage
    (2007), 'Feminist Perspectives on Sex Markets', *Stanford
    Encyclopedia of Philosophy.*
31. *See* Assiter, 1988: 65.
32. *See* Shrage, 2007.
33. *See* Pateman, 1988: 207.
34. *See* Anderson, 1993: 154–55.
35. *See* Satz, 1995: 78.
36. Ibid., 79.
37. *See* Nussbaum, 1999: 214.
38. Exchangeability: the quality of being capable of exchange or
    interchange.
39. *See* Nussbaum, 1999: 218.
40. Ibid., 238–39.
41. *See* Shrage, 2007.
42. *See* Valverde, 1989.
43. *See* Nussbaum, 1999: 277.
44. *See* Nussbaum, 1999: 288–97.
45. *See* Doezema, 2001.
46. *See* Raymond, 1998.
47. *See* Farley, 2003: xiii.
48. Ibid., 148.
49. *See* Delacoste, 1987: 15.
50. *See* Ishida, 1993–94.
51. *See* Bell, 1994: 133.
52. *See* Farley, 2003: xii. 'As I talked with her, I felt as if I had
    jumped into a bunker in the middle of a war, asking questions
    about stress reaction to combat.'
53. Ibid., xv. 'The dailiness of the rapes of San Francisco women in
    prostitution appeared chillingly similar to the rapes of women
    during that [Bosnia-Herzegovina] genocide.'

54. Ibid., xvi. 'Prostitution is to the community what incest is to the family.'

55. Ibid., xix. 'People don't want to hear details about it, just as they don't like to hear about torture.'

56. Ibid., 17. 'Sister oppressions: a comparison of wife battering and prostitution.'

57. Ibid., 23. 'Unless human behaviour under conditions of captivity is understood, the emotional bond between those prostituted and pimps is difficult to comprehend... This emotional bonding to an abuser under conditions of captivity has been described as the Stockholm Syndrome.'

58. Ibid., 53. 'Equating prostitution with death, one woman stated: "Why commit suicide? I'll work in prostitution instead." [Prostitution is] a worldwide enterprise that condemns millions of women to social death and often to literal death...'

59. Ibid., 173. 'Thus for prostituted women and girls, the rape-like experience they must endure is not a single assault but a prolonged, numbing series of sexual violations, carried out by multiple violators, that resembles nothing so much as gang rape, and not just a single gang rape, but gang rape carried out day after day, often over the course of years.'

60. Ibid., xiv.

61. Ibid., xvi.

62. Ibid., 4.

63. Ibid., 127.

64. Ibid., xi.

65. Ibid., xiv.

66. Ibid., xiv.

67. Ibid., 2.

68. Ibid., 22.

69. Ibid., 22.

70. Ibid., 21.

71. Ibid., 24.

72. Ibid., 23.

73. Ibid., 34.

74. Ibid., 35.

75. Ibid., 34.

76. www.swimw.org, Notes for Journalists.

77. *See* Raymond, 1998.

78. 1a: belonging or native to a particular people or country; b: characteristic of or prevalent in a particular field, area,

or environment <problems *endemic* to translation> <the self-indulgence *endemic* in the film industry> 2: restricted or peculiar to a locality or region <*endemic* diseases> <an *endemic* species>

79. *See* Doezema, 2001: 11.

80. *See* Kinnell, 2008: 151.

81. Restore International had raided a red-light area with 60 policemen, 17 female police constables, and 8 police officers. The raids, conducted with missionary zeal and thug-like brutality, spared no one, including two school girls visiting their families. A medical report showed that only 4 out of the 35 were minors who could be thus removed; the others were released.

References

Alexander, Priscilla and Frederique Delacoste (eds.) (1987): *Sex Work*. San Francisco: Cleis Press.

Agustin, Laura (2007): *Sex at the Margins: Migration, Labour Markets and the Rescue Industry*. London: Zed Books.

Barry, Kathleen (1979): *Female Sexual Slavery*. New York University Press: New York.

Bell, Laurie (ed.) (1987): *Good Girls/Bad Girls: Feminists and Sex Trade Workers Face to Face*. Seattle: Seal Press.

Bell, Shannon (1994): *Reading, Writing and Rewriting the Prostitute Body*. Bloomington: Indiana University Press.

Bernstein, Elizabeth (2007): *Temporarily Yours: Sexual Commerce in Post-Industrial Culture*. Chicago:University of Chicago Press.

Bernstein, Elizabeth and Laurie Schaffner (eds.) (2004): *Regulating Sex: the Politics of Intimacy and Identity*. New York: Routledge.

Bindman, Jo, with the participation of Jo Doezema (1997): *Redefining Prostitution as Sex Work on the International Agenda*.Vancouver: CSIS. Online at www.walnet.org/csis/papers/ redefining.html.

Chapkis, Wendy (1997): *Live Sex Acts: Women Performing Erotic Labor*. New York: Routledge.

Coomaraswamy, Radhika (2000): 'Integration of The Human Rights of Women and the Gender Perspective: Violence Against Women'. 29 February. New York:United Nations Economic and Social Council. Online at http://www.unhchr.ch/Huridocda/ Huridoca.nsf/0/e29d45a105cd8143802568be005   1fcfb/ $FILE/G0011334.pdf.

Datta, Bishakha (2005): 'Not a Sob Story: Representing the Realities of Sex Work in India', in Geetanjali Misra and Radhika Chandiramani (eds.), *Sexuality, Gender, and Rights: Exploring Theory and Practice in South and South-east Asia.* New Delhi: Sage.

Delacoste, Frederique, and Priscilla Alexander (eds.) (1987): *Sex Work: Writings by Women in the Sex Industry.* San Francisco and London: Cleis Press and Virago.

Ditmore, Melissa (1999): 'Addressing Sex Work as Labor' (prepared for the Working Group on Contemporary Forms of Slavery, Geneva). Online at www.swimw.org.

Doezema, Jo (1998): 'Forced to Choose: Beyond the Voluntary v. Forced Prostitution Binary', in Kamala Kempadoo and Jo Doezema (eds.), *Global Sex Workers: Rights, Resistance, Redefinition.* New York: Routledge.

—— (2001): 'Ouch!: Western Feminists' 'Wounded Attachment' to the 'Third-World Prostitute', *Feminist Review*, 67: 16–38.

Farley, Melissa (ed.) (2003): *Prostitution, Trafficking, and Traumatic Stress.* Binghamton, New York: Haworth Press.

Gangoli, Geetanjali (2007): 'Immorality, Hurt or Choice: How Indian Feminists Engage with Prostitution', *International Feminist Journal of Politics*, 9(1), 1–19.

—— (2001): 'Silence, Choice and Hurt: Attitudes to Prostitution in India and the West,' Asia Research Centre Working Paper Series 2001. London: London School of Economics.

Ghosh, Swati (2007): 'Across (B)order and Back: The Everyday Reality of Kolkata's "Flyings"', in *Sarai Reader 07: Frontiers.* New Delhi: Centre for the Study of Developing Societies.

Ishida, Tomiya (1993–94): *Morals Cost Money.* Online at http://www.walnet.org/csis/papers/ishida_morals.html.

Jeffreys, Shiela. (1997): *The Idea of Prostitution.* Melbourne: Spinifex Press.

Kasl, Charlotte Davis (1989): *Sex and Addiction: A Search for Love and Power.* New York: Tickner & Fields.

Institute for Propaganda Analysis (1939): *The Fine Art of Propaganda.* New York: Harcourt, Brace & Co., 1939.

Jhaveri, Priya and Bishakha Datta (eds.) (2002): *Unzipped: Women and Men in Prostitution Speak Out.* Mumbai: Point of View.

Kempadoo, Kamala and Jo Doezema (eds.) (1998): *Global Sex Workers: Rights, Resistance, and Redefinition.* New York: Routledge.

Kinnell, Hillary (2008): *Violence and Sex Work in Britain.* Devon: Willan Publishing.

Kulick, Don (1998): *Travesti: Sex, Gender and Culture among Brazilian Transgendered Prostitutes.* Chicago: University of Chicago Press.

Leidholdt, Dorchen (2003): 'Prostitution and Trafficking', in Melissa Farley (ed.), *Prostitution, Trafficking and Traumatic Stress.* Binghampton, New York: Haworth Press.

Leigh, Carol (1997): 'Inventing Sex Work', in Jill Nagle (ed.), *Whores and Other Feminists.* New York: Routledge.

McElroy, Wendy (2008): 'A Feminist Defense of a Woman's Right to Sell Sex'. Online at http://www.wendymcelroy.com/e107_plugins/content/content.php?content.102.

Nagle, Jill (ed.) (1997): *Whores and Other Feminists.* New York: Routledge.

National Alliance of Women (2006): *India Second Shadow Report on CEDAW.* Bangalore: NAWO. Online at www.iwraw ap.org/ .../India%20FINAL%20shadow%20report%20Jan%202007.pdf.

Nussbaum, Martha (1999): *Sex and Social Justice.* Oxford: Oxford University Press.

O'Connell Davidson, Julia (1998): *Prostitution, Power, and Freedom.* Anne Arbor: University of Michigan Press.

Outshoorn, Joyce (ed.) (2004): *The Politics of Prostitution: Women's Movements, Democratic States and the Globalisation of Sex Commerce.* Cambridge: Cambridge University Press.

Overs, Cheryl and Paulo Longo (1997): *Making Sex Work Safe.* London: Network of Sex Work Projects.

Pateman, Carole. (1988): *The Sexual Contract.* Cambridge: Polity Press.

Pheterson, Gail (ed.) (1989): *A Vindication of the Rights of Whores.* Seattle: Seal Press.

—— (1996): *The Prostitution Prism.* Amsterdam: Amsterdam University Press.

Raymond, Janice (1998): 'Prostitution as Violence Against Women: NGO Stonewalling in Beijing and Elsewhere'. *Women's Studies International Forum,* 21, 1–9.

Roberts, Nickie (1992): *Whores in History: Prostitution in Western Society.* London: HarperCollins.

Rubin, Gayle (1975): 'The Traffic in Women: Notes on the "Political Economy" of Sex', in R. Reiter (ed.), *Toward an Anthropology of Women.* New York: Monthly Review Press.

Sahni, Rohini, Kalyan Shankar, and Hemant Apte (eds.) (2008): *Prostitution and Beyond: An Analysis of Sex Workers in India.* New Delhi: Sage.

SANGRAM (2000): *Of Veshyas, Vamps, Whores and Women.* Mumbai: Point of View.

Sen, Amartya (2006): *Identity and Violence: The Illusion of Destiny.* New Delhi: Penguin Books.

Shah, Svati (2008): 'Producing the Spectacle of Kamathipura: The Politics of Red Light Visibility in Mumbai', in R. Sahni, et al. (eds.), *Prostitution and Beyond: An Analysis of Sex Workers in India.* New Delhi: Sage.

Seshu, Meena (2008): 'Surfacing Voices from the Underground', in R. Sahni, et al. (eds.), *Prostitution and Beyond: An Analysis of Sex Workers in India.* New Delhi: Sage.

Shrage, Laurie (1989): 'Should Feminists Oppose Prostitution?', *Ethics,* 99: 347–61.

—— (1994): *Moral Dilemmas of Feminism: Prostitution, Adultery, and Abortion.* New York: Routledge.

—— (2007): 'Feminist Perspectives on Sex Markets'. *Stanford Encyclopedia of Philosophy.* Online at http://plato.stanford. edu/ entries/feminist-sex-markets/

Soderlund, Gretchen (2005): 'Running from the Rescuers: New U.S. Crusades Against Sex Trafficking and the Rhetoric of Abolition', *NWSA Journal* 64, 17(3). Indiana: Indiana University Press.

Truong, Thanh-Dam (1990): *Sex, Money and Morality: Prostitution and Tourism in Southeast Asia.* London: Zed Books.

Vance, Carole (ed.) (1984): *Pleasure and Danger: Exploring Female Sexuality.* London: Routledge & Kegan Paul.

Valverde, Mariana (1989): 'Beyond Gender Dangers and Private Pleasures: Theory and Ethics in the Sex Debates', *Feminist Studies,* 15(2): 241.

Weitzer, Ronald (2007): 'The Social Construction of Sex Trafficking: Ideology and Institutionalization of a Moral Crusade', *Politics and Society,* 35(3): 447–75.

11

River Song

Sonia Jabbar

It's been an unusually hot summer. The sun burns with a fierce, unfamiliar power bleaching the skies white. The paddy fields have ripened early this year, and the entire length and breadth of Kashmir blazes with the pure madness of Van Gogh's palette, all cadmium and chrome yellows. When the clouds come, they don't bring hope or relief, but simply glower from above like a sullen, demonic presence. In the green shade of the poplars, where it is no less warm and humid, the cicadas keep up their maddening, metallic hum. The air is blue and acrid with the belched fumes of army trucks, the long convoys that ceaselessly ply the highways from dawn to dusk. And yet here, standing at the lip of a hill overlooking Baramulla, I feel I have escaped to an older Kashmir. The valley swoops out before me, a large bowl ringed by tall mountains that throw a protective cordon around it, sentinel-like. It is easy to understand how the old myths were moulded and shaped on the armature of this magnificent geography.

Kashmir was once an inland sea, they say, or a large lake. They called it Satisar, after the goddess Uma because the lake was a manifestation of her. But within its waters lived the demon Jalodbhav. He grew proud, overweening, and wreaked havoc on mankind. And what power did the gods have against his cunning and ability to hide underwater? At last Vishnu ordered Ananta to break open the mountains so that the waters could be drained. Heaving his plough,

Ananta delivered a thunderous blow, splitting the Himalayas at Baramulla. The sea drained away, the land appeared, Jalodbhav was killed and order restored.

Here where I stand, it is utterly peaceful. The slope tumbles away gently to where the town nestles in violet shadow, cupped in the palm of the valley, its tin roofs winking in the dying light like so many uncut jewels. The river moves past the town and leaves Kashmir through Ananta's crack, a narrow gorge in the north. A constant, cool breeze brushes past my cheek. Baramulla. Tempting to think of the name having something to do with *bara mullah*, or 'twelve Muslim priests', but it's nothing of the sort. Kashmiris still call it Varmul, a corruption of Varahamul, from Varaha, Vishnu's third incarnation as the boar.

Suraiyya's face has turned a pretty shade of pink. She huffs and trots to keep pace, the generous rolls of fat and ample bosom jiggling under the folds of her dupatta. 'Stop!' she cries. 'Ya Allah! You will be the death of me, dragging a poor woman around like this.'

'Come on,' I glare at her. 'It's good for you to get this exercise. As for your "poor woman" business I should take a photograph of you and go around India asking for alms for the poor of Kashmir. How much money do you think I'd collect, eh?'

'Nothing,' says Shazia giggling.

'Yes, a big fat zero, that's for sure. But shoes, yes. Those I'd gather after they're thrown at my head.' Shazia howls with laughter, 'You're right, mamma is very lazy. If she walked like this every day she'd be slim and very pretty.' Suraiyya sniffs indignantly and then bursts out laughing. It is good to see them like this, mother and daughter, out of the house, enjoying a joke, laughing together.

It was different at their home in Ladoora: a small, dishevelled house that stood in an unfenced, unkempt yard. A strange feeling of ennui pervaded everything. Ghulam Hassan, Suraiyya's husband, sat around ineffectually, conscious of the patches of leucoderma on his face and the fact that he lacked the will to work. They smiled but rarely and when they did, it seemed with much effort. All conversation revolved around Javed's disappearance, Shazia dropping out of school, and the poverty that they confronted having sold their lands and spent their resources in the search.

It was good to get out of the house and walk from the village down the pleasant, narrow winding lane that cut through apple orchards laden with fruit. The sky was overcast and the green of the countryside glowed with a neon intensity. 'Well, thank God, we are nearly there,' Suraiyya said, pointing to the river. 'You and Shazia go ahead, I'll rest under these trees for a bit.' The river twisted lazily before disappearing behind a stand of tall poplars. The water was a silky olive green and not very deep. We rested a while on a patch of grass on the high mud embankment. Shazia pointed to the punts and barges upriver that were engaged in dredging the silt-heavy waters. A few kites circled overhead, mewling softly. I figured we were somewhere mid-river between Sopore and Baramulla. Sopore, I recalled, was Suyyapura of old, named after the engineer Suyya, who lived and worked in the time of Avantivarman (mid-ninth century), and who saved the valley from devastating floods by successfully dredging and regulating the course of the river.

There was no fear of floods now. Kashmir was drying up, its magnificent water bodies shrinking, and the once-luxuriant rivers now reduced to muck-carrying drains. And yet, as of old, there were so many stories linked to its waters, contained within its waters, some floating on top, serene and splendid as the many lotuses and water lilies that embellished its lakes; some gliding beneath the surface only to reveal themselves in brief, dazzling flashes like trout leaping out of rushing mountain streams; and some stories remaining mysteriously hidden forever, buried and silted over, like ancient submerged cities.

There was a neglected children's park by the river. Shazia and I watched as two teenage boys flung flat stones onto the river, hooting with excitement at each successful leap and skip. Maybe this is what Javed was doing when he was picked up, I thought, suddenly feeling depressed. The boy was eight years old, what could they possibly have done with an eight-year-old? I looked over to where Suraiyya sat under a tree. She waved cheerfully and we waved back.

I had first met her at a protest of the mothers of the disappeared. She sat holding a laminated photograph of the missing child. I thought it was a mistake. Perhaps the boy had been older when he was picked up, and that she had only brought this along because she had no other. But it became clear soon enough that Javed Ahmed Dar was born in 1982, and that he was only 8 years old on the afternoon of 3 October 1990, when he was playing near the river at Zero Bridge in Srinagar just outside his grandparents' home. Some say he threw stones at a patrolling CRPF[1] Gypsy and they stopped and a few soldiers leapt out and bundled him into the vehicle.

It seemed absurd, a mistake surely. Suraiyya and Ghulam Hassan thought so too, for they went to the local police station to file a complaint the next day, certain that Javed would be returned soon. A few days later a militant who had now switched sides met Ghulam Hassan and told him that he'd seen a little boy who looked like Javed at the Joint Interrogation Centre at the Old Airport in Srinagar. By mid-1990, militancy[2] had erupted in full force and there were fierce encounters and dreaded crackdowns all around. The facilities at the Old Airport were one of the 4 sites where suspected militants were held and tortured. It was said that those who had the misfortune to leave the centres alive groaned and prayed for death to quickly claim their broken bodies and spirits. Alarmed now, Suraiyya and Ghulam Hassan joined scores of other petitioners at the office of the Advisor to the Governor.

Jameel Qureishi seemed to be a kind man. I saw his letter to the Director General of Police, JM Saxena, that said Javed had been apprehended by the security forces, and that the DGP should kindly provide assistance to his parents. On their fifth visit to DGP Saxena, they were told that they had lied, that the boy was not 8 as they claimed but 16, and that is why he was still in jail as a suspect. Horrified, they returned to Qureishi who, in a letter dated 1 November 1990, again requested Saxena to help. This time he sent them to SS Semyal (Superintendent of Police, CID, CIK).[3] Semyal wrote to Mr. Mir*, his counterpart in Jammu, on 1 January 1991, three months after Javed's disappearance. I saw a copy of the letter. It says clearly: 'One Javed Ahmed Dar, S/o Ghulam Hassan, R/o Zero Bridge is lodged in JIC, Jammu. His parents want to see him. They may kindly be permitted to meet him under rules.'

Sixteen years later, when I held the copy in my hands I felt my spirits rise. The letter was a clear admission of culpability. Within three months Javed had been moved from Srinagar to Jammu. The letter clearly says 'is lodged,' not 'may be lodged.' Fortuitously, the officer in Jammu was now in Srinagar and turned out to be someone I knew well enough over the years to call a friend. Surely it was possible to find out what had happened? I just needed to talk to him and a few others, somehow get the files out, piece the story together. Though the prospect of ever seeing him again had dimmed over the years, Suraiyya still hoped that Javed was alive. Someone had once told her that while he was in custody, a childless CRPF officer had taken a shine to him. Javed was a beautiful boy, with sparkling blue eyes. Perhaps the officer had adopted him and sent him away to a small town in India, somewhere far away. It was an unlikely story, something out of a Hindi film, but it was difficult not to want to believe it when Suraiyya introduced me to her nephew one day. 'This is my sister's son,' she had said with a queer half-smile. 'He was born around the same time as Javed. Everyone says they looked alike.' I regarded the boy carefully as he greeted me. He was in his twenties, wore jeans and a T-shirt and the light insouciance of youth. Yes, it seemed crazy to think that Javed was killed. Why would they do that to an eight-year-old?

Early in 1991, Ghulam Hassan told me, he made his way to Kot Balwal jail in Jammu, armed with Semyal's letter. He was directed to a room and asked to wait. A Sikh police officer sat at a desk, examined Ghulam Hassan's papers and then turned

* Name changed

to a subordinate and said, 'Bring Javed.' The man left, but returned alone fifteen minutes later. 'He's not there,' he said. The police officer got up and left the room. When he returned he looked perplexed and upset and said, 'He's not there.'

'What do you mean, he wasn't there?' I asked. 'What happened exactly?'

'I don't know,' Ghulam Hassan replied dully. 'I've told you all I know. This is exactly what happened. All I could tell was that the officer looked upset.'

The system, with its loops and dead ends and forms in triplicate in English, its manifold departments, its offices with bewildering, long corridors, its officers who are regularly transferred, was designed to confound, no, to drive one insane. If I could feel paralyzed, what of someone like Ghulam Hassan – uneducated, without resources or connections?

'Then…?'

'Then what could I do? There was nothing more I could do in Jammu. I returned to Kashmir and met all the high-up officers like Wajahat Habibullah and Thakur Jaswant Singh.'

Habibullah helped with letters. 'He even gave me air tickets to Jammu the second time I went – in June 1991, eight months after Javed disappeared.' This time the letter facilitated a meeting with Mir himself. Suraiyya and Ghulam Hassan were elated. They were sure they'd meet the boy. But in Jammu, Mir pulled out all the records and showed Ghulam Hassan. They went through the list together. Javed Ahmed Dar's name was not there. 'If he isn't here, there's nothing I can do,' Mir had told Ghulam Hassan. Bewildered, they returned to Kashmir. 'Much later, there was this officer, a good man… yes, Masood Chowdhry was his name. He was SSP, Srinagar, he told me, we know they pulled the child, but there's nothing we can do.'

Sometime in the middle of 1991 someone told the parents about the noted human rights activist, H.N. Wanchoo. Wanchoo was an old trade unionist, a leftist and a Kashmiri Pandit. When the exodus of the Pandits took place in 1990, he vowed to remain in the valley and continue fighting human rights violations by the Indian security forces. He was an upright, hardworking and decent man. Suraiyya and Ghulam Hassan went to him and he promised to fight the case in the High Court at Srinagar. 'I'll fight this case without money,' he said. 'I promise I'll get you justice.' But within a year he was abducted and his body was found riddled with bullets. For Suraiyya and Ghulam Hassan, Wanchoo's murder was just another bewildering event in a universe gone mad. There was no hope of finding him now, and years later when I showed up in their lives and attempted to help find Javed, I could see the kindness in their eyes, and the patience, the kind that the very old and wise reserve for the very young and foolish.

I called Mir and it was kind of him to invite me home to lunch, but I knew I was going to get nowhere that day. I stared moodily out over the wooden deck, through the thick foliage of trees onto the glinting waters of the Dal Lake. 'Come on, Mir Sahab, don't stonewall me. The child was eight years old. He's playing near the river one afternoon and he is picked up and disappears. How can he disappear without a trace? There's no question of this boy being involved in militancy, you'd have to be insane to believe that.'

'Look, you yourself said the father saw the records. If there was no name there was no boy,' he said gently.

'No name, no boy? No, there *was* a boy, I'm afraid, and he *was* picked up, there *were* witnesses, and you *can* help me by pulling out old records.'

'Let me explain something, how the whole thing worked,' he said. 'The CID was involved purely in logistics. All the state security forces – when they had to show an arrest they'd bring the fellow over to us. We'd record the date, fingerprint the suspect, do the interrogation and deal with their relatives. Then we'd present the suspect to the judicial magistrate and get a remand for fourteen days. Thereafter, the suspect had to be handed over to judicial custody.'

'So?'

'So, we just recorded the cases that they brought to us. There were many that they didn't.'

'OK. So what do you think happened? Even they couldn't have tortured an eight-year-old child to death…'

'Maybe he fell ill. Maybe someone slapped him and he fell and hit his head and died…'

'The mother thinks an officer may have adopted him, taken him away somewhere. Do you think…?'

'What do you think?' he cut me short and looked away.

A lesson in geography, best illustrated by catching the Delhi-Srinagar flight: I often peer out to watch the drama unfold as the land gathers itself, swells into gentle rises and then billows into the Jammu hills, green and khaki. Further north it bucks and rears into the sharp crests of the Pir Panjal range: wave upon wave of high snow-capped peaks running east to west before veering off towards the northwest. Crossing these, we enter the Kashmir valley, bound on the east and northeast by the tall, serrated peaks of the Great Himalayan range, and in the north by the ramparts of the Shamshabari range. The Mughals once described it as an emerald set within a ring of pearls, their jewel in the crown. But the jewel is imperfectly set, as if deflected by a blow, to settle slightly left of the perpendicular, southeast to northwest. And running like a vein through its entire length is the river. Unlike other rivers in the Indian peninsula that follow the laws of gravity, rising in the Himalayas to the north to flow southeast or southwest, the river in Kashmir rises in the Pir Panjal range that marks the southern boundary of the valley. Moving northwards, it unites the entire drainage of Kashmir before flowing out of the Baramulla gorge in the northwest. It is only at Muzaffarabad, now in Pakistan-administered Kashmir, that the river bends and moves southwards through Pakistani Punjab towards its final destination in the Arabian Sea.

The Punjabis call it the Jhelum. Here the river is still called Vyeth by the Kashmiris, a reduction and corruption of the ancient name, Vitasta. Just as the mountains establish the outer boundaries of Kashmir, the Vyeth marks the valley, *is* Kashmir, and has traditionally been so, notwithstanding the larger political boundaries of the state today. The measure of the valley is surprisingly small: only about 84 miles long and 20–25 miles wide. In spite of the bad roads, I have comfortably driven from its source at Verinag in the south to Baramulla in half a day. If you followed the river, you'd pass Bijbehara, where the river first becomes navigable, then the ancient temple town of Avantipora before arriving at Srinagar. From here the river moves northwards and drains into the Wular Lake at Bandipora. Then it leaves the lake at its western corner and flows past Sopore towards Baramulla in the northwest.

The Vyeth is still considered sacred. Before the Kashmiri Pandits were driven away by the fundamentalists in 1990, they would celebrate the Vyeth Truvah, the river's birthday, every year in August or September. The men would offer water while reciting Sanskrit shlokas (invocations) and the women and children would offer diyas (little clay lamps), that they would float on the river at dusk. The waters would come alive with thousands of flickering lights floating gently past fields and villages and the houseboats of the poor fisherfolk.

The Pandits took their cue from the *Nilmata Purana*. After the demon Jalodbhav was killed, or so says the sixth- or seventh-century text, the great sage Kashyapa Rishi asked his daughters the goddesses to bless the country of Kashmir with the gift of water. All but Uma agreed. She was puzzled. Recalling the Satisar legend she argued, 'Why, that country being my body is already purified, what else is to be done there?' The sins of the new inhabitants, the old sage explained, the black stains of black deeds of human beings, needed cleansing, and only the purest of rivers would do. Uma, known also as Kashmira, had great stores of compassion, and though she was reluctant, she agreed. Then Shiva, her consort, pierced the mountain at Verinag with his spear and out poured the gentle Uma, now in the form of the pure, clean Vitasta.

When the people of Kashmir heard that the goddess had assumed the form of a river, they rushed to bathe in it. But when Kashmira smelt the great sins of the inhabitants, she grew afraid of contamination and ducked deep down into the nether world. Her journey across the floor of the valley was not easy. Each time she grew skittish and dived into the

netherworld, she was propitiated by Kashyapa and thousands
of Brahmins and persuaded to reappear. The first time it was
merely the sight of someone who was an ingrate that sent her
diving down, the second time she came across a man who
had betrayed his friend by sleeping with his wife, the third
time her journey brought her face to face with a murderer.
Kashyapa realized the seriousness of the situation. Nothing,
he knew, could make Kashmira appear again. The taking of a
human life was too great a burden for the Vitasta to bear. But
he went to her nevertheless and tried to explain the nature of
sin. He sang,

Salutations to you, O daughter of the king of mountains;
Salutations to you, beloved of the best sages;
Salutations to you, O giver of boons,
Worthy of praise, of sacred nature, consort of Hara,
O goddess, free of impurities and grief,
Having the nature of holy and cool water,
O goddess, just as a thing burnt in the fire is made pure,
So is purity achieved by merely looking at you,
All sins are purified in the same way.
O great goddess, be favourable!
O great river, you have been summoned here for the purification
of the sinners,
So purify the sins! O swiftly-going one, do not disappear![4]

Although Kashmira understands, she confesses that the sins
are too much for her to handle alone. She cannot bear it, she
feels incapable and cannot purify 'those who are associated
with too much sin.' She begs her father to obtain the help
of the goddess Lakshmi, who is capable of purifying 'even
the three worlds'. Kashyapa approaches Lakshmi and tells
her, 'The water of the Vitasta, mixed with your water, will be
such as is honey mixed with nectar. Bathed in your waters,
even sinners become free at once and are purified.' Hearing
this, Lakshmi, the great goddess, the giver of boons, becomes
devoid of grief. She takes on the form of the river that the
people call Vishoka, Griefless, and joins her sister, Vitasta.
Later, Aditi, Sati, Saci, Ganga, Diti and Karsini – who become

the other sacred rivers of Kashmir – flow into the Vitasta, and together they purify the sins of Kashmir.

They arrive at 3 a.m. The *mukhbir* (informer), points to the house. The National Security Guard moves silently and lays a cordon around the house. Javed and his friend are the only ones awake, studying, when there is loud rapping on the door. They freeze. One of the older men of the house wakes up and goes sleepily to the door.

'Javed there?' a voice barks in the darkness.

The boys peer out of the window and can see men with guns in the shadows. Then, more angry voices and the sound of boots echoing harshly in the front hall. Javed panics, skips to the back window and jumps out, hoping to escape through the alleyways back to his home. He runs straight into the cordon. They thrash him silently before bundling him into the back of a waiting Gypsy. Then they climb into their vehicles and race away. It is all over within a few minutes.

18 August 1990. Not even a full year into the insurgency. Azadi, independence, seems around the corner. The Indian State is as yet floundering, unable to get on top of things. Arms of the state are lashing out in desperation. Parveena and her family live in Batmaloo, a poor, sprawling quarter just north of the Vyeth in Srinagar. Javed, her son, eats his dinner quickly, picks up his books, kisses his laughing mother goodbye, and rushes off to study for his exams. The plan is to cram all night. The friend lives only a few hundred yards away so Parveena shouldn't be worried, but the times are dangerous and she stays up fretting. At dawn there is banging on the front door. It is a neighbour who says between gasping breaths that the NSG took Javed away in the middle of the night, that they had been too terrified to come earlier and waited until first light to tell her. Parveena is stunned, but calms herself soon after because it is clearly a case of mistaken identity. They live in Batmaloo, after all, a locality notorious for producing an unlimited supply of militants, and the NSG, it is soon learnt, had been looking for an unsavoury character by the name of Javed Butt who lived nearby. The *mukhbir* had gotten the

houses mixed up in the dark. She is fairly confident that Javed will be released soon and allowed to return home unharmed.

What follows is a long and unproductive search, a confrontation with silence, leads which exhaust themselves into dead ends, walls. In the beginning, when the flame of hope in her heart is still unwavering, a sympathetic policeman tells her that the boy is in the Badami Bagh army hospital. She rushes over. She is barred from entering the ward but someone says, yes, he is there; he's just a little hurt. Don't worry, we'll release him soon. She returns home and cries with relief. Then she waits. After a week she returns to the hospital, armed with a pass that she's procured from the local police station. Who Javed? they ask. We have no one here by that name or description. She begs them. Tells them she is a poor woman with few resources, that the boy is innocent. They turn her away.

Later, she is visited by an Intelligence officer or someone in plain clothes who says she should be patient, that he knows where the boy is, that he will return soon. The years pass. Her hopes are buoyed and then dashed with every rumour, which later proves to be false. In 1994 a young militant is released. Parveena hears that he was in hospital around the same time as Javed and rushes over to him with a photograph of her son. Yes, the man had said, this boy was with me in jail. We had talked, and he spoke at length about his family. A barber who worked in Badami Bagh confirmed it later. He said he'd seen the boy. He was very dirty and dishevelled. The guards said he doesn't eat, doesn't speak. The years pass. Parveena still believes that he is alive, somewhere. 'Perhaps,' she says, 'he is in an underground prison somewhere, and one day when the war is over and they release all the prisoners Javed will return home.'

I think of Parveena Ahangar often, remember how her fingers caressed a large laminated photograph of the boy. He had an angular face, unlike the soft contours of his mother's, and the beginnings of a wispy moustache and beard. He looks directly into the camera. Then she pulled out another, smaller photograph. We hunched over it together and I felt the leaden weight of her sorrow sheathed in her body as it leaned heavily against my left shoulder. It was a formal annual school portrait where the entire class turns out scrubbed and clean, the shorter children seated in front, the taller at the back, the favourites on chairs flanked on either side of the teacher and principal.

'This boy has become a policeman,' she murmured. 'This boy runs his father's business, this is one of Javed's closest friends – he is a doctor now and comes around here sometime... and that's Javed.' Then she puts the photographs away briskly and brings us tea.

I first met the major in 2001 when he was still in uniform, working for Military Intelligence. He was genial enough, and I needed information, so we became friends. I hadn't realized then that he would develop a need to talk, that I would also become his confessor. He had been in interrogation. Some of the Kashmiri men who survived it later told stories that circulated and became an inherent part of the narrative of the war: electric shocks to the genitals, slaps, punches, kicks, beatings on the soles of the feet with iron rods; iron rods inserted in the anus, burning cigarette butts stubbed out on raw skin, suffocation, drowning; and 'rollering', which involved passing a heavy-duty roller over the thighs and genitals. It was difficult to imagine the amiable major doing any of this. But yes, he says, he did.

I heard it all, silently for the most part.

'You know we are not really allowed to...' he had said at one point.

'It's against the law? Against war conventions?'

'Yes, it is, according to the manual and our training. We're supposed to hand the guy over to the police, but in Kashmir, this was not practical when the insurgency first started. You weren't here then. Now it's different. Too many people involved and we couldn't trust the police at the time, so we had to do it.'

'The IB and CID?'[5]

'IB?' he laughed. 'Those shits? Let me tell you, we didn't get two paise – what you call a tuppenny – worth of information from them. We had to create our own network and break down the enemy's.'

'So, the disappearances, tell me why did those happen?'

'Well, some of us exceeded the brief, I'll admit it. We'd be interrogating and sometimes it would go on for days, the beatings and suddenly you'd switch tactics, like produce a Koran and ask him to swear on it, and then boom, out it would come, all the secrets he'd been hiding through the torture! But at other times you'd be interrogating someone and the bloke would just die on you without warning,' he said, in a tone which sounded like mild complaint. 'And then if there were three other guys in the room who witnessed it, it was too bad. You had to get rid of them too. In the early nineties it was war, my dear, no holds barred, no rules. They were ruthless and we matched them bullet for bullet. We had to, in the interests of the nation... and should the Jhelum ever dry up completely,' he giggled nervously, 'you'll find the river bed white with the bones of the bodies we dumped.'

As he was speaking an image formed before my eyes of Parveena's son among the broken bodies in large gunny sacks, anchored to weights like mariners of ancient times who were buried at sea, being rocked ever so gently by the river's currents. It was too much. I gasped, 'How could you do those things?' He stopped, alerted to the censure that had crept into my voice. He cocked an eyebrow. 'Listen, friend,' he said, 'we just followed orders. If there's a policy that needs to be carried out, it's done. No questions asked.' He lit another cigarette and fell silent. I watched the smoke curl lazily up to the ceiling. I studied the large map on the wall behind his head.

'So how is this done?' I said at last, keeping my voice level. 'Aren't interrogation and torture carefully calibrated by trained specialists, or is it a kind of free-for-all? You know, anyone wanting to let off a bit of steam is allowed to have a go.'

He laughed, a harsh, derisive bark. 'No, obviously not everyone is allowed. There are trained specialists on the job.'

'Then how did so many of these guys die on you?'

He slumped very slowly in his chair, as if the wind had been let out of him. 'Well, listen, sometimes you get really frustrated, you've been at it for days, you know the man is hiding something. He has information that is vital to winning the battle. Sometimes your emotions get the better of you... it happens, it just happens.'

Not far from Suraiyya's home, if one moves northwest downriver towards Baramulla, is a large village called Tragpora. We walked among the gigantic chinar trees, Suraiyya, Parveena, Bakhti and I, until we came upon the small wooden shrine. We lit some incense and offered prayers. I went inside for a quick look and when I returned I found the three women kissing the lattice windows, beseeching the old saint for favours. I had no doubt what these were, for all three were sobbing freely now. As we walked back to her home at the edge of the compound, I asked Bakhti, 'So did Manzoor bring his bride here?'

'Of course, all newly married couples do for blessings, I told you. He was very attached to this shrine, used to pray here a lot.'

Manzoor Ahmed Wani, Bakhti's son, was a poor, handsome bus driver whose undoing was that he had married well. His bride, Jabina, was the only child of a rich father. Everyone was happy but for Jabina's cousin, Gulzar Ahmed Butt, who had not only loved her for many years but also coveted her fortune. The marriage had ruined all his plans. It's only after he confided in his friend, the Ikhwani thug Qayoom Tantray, that he realized something could still be salvaged. Soon after the wedding, Jabina conceived. A month-and-a-half later Manzoor was taking her to the hospital for her first check-up when their bus was stopped at the Tragpora army check post. All the men were asked to step down. After being frisked everyone was allowed to board the bus except Manzoor Ahmed Wani. That was the last anyone ever saw him alive.

Bakhti fought. She was poor, she was widowed, she was uneducated, but she fought. She filed an FIR,[6] she followed

up on the courts. At last the police investigations named
three people responsible for Manzoor's disappearance: Butt,
Tantray, and Major Bhattacharya of the 28 Rashtriya Rifles.
The police arrested Butt and Tantray. Bhattacharya was
transferred out of Kashmir and that was the end of that.

We sat in Bakhti's house, among files and a pile of papers
in English, all relating to her case. I marvelled at her pluck
and determination. The house was bare, the windows did
not even have shutters, she herself was painfully thin, and
yet she had somehow gathered the resources to fight the
case. Just her bus fare to Srinagar and back must cost her
over a hundred rupees each time. While we were talking her
daughter brought in a tray and placed it before us. The cups
were chipped and full of milky tea. The plates had pastries
with bright pink icing. I demurred.

'Please,' Bakhti said in a small, thin voice. 'We are poor, but
please, you have come from so far away. You are my guest.'

I ate a pastry and drank the tea. I wanted to get up and hug
her and take away her pain. I said, 'Bakhti, your case, unlike
many others I know, is proceeding well. Tell me please, what
can I do for you?'

'I don't want money,' she said without hesitation, 'or jobs
for my other children. Please... please just tell them to give
me his bones, my baby's bones. I will hold them to my breast
one last time.'

All the horror and stupidity of Kashmir seemed to constellate
and settle around Hajra's home. It stood, a two-storeyed,
dun-coloured building in a corner of a small hamlet by the
lake near Bandipora, not far from the river, which broke up
among the rushes and duckweed before draining into the
lake. Reflecting off the shrinking expanse of the Wular, the
fierce noon sun beat down on the village, exacerbating the
gagging stench of human excreta. The open drains lay choked
with discarded plastic bags. I followed Parveena, and ducked
into the shade of the house with gratitude. Hajra lay propped
against pillows on the floor, a grimy old quilt covering her
knees. The room was bare, but filled up soon enough with a

group of women, some with children and squalling infants. It
smelt of stale urine.

Hajra welcomed me with kisses and thanked me for taking
the trouble of coming all the way to see her as I had promised
the last time we had met. I looked at her closely. Her skin
had taken on a yellowish tinge; the faded blue eyes seemed a
shade paler. She clearly needed the surgery the doctors had
recommended if she wanted to live. I poured her a glass of the
orange juice that I had brought and she drank it, whispering
thanks between each gulp. Her relatives pounced on the bags
of food and began distributing the bread, biscuits and kababs
excitedly among themselves. I arched an eyebrow at Parveena.
'It's all right, let them eat,' she said reassuringly. 'Hajra doesn't
have much of an appetite anyway.' I felt irritated nonetheless.
I had brought the food for her. She needed to build up her
strength. A bespectacled old man wearing a filthy pheran
appeared and sat down beside me. It was Hajra's husband,
a halfwit, who grinned idiotically and toyed absentmindedly
with my camera bag. 'Leave that alone,' I snapped, and pulled
the bag close to me. Then I turned to Parveena, 'Come on,'
I growled. 'Let's not waste more time. I want to record her
story today.'

I pulled out my notebook and pen. Everyone sat up straight
and expectant. Hajra reached out to the closet by her side and
pulled out a large, laminated photograph. It was a collage of
pictures of bearded young men, clearly mujahideen with their
AK-47s, baggy shalwars and Chitrali topis in the manner of
the Afghans, bandoliers of cartridges slung casually across
their chests. 'Hajra's boys,' Parveena whispered in my ear.
'Of her eight children, four were martyred.'

'Four?' I exclaimed, 'I thought she had *one* disappearance
in her family.'

'Yes,' Hajra said pointing to the tall, dark man in the
photograph. 'This is Basheer. This is the one that's missing.'

'But he has a gun,' I spluttered. 'Was he involved with a
militant group?'

'Yes, with Jihad Force,' she said simply. 'He trained in
Pakistan for two years and then returned to Kashmir. He did

some operations here and then surrendered. Then one night
the military cordoned the village and took Basheer away. I
met him a week later at the camp. He seemed okay. Then
the army men returned one night and banged on our door.
Where's Basheer? they demanded. He has run away from the
camp. There was snow on the ground. They kept us out all
night, beating my other sons...'

'Then?'

'Then nothing, we never heard from him again. We knew
they had killed him.'

'Did you lodge an FIR with the police?'

'No.'

'And your other boys?'

'Rafiq was the first one to go to Pakistan for training. He
returned twenty two days later and was killed. Then Nazir
went and stayed there for four years; and then Aijaz, my
youngest child, went. Both were killed in encounters,' she said
quietly, cradling the photograph under her chin.

I couldn't believe it. I felt a sudden and irrevocable alienation
from this woman for whom I had thus far only felt sympathy
and affection. Why had she allowed this to happen? When
the first body was brought home, why had she not protected
her other children from the same fate? The men were hot-
blooded and foolhardy, but surely her instinct was sharper?
I recalled my conversations with other mothers and fathers
who had ferreted their children away from danger, and I was
perplexed at this woman who sat before me, who had been so
careless with the lives of her own children.

'Where are you from, Hajra? What is the name of your
village before you were married here in Oonagam?' I asked
gently.

'Til, Paykyistaen.'

'I didn't hear properly, did she say Pakistan?' I turned to
Parveena, who asked again in Kashmiri.

'Tilel, Pakistan,' Parveena repeated, looking impressed.

I looked at the old woman and suddenly didn't know
whether I should laugh or cry. I felt horribly sorry for her. She
was a tribal masquerading as a Pakistani for everyone who

didn't know better. I knew of course the fact of the Kashmiris looking down upon Gujjars and Bakerwals and the hill tribes of Gurez and Tilel. '*Gurezi*' was a term of abuse in Kashmir. Perhaps both she and the boys had felt a need to prove their loyalty, to feel accepted – no, honoured – by the Kashmiris. Who knows?

'Tell her,' I said to Parveena, aware I was being cruel. 'Tilel is not in Pakistan, it is beyond Gurez on the LoC.[7] I have been there.'

Driving back from Bandipora, I wrestled with Hajra's case, and my own complex feelings about it. Obviously, even militants had rights and could not simply be 'disappeared'. But how could a militant claim the immunity, rights and privileges of an ordinary citizen, of a non-combatant, just because part of the time he pretends to be one? Even though I felt sympathy for the woman, I could hardly place Hajra's case on par with Parveena's or Suraiyya's or Bakhti's or the hundreds of others I had come across who were fully and completely innocent. One could look at the problem legally and morally, look at the positions fairly from both sides, wrestle with it for years, and never come up with a straight answer.

Returning to Srinagar from Hajra's I made my way directly to Ghulam Qadir's house for the night. He was my friend Aslam's father, Aslam[*] being a former militant commander in the early nineties. When Aslam picked up the gun in 1989, Ghulam Qadir left Kashmir. He returned only after Aslam surrendered. Now, as we sat together in the hour before dinner, I told him about Hajra's sons. 'This is a problem I've been wrestling with for some years now and sometimes I think this and sometimes that. What do you think?'

He stroked his grey beard thoughtfully and said, 'Well, if we speak of morality, then the first thing we have to think about is how we ought to look at it as Muslims. Jihad, first and foremost, is against *nafs*, our own capacity to sin. Only after that comes waging war against the external enemy. But here Islam is clear: jihad must be declared by a group of

---

[*] Name changed

learned *ulema* (Muslim scholars) after great consideration. It
should never be declared in a hurry, and as our Prophet,
peace be upon him, said, if war can be avoided it should. In
the case of Kashmir, how can the Pakistani state decide to
launch a jihad? And then we have to think and ask, is it right
to declare jihad against India which is home to a hundred
and fifty million Muslims?'

I hadn't thought of it in the context of religious ethics, but
for an ordinary Kashmiri like Ghulam Qadir, the 'legal' was
just one part of the idea of justice. What was right and what
was wrong was also determined by morality and ethics.

If Abba had made things clearer then Amin muddied them
again. Amin Bhatt was a Kashmiri playwright with an oeuvre
that was largely satirical and very successful. He worked with
a small team of dedicated young actors on a small stage in
Baramulla. He also wrote and directed television plays in
Srinagar. Like many young Kashmiris he was a liberal, secular
nationalist and had come under attack from the Islamists in
the early 1990s. We met for a chat at Café Arabica, and as it
always happens with thinking Kashmiris, ended up talking
about the violence. He said, 'So to get one militant it's all right
to kill ten innocents.'

'I didn't say that,' I said sharply.

'Listen, I understand there is militancy and that the army
is needed to fight it, but tell me, doesn't an ordinary man
deserve to be treated like a human being?' he asked, taking
a drag from his cigarette. 'This issue can be fought militarily,
but it cannot be solved militarily. In the old days the army was
different in Kashmir. You know, we always had a garrison in
Baramulla. In the early eighties one of my theatre friends was
beaten up by a soldier. We went and complained and Colonel
Sukh Lal took off the man's uniform in front of us. Today
it's different. Every Kashmiri is suspect. Sometimes, when I
look at kids who are in their early twenties who have seen no
other Kashmir but this, I wonder whether it is extraordinary
patience that allows them to tolerate such humiliation or
whether it's something that is burning quietly inside, a rage
that is quietly being nursed. It's frightening.'

'And now that it isn't possible to think of violence as an alternative?'

'For most of us it was never an alternative. When I was a child, you couldn't get a person to slaughter a chicken...'

'Oh come on!'

'No, I'm not exaggerating. There'd only be one or two people in the village who were considered brave enough to do the job. And then we'd have to take a sharp knife from the house along with the chicken. My grandmother would drop the knife on the floor from where I'd have to pick it up because it was said that if you handed a knife directly, the child would grow up to be a murderer. Yes, very few villagers had the guts to *zaba karo*. So, many chickens survived and grew old in the village.' He paused for effect. We looked at each other and laughed. 'But then,' he said growing serious once more, 'you have to ask yourself how a place like this can turn violent. This is not to justify or defend the madness, but we must ask ourselves why.'

'So what's the answer, Amin, how do we get out of this mess?'

'There is a screenplay I'm working on for a short television film: two bulls fighting, two boys watching. There is dust kicked up and both bulls are bleeding profusely.

'Why are they fighting?' one boy asks the other.

'They have a problem with each other.'

'What will happen?'

'One, the other or both will die.'

'If you and I have a problem with each other, what will happen?'

'We can talk. We are human. We don't have to fight and die like animals.'

Of all the pleasure gardens that the Mughal emperor Jehangir planted in Kashmir, Verinag must have been his favourite, or why should he have – as he lay dying in Rajouri – wished to be buried there among the shady trees, cooled by the pine-scented breeze and the icy waters? In 1627 Shah Jehan completed the construction of the octagonal basin and arcade that was begun by his father. An inscription in Persian reads something like this:

Haider, by the order of Shah-i Jahan, the Monarch of the Universe,

The Lord be praised for that, constructed such a cascade and such a water course…

The invisible angel whispered in my ear

This stream has sprung from the fountain of heaven.[8]

I have always wanted to go to the source of the river at Verinag. The spring from which the Vyeth issues is supposed to be a deep, azure blue. The only time I passed it was in the summer of 2000, on my way to Halan, and I suppose I was too distraught at the time to notice anything but the vague shape of the old Mughal masonry slumbering under large chinars. Halan was the last stop on my list, the southernmost point. I had already been to two homes in Brariangan in southwest Kashmir, and one just outside Anantnag in the past week.

Those familiar with Kashmiri politics will recall the names of Chittisingpora and Panchalthan-Pathribal. The first is a village in south Kashmir where 36 Sikhs were massacred on the eve of then US President Bill Clinton's visit to India in March 2000. Panchalthan-Pathribal is the site where the Indian army claimed it cornered the killers in their hideout and killed them. I was there at Chittisingpora and it is difficult to explain the burning need I had to personally track down the killers and bring them to justice. Although it was tempting to believe the obvious, unlike many journalists and writers I did not hold the Indian state responsible for Chittisingpora. But I smelt the lie the moment the army claimed it had got the killers at Panchalthan-Pathribal. It made big news. A huge cache of arms had been recovered from the hideout. The case had been dealt with swiftly, efficiently. The Americans were sure to be impressed. The Home Minister announced a large cash reward plus medals for the officers of the 7 Rashtriya Rifles.

A few days later there was a huge row around Anantnag.

Five families claimed that their men were victims of enforced disappearances, and that they feared the five militants killed by the army were possibly their kin. At first the government refused to do anything. Protests followed. One, at Brakpora, just outside Anantnag, grew large and unruly. The police fired in panic and seven people were killed. The protests grew shriller. The government was forced to exhume the bodies.

For me there was something beyond terror in exhumations, something almost apocalyptic in the earth disgorging the dead, so I stayed away. I went later, dragging a reluctant journalist from Anantnag to guide me through militant-infested countryside. At the last army checkpoint I was advised to blow my horn at every turn of that winding mountain road so that the militants would know it was a civilian vehicle and, hopefully, desist from blowing us up with an IED.[9] It was late afternoon, I remember, and the sun slanted in, a pretty, pale gold. Veeray cowered in the passenger seat. '*Khuda ke vaastey* (for God's sake), drive slowly, please. See!' he shrieked from time to time, 'There, that crater in the middle of the road is from an IED.' I drove on grimly, silently, until we reached the small hamlet of Panchalthan.

The villagers came out. We went on foot up a steep track to the top of a small hill where the encounter took place. There in the clearing stood a small, but solidly-built log hut used by Gujjar shepherds while pasturing their animals in summer. 'Zoon Tingri,' said the young man who walked beside me.

'What?'

'This hill is called Zoon Tingri.'

'It's a pretty name,' I said, catching my breath, 'What does it mean?'

'Moon Hill. This is where we come at the end of Ramzaan to try and spot the first sliver of the Eid moon. But sometimes on a full moon night we just come up here at night to enjoy the moonlight.' An image hovered before my eyes for a brief moment, of something infinitely delicate – a light breeze, silver moonlight, whispers, and the quick, furtive embrace of lovers. It vanished and I regarded the log hut in front of me. Inside, the floor was black with soot. A faint burnt smell still lingered.

If mortars had been used in the encounter, as was claimed by the army at the time, the hut would have been burnt down or at least damaged. The headman spoke up. 'We saw them take kerosene up when the siege was on. They had laid a cordon around our village. No one was allowed to witness what was happening. Later, when it was all over, they forced us to bury the bodies. We knew they were not militants.'

Zoon Tingri, what a pretty name, I thought as I drove away. Will the village ever return to a state of innocence, where it could remember the hill as it once was, pure and uncontaminated by the present?

The hospital room was large, dimly lit and poorly furnished. Dr Balbir Kaur, Head of Forensics, Government Medical College, was in charge of the autopsies done on the exhumed bodies. Now she was insisting I drink more tea and eat the kanti kababs she had ordered as if she were entertaining me in her living room. She had been very reluctant to meet and had finally agreed after much pressure, but when I entered her office I found her accompanied by two men – her husband, and someone she claimed was a colleague, who looked less of a doctor and more of an officer from the Intelligence Bureau. I didn't care and carried on as if they did not exist. She was tight-lipped and kept stealing glances at the men every time I asked a question, but in the end I gleaned all that I needed to know: two cases, death by bullet wounds. Two cases, 50–60 per cent burns and bullet wounds. One case, no bullet wounds.

'No bullet wounds? So how did he die?'

'His body was charred.'

'You mean he was burnt to death?'

'Yes, you could say that.'

'What happens next?'

'I will prepare the post-mortem reports and then we will send samples for DNA tests.'

'DNA? But the families have already identified the bodies...'

'Yes, but the government needs irrefutable proof.'

'Ah, I see. Thank you very much for your time,' I said getting up. 'I really must be going.'

'Please, you haven't eaten anything, have a piece of kanti at least,' she said genially, holding up the white quarter-plate with its few shrivelled pieces of meat that looked horribly, horribly like burnt human flesh.

The road petered out far below Brariangan. I locked the car, and asking directions from a young shepherd boy climbed the hill to the first of the two homes. The hills were bare but for the blonde stubble of grass, and the two-storeyed house stood alone and desolate in a shabby yard where a few scrawny chicken scratched at the dirt. The family trickled out one by one, men, women and many children. We stood about while Roshan Jani, a squat but handsome woman, told me the story. They were from the Gujjar tribe, had a few goats and buffaloes. Her husband was called Jumma Khan and sported the appellation Darwaish, dervish or sufi, because of his spiritual proclivities. A man of peace: odd how knowing this little detail made his death seem even more tragic.

'On the night of 23 March,' Roshan Jani told me, 'they broke the front door down and entered the house, six men inside, God alone knows how many outside. Give us food, they said. We had nothing. Jumma Khan Darwaish had taken to fasting on Fridays and Saturdays and he had kept some rotis aside for breaking his fast at dawn. He took these out and offered it to the men. They ate hurriedly and then took him by the hand. 'Come with us, they said, show us the way to Shangus Nala.'

Roshan Jani had stepped forward. 'We'll go with you,' she said.

'Shut up and sit down,' snarled one of the men, pushing her down roughly. Then they took him away, as they had done last year when they had asked him to guide them to Wadran. But when Jumma Khan Darwaish did not reappear at dawn the following morning, Roshan Jani and her son decided to go to the 7 RR camp to enquire.

Brariangan fell under their area of operations, but the army claimed that no one had gone out on patrol the night before and turned Roshan Jani away. On the 24th mother and son filed an FIR at the Acchabal police station. On the 25th they scoured the jungles around the village. That afternoon they heard the news on the radio. They said some militants had been killed in Panchalthan-Pathribal. Fearing the worst, they returned to the police station and offered to identify the bodies. 'They are militants,' the Station House Officer insisted, and turned the family away. On the 26th morning they went to Panchalthan but the army had cordoned the area and wouldn't allow the family to proceed. Yusuf Khan, Jumma Khan Darwaish's young nephew, hid in the forest until night fell, and when the army left, climbed up to Zoon Tingri and in the woods around found Jumma Khan's turban and ID card, and another turban and a burnt piece of a sweater that belonged to the other Jumma Khan, their neighbour in Brariangan.

Yusuf Khan escorted me over the hill to the other Jumma Khan's house. His son Shukur Khan greeted me at the door and took me inside. It was a neat, well-proportioned and prosperous house. Over tea and biscuits Shukur Khan told me their story. It sounded close to what I'd just heard. Then he went to the tin trunk that stood in a corner and pulled out some photographs. 'This is my father,' he said solemnly, and I saw a handsome face with a bright red, hennaed beard and a confident smile. I flipped through a few pictures, Jumma Khan with his flock of sheep, Jumma Khan in a Jammu studio with kohl lining his eyes, Jumma Khan sitting on a hillside, and then something I didn't recognize at first as even human. It looked like a gnarled, charred, tree trunk. I was about to put it away, when an involuntary cry burst from my lips. The shape materialized, legs bent at the knees, belly full and distended like a pregnant woman's, a white mass where the genitals should have been, stumps for arms. I felt faint with horror.

'Wha... what's this now?!'

'The pictures at the exhumation. There are more...'

After the exhumation, as Dr Balbir Kaur had said, the post-mortem report was prepared and sent to the government. DNA samples were collected from the bodies and the families and sent to two independent labs, one in Kolkata and the other in Hyderabad. I got their details from a friend

who worked in the police department in Anantnag, and then
waited the stipulated three weeks that the labs had requested
for preparing the report before I got in touch with the
authorities. Sorry, nothing yet, I was told. A week later, the
same response. Six weeks after the samples were sent I got
in touch with the lab in Hyderabad. I received a polite email
informing me that they had not as yet received any samples
from the J&K Government. I called my contact, furious. He
swore on his mother and offered to show me the registered
post receipts. Someone must have nicked it en route, he cried.
I threatened to go public with it. The Inspector General of
Police, Kashmir range, called and reassured me that another
lot of samples would be sent forthwith. They were, but on 26
February 2001, the Hyderabad lab wrote to the J&K Police
in protest. The DNA samples were fudged. The press got
wind and all hell broke loose. DNA samples were collected
and sent for the third time. Finally on 16 July 2002, based
on the forensic reports, the Chief Minister admitted, 'It has
been clearly established that the deceased were not foreign
terrorists as claimed by the forces who led the operations, but
were innocent civilians.'

The government ordered a Central Bureau of Investigation
(CBI) enquiry into the Panchalthan-Pathribal incident. On 11
May 2006 the CBI completed its investigation, exonerated
the J&K Police officers who had accompanied the army at the
time, and filed murder charges against the five army officers
of 7 Rashtriya Rifles who had led the operations: Brig. Ajay
Saxena, Lt. Col. Brajendra Pratap Singh, Maj. Amit Saxena,
Maj. Saurabh Sinha, and Subedar Idrees Khan. On 15 May
2006, the *Indian Express* reported that Brig. Ajay Saxena had
written a letter to the Director General of Military Operations
complaining that the five had 'been singled out for "harassment,
ignominy, humiliation, agony and financial strain" over an
operation conducted jointly by the Army and J&K Police.'
His wife, Sushma Saxena, wrote to the Army chief's wife who
was the president of the Army Wives' Welfare Association.
Claiming to speak on behalf of the wives of all five officers,
she wrote, 'If our husbands are prosecuted in this case, then

every husband who is fighting in the valley in the future is also liable to face such action... all our husbands have done is obey orders and carry out operations based on information provided by a Senior Commander and the police.'

Seven years after the murders at Panchalthan the army decided to fully and publicly back the five officers. There would be no court martial and certainly no trial in a civil court. On 9 September 2007, the army prepared to petition the Supreme Court. The Additional Solicitor General, who acted as the army's defence counsel, argued that army personnel operating in Kashmir were protected under Para 7 of the Armed Forces Special Powers Act, 1990, and therefore permission of the Central Government had to be sought before they could be charged for murder. Since this was not done, neither the CBI nor the police had any jurisdiction and therefore the chargesheet against the officers was invalid.

No, I didn't stop at the source of the river at Verinag, but I couldn't help but notice how many pretty streams we crossed en route to Halan. Many didn't have bridges, but my car pitched and bucked and forded each one valiantly. At Halan I went to see Mohammad Yusuf Malik's family. His wife looked shellshocked and didn't say much. His brother told me the story while his two little boys, aged 14 and 6, sat in the corner regarding me silently. Mohammad Yusuf Malik and Basheer Ahmed Butt were sheep traders and business partners for twenty years. Unfortunately, they chose the evening of 24 March 2000 to travel to Anantnag to pick up money from their sundry debtors. They never returned. Their families later identified their bodies at the exhumation at Panchalthan.

I didn't stay long. There was nothing left to ask and nothing more to say. I felt drained and exhausted as I took my leave. Malik's brother and elder son walked me back to the car. On the way we passed some fresh graves by the road. 'Mohammad Yusuf's and Basheer Ahmed's,' said the brother. 'We brought them back and buried them here properly. We did all the prayers and ceremonies properly this time.'

'Yes, but, but...' I turned and saw Malik's elder boy, pink in the face, struggling to say something.

'What is it, son?' I said gently.

'They, they murdered my father,' he said, fighting back the tears.

'I know, I know,' I said, feeling the sting of tears in my own eyes and reached out to stroke his head.

'No!' he cried out, brushing my hand aside, 'You don't know anything! We got his body but his body had no head.'

New Delhi, February 2007.

Sixty of them were there that day – Parveena, Suraiyya, Mughli, the old greybeard whose two sons had been picked up by Indian intelligence in Kathmandu and disappeared, Hajra, Hafeeza whose 13-year-old son was abducted, Muntazer, Muneer and his mother, Pal who made us all weep every time he spoke of his son, Ghulam Hassan Padder, Sartaj Ganie's father, Abdul Majid, Rafiqa, and the others. It was strange to see them milling about the Boat Club lawns, chattering animatedly with India Gate looming behind them. They could have been mistaken for a large group of tourists out on a lark, but for the posse of pathetic policemen who tailed them. It was hard for me to keep a straight face after all that had transpired that day. What did they think we'd do, storm the Eternal Flame?

As soon as poor old Ghulam Hassan Padder identified his son's body at the exhumation at Ganderbal, Parveena had swung into action. Like Panchalthan-Pathribal, a unit of the J&K Police (this time the army was not involved) claimed to have killed five dreaded Pakistani militants. Soon enough it became clear that the five were poor, young Kashmiri men who had been kidnapped and murdered so that the unit could claim the rich rewards and promotions that the government was offering as incentives to the security forces to improve their 'kill rate'. Parveena phoned me. 'The disappearances and murder of our children continue at the hands of the security forces,' she said. 'It doesn't seem to matter whether it's the chief minister or prime minister who gives reassurances that

it will never happen again. Now we want to come to Delhi to
appeal to the conscience of the people of India. We feel this
is our only hope.'

And so they came all the way from Kashmir, sixty mothers,
fathers, sisters, brothers and wives of the young men who had
been victims of enforced disappearances, and at hurriedly-
called meetings at the universities in Delhi they told their
stories. I don't know what effect they had on the young
students. I saw a few of them weeping for sure, but would the
trembling indignation they felt then transform into something
else, a clamour for justice that would resound across the
country and wake up this rotten system? No, I wasn't sure at
all. The only thing I felt confident about was that one had to
keep at it doggedly, and this I had learnt from Parveena.[10]

Today was the big day, the culminating event, a daylong
public hearing at Jantar Mantar.[11] Of course I wasn't happy
with the venue, but there was no other to be had. In the early
1990s, I remember, it was still possible to attend large rallies
outside Red Fort and India Gate, march down Daryaganj
and join the pamphleteers at Patel Chowk. Now it's only the
narrow strip of pavement off Parliament Street, near Jantar
Mantar, or nothing. Every other public space is under Section
144 of the Criminal Procedure Code, meaning the police can
arrest you if you are an assembly of four or more persons.

But we are a democratic country, and protest being an
integral part of democracy, we are granted space at the
pavement at Jantar Mantar.

Elbow your way between the displaced farmers from
Jodhpur and disgruntled workers from Gurgaon, holler
yourself hoarse through the din and watch how the onlooker
moves on after shrugging his shoulders in resignation at the
many problems that bedevil this country. Still, it wasn't that
bad, I suppose. The tent-house people had laid a smart green
carpet on our side of the pavement, upon which we sat. A
scalloped canvas tied to trees overhead provided respite
from the midday sun. Parveena had brought large orange
banners with 'APDP, Association of Parents of Disappeared
Persons' and 'We Want Justice' emblazoned across them. We

tied them to the railing behind us. It took all day for the
testimonies. Women, men and children got up one by one and
said their piece. Sometimes they broke down. A scattering
of people witnessed the proceedings: human rights activists,
lawyers, a few feminists and a few Gandhians, professors
and students from the university. I think they were moved.
I kept wishing we were somewhere more public, where
ordinary people could listen and engage. At about 4 p.m.
the press descended on us and all of a sudden there was
a jungle of mikes and jostling cameramen and no space to
move. And then suddenly it was all over. The journalists
left, the tent-house men came and took down the canvas and
rolled up their carpets. We broke our one-day hunger strike
with water, fruit and biscuits. Parveena came up and hugged
me. 'Thank you,' she said beaming. 'What a tremendous
response. Now surely something will happen.' I smiled at
her and felt like crying.

Then we gathered our things and boarded the waiting
bus. The idea was to proceed to India Gate to light candles
and then to visit the shrine at Nizamuddin Dargah before
returning to the guesthouse for the night. But as the driver
fired the ignition, a line of policemen suddenly materialized
and blocked our way. T. and a few other men got off. 'What's
the problem?' he asked the officer.

'This bus is not allowed to proceed to India Gate,' came the
reply. I heard it but I couldn't believe it. I started reasoning
with him and then when he saw the officer wasn't going to
budge, started arguing. Someone shouted, another pushed.
Suddenly there was a situation. I could see from the bus
window that the police had their batons out. Damn. I got off
the bus, pushed my way out to the front of the crowd and
placed myself between T. and the officer.

'Sir,' I asked politely, 'what is the problem? Why won't you
allow us to go to India Gate.'

'Because there is Section 144 and you are not allowed to
stage a protest there.'

'But we weren't planning to stage a protest. Our protest was
here and now it's over.'

'No, madam,' he said triumphantly. 'I know you were planning to light candles there.'

'But sir, everyone lights candles there. Only last week the papers were full of photographs of people lighting candles for the Jessica Lall murder case.'

'Yes, yes, madam, but you cannot be allowed to light candles there. I have my orders.' I could see he wasn't going to budge, so I thought, Oh eff you and your damned candles.

'All right,' I turned around and addressed the women who had gotten off the bus. 'This gentleman has a problem with our lighting candles at India Gate and therefore he isn't allowing us to move. I suggest we forget the candles. Let's just go and have a stroll around the lawns. It's been a long day. Let's just go and relax and we can light the candles at the shrine. It'll be more meaningful there anyway.' Everyone readily agreed, so I turned to the officer and smiled.

'No,' he said sternly, 'I cannot allow you to proceed.'

'Why?'

'Because you will light candles, I know.'

'No, we don't want to anymore, you heard them.'

'But I cannot allow it.'

'Why?'

'You will light candles, I know.' I sighed. We could go on all night.

'OK, sir, listen, you have my word.' I pulled out my press card and showed him. ' I give you my word that we will not light candles at India Gate. Everyone is tired. We would just like to go and take a stroll on the lawns and relax for a bit. We will be tourists from Kashmir. There is no law against tourists visiting India Gate.'

He wavered and then relented, 'OK, then go on. But no candles, remember.'

But by the time the bus wended its way through the evening traffic to India Gate a posse of policemen awaited our arrival. They were armed with long canes and threw a protective ring around the monument as if the old ladies had planned to storm it. I was furious. But if the Kashmiris noticed, they didn't say anything. They just seemed happy to be out on

a well-deserved excursion. I played tour guide and pointed
out Rashtrapati Bhavan. 'That's where the President lives. It
was built during the British period as the Viceroy's Palace.
The road leading up to it is called Raj Path. The British
used to call it King's Way, and I guess Raj Path is a straight
translation...' They nodded happily as we walked among the
other tourists on the north side of the Boat Club lawns. Soon
we had a bhelpuriwala and a balloon man trailing us. Muneer
and a few others had stopped to watch the candyfloss man
twirl his creations. 'And this behind us is called India Gate,' I
said waving my hand at the Arc de Triomphe-like monument
that was now floodlit. 'This was also built by the British to
commemorate the Indian soldiers who died during the First
World War. And then Mrs Gandhi added the Amar Jyoti, the
Eternal Flame, after the 1971 war to honour the soldiers who
died there...' I faltered and stopped. All bloody monuments
to bloody imperialism, I suddenly realized.

Here I lived among them, passed them every other day
as I drove to meetings or appointments, or stopped for an
ice cream and, admiring the architecture, just took them for
granted as symbols of the national capital. But these were
unapologetic tributes to Empire and the imperial project.
They were designed to tower above the subject races, to elicit
awe, fear, submission. I recalled that the Mahatma had wanted
the Viceroy's palace to be turned into a hospital after India's
independence but the idea had been shot down along with
him. And so, with its buildings we had inherited the colonial
attitudes of governance towards our own people. I turned and
looked at the Kashmiris. Abdul Majid Ganie gave me a big
smile. I waved back. His son was just 17... Next to him stood
Muneer whose brother had been 15 and mentally unsound,
and there was Hafeeza, whose son was 13 and Suraiyya whose
little boy was 8... We will do anything to preserve the nation.
We will wage war on children if we have to. We will treat
you the way we do because we've inherited the mantle of
our colonial masters and we're too lazy or too stupid or too
arrogant to want to change. What was it that George Orwell
had written justifying the rationale of bombing German cities

during the Second World War? Something about shattering
the immunity of civilians who had supported the war, the
immunity that had made war possible in the first place...

'Can we walk over to the other side?' Parveena asked,
interrupting my thoughts.

'Of course,' I said and led them across to the south lawns.
To my irritation I saw the posse of policemen follow suit.

'Shall we sit for a while?' Hajra suggested after a while. 'My
old bones are too tired to be hauling across Delhi like this.' We
all laughed and sat down in a circle on the grass. It was a pretty
evening. Though the days had started to warm, the evenings
still held the chill of winter. All around us families sat together
in small circles while children darted in and out between them.
A group of Japanese tourists strolled by followed by a gang of
local boys who held hands and laughed loudly.

I don't know who started it first, but someone from our
group hummed a few tentative bars of a song. 'Oh yes, let's
sing,' one of the toothless old ladies suggested and started
clapping a slow beat. Soon she was joined by Muntazer and
Muneer, and then Rafiqa, Suraiyya and some of the other
younger women started singing a wedding song in praise
of the bridegroom, but here they substituted the name with
mine. I got up and bowed theatrically and did a slow twirl in
the middle of the circle to great hoots of laughter. And then I
heard a voice above the rest, high-pitched and clear. I turned
to see it was Rafiqa, the shy young widow. I stopped dancing
and sat down within the circle. The song was haunting, slow
and sad. Everyone became quiet and watchful.

Vaad dit baaliyara aao ma
He promised me he would return

Chu pheran Shalimaran aao ma
After he visited the gardens of Shalimar

Zooni khotay yaar myoni dui hasin

Yash temsunt chui sitaran aao ma.

I thought Rafiqa was singing the sixteenth century
composition of a famous Kashmiri poet, it somehow sounded

so familiar. Months later I was to ask her, 'That night, was it
Habba Khatoon you sang?'

'No,' she would say, smiling shyly, 'my own.'

Vaad dit baaliyara aao ma, she sang now, her voice taking
flight, soaring above us. *Chu pheran Shalimaran aao ma,* joined
the old ladies in refrain. A tear ran down my cheek. Soon a
large crowd surrounded us: students from Madhya Pradesh,
the families from Delhi, the Japanese tourists, and the balloon
man. The policemen gathered closer, but since we weren't
lighting candles there was nothing they could do and so they
leaned on their canes and listened. *Vaad dit baaliyara aao ma,*
he promised me he would return, sang Rafiqa in a voice
that broke all our hearts. Not one of them understood the
words as she sang, but there among the Delhi families, I saw a
woman lean over to her husband and say, 'They are Kashmiri
women.' And I heard the strength of Rafiqa's voice: it flowed
through us, clear and boundless, and I recognized its power
at last in the way it moved around the policemen, the way a
river flows around mountains and boulders to make its way
towards the sea.

Notes

1. Central Reserve Police Force.
2. 1989 marks the beginning of a full-blown violent insurgency
    in Kashmir that has pitted Kashmiri and Pakistani militants
    against Indian security forces. The roots of this war lie in the
    partition of India in 1947 into India and Pakistan with both
    countries laying claim to the erstwhile kingdom of Jammu &
    Kashmir. Since the division was on religious lines with Muslim-
    majority areas of eastern and western British India constituting
    the new state of Pakistan, it was anticipated that Kashmir
    having a Muslim majority would form a part of Pakistan.

    However, a tribal invasion from the North West Frontier
    Province of Pakistan in October 1947 precipitated events
    leading to the Maharaja of Kashmir acceding to India. With
    Pakistan crying foul, Indian Prime Minister Jawaharlal Nehru
    took the matter to the United Nations and assured the people
    of Kashmir of a plebiscite to ascertain their wishes before
    the accession became fact. But by the end of 1947 India and

Pakistan were at war, with Pakistan gaining control over the western (Mirpur and Muzaffarabad) and northwest parts (Gilgit and Baltistan) of the state, while India retained the Kashmir valley, Jammu and Ladakh.

Since then India has maintained that Jammu & Kashmir is an integral part of India, that the Instrument of Accession is the legal basis of its claim to and control of the state, and that its army is stationed there as a right of nation-states to defend their territories. It claims the loyalty of the Hindu-majority Jammu region as well as Buddhist-majority Ladakh. It regards the numerous elections held in the state since 1947, the presence of the state assembly, the Constitution of Kashmir (drafted by Kashmiris and separate from the Indian Constitution), and the special provisions of Article 370, as acts which have more than compensated for the absence of the plebiscite. It views political disturbances in Kashmir since the early 1950s as an 'internal matter'. It regards Pakistan as having no locus standi and its presence in western and northwest Jammu & Kashmir as illegal (though India is willing to relinquish claim over those territories if Pakistan was amenable to give up its claim on hers, and to convert the Line of Control into an international border). Lastly, India describes the insurgency as a 'proxy war' conducted by Pakistan through its agents on Indian soil, particularly since the mid-nineties when terrorist strikes, hitherto confined to the Kashmir valley, have become commonplace in Indian metropolises.

Pakistan's position is that by the logic of the partition of India, Jammu & Kashmir ought to have naturally gone over to it; that the accession was illegal since the Maharaja of Kashmir had no authority to execute the Instrument of Accession when the people had revolted against him; and that it considered itself a party to the dispute. Pakistan re-named the region of Mirpur and Muzaffarabad as Azad (Free) Kashmir, which (though it has its own Prime Minister and President) is administered by the Ministry of Kashmir Affairs in Islamabad. Prospective candidates for the forty two-seat legislative assembly have to sign an affidavit declaring that they support the accession of Azad Jammu & Kashmir to Pakistan. In 1949 Pakistan issued a proclamation separating Gilgit and Baltistan from Azad Kashmir and placing them under the administration of the federal government under the name of Northern Areas of

Pakistan. However, there is no adult franchise, no constitution guaranteeing fundamental rights, or democratic representation. On India's charge of fomenting terrorism in Kashmir, Pakistan claims to provide only moral support to the secessionists.

The Kashmiris themselves are divided on the dispute. Jammu and Ladakh prefer closer ties with India, and though the 'azadi' (freedom) sentiment is ubiquitous in the Kashmir valley, what this means is disputed. For some it means a merger with Pakistan; and for others an independent nation-state. A third, sizeable group of people reject the separatists altogether, preferring strong regional parties like the National Conference and the People's Democratic Party that operate within the Indian Constitution. Also involved in Kashmir's electoral politics and fairly popular are mainstream Indian parties like the Congress, Communist Party of India, and the Bharatiya Janata Party.

3. Criminal Investigation Department, Counter Intelligence, Kashmir.

4. *See* p. 69, *The Nilmata Purana*, Vol. II, translated by Dr. Ved Kumari (1973). J&K Academy of Art, Culture & Literature, Srinagar.

5. The Intelligence Bureau and the Criminal Investigation Department.

6. First Information Report, the first step in a police complaint, case or investigation.

7. The Line of Control demarcates and separates the Indian-controlled and Pakistan-controlled areas of Jammu & Kashmir.

8. Kak, Ram Chandra (1933). *Ancient Monuments of Kashmir*. Reprinted 2000. New Delhi: Aryan Books International.

9. An improvised explosive device (IED) is a bomb constructed and deployed in ways other than in conventional military action.

10. When tragedy first struck Parveena she had fought back. In her many rounds of the courts and lawyers' offices she found other women like her. Channelling her grief into action, she formed the Association of Parents of Disappeared Persons (APDP), largely consisting of poor, uneducated women and men who meet once a month to try and keep the issue alive.

11. Jantar Mantar is an eighteenth century observatory set in a garden on Parliament Street, New Delhi.

12

What Poetry Means to Ernestina in Peril

Mona Zote

What should poetry mean to a woman in the hills
as she sits one long sloping summer evening
in Patria, Aizawl, her head crammed with contrary
   winds,
pistolling the clever stars that seem to say:
Ignoring the problem will not make it go away.

So what if Ernestina is not a name at all,
not even a corruption, less than a monument. She
   will sit
pulling on one thin cigarillo after another, will lift her
   teacup
in friendly greeting to the hills and loquacious stars
and the music will comb on through her hair,
telling her: *Poetry must be raw, like a side of beef,*
should drip blood, remind you of sweat
and dusty slaughter and the epidermal crunch
and the sudden bullet to the head

The sudden bullet in the head. Thus she sits, calmly
   gathered.
The lizard in her blinks and thinks. She will answer:
The dog was mad that bit me. Later, they cut out my third
   eye
and left it in a jar on a hospital shelf. That was when the
   drums began.

Since then I have met the patron saint of sots and cirrhosis
  who used to stand
in every corner until the police chased her down. She jumped
  into a taxi.
Now I have turned into the girl with the black guitar
and it was the dog who died. Such is life.

The rustle of Ernestina's skirt will not reveal the
  sinful vine
or the cicada crumbling to a pair of wings at her feet.
She will smile and say: *I like a land where babies*
are ripped out of their graves, where the church
leads to practical results like illegitimate children and bad
  marriages
quite out of proportion to the current population, and your
  neighbour
is kidnapped by demons and the young wither without
  complaint
and pious women know the sexual ecstasy of dance and
  peace is kept
by short men with a Bible and five big knuckles on their
  righteous hands.
Religion has made drunks of us all. The old goat bleats.
We are killing ourselves. I like an incestuous land. Stars,
  be silent.
Let Ernestina speak.

So what if the roses are in disarray? She will rise
with a look of terror too real to be comical.
The conspiracy in the greenhouse the committee of
  good women
They have marked her down
They are coming the dead dogs the yellow popes
They are coming the choristers of stone

We have been bombed silly out of our minds.

Waiter, bring me something cold and hard to drink.
Somewhere there is a desert waiting for me
  and someday I will walk into it.

Notes on Contributors

BISHAKHA DATTA is an independent writer and documentary filmmaker in Mumbai. Her first book *And Who Will Make the Chapatis?* (1998) focused on rural women in politics; she is currently writing a book on the sex workers' rights movement in Kolkata. Her two most recent documentary films include *In The Flesh* (2002), which explores the lives of three people in prostitution, and *Taza Khabar* (2006), about a women-run and managed rural newspaper. Bishakha is the executive director of Point of View, a non-profit organization that promotes the points of view of women through media, art and culture.

FARAH NAQVI is a Delhi-based writer, activist and consultant working on gender rights, minority rights, communalism, and women's education. She is the author of *Waves in the Hinterland* (2008, Zubaan) and has been involved in the women's movement for nearly 20 years.

MANJIMA BHATTACHARJYA is an independent writer, researcher and consultant with NGOs from across the world. She has a PhD in Sociology from Jawaharlal Nehru University, New Delhi, and has been active in the Indian women's movement for over a decade. She writes for various publications as well as a monthly column on feminism's 'Third Wave' for the web magazine *Inforchangeindia* (www.infochangeindia.org). She lives in Mumbai.

MAYA GANESH began her career with feminist organizations in New Delhi, India, working on gender-based violence, women's rights and sexuality. She has also worked with UNICEF in Mumbai and New Delhi, developing training and learning materials on gender, adolescent health and HIV/AIDS prevention. More recently she has married her experience of working on gender and sexuality with media technologies and communications rights issues on research and documentation projects for the Association for Progressive Communications (APC) and Tactical Technology Collective. She has a Masters degree in Psychology from Delhi University, and a Masters degree in Media and Cultural Studies from the University of Sussex in Brighton.

MONA ZOTE lives in Aizawl in the Northeast Indian state of Mizoram. She describes herself a poet 'disguised as a government employee'. She writes in English. She has published her poetry in various journals, including *Indian Literature* and *Carapace.* Her work was also featured in the *Anthology of Contemporary Poetry from the Northeast* (2003), edited by Kynpham Sing Nongkynrih and Robin Ngangom and in *Dancing Earth: An Anthology of Poetry from NorthEast India* (2010). She publishes sparingly.

PUJA ROY has a Masters in Social Work, specializing in Family and Child Welfare, from the Tata Institute of Social Sciences, Mumbai. She has over a decade of experience in development aid with organizations like Oxfam, Terre des Hommes, and the Sir Dorabji Tata Trust, where she monitored more than 50 projects across India on women's and children's rights issues. Currently a freelance consultant, Puja works with organizations such as CARE International, HIVOS, Novib, UNFPA, UNIFEM and others in promoting gender and human rights in development. She is based in Mumbai.

PURNIMA MANGHNANI holds an MPH in Community Health Sciences with a concentration in socio-cultural aspects of health. For the past ten years she has worked as a researcher in the applied social science field, focusing in the areas of violence prevention, intergroup relations, and prisoner health rights. Born and brought up in Honolulu, Hawai'i, she has made India her home.

RAJASHRI DASGUPTA started her career as a business journalist but moved quickly to social and political reporting. In her last job in *The Telegraph*, she was the Themes Editor responsible for assigning, conceptualizing, writing and editing the weekly feature pages. She is currently an independent journalist and specializes on issues related to gender, health, human rights, development and social movements. She is a contributing editor to *Himal Southasian* and a commissioning editor of the web magazine *Infochangeindia* (www.inforchangeindia.org). She is active in the movements for peace and women's rights and a member of several boards of organizations for social change.

SHAMITA DAS DASGUPTA is a cofounder of Manavi (New Jersey), the first organization in the US to focus on violence against South Asian immigrant women. She is currently as an adjunct professor at NYU Law School. Her research interests are in the areas of domestic violence, ethnicity, gender, and immigration. In addition to several articles, she is the author of *The Demon Slayers and Other Stories: Bengali Folktales* (1995), *A Patchwork Shawl: Chronicles of South Asian Women in America* (1998), *Body Evidence: Intimate Violence Against South Asian Women in America* (2007), and *Mothers for Sale: Women in Kolkata's Sex Trade* (2009).

SHARMILA JOSHI is a journalist and researcher. Her areas of interest cover a broad spectrum of issues related to globalization and gender. As a researcher her work includes chapters in different books, and as a journalist she has written for many years on development issues for many national and international publications; some of these articles have also been re-printed in academic texts. She has an MA in Historical Sociology from SUNY, Binghamton, and is working towards a prolonged PhD in Mumbai.

SHILPA PHADKE is Assistant Professor at the Centre for Media and Cultural Studies, Tata Institute of Social Sciences,

Mumbai. She conceptualized and led the Gender & Space Project at Partners for Urban Knowledge Action and Research (PUKAR), Mumbai from September 2003 to September 2006. She co-authored *Why Loiter: Women and Risk on Mumbai's Streets* (forthcoming) based on research done during the Gender and Space project. She has been educated at St. Xavier's College, Mumbai, SNDT University and the University of Cambridge. Her areas of concern include gender and the politics of space, the middle classes, sexuality and the body, feminist politics among young women, reproductive subjectivities and pedagogic practices.

SONIA JABBAR is an independent writer, photographer and filmmaker who spends her time between Delhi, Kashmir and Kolkata. She is presently working on a book on Kashmir.